Criminal Litigation and Sentencing

Criminal Litigation and Sentencing

Inns of Court School of Law

Institute of Law, City University, London

OXFORD

UNIVERSITY PRESS

OXFORD
UNIVERSITY PRESS

Great Clarendon Street, Oxford OX2 6DP

Oxford University Press is a department of the University of Oxford.
It furthers the University's objective of excellence in research, scholarship,
and education by publishing worldwide in

Oxford New York

Auckland Cape Town Dar es Salaam Hong Kong Karachi
Kuala Lumpur Madrid Melbourne Mexico City Nairobi
New Delhi Shanghai Taipei Toronto

With offices in

Argentina Austria Brazil Chile Czech Republic France Greece
Guatemala Hungary Italy Japan Poland Portugal Singapore
South Korea Switzerland Thailand Turkey Ukraine Vietnam

Oxford is a registered trade mark of Oxford University Press
in the UK and in certain other countries

Published in the United States
by Oxford University Press Inc., New York

A Blackstone Press Book

British Library Cataloguing in Publication Data
Data available

Library of Congress Cataloging in Publication Data
Data available

Typeset by Newgen Imaging Systems (P) Ltd., Chennai, India
Printed in Great Britain
on acid-free paper by
Ashford Colour Press, Gosport, Hampshire

ISBN 0-19-928151-3   978-0-19-928151-0

1 3 5 7 9 10 8 6 4 2

FOREWORD

It is a privilege to write this Foreword, following the tradition set by my predecessor, the Hon. Mr Justice Elias.

The Bar Vocational Course (BVC) bridges the gap between completion of a university degree and the start of a professional working life, whether by way of pupillage preliminary to a career at the Bar, or otherwise. These Manuals are geared to the practical and professional approach that is central to the BVC. Updated and revised, the Manuals form an integral part of the student's vocational training; as such, they are an important ingredient in the constant drive to raise standards in the public interest.

The Manuals are written by staff at the Inns of Court School of Law (ICSL). The range and coverage of the Manuals have grown steadily. They are intended to provide a useful resource for all concerned in the training of legal skills, hopefully at whichever validated institution such training takes place.

Legal vocational training does not stand still; the ICSL and authors would welcome feedback from any source, which may assist to improve the Manuals in the future. Any such comments should be addressed to the BVC Course Director at the ICSL.

Finally a word of thanks is appropriate to the publishers for their enthusiasm and efficiency in arranging production and publication of the Manuals.

The Hon. Mr. Justice Gross
Chairman, Advisory Board of the Institute of Law
City University, London
October 2004

OUTLINE CONTENTS

DETAILED CONTENTS

PREFACE

It is essential that practitioners in the criminal courts master the rules of criminal procedure and sentencing and frequently update their knowledge of the relevant statutory provisions and case law. This task has grown more onerous over the last two decades as there has been a steady stream of legislation in this field.

This Manual endeavours to provide a clear guide to the law and rules which apply to practice in the magistrates' courts, youth courts, Crown Court and appellate courts. Questions for discussion in small group sessions are provided in Appendix 1 and are designed to enable Bar Vocational students to apply the rules in a practical context. Sample multiple choice questions are also included in Appendix 2 and give students practice in answering a wide range of questions.

This Manual has been updated to include all relevant legislation to 4 May 2005.

TABLE OF CASES

TABLE OF STATUTES

Introduction

1.1 The new Criminal Procedure Rules 2005

1.1.1 Generally

Normally, we begin this Manual by introducing the Criminal Litigation and Sentencing course on the Bar Vocational Course and explaining its aims and objectives. However, there has been a very significant development in 2005, namely the introduction of the first comprehensive collection of rules governing the work of the criminal justice system — the Criminal Procedure Rules 2005. These Rules came into effect on 4 April 2005 and although the first edition is expressly intended to be largely a codification of the existing disparate rules for the various criminal courts, there are already some significant changes and additions.

In particular, the Rules set out case management powers for the magistrates' and Crown Courts (in Part 3) and, perhaps most significantly, an overriding objective for the code. This is an echo of the insertion of an overriding objective into civil litigation via the Civil Procedure Rules in 1998 and is no doubt intended to be equally important for the conduct of criminal litigation.

Rule 1.2 states that those involved in the conduct of a case must act in accordance with the Rules (and Practice Directions) and inform the court at once of any significant non-compliance.

Reference will be made to the Rules, where appropriate, in the Manual. The Rules can be found in SI 2005/384 and online at www.hmso.gov.uk/si/si2005/20050384.htm. For a swift critique of the Rules, see the two articles by Philip Plowden in New Law Journal, 4 and 18 March 2005.

1.1.2 The overriding objective

The overriding objective is set out in rule 1.1 and is as follows:

(1) The overriding objective of this new code is that criminal cases be dealt with justly.

(2) Dealing with a criminal case justly includes—
  (a) acquitting the innocent and convicting the guilty;
  (b) dealing with the prosecution and the defence fairly;
  (c) recognising the rights of a defendant, particularly those under Article 6 of the European Convention on Human Rights;
  (d) respecting the interests of witnesses, victims and jurors and keeping them informed of the progress of the case;
  (e) dealing with the case efficiently and expeditiously;
  (f) ensuring that appropriate information is available to the court when bail and sentence are considered; and

> (g) *dealing with the case in ways that take into account—*
> (i) *the gravity of the offence alleged,*
> (ii) *the complexity of what is in issue,*
> (iii) *the severity of the consequences for the defendant and others affected, and*
> (iv) *the needs of other cases.*

1.1.3 Case management powers

Under Part 3 of the 2005 Rules, courts are given significant new powers to manage cases through the criminal justice system efficiently and effectively. These powers apply to all cases in the magistrates' courts and Crown Courts. The principle behind them is to facilitate the overriding objective through enabling courts to engage in active case management. Appropriate directions are to be given in each case as early as possible and the parties are to actively assist the court, where necessary by applying for directions. This will be promoted through the appointment, for every case, of an individual — the case progression officer (c.p.o.) — to be responsible for progressing the case. Prosecution, defence and court must each have a c.p.o. and their contact details must be exchanged.

In actively managing a case, a number of objectives are identified (in rule 3.2) —

- identifying the real issues at an early stage;
- identifying the needs of witnesses at an early stage;
- setting a timetable for the progress of the case, and deciding what must be done, by whom and by when;
- monitoring case progress and compliance with any directions;
- ensuring that evidence is presented in the most succinct and clear way;
- avoiding unnecessary hearings;
- encouraging co-operation;
- using technology.

In particular, applications for directions, representations and any resultant hearings may take place via letters, telephone or electronic communications (presumably this includes e-mails). Alternatively, the court may give a direction without a hearing and can specify 'the consequences' of failure to comply with a direction (rule 3.5). Directions must be given at every hearing, to enable the case to conclude at the next hearing, if possible, or as soon as is possible thereafter. The punitive sanction alluded to in rule 3.5 (above) appears again in rule 3.8 — 'where a direction has not been complied with, [the court is to] find out why, identify who was responsible, and take appropriate action'. Each party must ensure that their case is ready for trial and, as part of this process, the court may require a party to identify those witnesses which he intends to call to give oral evidence, the order in which they will be called, any arrangements for facilitating the giving of evidence and to identify what other material he intends to make available to the court (see rule 3.9 and 3.10).

These changes are further developed in *Amendment No.11 to the Consolidated Criminal Practice Direction (Case Management)*, published on 22 March 2005 by the Lord Chief Justice. Cases which are tried summarily in the magistrates' court will require completion of a case progression form (set out in Annex E of the Practice Direction). This form, together with its guidance notes, sets out a case progression timetable for effective preparation of the case (see Part V.56.2 of the amended Practice Direction). Where a case is sent to Crown Court for trial, a plea and case management hearing (PCMH) will be scheduled. The PCMH should take place within about 14 weeks after sending the case for trial if the defendant is in custody (or about 17 weeks, if he is on bail). According to the amended Practice Direction, a PCMH 'should reduce the number of ineffective and cracked trials and delays during the trial to resolve legal issues'. Where possible, courts should fix the dates of cases so that the trial advocates are also able to attend the PCMH.

1.2   Aims of the course

The main intention of those responsible for designing both the Criminal Litigation element of the Bar Vocational Course, and this Manual, has been to make the subject both real and practical. The Criminal Litigation Course should instil you with a knowledge of how the criminal justice system actually works; then give you the opportunity to demonstrate that you have assimilated such knowledge and are able to make the decisions which a barrister could find himself or herself making in practice.

1.3   Objectives of the course

By the end of the course, and having read this Manual, you should be:

(a) Familiar with the progress of a case through the criminal courts, understanding the various stages and what each stage involves.

(b) Able to prepare for a hearing in the magistrates' court or Crown Court, knowing what the procedure will be in court and what matters will need to be covered.

(c) Capable of taking informed decisions (and, if necessary, advising your client on how to act) with regard to the various different paths that a case can take, both as to its final resolution and the intermediate hearings.

(d) Able to decide whether or not a decision taken in criminal proceedings merits an appeal — whether it be in relation to conviction, sentence or some procedural matter.

(e) Able to prepare properly for an appeal and advise your client which is the most suitable method of appeal (where a choice exists).

1.4   The Manual

1.4.1   Its contents and other sources

The Manual is designed primarily for use in conjunction with the Criminal Litigation classes on the Bar Vocational Course. It should prepare you to deal with a particular topic as well as supporting specific classes through the material it contains. It is also designed to stand alone as a practical and sensible guide to legal practice in the criminal courts of England and Wales. It contains most of the 'bare bones' of what anyone needs to know when starting on a career in the criminal courts; it devotes rather less space to the remoter world of the Court of Appeal and the House of Lords.

Throughout the text, references will be found to other sources (see **1.7** below). These include law reports and statutes, and there are also references to relevant chapters in the two main works used by practitioners, *Archbold* and *Blackstone's Criminal Practice*. Occasional reference is also made to *Stone's Justices' Manual* (everything you need to know for the magistrates' court), the excellent books by John Sprack (*A Practical Approach to Criminal Procedure*, 10th edn) and Peter Hungerford-Welch (*Criminal Litigation & Sentencing*, 6th edn), and to articles in periodicals (notably the *Criminal Law Review*). These references are intended to indicate other sources of information either more eloquent, more authoritative or more detailed than this Manual. They should all promote an understanding of the subject. The Manual is a concise and, it is hoped, readable guide, both by way of introduction and as a source of practical knowledge.

1.4.2 Its structure

The Criminal Litigation Course starts at the beginning of the process (eg an individual being charged with an offence) and works its way through to the possible endings — acquittal, conviction and sentence, appeal. This Manual reflects that pattern because this seems to be the best way to promote an understanding of the various practices and procedures that govern the passage of a case through the criminal courts. The Manual begins with preliminary matters, such as powers of arrest, then the commencement of criminal proceedings against an accused person. Having dealt with the subject of bail, the Manual then looks at what happens when an accused person first appears in court and how a decision is made on which court should try the accused. The usual way of disposing of a case is summary trial by magistrates, so that is next on the list. The Manual then examines the treatment of juveniles in the criminal justice system, in particular trial venues and procedures. Our focus then shifts to the Crown Court — how a case may get there (sent for trial or sentence or on appeal from a decision of the magistrates) and then pre-trial issues (such as disclosure, drafting an indictment and pleas). This leads us on to consideration of the trial in the Crown Court and then the possibility of further proceedings in the Court of Appeal and House of Lords. Finally, we look at sentencing powers and procedures in each of the three types of trial court — magistrates', Youth and Crown Courts.

1.5 Structure and relationship of the courts

All cases begin in the magistrates' court. A youth court is a type of magistrates' court which deals exclusively with juveniles. The vast majority of cases will be tried in the magistrates' court and will end there (unless the accused is committed to the Crown Court for sentence, or appeals to either the Crown Court or the High Court). The remaining cases will begin in the magistrates' court but be committed for trial to the Crown Court with the possibility of an appeal to the Court of Appeal. From both the Court of Appeal and the High Court it is possible, though rare, to appeal to the House of Lords on matters of law. The inter-relationship of the courts is set out in **Figure 1.1**.

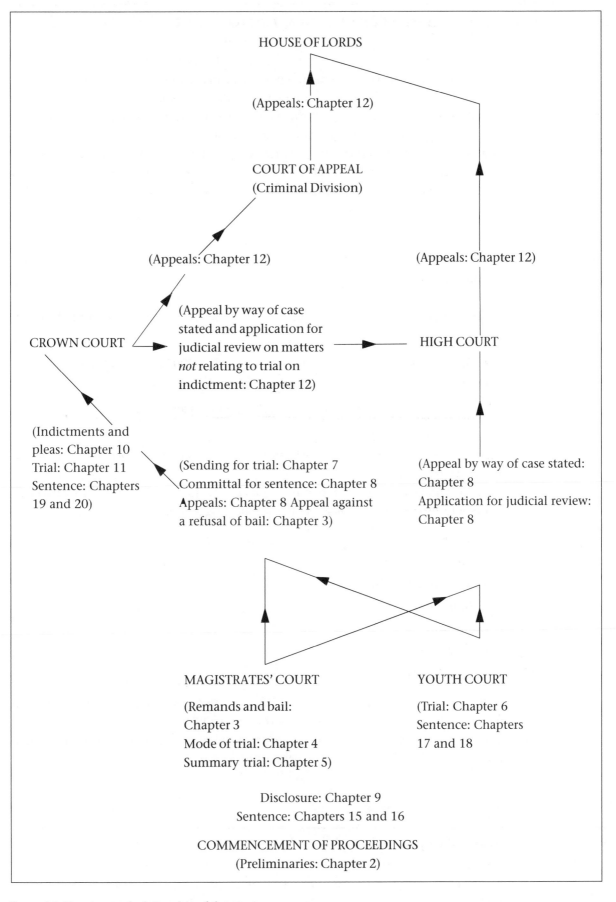

HOUSE OF LORDS

(Appeals: Chapter 12)

COURT OF APPEAL
(Criminal Division)

(Appeals: Chapter 12)

(Appeals: Chapter 12)

CROWN COURT

(Appeal by way of case stated and application for judicial review on matters *not* relating to trial on indictment: Chapter 12)

HIGH COURT

(Indictments and pleas: Chapter 10
Trial: Chapter 11
Sentence: Chapters 19 and 20)

(Sending for trial: Chapter 7
Committal for sentence: Chapter 8
Appeals: Chapter 8 Appeal against a refusal of bail: Chapter 3)

(Appeal by way of case stated: Chapter 8
Application for judicial review: Chapter 8

MAGISTRATES' COURT

(Remands and bail: Chapter 3
Mode of trial: Chapter 4
Summary trial: Chapter 5)

YOUTH COURT

(Trial: Chapter 6
Sentence: Chapters 17 and 18

Disclosure: Chapter 9
Sentence: Chapters 15 and 16

COMMENCEMENT OF PROCEEDINGS
(Preliminaries: Chapter 2)

Figure 1.1 Structure and relationship of the courts

1.6 The civil jurisdiction of the magistrates' court

It is appropriate at this stage to note that the magistrates' court has a civil jurisdiction, in addition to its criminal work. Whatever powers the magistrates' court has are given to it by Acts of Parliament — it has no inherent jurisdiction. Numerous Acts establish the jurisdiction of magistrates to deal with a considerable variety of work. Perhaps the most significant aspects of their work, for a barrister, are their jurisdiction over family and domestic proceedings and their role in licensing matters. This may change as more civil matters are determined by magistrates despite their apparently criminal nature, for example, granting anti-social behaviour orders.

1.7 Research

You are advised to read further about the topics covered in this course in the following books:

- Archbold, *Criminal Pleading, Evidence and Practice*, 2005 edn, Sweet and Maxwell;
- *Blackstone's Criminal Practice*, 2005 edn, Oxford University Press;
- Sprack, *Emmins on Criminal Procedure*, 10th edn, Oxford University Press.

A thorough work of reference for magistrates' courts is *Stone's Justices' Manual* (annual editions). Other specialist works exist and are used by practitioners, eg *Wilkinson on Road Traffic Offences*.

You will find cross-references to other publications throughout the text which follows but should also refer where necessary to the following Manuals:

- *Advocacy;*
- *Conference Skills;*
- *Negotiation Skills;*
- *Opinion Writing;*
- *Drafting;*
- *Evidence;*
- *Case Preparation*.

Note: In some chapters of **Criminal Litigation and Sentencing**, statistical tables are reproduced with the kind permission of the Home Office Statistics Department. Due to different recording procedures in some areas of the country and some incomplete data, the figures in these Tables should be taken only as a guide.

1.8 Abbreviations

Abbreviations are often used in the text. Some are probably familiar, eg *Archbold, Stone's*, WLR for Weekly Law Reports. Others will become familiar in time. The following list of common abbreviations should help.

BA 1976 (Bail Act 1976);

CAA 1968 or 1995 (Criminal Appeal Act, either 1968 or 1995);

CDA 1998 (Crime and Disorder Act 1998);

CICB (Criminal Injuries Compensation Board);

CJA (Criminal Justice Act, various years but most notably 1991 and 2003);

CJCSA 2000 (Criminal Justice and Court Services Act 2000);

CJPOA 1994 (Criminal Justice and Public Order Act 1994);

CLA (Criminal Law Act, various years);

CPIA 1996 (Criminal Procedure and Investigations Act 1996);

CPS (Crown Prosecution Service);

Cr App R (Criminal Appeal Reports. A specialist series, reporting cases from the Divisional Court of the Queen's Bench Division, Court of Appeal (Criminal Division), and the House of Lords);

Cr App R (S) (Criminal Appeal Reports (Sentencing). A companion to the Cr App R but concentrating on sentencing decisions);

Crim LR (Criminal Law Review. A monthly publication with brief, up-to-date reports of cases and useful articles);

C(S)A 1997 (Crime (Sentences) Act 1997);

CYPA 1933 or 1969 (Children and Young Persons Act, either 1933 or 1969);

DTO (Detention and Training Orders);

DTTO (Drug Testing and Treatment Orders);

ECHR (European Convention on Human Rights and Fundamental Freedoms);

HRA 1998 (Human Rights Act 1998);

JA 1974 (Juries Act 1974);

MCA 1980 (Magistrates' Courts Act 1980);

MHA 1983 (Mental Health Act 1983);

PACE 1984 (Police and Criminal Evidence Act 1984);

PCC(S)A 2000 (Powers of Criminal Courts (Sentencing) Act 2000);

ROA 1974 (Rehabilitation of Offenders Act 1974);

SCA 1981 (Supreme Court Act 1981);

t.i.c. (taken into consideration);

YJCEA 1999 (Youth Justice and Criminal Evidence Act 1999).

2

Preliminaries

Not tested on pgs 9 - 27.

2.1 Preamble

There are essentially two methods of commencing prosecutions, namely the arrest and charge of the suspect, described at **2.2** below, and the issue of process, described at **2.3** below. Two matters may be conveniently dealt with now by way of preamble.

2.1.1 Jurisdiction and immunity

English courts accept jurisdiction to try an accused for an offence committed in England and Wales, regardless of the nationality of the offender. In addition, English courts have jurisdiction over some offences committed abroad in certain circumstances, such as offences of murder and manslaughter where the accused is a British subject, and offences of hijacking regardless of the nationality of the accused. For a complete list of such offences, see *Archbold* (2005 edn), para 2–33 et seq and *Blackstone's Criminal Practice* (2005 edn), para A8.1 et seq. For the limited jurisdiction of magistrates' courts, see **2.5** below.

Certain persons are entitled to immunity from prosecution. The Queen is immune, as are foreign sovereigns and heads of state, their families and personal servants. Diplomatic agents, their staff and families are also immune. For a complete list of those immune from prosecution, see *Archbold* (2005 edn), para 1–82 et seq, *Blackstone's Criminal Practice* (2005 edn), para.D1.75.

2.1.2 The right to prosecute

The Crown Prosecution Service (CPS) was created by the Prosecution of Offences Act 1985, and is a single, national, prosecution service, with the Director of Public Prosecutions (DPP) at its head, and under the 'superintendence' of the Attorney-General. The main duty of the CPS is to take over and conduct all criminal proceedings commenced by the police, which includes the power to discontinue proceedings or to change or amend any charges originally preferred.

The right of an individual, and of certain statutory bodies such as the Inland Revenue, to institute and conduct criminal proceedings, is expressly preserved by the Act. However, under s 6(2), the DPP has an unfettered discretion to intervene in any proceedings, and conduct them on his or her own behalf.

2.2 Arrest and charge

Most police powers of arrest, interviewing and charging a suspect are contained in the Police and Criminal Evidence Act 1984 (PACE 1984) and the Codes of Practice created thereunder. In general terms, the Act provides the overall framework, and the Codes provide the fine detail. There are five Codes of Practice, namely:

- Code A: Code of Practice for the Exercise by Police Officers of Statutory Powers of Stop and Search.
- Code B: Code of Practice for the Searching of Premises by Police Officers and the Seizure of Property found by Police Officers on Persons and Premises.
- Code C: Code of Practice for the Detention, Treatment and Questioning of Persons by Police Officers.
- Code D: Code of Practice for the Identification of Persons by Police Officers.
- Code E: Code of Practice on Tape Recording.

The Codes contain detailed regulations on the exercise of police powers, and 'notes for guidance'. The notes for guidance are not provisions of the Codes, but are guidance to police officers and others about their application and interpretation.

The Codes of Practice apply to:

- police officers (PACE 1984, s 67(8) and (10)); and
- persons 'other than police officers who are charged with the duty of investigating offences or charging offenders' (PACE 1984, s 67(9)). This includes local authority officials, post office investigators, officers of the Serious Fraud Office, customs officers and store detectives. Whether a body or person conducting an enquiry is subject to s 67(9) is a question of fact in each case *(R v Seelig* [1992] 1 WLR 148).

Revised Codes of Practice to take into account the changes made by the CJA 2003 came into effect in August 2004. By CJA 2003, s 11, any further revisions may be brought into effect by the Home Secretary without the requirement to publish a draft code for consultation. Students are advised to consult the Codes in detail for their full terms and effect.

While students should be familiar with all five Codes, this Manual is mainly concerned with Code C, and any reference to 'The Code' should be understood accordingly. Students should consult the *Evidence Manual* and standard texts for a full discussion of this area.

2.2.1 Powers of arrest without warrant

A police officer has a number of powers of arrest in a number of circumstances, the most important of which are as follows:

(a) If the offence is designated by PACE 1984, s 24 as an arrestable offence, ie:
  (i)   where the sentence for the offence is fixed by law (eg murder);
  (ii) where the offence carries at least five years' imprisonment (eg theft);
  (iii) specified offences in s 24(2), for example, taking a motor vehicle without authority or going equipped for stealing under ss 12(1) and 25(1) respectively of the Theft Act 1968.

(b) Under PACE 1984, s 25, if a police officer has reasonable grounds for suspecting that an offence, not included within s 24, has been committed or attempted, he may arrest the person he suspects of committing the offence if one of the following conditions, known as the general arrest conditions, is satisfied:
  (i)   it is impossible to ascertain accurately the suspect's name and address;
  (ii) the officer has reasonable grounds for believing that arrest is necessary to prevent the suspect:
    — causing physical injury to himself or herself or any other person;
    — suffering physical injury;

> — causing loss of or damage to property;
>
> — committing an offence against public decency; or
>
> — causing an unlawful obstruction of the highway; or

(iii) the officer has reasonable grounds for believing that arrest is necessary to protect a child or other vulnerable person from the suspect.

(c) Schedule 2 to PACE 1984 preserves pre-existing powers of arrest created under earlier statutes, for example, where a suspect fails to provide a breath test under the Road Traffic Act 1988, s 6(5) or is unlikely to comply with the conditions of his bail under the Bail Act 1976, s 7 (see further **3.15**).

(d) PACE 1984, s 46(1), inserted by s 29 of the Criminal Justice and Public Order Act 1994 (CJPOA), provides the police with a power to arrest any person who, having been bailed by police subject to a duty to attend at a police station, fails to do so.

(e) The Public Order Act 1986 contains specific powers of arrest relating to offences of fear of provocation of violence (s 4(3)), and harassment, alarm or distress (s 5(4)).

(f) The CJPOA 1994 gives a constable in uniform the power to remove trespassers from land (s 61), to seize or remove any vehicle after a request to remove has been refused (s 62), and certain other powers to deal with raves.

(g) The Terrorism Act 2000, ss 40 and 41 confers powers of arrest in relation to persons who are reasonably suspected of being terrorists.

(h) CJA 2003, s 3 confers powers of arrest in relation to:

(i) CJA 1925, s 36;

(ii) having possession of a controlled drug in relation to cannabis or cannabis resin, under Misuse of Drugs Act 1971;

(iii) false statements and withholding material information under RTA 1988, s 174.

Important note. Under the Serious Organised Crime and Police Act 2005 (SOCPA), s 110, the present powers of arrest under PACE 1984, ss 24 and 25 will go. A new s 24 will be substituted along with a new provision, s 24A, detailing a citizen's powers of arrest. One of the consequences is that the many references in PACE 1984 to 'arrestable offences' and 'serious arrestable offence' (see **2.2.2**) will be simply replaced by references to 'indictable offences'; see SOCPA 2005, Sch 7. None of these provisions is in force at the time of writing.

2.2.2 Serious arrestable offences

PACE 1984 defines certain offences as being serious arrestable offences. While these offences do not carry any greater power of arrest, the fact that the defendant is charged with a serious arrestable offence gives the police additional powers during detention (see **2.2.10**) and it is convenient to include them here. Under PACE 1984, s 116 and Sch 5 (as amended), the following are always serious arrestable offences:

(a) Treason.

(b) Murder.

(c) Manslaughter.

(d) Kidnapping.

(e) Being knowingly concerned, in relation to any goods, in any fraudulent evasion or attempt at evasion of a prohibition on importing indecent or obscene articles contrary to Customs and Excise Management Act 1979, s 170.

(f) Causing explosions likely to endanger life or property contrary to the Explosive Substances Act 1883, s 2.

(g) Possession of firearms with intent to injure contrary to the Firearms Act 1968, s 16.

(h) Use of firearms and imitation firearms to resist arrest contrary to the Firearms Act 1968, s 17.

(i) Carrying firearms with criminal intent contrary to the Firearms Act 1968, s 18.

(j) Hostage-taking contrary to the Taking of Hostages Act 1982, s 1.

(k) Hijacking contrary to the Aviation Security Act 1982.

(l) Torture contrary to the Criminal Justice Act 1988, s 134.

(m) Causing death by dangerous driving contrary to the Road Traffic Act 1988, s 1.

(n) Causing death by careless driving when under the influence of drink or drugs contrary to the Road Traffic Act 1988, s 3A.

(o) Endangering safety at aerodromes contrary to the Aviation and Maritime Security Act 1990, s 1.

(p) Hijacking of ships contrary to the Aviation and Maritime Security Act 1990, s 9.

(q) Seizing or exercising control of fixed platforms contrary to the Aviation and Maritime Security Act 1990, s 10.

(r) Hijacking Channel Tunnel trains contrary to Channel Tunnel Security Order 1994 (SI 1994/570), art 4.

(s) Exercising or seizing control of the tunnel system contrary to Channel Tunnel Security Order 1994 (SI 1994/570), art 5.

(t) Taking and distributing indecent photographs or pseudo-photographs of children and the publication of obscene matter under the Protection of Children Act 1978, s 1 and the Obscene Publications Act 1959, s 2.

(u) Rape or rape of a child under 13 contrary to the Sexual Offences Act 2003, ss 1 and 5.

(v) Assault by penetration or assault by penetration of a child under 13 contrary to the Sexual Offences Act 2003, ss 2 and 6.

(w) Causing a person (or a child under 13) to engage in penetrative sexual activity without consent contrary to the Sexual Offences Act 2003, s 4 (or s 8)

(x) Engaging in penetrative sexual activity with, or causing or inciting the engagement in penetrative sexual activity by, a person with a mental disorder impeding choice contrary to the Sexual Offences Act 2003, s 30 and 31.

(y) Causing or allowing the death of a child or vulnerable adult contrary to the Domestic Violence, Crime and Victims Act 2004.

Under PACE 1984, s 116(3), any other arrestable offence is also a serious arrestable offence if its commission has led to, is intended or is likely to lead to, or consists of making a threat which if carried out would lead to:

(a) Serious harm to the security of the State or to public order.

(b) Serious interference with the administration of justice or with the investigation of offences or particular offence.

(c) The death of any person.

(d) Serious injury to any person. Injury includes any disease and any impairment of a person's physical or mental condition.

(e) Substantial financial gain to any person.

(f) Serious financial loss to any person. Loss is serious if it is serious for the person who suffers it (see for example *R v McIvor* [1987] Crim LR 409). *Blackstone's Criminal Practice* has in the past suggested that this provision may therefore apply to a series of petty thefts or burglaries upon the old or vulnerable.

Important note. The Serious Organised Crime and Police Act 2005 will remove the concept of the 'serious arrestable offence', when Sch 7 comes into force.

2.2.3 Effecting the arrest

A person is arrested by:

- being informed by a police officer that he or she is under arrest; or
- being physically seized by a police officer, in which case he or she must be informed that he or she is under arrest as soon as is practicable after the arrest (PACE 1984, s 28(1)); or
- a combination of words and conduct which makes it clear that the officer will, if necessary, use force to prevent the person from leaving *(Murray v Ministry of Defence* [1988] 1 WLR 692).

The arrested person must be told the reason for the arrest, even if it is obvious (s 28(3) and (4)). ECHR, Article 5(2) also provides that an arrested person should be told promptly and in language which he understands of the reason for his arrest and any charge against him.

If the reason given renders the arrest unlawful, it is irrelevant that there was a valid reason for the arrest if it was not communicated to the arrested person at the time *(Christie v Leachinsky* [1947] AC 5 73; *Abassy v Commissioner of Police of the Metropolis* [1990] 1 WLR 385).

It is not a requirement of s 28 that the arresting officer supply the reason for the arrest, as long as a reason is provided as soon as practicable thereafter *(Dhesi v Chief Constable of the West Midlands* The Times, 9 May 2000, where the defendant was arrested by one officer and directed towards another nearby who supplied the reason).

The arrested person must be taken immediately to a police station, unless it is reasonable to carry out other investigations first (PACE 1984, s 30(1), (10) and (10A) and *Dallison v Caffery* [1965] 1 QB 348), or released on street bail (see **2.2.4**).

In each police area, certain police stations are designated as being suitable for the detention of arrested persons (PACE 1984, s 35(1)). If it is anticipated that the detention will exceed six hours, the arrested person must be detained in a designated police station (s 30(2) and (3)).

There is nothing improper in arresting a suspect on a holding charge provided there are reasonable grounds for arresting that person on that charge. It makes no difference, if the arrest is proper, that the motive is to investigate other and more serious offences *(R v Chalkley and Jeffries* [1998] QB 848). But if the arresting officer knows that there is no possibility of a charge being brought, the arrest will be improper even if there are in fact reasonable grounds for suspecting that an offence has been committed *(Holgate-Mohammed v Duke* [1984] AC 437).

Powers of arrest are also governed by ECHR, Article 5, to which students are referred. Article 5 is construed narrowly, and sets out an exhaustive list of the circumstances in which a person may properly be detained. UK domestic law has been held to be formulated with 'the degree of precision required by the Convention' in *Steel v UK* [1988] 28 EHRR 602.

2.2.4   Street bail

By virtue of PACE 1984, s 30A, as inserted by the CJA 2003, the police officer has the power to release the arrested person on bail, even before he is taken to the police station. The only condition which the police may impose on street bail is to attend a police station. There is no restriction on which police station. However, the police officer must give the bailed person a notice, specifying the offence for which he was arrested, the ground on which he was arrested and certain other practical matters (s 30B). If the bailed person fails to attend as required, he may be arrested (s 30D).

2.2.5   At the police station

The following, rather complicated, timetable for the detention of the arrested person (hereafter called the 'suspect') is contained in PACE 1984, ss 34–46. When reading it please note that references to 'arrestable offence' and 'serious arrestable offence' will be replaced with 'indictable offences' when SOCPA 2005, Sch 7, comes into effect.

Note that a person who attends at a police station voluntarily, or any other place where a police officer is present, is entitled to leave at any time, or he or she must be arrested to prevent his or her leaving.

Stage 1: At the police station, the suspect is taken to the custody officer. Each designated police station has one or more officers, of at least the rank of sergeant, appointed as custody officers. The custody officer must not, except in exceptional circumstances, be an officer involved in the investigation.

As regards the suspect, the custody officer has several duties, including, under the revised Code, specific duties in relation to vulnerable suspects. The most important duties are:

(a) To inform the suspect of his or her rights to consult a solicitor, to have someone informed, and to examine the Codes of Practice (see **2.2.10** below).

(b) To determine whether the suspect:

  (i)   is in need of medical treatment or attention (see **2.2.6** below);

  (ii) requires either an appropriate adult, help to check documentation, or an interpreter;

and to record the decision.

(c) To maintain a custody record, being a complete record of the suspect's detention, including such matters as times of meals, interviews, the caution, if given, and the charge. A solicitor or appropriate adult must be permitted to consult a suspect's custody record as soon as practicable after the suspect's arrival at the police station and at any other time during the suspect's detention (Code C, para 2.4).

(d) To ascertain and record everything which the suspect has with him when detaining him. Prior to CJA 2003, every item in the suspect's possession was individually recorded. This was useful to the defence solicitor in that it may reveal other reasons behind the suspect's arrest. It also protected the police themselves from allegations of tampering with the possessions. Recording possessions, however, was also seen as time-consuming and unnecessary. CJA 2003, s 8 therefore provides that though the custody officer will still have to ascertain everything that the detained person has with him, he will no longer have to record it on the custody record. Any record that is made does not have to be part of the custody record under s 54(2A), but the suspect must be allowed the opportunity to check and sign it as correct. There is no provision that the suspect's solicitor is given the opportunity to examine the record if not in the custody record.

It is a matter for the custody officer to decide whether a record should be made and that if the record is not on the custody record, the custody officer should record where the record exists. Home Office Circular 60/2003 para 5.3 indicates in deciding whether to record property, the custody officer should have regard to:

- the circumstances of the case, eg whether the property could be the proceeds of crime, could have been used in the commission of crime or could be relevant evidence;
- the nature and volume of the property — drugs, money and property of substantial value should always be recorded;
- the wishes of the suspect — he should be asked if there are any items he wants to be recorded and his wishes should, 'within reason and if practicable' be complied with;
- the facilities for securing property — detailed records may not be necessary if placed in a sealed bag in the presence of the suspect.

(e) To oversee the whole of the suspect's detention. As the custody officer is unconnected with the investigation, he or she can take a more detached view when assessing whether the suspect should be released or detained, or whether there is sufficient evidence to charge the suspect.

(f) To order the release of the suspect, or his or her charge, unless continued detention without charge is necessary:

(i)   to secure or preserve evidence relating to the offence; or

(ii) to obtain such evidence by questioning the suspect.

The CJA 2003, ss 9 and 10 amend PACE 1984 s 61 and abolish previous requirements that the taking of fingerprints and non-intimate samples be subject to the suspect's consent. This change now allows them to be taken by the police as a matter of routine, where the suspect has been arrested for a recordable offence.

The CJA 2003 also provides that the fingerprints and samples may be kept indefinitely. This was challenged in *R v Chief Constable of South Yorkshire; R v Chief Constable of South Yorkshire* [2004] 4 All ER 193 where the right to retain such data for ever was challenged but upheld.

Under PACE 1984, s 63B, the police may test detained persons over the age of 18 for drugs. This power applies to certain trigger offences only, listed in the Criminal Justice and Court Services Act 2000, and includes certain offences under the Theft Act 1968 and under the Misuse of Drugs Act 1971. The police must first have reasonable grounds to suspect that that the offender's offending is contributed to or caused by his drug habit. Once a sample has been taken, it can be used to inform decisions in relation to bail and sentencing, and guides supervision while in detention.

Stage 2: If the custody officer authorises detention, periodic reviews of the detention must be made by a review officer to determine whether that detention is still necessary. The review officer must give the opportunity to the suspect, his solicitor (if available) or an appropriate adult (if available) to make representations about the detention. If the suspect has not yet been charged, the review officer must be:

- an officer of at least the rank of inspector; and
- not directly involved in the investigation.

The first review must be held within six hours of the original decision to detain. Note that, in any event, a suspect who is detained in a cell should be visited at least every hour.

Note that there are a number of persons who are not subject to statutory review, eg those who attend the police station voluntarily. The Notes for Guidance, para 1513 of the Code, however, states that those persons should nevertheless still have their detention reviewed as a matter of good practice.

Stage 3: A second review of the detention must be held within nine hours of the first review. Reviews must thereafter be held at no more than nine-hourly intervals. According to *Roberts v Chief Constable of the Cheshire Constabulary* [1999] 1 WLR 662, failure to review renders a previously lawful detention unlawful, and amounts to the tort of false imprisonment.

Generally the review officer must be present at the police station holding the suspect. CJA 2003, s 6 however, permits the reviews of detention under s 40 to be conducted by telephone without any pre-conditions. In other words, reviews by telephone may take place as a matter of course, and there is no requirement of, for example, practicability or impracticability of reviews on site.

The revised Code C, para 15.3 states that the decision on the type of review 'must always take full account of the needs of the person in custody'. The benefits of carrying out a review in person should always be considered, based on the individual circumstances of each case with specific additional consideration being given if the person is a juvenile, mentally vulnerable, has been subject to medical attention other than routine minor ailments or there are presentational or community issues around the person's detention.

Even though the review may be conducted by telephone, the review officer must still give the suspect or his/her solicitor, the opportunity to make representations which may be made orally or by fax, if fax facilities are available.

Telephone reviews are not permitted where video-conferencing facilities are available and practicable to use. At present, video-conferencing facilities are not available.

Stage 4: After a maximum of 24 hours after arrival at the police station, the suspect must be released or charged, unless the following conditions are satisfied:

  (a) The continued detention is authorised by an officer of at least the rank of superintendent.

  (b) The suspect is under arrest in connection with an arrestable offence.

  (c) The authorising officer has reasonable grounds for believing that the suspect's continued detention is necessary to:

    (i)   secure or preserve evidence relating to the offence; or

    (ii) obtain such evidence by questioning the suspect.

  (d) The authorising officer has reasonable grounds for believing that the investigation is being conducted diligently and expeditiously.

At para 15.2, the Code states that in the case of a juvenile or mentally vulnerable person detention beyond 24 hours will be dependent upon the circumstances of the case and with regard to the person's:

  (a) special vulnerability;

  (b) the legal obligation to provide an opportunity for representations to be made prior to a decision about extending detention;

  (c) the need to consult and consider the views of any appropriate adult; and

  (d) any alternatives to police custody.

Home Office Circular 60/2003 provides that the power to detain beyond 24 hours:

  • should be used sparingly and only where there is full justification;

  • should only be used where the authorising officer is satisfied that alternatives to continued detention, such as bail or restorative justice, have been considered and determined to be inappropriate;

  • in the case of a juvenile or mentally vulnerable person, should normally be used only where he or she is detained in respect of a serious arrestable offence.

Stage 5: After a maximum of 36 hours, the suspect must be released or charged unless a warrant of further detention is issued by a magistrates' court. A court may authorise detention for a further 36 hours if:

(a) The court comprises at least two magistrates.

(b) The application for the warrant is made on oath and supported by written information which is also supplied to the suspect.

(c) The suspect is present in court.

(d) The suspect is detained in connection with an arrestable offence (amended by CJA 2003).

(e) The court is satisfied of the matters in paras (c) and (d) of Stage 4 above.

Stage 6: After a maximum of 72 hours the court may authorise further detention if all the conditions of Stage 5 above are satisfied. This further detention is for a maximum of 36 hours, and, in any event, the court may not authorise detention for a period of more than 96 hours.

Stage 7: No detention without charge is permitted after 96 hours. Thereafter the suspect must be charged and/or released.

Notes:

1. Code C, para 1.1 provides: 'All persons in custody must be dealt with expeditiously, and released as soon as the need for detention no longer applies.'

2. A person who has been released may not be re-arrested without a warrant for the offence for which he was originally arrested unless new evidence justifying a further arrest has come to light (PACE 1984, s 41(9)).

3. These time limits do not apply to those who are detained under the Terrorism Act 2000. Under s 41, a person arrested under the 2000 Act must be released not later than 48 hours from the time of his arrest. If it is intended to make an application for further detention, however, he may be detained pending the making of that application, or detained pending the outcome of the application if one has already been made. As amended by the CJA 2003, s 306, the Terrorism Act 2000 permits second and subsequent periods of further detention to last for a period of 14 days from the time of the arrest. Students are referred to the Terrorism Act 2000 for its full terms and provisions.

2.2.6   The risk assessment

Paragraphs 3.6–3.10 of the Code require the custody officer to initiate a structured risk assessment of whether the suspect is likely to present a specific risk to custody staff or to him or herself, and to make an appropriate response if such risks are identified. Guidance as to risk assessments is set out in HO Circular 32/2000, and includes the following points:

(a) The requirement to carry out a risk assessment applies to all persons entering into police custody, and all persons must be asked the questions set out in (b) below.

(b) The questions include whether the suspect has any injury or illness, whether they are taking any medication, whether they are suffering from any mental health problems or depression, and whether they have ever tried to harm themselves.

(c) The result of the risk assessment must be entered into the custody record, indicating whether any risks have been identified and the answers to the questions.

(d) Risk assessment is an ongoing process and must be reviewed if circumstances change.

(e) Risk categories include medical or mental conditions, medication issued, special needs, violence, escape risk, suicide or self-harm, injuries, vulnerability and any force, restraint or spray used.

(f) It is the responsibility of the custody officer to decide on the appropriate response to any risk identified.

(g) If the suspect is to be transferred from a police station, a Prisoner Escort Record must be completed setting out the details of the risk assessment.

It is essential that health care professionals who are consulted consider the functional ability of the suspect, rather than simply relying on a medical diagnosis, eg is it possible for a person with a severe mental illness to be fit for interview? (See Annex G, para 4 and see above.)

Health care professionals should also advise on the need for an appropriate adult to be present, whether a reassessment of the suspect's fitness for interview may be necessary if the interview lasts beyond a specified time, and whether a further specialist opinion may be required (Annex G, para 5).

The role of the health care professional is to consider the risks and advise the custody officer as to the outcome of that consideration. The health care professional's determination and any advice or recommendations should be made in writing and form part of the custody record (Annex G, para 7). This leaves open the issue of whether all the symptoms of which the suspect complains are to be included, and also the question of just how much of the suspect's medical history may be available to the police.

2.2.7 The caution

Under para 10.1 of the Code, where there are 'grounds to suspect' a person of an offence, he or she must be cautioned before questioning if either the suspect's answers or silence may be put before a court in a prosecution. There must be some reasonable, objective grounds for suspicion, based on known facts or information relevant to the likelihood that the person to be questioned has committed the offence.

Because a caution is required only where there are 'grounds to suspect' the person of an offence, it need not be given where the questions are merely general, preliminary questions, to establish, for example, identity or ownership, in furtherance of a proper and effective search, or to obtain verification of any written record of comments made outside the context of an interview.

In addition, para 10.4 provides that the caution must be given on arrest unless the suspect has already been cautioned immediately prior to arrest, or because it is impracticable to administer the caution by reason of the suspect's behaviour at the time.

The caution should be re-administered after a break in questioning, but see *R v Oni* [1992] Crim LR 183, where it was held to be unnecessary after a break of only two minutes. It should always be re-administered, however, if there is any doubt as to whether or not it is necessary.

The wording of the caution arises from the provisions of the CJPOA 1994, s 34. Section 34 provides that a court 'may draw such inferences as appear proper' if evidence is given that the suspect:

(a) at any time before he was charged with the offence, on being questioned under caution by a constable trying to discover whether or by whom the offence had been committed, failed to mention any fact relied on in his defence in those proceedings; or

(b) on being charged with the offence or officially informed that he might be prosecuted for it, failed to mention any such fact, being a fact which, in the circumstances existing at the time, the accused could reasonably have been expected to mention when so questioned, charged or informed, as the case may be.

The caution is in the following terms:

You do not have to say anything. But it may harm your defence if you do not mention, when questioned, something which you later rely on in court. Anything you do say may be given in evidence.

Provided that the sense of the caution is preserved, minor deviations from the stated form do not constitute a breach of the Code.

This caution will be used in the majority of cases. However, s 58 of the Youth Justice and Criminal Evidence Act 1999 amends the CJPOA 1994 by providing that no inferences may be drawn where the suspect has not been given the opportunity to obtain legal advice. In these circumstances, the above caution is not to be used. In these circumstances, the appropriate caution is:

juveniles

You do not have to say anything, but anything you do say may be given in evidence.

Note that this is the same caution which is used in the exceptional cases where the suspect is questioned after charge.

The circumstances in which the latter form of caution should be used instead of the former are set out in a new Annex C as follows:

1. *The Criminal Justice and Public Order Act 1994 sections 34, 36 and 37 as amended by the Youth Justice and Criminal Evidence Act 1999 section 58 describe the conditions under which adverse inferences may be drawn from a person's failure or refusal to say anything about their involvement in the offence when interviewed* [note that this does not accurately reflect the wording of s 34, 36 or 37], *after being charged or informed they may be prosecuted. These provisions are subject to an overriding restriction on the ability of a court or jury to draw adverse inferences from a person's silence. This restriction applies:*

    (a) *to any detainee at a police station (see Note 10C) who, before being interviewed (see section 11) or being charged or informed they may be prosecuted (see section 16) has:*
      (i) *asked for legal advice (see section 6, paragraph 6.1);*
      (ii) *not been allowed an opportunity to consult a solicitor, including a duty solicitor as in this Code; and*
      (iii) *not changed their mind about wanting legal advice (see section 6, paragraph 6.6(d)).*

Note that the condition in (ii) will:

- apply when a detainee who has asked for legal advice is interviewed before speaking to a solicitor as in section 6, paragraph 6.6(a) or (b);

- not apply if the detained person declines to ask for the duty solicitor (see section 6, paragraph 6.6(c) and (d)).

    (b) *to any person charged with, or informed they may be prosecuted for an offence who:*
      (i) *has had brought to their notice a written statement made by another person or the content of an interview with another person which relates to that offence (see section 16, paragraph 16.4);*
      (ii) *is to be interviewed about that offence (see section 16, paragraph 16.5; or*
      (iii) *makes a written statement about that offence (see Annex D, paragraphs 4 and 9).*

Note that it would be possible for a suspect to be given both cautions at different times, eg where the usual caution is given on arrest, but the shorter caution is administered later when a decision to delay access to a solicitor is made at the police station by an officer of not less than superintendent rank. Further, the usual caution would need to be administered if and when legal advice is obtained, and then the shorter caution once again if the suspect is, unusually, questioned after charge.

2.2.8 Interviews

An interview is defined by Code C, para 11.1A as:

the questioning of a person regarding their involvement or suspected involvement in a criminal offence or offences which . . . is required to be carried out under caution.

Many defence solicitors found that there was confusion between deciding whether a suspect was fit to be *detained* and whether he or she was fit to be *interviewed*. Paragraph 9.13 of the revised Code requires a custody officer to ask a health care professional called to see a suspect, both about the risks or problems associated with continued detention and about 'when to carry out an interview' as well as any safeguards that are required.

Further, the revised Code includes a new Annex G, 'Fitness to be Interviewed', which provides guidance as to whether a detainee might be at risk in an interview. 'Risk' here means, according to Annex G, para 2, that:

- conducting the interview could significantly harm the detainee's physical or mental state;

- anything the detainee says in the interview about his or her involvement or suspected involvement in the offence about which he or she is being interviewed might be considered unreliable in subsequent court proceedings because of his or her physical or mental state.

The arrested person must not be interviewed except at a police station, unless any delay would be likely to lead to interference with evidence, harm to persons, the alerting of suspects or the hindering of the recovery of property (Annex G, para 11.1).

Any interview at a police station should take place in an adequately lit, heated and ventilated interview room. At the beginning of the interview, the interviewing officer must identify himself or herself and any other officer present. The suspect must not be required to stand during the interview, and should be given breaks at recognised mealtimes. In addition, there should be short breaks for refreshment every two hours. The Code specifically provides that in any period of 24 hours, the suspect should be allowed a continuous period of eight hours' sleep without interruption, normally at night.

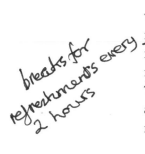
breaks for refreshments every 2 hours

All interviews with persons cautioned in respect of an indictable offence, or where questions are put to, or a statement of another person is shown to, a person who has been charged, should be tape-recorded. Tapes need not be made if it is not reasonably practicable to do so for reasons such as the failure of the equipment, and the custody officer considers that the interview should not be delayed. For detailed provisions relating to tape-recording, see Code E.

Problems occasionally arise where a brief conversation or 'exchange' takes place between police officers and a suspect outside a police station, for example, after a speeding or stolen car has been stopped. If the exchange goes beyond a mere request for information and the suspect is, in effect, questioned about his or her involvement in an offence, then the exchange has become an interview. It is the nature of the questioning rather than the length which is relevant (*R v Ward* (1994) 98 Crim App R 337). If the questioning has become an interview, then the defendant is immediately protected by the provisions of the Code, including the requirement to caution, and any breaches will be taken into account by the court at any subsequent trial in determining the reliability of any confession that may have been made (see for example *R v Cox* (1993) 96 Cr App R 464). For a full discussion of the law relating to confessions, see the ***Evidence Manual***.

A problem unresolved under the 1995 Code was the point at which an interview must cease. Paragraph 11.4 of the 1995 Code provided that as soon as the officer believed that a prosecution should be brought against the suspect, and there was sufficient evidence for a prosecution to succeed, the officer should ask the suspect if he or she had anything further to say and, if not, the officer should stop the interview. It has consequently been held that anything said after that moment should not be admissable as evidence (*R v Pointer* [1997] Crim LR 676, *R v Gayle* [1999] Crim LR 502). Other cases, however, have held that the term 'sufficient evidence to prosecute' must involve some consideration of any explanation given by the suspect (*R v McGuinness* [1999] Crim LR 318, *R v Elliott* [2002] EWCA Crim 931, *R v Howell* [2003] EWCA Crim 1).

Paragraph 11.6 of the revised Code seeks to resolve this issue and provide the police with some leeway. Paragraph 11.6 provides as follows:

The interview or further interview of a person about an offence with which that person has not been charged or for which they have not been informed they may be prosecuted, must cease when the officer in charge of the investigation:

(a) *is satisfied all the questions they consider relevant to obtaining accurate and reliable information about the offence have been put to the suspect, this includes allowing the suspect an opportunity to give an innocent explanation, and asking questions to test if the explanation is accurate and reliable eg to clear up ambiguities or clarify what the suspect said;*

(b) *has taken account of any other available evidence; and*

(c) *the officer in charge of the investigation, or in the case of a detained suspect, the custody officer . . . reasonably believes there is sufficient evidence to provide a realistic prospect of conviction for that offence if the person was prosecuted for it.*

This paragraph does not prevent officers in revenue cases or acting under the confiscation provisions of the Criminal Justice Act 1988 or the Drug Trafficking Act 1994 from inviting suspects to complete a formal question and answer record after the interview is concluded.

2.2.9   Persons at risk

Special rules apply when the police are dealing with persons at risk, that is, juveniles, the mentally disordered or otherwise mentally vulnerable persons. The reason, according to the Notes for Guidance, is that, although such persons are often capable of providing reliable evidence, they may, without knowing or wishing to do so, be particularly prone in certain circumstances to provide information that may be unreliable, misleading or self-incriminating. Special care should always be taken when questioning such a person and, because of the risk of unreliable evidence, corroboration should be obtained wherever possible.

Paragraph 1G of the Code (Notes for Guidance) provides that the term 'mentally vulnerable' applies to those who 'because of their mental state or capacity, may not understand the significance of what is said, of questions or of their replies'. This would appear to be a much wider definition than under the 1995 Code and would appear to include those whose mental state is adversely affected by drink or drugs, as the term is not restricted to those whose mental state is affected by some kind of mental disorder.

'Mental disorder' is defined by the Mental Health Act 1983, s 1(2) as 'mental illness, arrested or incomplete development of mind, psychopathic disorder and any other disorder and any other disorder or disability'. When a custody officer has any doubt as to the mental state or capacity of any detainee, the officer should treat the detainee as mentally vulnerable and call an appropriate adult.

A juvenile or person who is mentally disordered or otherwise mentally vulnerable should not be interviewed regarding their involvement or suspected involvement in a criminal offence or asked to provide a statement under caution except in the presence of an appropriate adult. If an appropriate adult is present at the interview, he or she should be informed that:

- he or she is not expected to act simply as an observer; and
- the purpose of his or her presence is to:
  — advise the person being interviewed;
  — observe whether the interview is being conducted properly and fairly; and
  — facilitate communication with the person being interviewed.

An appropriate adult is, for example, the parent or guardian of a juvenile, or the guardian of the person who is mentally disordered. The adult must be 'appropriate' both in the sense of being capable of understanding what is happening and in the sense of being someone the person at risk wishes to have present and not, for example, an estranged parent (see *R v Morse* [1991] Crim LR 195 and *DPP v Blake* (1989) 89 Cr App R 179).

In an emergency, however, a person at risk may be interviewed without delay under para 11.18 of the Code if an officer of not less than the rank of superintendent is satisfied that the interview would not significantly harm the person's physical or mental state, and considers that delay would be likely to:

- lead to interference with or harm to evidence connected with an offence;
- lead to interference with or physical harm to other people or serious loss or damage to property;
- lead to the alerting of other people suspected of committing an offence but not yet arrested for it; or
- hinder the recovery of property obtained in consequence of the commission of an offence.

This provision also applies to:

- any person other than persons at risk who at the time of the interview appears to be unable to:
  — appreciate the significance of questions and their answers; or
  — understand what is happening because of the effects of drink, drugs or any illness, ailment or condition;
- a person who has difficulty understanding English or has a hearing disability if at the time of the interview an interpreter is not present.

An appropriate adult should always be involved if there is any doubt about a person's age, mental state or capacity.

2.2.10   The rights of the suspect

The suspect has three important rights in the police station.

2.2.10.1   The right to see a solicitor

PACE 1984, s 58(1) provides that a person who has been arrested and is being held in custody is entitled, upon request, to consult privately with a solicitor at any time, whether in person, in writing or by telephone. The suspect must be informed of this right by the custody officer on arrival at the police station and, if he or she declines legal advice, the suspect must be asked why, and any reasons should be recorded on the custody or interview record as appropriate. The request must be complied with as soon as is practicable.

Note that s 58 gives the suspect the right to consult a solicitor but not specifically the right to have the solicitor present during the interview. However, para 6.7 of the Code provides that if the solicitor is available at the time the interview begins or is in progress, the suspect 'must be allowed to have his solicitor present while he is interviewed'.

The right must not be denied, and may not be delayed for more than 36 hours after the suspect's arrival at the police station. Access to legal advice may be delayed only if:

(a) the suspect is in police detention in connection with a serious arrestable offence, and has not yet been charged with an offence;

(b) an officer of not less than the rank of superintendent authorises the delay; and

(c) that officer has reasonable grounds for believing that the exercise of the right at the present time will lead to:
  — interference with, or harm to, evidence connected with a serious arrestable offence; or
  — interference with, or physical harm to, other people; or
  — lead to the alerting of other people suspected of having committed a serious arrestable offence but not yet arrested for it; or
  — hinder the recovery of property obtained in consequence of the commission of such an offence.

See PACE 1984, s 58(6) and (8), and Code C, Annex B. Note also that, when SOCPA 2005, Sch 7, comes into force, it will replace 'serious arrestable offence' in PACE 1984, s 58, with 'indictable offence'. The same change will be made in PACE 1984, s 56.

Code C, Annex B, para 2 further provides that access to legal advice may also be delayed if the serious arrestable offence is a drug trafficking offence or an offence to which the Criminal Justice Act 1988, Pt VI (confiscation orders) applies, and certain other conditions are satisfied.

Once a suspect has requested legal advice, he or she may not be interviewed (or an interview continued) unless:

(a) PACE 1984, s 58(6) applies (see above); or

(b) an officer of superintendent rank or above has reasonable grounds for believing that:
  (i) the consequent delay might (note that the earlier version of the Code used the word will):
    — lead to interference with, or harm to, evidence connected with an offence,
    — lead to interference with, or physical harm to, other people;
    — lead to serious loss of, or damage to, property;
    — lead to the alerting of other people suspected of having committed an offence but not yet arrested for it;
    — hinder the recovery of property obtained in consequence of the commission of an offence; or
  (ii) when a solicitor, including a duty solicitor, has been contacted and has agreed to attend, awaiting their arrival would cause unreasonable delay to the process of investigation; or

(c) the solicitor that the suspect has nominated or selected from a list cannot be contacted, has previously indicated that he or she does not wish to attend, or declines to attend and the suspect has declined to ask for the duty solicitor having been advised about the Duty Solicitor Scheme; or

(d) the detainee has changed his or her mind about wanting legal advice and consented to the interview beginning (or continuing).

See Code C, para 6.

The rights may be delayed only for as long as the grounds exist, and in no case for longer than 36 hours.

The suspect must be told why access to a solicitor has been delayed, and that reason must be entered in the custody record.

Both PACE 1984, s 58 and para 6 of the Code provide for the right of the suspect to consult *privately* with a solicitor at any time. The only exception to this is under s 41 and Sch 7 of the Terrorism Act 2000, which provide that, if certain conditions are met, an Assistant Chief Constable may direct that any consultation take place in the sight and hearing of a qualified officer. Defence solicitors, however, have long been concerned that consultations between a suspect and his or her solicitor have on occasion been the subject of covert surveillance. No provisions are included in the Code to prevent or control such surveillance.

Wrongful denial of access to a solicitor may lead to a confession made without having taken legal advice being excluded at any subsequent trial. See for example R *v Samuel* [1988] 1 WLR 920 and *R v Alladice* (1988) 87 Cr App R 380. For a full discussion of the cases where a confession has been obtained in such circumstances, students should refer to the ***Evidence Manual***.

2.2.10.2 The right to have someone informed

Under PACE 1984, s 56(1) the suspect has the right to have a friend or relative, or some other person who is known to him or her, or who is likely to take an interest in his or her welfare, told of the arrest. The request must be complied with as soon as is practicable.

This right may be delayed in circumstances similar to the circumstances permitting the delay of access to legal advice.

In addition, the suspect must be given writing materials on request and allowed to make one phone call for a reasonable time, unless the above circumstances apply.

2.2.10.3 The right to consult the Codes

The suspect has the right to consult all the Codes of Practice. This does not entitle him or her to delay unreasonably any investigation or administrative action while this is done (Code C, paras 3.1 and 3D).

2.2.11 The charge

Except for routine cases or where the police need to make a holding charge, the decision as to which offence the suspect is charged with is a matter for the CPS rather than the police.

PACE 1984, s 37(7) as amended by CJA 2003, s 28 and Sch 2, provides that once the custody officer has sufficient evidence upon which to charge, he has the following options:

(a) to release the suspect without charge, and on bail for the purpose of enabling the DPP to make a decision as to the charge. The suspect must be informed that there will be a consultation with the DPP as to the charge. Consultation with the DPP should take place as soon as is reasonably practicable.

The ultimate aim is that the CPS will decide on charge in all indictable only, triable either way and summary only offences where the custody officer has decided that there is sufficient evidence to charge, except for specified offences. The specified offences include most road traffic offences, absconding under the Bail Act 1976 and various other summary only offences. The custody officer has to have regard to the decision of the DPP.

In the interim, except for certain specified offences, listed in Annex A of the Notes of Guidance to the Code, (which include serious offences of violence, certain public order offences and deception under the Theft Acts 1968 and 1978) the police may decide on charge:

- in any summary or either way offence;
- where it appears to the custody officer that a guilty plea is likely;
- where the case is suitable for sentencing in the magistrates' court.

Under PACE 1984, s 37A (inserted by CJA 2003, Sch 2) the DPP may issue guidance for the purposes of enabling custody officers decide how to deal with persons under s 37(7) and what information should be forwarded to the DPP.

Section 37B provides details as to the consultation with the DPP. It provides as follows:

(1)   *Where a person is released on bail under section 37(7)(a) above, an officer involved in the investigation of the offence shall, as soon as reasonably practicable send to the Director of Public Prosecutions such information as may be specified in guidance under section 37A above.*

(2)   *The Director of Public Prosecutions shall decide whether there is sufficient evidence to charge the person with the offence.*

(3)   *If he decides that there is sufficient evidence to charge the person with an offence, he shall decide —*
    (a)   *whether or not the person should be charged and, if so, the offence with which he should be charged, and*
    (b)   *whether or not the person should be given a caution and, if so, the offence in respect of which he should be given a caution*

(4)   *The DPP shall give written notice of his decision to an officer involved in the investigation of the offence.*

(5)   *If his decision is —*
    (a)   *that there is not sufficient evidence to charge the person with an offence*
    (b)   *that there is sufficient evidence to charge the person with an offence but that the person should not be charged with an offence or given a caution in respect of the offence,*
    a custody officer shall give the person notice in writing that he is not to be prosecuted.

(6)   *If the decision of the Director of Public Prosecutions is that the person should be charged with an offence or given a caution, in respect of the offence, the person shall be charged or cautioned accordingly.*

(7)   *But if his decision is that the person should given a caution in respect of the offence and it proves not to be possible to give the person such a caution, he shall instead be charged with the offence.*

(8)   *For the purposes of this section, a person is to be charged with an offence either —*
    (a)   *when he is in police detention after returning to a police station to answer bail or is otherwise in police detention at a police station, or*
    (b)   *in accordance with section 29 of the Criminal Justice Act 2003.*

(9)   *In this section 'caution' means —*
    (a)   *a conditional caution within the meaning of Part 3 of the Criminal Justice Act 2003, and*
    (b)   *a warning or reprimand under section 65 of the Crime and Disorder Act 1998.*

Sections 37C and 37D, inserted by CJA 2003, Sch 2 contain further provisions about the release of the suspect on bail;

(b) to release the suspect without charge and on bail but not for the purpose of deciding on charge, eg to enable further enquiries to be made. The suspect may apply to court for the conditions of bail to be varied under CJA 2003, Sch 2, para 6;

(c) to release the suspect without charge and without bail, eg where there is no immediate prospect of further proceedings being taken;

(d) to charge the suspect.

2.2.12   The decision to release

After the charge the custody officer must order the suspect's release from custody under PACE 1984, s 38(1) unless one of the situations contained in s 38(1)(a), as amended by s 28 of the CJPOA 1994, applies:

(a) The suspect's name or address cannot be ascertained.

(b) The custody officer has reasonable grounds for doubting whether the name and address supplied are genuine.

(c) The custody officer has reasonable grounds for believing that:

    (i)   the suspect will not surrender to bail; or

    (ii)   (imprisonable offences) the detention is necessary to prevent the suspect from committing an offence; or

    (iii) where the person has attained the age of 18, the detention is necessary for a sample to be taken;

    (iv) (non-imprisonable offences) the detention is necessary to prevent the suspect from causing physical injury to any other person or loss or damage to property; or

    (v)   the detention is necessary to prevent the suspect from interfering with the administration of justice or with the investigation of any offence or offences; or

    (vi) the detention is necessary for the suspect's own protection.

If the suspect is to be released after charge, he or she is likely to be bailed to attend at the appropriate magistrates' court to answer to the charge on a specified day. CJPOA 1994, s 27 provides that s 3 of the Bail Act 1976 (BA 1976) (power of the court to impose conditions on bail) shall apply with certain modifications (see below) to bail granted by the police.

The bail decision is taken by the custody officer, who may not impose conditions on the grant of bail unless it appears, under s 3A(5) of the BA 1976 (inserted by s 27 of the CJPOA 1994) that it is necessary to do so for the purposes of preventing the bailed person from:

- failing to surrender to custody; or

- committing an offence while on bail; or

- interfering with witnesses or otherwise obstructing the course of justice, whether in relation to the bailed person or any other person.

The main differences between conditions imposed by police and those imposed by the court are as follows:

(a) The court, but not the police, has the power to order that reports be compiled on the bailed person (BA 1976, s 3A(3), as inserted by CJPOA 1994, s 27(3)).

(b) The court, but not the police, may require the bailed person to reside in a bail hostel (BA 1976, s 3A(2), as inserted by CJPOA 1994, s 27(3)).

(c) Where the custody officer has granted bail, either the custody officer or another officer serving at the same police station may vary the conditions of bail, at the request of the bailed person (BA 1976, s 3A(4), inserted by CJPOA 1994, s 27(3)). Further, the bailed person may apply to a magistrates' court to have conditions of bail varied, but should bear in mind that the court has the power to impose more onerous conditions (MCA 1980, s 43B, inserted by CJPOA 1994, Sch 3, para 3).

[handwritten margin note: If detained after charge suspect must be brought before Magistrates at first sitting]

If the suspect is detained after charge, he or she must be brought before a magistrates' court as soon as is practicable, and in any event not later than the first sitting after he or she has been charged with an offence. If no suitable court is sitting, the clerk of the court must be informed, and a special sitting will be arranged. See generally PACE 1984, s 46.

If release is authorised, the suspect is bailed to appear before the magistrates' court on a specified day to answer the charge (see PACE 1984, s 47).

A useful article is 'Detention in a police station and false imprisonment' by J Mackenzie, 142 NLJ 534.

2.2.13   Conditional cautions

As an alternative to the charge and prosecution of a suspect or his release without charge, CJA 2003, ss 22–27 introduce the conditional caution. Cautions are a very common method of dealing with offenders, often first-time adult offenders. These sections allow an adult offender to be released subject to being cautioned, but unlike other cautions, the conditional caution is 'a caution which is given in respect of an offence committed by the offender and which has conditions attached to it with which the offender must comply' (s 22(2)). Failure to comply may result in the offender being prosecuted for the offence.

The person giving the conditional caution is known as the 'authorised person' and is either a constable, an investigating officer or a person authorised by a relevant prosecutor, a group of people including the Attorney-General, the Director of Public Prosecutions, the director of the Serious Fraud Office and the Commissioners of Customs and Excise.

Before the conditional caution may be given, five conditions must be complied with, namely:

(a) the authorised person has evidence that the offender committed an offence;

(b) the authorised person decides that there is sufficient evidence to charge the offender and that a conditional caution should be given;

(c) the offender admits the offence;

(d) the authorised person explains the effect of the conditional caution to the offender and warns him that failure to comply with the conditions may result in his prosecution for the offence;

(e) the offender signs a document setting out:

   (i)   the details of the offence;

   (ii)   an admission by him that he committed the offence;

   (iii) his consent to the giving of a conditional caution;

   (iv) the conditions attached to the caution.

The conditions which are imposed have the following objects, under s 22(3):

(a) facilitating the rehabilitation of the offender;

(b) ensuring that he makes reparation for the offence.

The Conditional Cautioning Code of Practice states that the conditions must be:

• *Proportionate* to the offence — it should not be more onerous than the punishment that would be likely to be imposed if the offender were prosecuted

• *Achievable* within a reasonable time — having particular regard to any limitations on prosecution if the offender breaches the conditions.

• *Appropriate* — any conditions should be relevant to the offence or the offender.

Failure without reasonable cause to comply with any of the conditions renders the person liable to prosecution for the offence and the document referred to above is admissible as evidence: s 24(1)and (2).

The authorised person may seek the advice and assistance of the National Probation Service in deciding whether a conditional caution should be given and, if one is given, the conditions that should be attached (s 26).

If the offender fails to comply with the conditions he may be prosecuted for the original offence. In such proceedings, the notice which the offender signed is admissible (s 24).

2.3 Instituting proceedings

2.3.1 Written charge and requisition

The CJA 2003 replaced the existing, rather unwieldy, procedure for commencing proceedings with a new, simple, system of charge and requisition: s 29. This does not replace or alter the system for charging a suspect in custody: s 18 (and see **2.2**).

The old method of laying an information and issue of summons is abolished except for prosecutions brought by private individuals, and where the public prosecutor is required to lay an information for the purposes of obtaining the issue of a warrant: s 40(4).

Under s 29, the proceedings are started by issuing a document, called a 'written charge', charging the suspect with an offence. At the same time a document called a 'requisition' is issued requiring the suspect to appear before the magistrates' court to answer the written charge. These documents are issued by a person referred to as a 'public prosecutor' (defined below), and served on the person charged and on the court.

See CJA 2003, s 29:

(1)   *A public prosecutor may institute criminal proceedings against a person by issuing a document (a 'written charge') which charges the person with an offence.*

(2)   *Where a public prosecutor issues a written charge, it must at the same time issue a document ('a requisition') which requires the person to appear before a magistrates' court to answer the written charge.*

(3)   *The written charge and the requisition must be served on the person concerned and a copy of both must be served on the court named in the requisition.*

The 'public prosecutor' is defined in CJA 2003, s 29(5) as

(a) A police force or person authorised by a police force to institute criminal proceedings.

(b) The director of the Serious Fraud Office, the Director of Public Prosecutions, the Attorney-General, or a Secretary of State or any person authorised by any one of them to institute criminal proceedings.

(c) The Commissioners of the Inland Revenue or of Customs and Excise, or any person authorised by either of them to institute criminal proceedings.

(d) A person specified in an order made by the Secretary of State for the purposes of this section, or a person authorised by such a person to institute criminal proceedings.

Rules of court made under MCA 1980, s 144 provide for the form, content, recording authentication and service of written charges and requisitions: s 30(1).

There is no requirement that either the written charge or the requisition should be substantiated on oath: s 31(1).

Under s 30(5) all references in previous statutes referring to informations and summonses are to be interpreted as referring to written charges and requisitions.

2.3.2 Trying two or more written charges

If the accused stands before the court charged with more than one offence, or if several accused stand before the court together, the question arises whether all outstanding matters can be dealt with at once.

Where several accused are jointly charged with an offence, they will almost always be automatically tried together, despite any objection they may make.

Where one accused stands charged with several matters, or several accused stand charged of related offences, then they may be tried together as long as no objection is made. If objection is made, the magistrates will order separate trials unless they are of the opinion that the offences are so connected that the interests of justice would be best served by a single trial. See *Chief Constable of Norfolk v Clayton* [1983] 2 AC 473.

If the magistrates decide against a single trial, it would seem those magistrates are debarred from hearing the case at all, as they are supposed to be unaware of any charges outstanding against an accused (see *R v Liverpool City justices, ex p Topping* [1983] 1 WLR 119). In these circumstances, each case may have to be heard by a different bench. In *R v Gough* [1993] AC 646, the House of Lords held that the test in all cases of apparent bias is: Was there a real danger of bias?

2.3.3 Amendment

The court has wide powers to amend the charge as originally laid. Further, the MCA 1980, s 123 provides that defects in the information, or any variations between the information and the evidence subsequently adduced, are not grounds upon which objection may be taken.

The discretion to amend should ordinarily be exercised in favour of amendment, unless to do so would result in injustice (*DPP v Short* (2002) 166 JP 474).

It has been held that if the defect or variation was trivial, and the accused was not in fact misled, any subsequent conviction will be upheld. See, for example, *R v Sandwell Justices, ex p West Midlands Passenger Transport Board* [1979] Crim LR 56. On the other hand, if the defect or variation is substantial, the prosecution should seek to amend the information. The magistrates will then consider whether the accused has been misled by the defect, and if so, offer an adjournment so that he or she can prepare for and meet the case now put forward by the prosecution. Failure either to amend, or adjourn, in these circumstances is likely to lead to any subsequent conviction being quashed. See, for example, *Wright v Nicholson* [1970] 1 WLR 142.

It is assumed that these cases will still apply under the new system.

An information could be amended, even to allege a different offence, including a purely summary offence, more than six months after it was laid, provided that the offence arose from the same incident as the offence originally charged, and the amendment was in the interests of justice, and it is assumed that the same will apply to the written charge. See *R v Scunthorpe Justices, ex p M* The Times, 10 March 1998, where an information alleging robbery was amended to common assault, a purely summary offence. A similar point was made in *R v Newcastle Upon Tyne Magistrates' Court, ex p Poundstretchers Ltd* [1998] COD 256.

Late amendments cannot cure an information or charge which discloses no offence known to law (*Garman v Plaice* [1969] 1 WLR 19).

2.3.4 Duplicity

A written charge is said to be duplicitous when two offences are charged within it. In such a situation, the prosecution may elect which charge to proceed with (see the Criminal Procedure Rules 2005, rule 7.3, although currently this still refers to 'informations').

Students are referred to **Chapter 10** for a full discussion of duplicity.

2.4 Issue of a warrant

2.4.1 Information in a warrant

Instead of issuing a requisition, application may be made to a magistrate to issue a warrant for the arrest of the person named therein. A warrant should contain the following information:

- the name of the court;
- the name and address of the accused; the offence alleged;
- the signature of the magistrate (the signature of the clerk is insufficient);
- if the warrant is to be backed for bail, any conditions of bail imposed by the magistrate (see **3.13**).

2.4.2 Conditions for the issue of a warrant

Before the warrant can be issued the following conditions must be met:

- The information must be in writing. The former condition that the information should be supported by sworn evidence was removed by CJA 2003, s 31.
- The offence must be imprisonable (or the accused is a juvenile or resides at an unknown address).
- The proceedings must take place before a magistrate, not a clerk.

2.4.3 Warrants 'backed for bail'

In most cases a warrant will not be necessary. A less serious offence is likely to be commenced by the issue of a charge and requisition, and more serious offences are arrestable in any event. However, the warrant is important where the accused fails to appear in answer to the summons, or fails to surrender to bail. A warrant issued in these circumstances is often referred to as a 'bench warrant'.

If the magistrates think that the accused's absence is due to an error, they may order that the warrant be 'backed for bail', that is, the conditions of bail upon which the accused may be released once arrested are endorsed on the back of the warrant. After arrest, the accused must be released once the conditions are complied with (see also **Chapter 3**).

2.5   Jurisdiction to try offences

The jurisdiction of the magistrates' courts to try offences is similar to their jurisdiction to institute proceedings, described at **2.1** above. More specifically:

(a) Where the offence is triable either way: magistrates have the power to try offences which are triable either way wherever they were committed, as long as the accused has consented to summary trial as described at **4.2** (MCA 1980, s 2(3) and (4)).

(b) Where the offence is triable summarily only: magistrates have the power to try summary offences where:

[handwritten: within the county]

(i)   The offence was committed within the county for which they act (MCA 1980, s 2(1)).

[handwritten: offence committed outside the county but court trying accused for another offence.]

(ii)   The offence was committed outside the county, but the court is already trying the accused for another offence (MCA 1980, s 2(6)). See *Morgan v Croydon LBC* [1998] Crim LR 219 for an example.

(iii) The offence was committed outside the county, but it is necessary or expedient in the better administration of justice that the accused should be jointly tried with another person who is being proceeded against in that county (MCA 1980, s 1(2)(b) and s 2(2)).

Under the MCA 1980, s 3 an offence committed within 500 yards of the county border may be dealt with by the courts in either county. This is to avoid disputes as to exactly where the offence was committed, and which court, therefore, has jurisdiction.

[handwritten: Courts Act 2003 s44. Any Magistrates court has jurisdiction to try any summary offence.]

When the Courts Act 2003, s 44, comes into force, MCA 1980, s 2 will be amended so that any magistrates' court has jurisdiction to try any summary offence (and MCA 1980, s 3 will be repealed).

Useful reading: *Overhauling Criminal Procedures* by Peter Wilcock and Joel Bennathan 154 NLJ 778, examines the new criminal procedures under the Criminal Justice Act 2003.

2.6   Public funding for legal representation and advice

2.6.1   The Criminal Defence Service

The Access to Justice Act 1999 (AJA), s 1(1) created a body known as 'The Legal Services Commission' (LSC). It is an executive, non-departmental body, responsible for administration of two separate schemes in England and Wales:

- The Community Legal Service. As from 1 April 2001, the Community Legal Service replaced the old civil scheme of legal aid. See the *Civil Litigation Manual* for details.

- The Criminal Defence Service. As from 2 April 2001, the Criminal Defence Service (CDS) replaced the old criminal scheme of legal aid.

A full discussion of either the LSC or the CDS is beyond the scope of this Manual and the following points are intended as an introduction only. See the Government's website at www.legalservices.gov.uk for a complete review of the new law.

The CDS is created by the AJA 1999, s 12(1), which provides that the service is created:

For the purpose of securing that individuals involved in criminal investigations or criminal proceedings have access to such advice, assistance and representation as the interests of justice require.

The AJA 1999, s 12(2) provides that, in this part of the Act, 'criminal proceedings' means:

(a) *proceedings before any court for dealing with an individual accused of an offence;*

(b) *proceedings before any court for dealing with an individual convicted of an offence (including proceedings in respect of a sentence or order);*

(c) *proceedings for dealing with an individual under section 9 of, or paragraph 6 of Schedule 1 to the Extradition Act 1989,*

(d) *proceedings for binding an individual over to keep the peace or to be of good behaviour under section 115 of the Magistrates' Courts Act 1980 and for dealing with an individual who fails to comply with an order under that section,*

(e) *proceedings on appeal brought by an individual under section 44A of the Criminal Appeal Act 1968,*

(f) *proceedings for contempt committed, or alleged to have been committed, by an individual in the face of the court, and*

(g) *such other proceedings concerning an individual, before any such court or other body, as may be prescribed.*

The overview of the General Criminal Contract provided by the LSC (see **2.6.9**) provides as follows:

Objective

1 *We want to encourage committed, high quality providers of criminal defence services to become contracted providers. We want to establish and develop long-term relationships with these providers to ensure that those eligible to receive publicly funded criminal defence services have access to competent, appropriate, quality assured and value for money services that meet their needs.*

2 *The objective of this Contract, therefore, is to secure the provision of competent quality assured, best value Contract work from specified offices.*

Criminal Defence Service — Purpose and Objectives

1 *. . .*

2 *The purpose of the CDS is to ensure access for individuals involved in Criminal Investigations or Criminal Proceedings to such Advice, Assistance and Representation as the interests of justice require.*

3 *The objectives of the CDS within the legal framework established for it are to:*

(a) *ensure that the Government meets its statutory and international obligations which provide that:*

(i) *people arrested and held in custody have the right to consult a solicitor privately at any time; and*

(ii) *defendants have a right to defend themselves in person, or through legal assistance of their own choosing, or, if they have insufficient means to pay for legal assistance, to be given it free when the interests of justice so require;*

(b) *help to ensure that suspects and defendants receive a fair hearing at each stage in the criminal justice process, and in particular that they can state their case on an equal footing with the prosecution;*

(c) *protect the interests of the suspect or defendant, for example by making the prosecution prove its case or advising the defendant to enter an early guilty plea, if that is appropriate;*

(d) *maintain the suspect's or defendant's confidence in the system and facilitate his or her effective participation in the process.*

The Lord Chancellor has set objectives for the Commission regarding the CDS. These are:

(a) *to ensure that eligible individuals have access to appropriate CDS services — including at police stations and in magistrates' courts;*

(b) *to ensure that the services provided on its behalf — whether by contracted private practice suppliers or salaried defenders — are of appropriate quality, and that their quality improves over time;*

(c) *to ensure effective control over CDS expenditure, and progressively improve the value for money of the criminal defence services it provides and purchases;*

(d) *to ensure that the CDS contributes fully to achieving the overall Criminal Justice System (CJS) strategic plan, including by working with the other CDS agencies.*

2.6.2   Advice and assistance

There are two ways in which an individual may be helped. These are (a) Advice and Assistance, and (b) Representation.

The Commission funds advice and assistance, under the AJA 1999, s 13(1), as it considers appropriate to the following persons:

(a) *for individuals who are arrested and held in custody at a police station or other premises, and*

(b) *in prescribed circumstances, for individuals who are [otherwise] involved in investigations which may lead to criminal proceedings or are before a court in such proceedings or have been the subject of such proceedings.*

Advice and assistance also covers help from a solicitor including giving general advice, writing letters, negotiating, obtaining counsel's opinion and preparing a written case. It thus enables people of small means to obtain help from a solicitor.

In order to receive advice and assistance, the applicant must pass the merits test, ie establish that the case has sufficient merit to justify the grant of publicly funded assistance. In order to pass the merits test, the solicitor must be satisfied that the advice required involves a legal issue concerning English law, and there is sufficient benefit to the client, having regard to the matter and the client's personal circumstances, to justify the work being carried out. The sufficient benefit test will be satisfied automatically for the purposes of initial advice given in a police station.

There is no means test for advice and assistance given to a person who is questioned by the police whether or not he or she has been arrested, and whether or not he or she is questioned at a police station. The Commission will only fund other advice and assistance if the individual's capital and income are within the current financial limits (not included in this Manual). The individual will not be asked to pay a contribution.

Children may be given advice and assistance, and may be advised directly in some circumstances. Where the child is under 17 years of age and requires the help of a solicitor, a parent or guardian should apply on the child's behalf.

Advice and assistance does not cover representation in court, except in certain limited circumstances, in which case the individual should apply for AdvocacyAssistance.

2.6.3 Advocacy Assistance

Advocacy Assistance is defined in the CDS Solicitor Arrangements 2001 as 'advice and assistance by way of advocacy before a court or tribunal together with any necessary preparatory work'. It thus covers the cost of a solicitor preparing the case and initial representation in certain proceedings in both the magistrates' court and Crown Court. It also covers representation for those who fail to pay a fine or obey a magistrates' court order, and are at risk of imprisonment.

Under para 6.3(18) of the General Criminal Contract, in deciding whether the client is entitled to Advocacy Assistance, the solicitor should ask himself or herself the following questions:

(a) *Is the applicant before the court as a result of a failure*

(i) *to pay a fine or other sum which he or she was ordered to pay; or*

(ii) *to obey an order of the court*

where the failure is likely to lead to the applicant being at risk of imprisonment?

If the answer to this is no, or a duty solicitor is available and could deal with the case, Advocacy Assistance should be refused. If the case is not suitable for the duty solicitor because either it is unusual (particularly in that it raises complicated issues of fact, law or procedure), or the applicant's finances are complex, then the next question is whether it is in the interests of justice that Advocacy Assistance be granted. This involves the same issues as set out in Sch 3 (see **2.6.4**) with the additional factor of whether there is a real risk of an order being made which if breached could deprive an individual of his or her liberty. The final question is whether it is reasonable in the circumstances for Advocacy Assistance to be granted. If it is in the interests of justice for Advocacy Assistance to be granted, then it will almost always be reasonable.

If Advocacy Assistance is granted, an application should be made for a Representation Order at the earliest opportunity, if appropriate, and all work should be done under that order. If the Representation Order is refused, the Advocacy Assistance ceases unless the client continues to meet the qualifying criteria.

There is no means test for advice and assistance for a person who is granted Advocacy Assistance.

2.6.4   Representation

The Commission funds individuals who have a 'Right to Representation' under AJA 1999, s 14 and Sch 3. Schedule 3, para 1 provides that the right may be granted to an individual who is before the court for any of the matters mentioned in s 12(2), and to enable him or her to resist an appeal to the Crown Court otherwise than in an official capacity.

The court before which any proceedings take place, or are about to take place, has the power to grant a right of representation (Sch 3, para 2(1)). Where any such right is granted, it includes the right to representation for the purposes of any related bail proceedings and any preliminary or incidental proceedings.

Under Sch 3, para 5(1) the right to representation is granted 'according to the interests of justice'. The court, under para 5(2), will take into account the following factors in deciding what the interests of justice consist of in relation to any individual:

(a) *whether the individual would, if any matter arising in the proceedings is decided against him, be likely to lose his liberty or livelihood or suffer serious damage to his reputation,*

(b) *whether the determination of any matter arising in the proceedings may involve consideration of a substantial question of law,*

(c) *whether the individual may be unable to understand the proceedings or to state his own case,*

(d) *whether the proceedings may involve the tracing, interviewing or expert cross-examination of witnesses on behalf of the individual, and*

(e) *whether it is in the interests of another person that the individual be represented.*

These factors may be amended or added to by the Lord Chancellor by order.

A 'case', according to the General Criminal Contract, means work carried out in criminal proceedings in respect of:

- one offence (that is an offence for which the client is charged or summoned or otherwise required to appear in court); or

- more than one offence, where one or more charges or informations are preferred or laid at the same time, or where the offences are allegedly founded on the same facts or form part of a series of offences (these are further defined in para 5.8 of the General Criminal Contract).

2.6.5   The duty solicitor schemes

The Legal Services Commission operates two duty solicitor schemes as part of the CDS. These are:

- the Police Station Duty Solicitor Scheme; and

- the Magistrates' Court Duty Solicitor Scheme.

The primary object of these schemes, according to the CDS Solicitor Arrangements 2001, is:

> . . . to ensure that individuals requiring advice and assistance (including advocacy assistance) at a police station, or at a magistrates' court and who choose not to, or are not able to, obtain such help from an Own Solicitor [ie a solicitor who provides advice and assistance to a client other than as a duty solicitor] may have access to the services of a duty solicitor.

The duty solicitor schemes are not means tested.

2.6.6 Appeals against the refusal of Advice, Assistance or Representation

No appeal if refusal on grounds of means

If the defendant is refused Advice and Assistance otherwise than on the ground of means, a further application may be made to another court.

If the Right to Representation is refused, the court will write to the individual giving the reasons for refusal. If the refusal is on the ground of means, there is no appeal, but if it is on the ground of the interests of justice, an application may be made to another court to review the case. If the individual is refused representation in a magistrates' court in relation to a case which is going to be dealt with by the Crown Court, a further application may be made to the Crown Court.

2.6.7 Appeals against conviction or sentence

The Representation Order, if granted, covers obtaining advice on appeal and the preparation of any application for leave or giving notice of appeal against conviction or sentence, and no separate Advice and Assistance would be required.

If no Representation Order has been granted, then the applicant may apply for Advice and Assistance for those purposes.

Advice and Assistance is also available for an application to the Criminal Cases Review Commission.

Advice, Assistance and Representation themselves are included in the definition of 'criminal proceedings' (see **2.6.1**).

2.6.8 Use of counsel

Under the contract, solicitors may generally instruct counsel to undertake contract work on their behalf (other than in certain specific cases) and such instructions are generally a matter for the solicitor and counsel concerned.

Payment for the work done by counsel will be paid either directly to him or her by the LSC or by the instructing solicitor.

2.6.9 The General Criminal Contract

From 2 April 2001, solicitors in private practice have only been able to carry out criminal defence work funded by the Commission if they have a General Criminal Contract (GCC). There are three basic types of GCC, namely the 'All Classes' contract, the Prison Law contract and the Criminal Cases Review Commission contract. Most contracts will be 'All Classes', as the other contracts are designed to allow a small number of specialist firms to continue to provide services in their specialist area.

The LSC audits applicant firms of solicitors, and firms which pass that audit are awarded a Crime category franchise. Firms with a franchise are eligible for a contract, and, if eligible, will usually receive a three-year contract.

Firms with a GCC are audited to ensure that they meet the quality assurance standards set out by the contract.

Under AJA 1999, s 16, the LSC has prepared a Code of Conduct to be observed by employees of the Commission who provide services as part of the CDS.

The Code sets out a number of duties imposed on such employees, such as the Duty to Act with Integrity and Independence, and the Duty to Act Impartially and to avoid Discrimination. Two duties require closer examination.

2.6.9.1 The duty to protect the interests of the client

Paragraph 2 of the Code provides as follows:

2.1 *The primary duty of a professional employee is to protect the interests of the client so far as consistent with any duties owed to the court and any other rules of professional conduct. Subject to this, a professional employee shall do his or her utmost to promote and work for the best interests of the client and to ensure that the client receives a fair hearing. A professional employee shall provide the client with fearless, vigorous and effective defence and may use all proper and lawful means to secure the best outcome for the client.*

2.2 *A professional employee shall not put a client under pressure to plead guilty, and in particular, shall not advise a client that it is in his or her best interests to plead guilty unless satisfied that the prosecution is able to discharge the burden of proof.*

2.6.9.2 The duty of confidentiality

Paragraph 5 of the Code provides as follows:

5.1 *Subject to paragraph 5.2, an employee shall keep all information about a client confidential within the salaried service. This is an ongoing duty that does not cease once employment has terminated, and can be enforced in a court by the Commission or the client.*

5.2 *The duty of confidence to a client is subject to any statutory provision, any court order and any relevant rules of professional conduct or otherwise setting out circumstances where the duty of confidentiality may be overridden.*

See the General Criminal Contract for full details (at www.legalservices.gov.uk).

2.7 Costs

Under the Prosecution of Offences Act 1985, ss 16–21, the court finally disposing of a case has the power to make various orders as to costs, of which the most important are set out below.

2.7.1 Defendant's costs order

Under s 16, a defendant who has been acquitted may have an order made in his or her favour for the payment of sums out of central funds (ie the Government) for expenses properly incurred by him or her in the proceedings. This may, but need not, be the full amount which the defendant claims.

The making of an order for costs is discretionary, but the court will normally make an order for costs in the defendant's favour, unless there are positive reasons for not doing so. For example, where the defendant's own conduct has brought suspicion on himself or herself and has misled the prosecution into thinking the case against him or her was stronger than it was (*Practice Direction (Costs: Criminal Proceedings)* [2004] 2 All ER 1070).

The order may be made where a person:

- is not tried on an indictment for which he or she has been indicted or sent for trial; or
- has been acquitted on any count on the indictment.

The defendant's costs order cannot be rescinded under the MCA 1980, s 142, as the power under that section only applies where the defendant has been found guilty (*Coles v DPP* (1998) 162 JP 687; and see **5.1.12**).

A number of decisions have held that there is no absolute right to costs under the ECHR, but the cases indicate that as a general rule, costs should be awarded in favour of an acquitted defendant. Where the defendant has been acquitted or the case against him has been dismissed or discontinued, a refusal to award costs could amount to a violation of the presumption of innocence if such a refusal amounts to a finding of guilt.

2.7.2 Prosecution costs

[handwritten margin note: private prosecutor only – does not have to be successful may not be full amount]

Where the offence is indictable, under s 17, a private prosecutor (but not the CPS or other prosecuting authority) may be awarded, out of central funds, an amount which the court thinks reasonably sufficient to compensate him or her for expenses properly incurred. The prosecution does not have to be successful for such an order to be made. Again, this need not be the full amount.

2.7.3 Costs against the defendant *[handwritten: s18 ordered to pay costs to CPS]*

Under s 18, if the defendant is convicted, he or she may be ordered to pay to the prosecution such a sum as is just and reasonable. Proper account should be taken of the defendant's means.

[handwritten margin note: should not be applied if costs cannot be paid within a year but up to 3 years OK depending on case. Fines should be payable within weeks for those of lower income.]

Practice Direction (Costs: Criminal Proceedings) [2004] 2 All ER 1070 provides that the order may be made where the court is satisfied that the defendant or appellant has the means and ability to pay. This direction reflects the pre-existing case law. For example, in *R v Nottingham Justices, ex p Fohmann* (1986) 84 Cr App R 316, it was said that justices should not make an order for costs against a convicted person in such a sum that, through lack of means, he or she would be unable to pay that sum within a reasonable period of about a year. However, it has been held, in relation to the payment of fines, that a period of two years would seldom be too long, and that three years may be acceptable in appropriate cases (*R v Olliver and Olliver* (1989) 11 Cr App R (S) 10). However, in *R v Stockport Justices, ex p Conlon* [1997] 2 All ER 204 the court held that where fines were imposed on those of limited means, they should be lesser in amount so that they could be paid 'in a matter of weeks'.

Guidelines for the court in making an order for costs against a defendant, derived from the authorities, were set out in *R v Northallerton Magistrates' Court, ex p Dove* [2000] 1 Cr App R (S) 136:

- (a) The defendant's means and any other financial order should be ascertained so that the costs order does not exceed a reasonable sum that the defendant is able to pay.
- (b) The sum should never be more than the costs actually incurred.
- (c) It is clear from the fact that there is no right of appeal from the making of a costs order that the policy is to compensate the prosecutor and not to further penalise the defendant.

(d) A costs order should be proportionate to the level of the fine and where the total of fine and costs are excessive, the costs should be reduced accordingly. (On the facts, the defendant had been fined £1,000, where the maximum was £5,000, but ordered to pay over £4,600 in costs. It was held that the amount of costs was grossly disproportionate.) *ex parte bore*

(e) The onus is on the defendant to provide details of his or her means and in default, magistrates are entitled to deduce his or her financial circumstances from the available evidence.

(f) The defendant must be allowed the opportunity to produce information as to his or her means and should be given notice of any unusual application for costs that is to be made.

The courts have also taken the following matters into consideration when making an order for costs against a defendant:

(a) The choice of court of trial: the defendant should not be 'punished' for electing a trial on indictment by an excessive order for costs *(R v Bushell* (1980) 2 Cr App R (S) 77, where the order was, in fact, upheld). On the other hand, nor should he or she be punished for an election made by the prosecution *(R v Hall* [1989] Crim LR 228).

(b) The plea: if the defendant pleads guilty, an order for costs may still be made, although, taking into account any other relevant matters, the court may be persuaded not to make the order as great as it may otherwise have been. If, on the other hand, the defendant pleads not guilty in the face of an overwhelmingly strong prosecution case when he or she must have known he or she was guilty, an order for costs would be appropriate *(R v Singh* (1982) 4 Cr App R (S) 38; R v *Mountain* (1979) 68 Cr App R 41).

(c) The rest of the sentence: if the defendant is sentenced to a custodial sentence, an order for costs is unusual, as he or she will have no income with which to pay such costs. If the court, however, considers that the defendant has sufficient funds, it may make the order nevertheless *(R v Maher* [1983] QB 784).

(d) If the sentence is non-custodial, the defendant is responsible for his own costs. If there is more than one defendant, the amount of costs should be apportioned between them *(R v Ronson* [1991] Crim LR 794). *if more than one defendant.*

In *Hamilton-Johnson v RSPCA* [2000] 2 Cr App R (S) 390 the court observed that, in dealing with an unsuccessful appeal, the Crown Court should hesitate before interfering with a costs order made by the magistrates, but that the Crown Court has the power to do so under the Prosecution of Offences Act 1985, s 18(1) (the power to make such orders for costs as seems 'just and reasonable') or under the Supreme Court Act 1981, s 48(2) (the power to alter any part of the decision appealed against including elements which had not been appealed). In this case the Crown Court increased the costs awarded against the defendant, on her unsuccessful appeal, from £260 to £28,500.

2.8   Reducing delay in the criminal process

The Crime and Disorder Act 1998 (CDA 1998) contains a number of provisions designed to reduce delay in the criminal process. Two measures will be dealt with here.

2.8.1 Powers of magistrates' courts exercisable by a single justice

Section 49 of the CDA 1998 empowers a single justice of the peace for a particular area to exercise the powers of a magistrates' court, such as extending bail or imposing or varying conditions of bail, and dismissing an information where no evidence has been adduced by the prosecution. Further, under s 49(2), rules of court are to be developed to enable a justices' clerk to make a number of administrative (as opposed to judicial) decisions. Students should consult s 49 for a full list of these powers and the restrictions placed upon the decisions of a justices' clerk. The purpose of this section is to reduce the delays inherent in a system which requires the decision of three people, and to attempt to achieve continuity in the handling of a case, particularly prior to trial.

2.8.2 Early administrative hearings

The Early Administrative Hearing (EAH) is designed to take place very early in the proceedings with the purpose of dealing with the issue of legal representation. See CDA 1998, s 50.

Under s 50, the first appearance after charge (other than indictable only and related offences shall be before a court consisting of a single justice. At this hearing, under s 50(2):

- the accused shall be asked if he or she wishes to receive legal representation; and
- if he or she does, his or her eligibility for it shall be determined; and
- if it is determined that he or she is eligible, the necessary arrangements or grant to him or her shall be made.

In addition, the single justice may exercise any of the powers of the single justice contained in s 49(1) as he or she thinks fit (s 50(3)(a)). Section 50(3)(b) specifically provides that the single justice may remand the accused in custody or on bail.

The powers of the single justice under s 50(1) may be exercised by a justices' clerk, except that the justices' clerk has no power to remand the accused in custody or remand the accused on bail on conditions other than any previously imposed.

Remands and bail

3.1 What is a remand?

Put in very simple terms, a remand is another name for an adjournment of a case — the postponement of its final resolution. However, the criminal justice system knows the remand as having a particular meaning. When a case is adjourned, the court may have the power or duty to remand the accused, rather than simply adjourn the case to another day. It would be accurate to say that, while all remands are adjournments, not all adjournments are remands.

The main Acts of Parliament referred to in this chapter are:

- the Magistrates' Courts Act 1980 (MCA 1980);
- the Bail Act 1976 (BA 1976);
- the Criminal Justice Act 2003 (CJA 2003).

Bail and remands are dealt with in the main practitioner works at *Archbold* (2005 edn), paras 3–1 to 3–195 and *Blackstone's Criminal Practice* (2005 edn), paras D5.1–D5.57.

3.1.1 Remands in the criminal justice system

If a criminal case before a court in England and Wales is not disposed of conclusively on one day, it will have to carry over into another day. For an analysis of how many cases are concluded on the first appearance in court, see **Figure 3.1**, Column 5.

Examples of such 'carry over' are:

(a) A trial which is too long to finish in a single day.

(b) A trial which has finished in a single day but the court wants more information on the offender before passing sentence (eg getting a pre-sentence report).

(c) A case which has been listed for a preliminary matter only to be determined (eg which court will try a defendant charged with an offence triable either way).

(d) A case which has been listed for trial but either party (or perhaps the court, if it has insufficient time that day) is unable to proceed with the case there and then.

(e) A case which has finished in one court but is going to another — on appeal or committal.

Note that, with regard to (a) above, a part-heard trial in the Crown Court continues on the next day. A part-heard case in the magistrates' court may continue the next day or may resume in several weeks' time (depending upon the availability of the courtroom and of the district judge or justices of the peace who are trying the case).

England and Wales

| Offence type | Average number of days: | | | | | | | | Percentage of defendants dealt with on first court appearance | | Average number of times case listed in court | | Average length of adjournments in days | | Percentage of defendants pleading: | | | | Number of defendants in sample (thousands) | |
| | From offence to completion | | From offence to charge or laying of Information | | From charge or laying of Information to first listing | | From first listing to completion | | | | | | | | Guilty[2] | | Not guilty[2] | | | |
	Old basis	New basis	Old basis	New basis	Old basis	New basis	Old basis	New basis	Old basis	New basis	Old basis	New basis	Old basis	New basis	Old basis	New basis	Old basis	New basis	Old basis	New basis
Indictable offences (including triable either way)																				
1992	129	*	43	*	22	*	64	*	20	*	3.4	*	27	*	48	*	19	*	26.3	*
1993[3]	120	*	39	*	25	*	56	*	21	*	3.3	*	24	*	48	*	19	*	24.1	*
1994[3]	128	*	43	*	25	*	60	*	20	*	3.5	*	24	*	50	*	19	*	22.0	*
1995[3]	130	*	43	*	26	*	61	*	20	*	3.6	*	24	*	50	*	19	*	22.2	*
1996[3]	132	*	45	*	28	*	60	*	19	*	3.6	*	23	*	50	*	17	*	51.6	*
1997[3]	135	*	46	*	29	*	60	*	20	*	3.6	*	23	*	50	*	17	*	22.7	*
1998[3]	127	*	46	*	26	*	55	*	22	*	3.4	*	23	*	54	*	17	*	23.5	*
1999[4]	120	124	46	46	21	21	52	56	23	23	3.3	3.3	23	24	55	55	18	18	23.3	23.5
2000[4]	108	114	46	46	8	9	54	59	25	25	3.2	3.3	24	26	55	55	20	20	29.9	30.2
2001[4]	105	111	48	48	7	8	50	55	28	28	3.1	3.1	24	26	54	54	22	21	30.0	30.3
2002[4]	104	109	48	48	7	8	49	54	29	29	3.1	3.2	23	25	55	55	22	22	32.1	32.4
Summary non-motoring offences																				
1992	137	*	79	*	37	*	21	*	70	*	1.5	*	42	*	52	*	10	*	11.0	*
1993[3]	132	*	75	*	38	*	19	*	67	*	1.6	*	32	*	52	*	10	*	9.4	*
1994[3]	137	*	81	*	37	*	20	*	68	*	1.6	*	32	*	47	*	10	*	9.2	*
1995[3]	138	*	80	*	40	*	18	*	75	*	1.6	*	30	*	46	*	9	*	10.4	*
1996[3]	133	*	79	*	39	*	15	*	76	*	1.5	*	28	*	49	*	8	*	10.4	*
1997[3]	128	*	70	*	36	*	21	*	68	*	1.8	*	27	*	47	*	12	*	7.2	*
1998[3]	131	*	78	*	34	*	18	*	72	*	1.7	*	28	*	45	*	11	*	8.2	*
1999[4]	129	133	76	76	33	34	20	23	69	68	1.7	1.8	27	30	42	42	13	13	7.2	7.3
2000[4]	127	129	76	76	32	32	20	22	70	70	1.7	1.7	28	30	42	42	14	14	14.3	14.4
2001[4]	129	132	78	78	33	34	18	21	73	73	1.7	1.7	28	31	42	42	11	11	16	.0
2002[4]	137	139	87	87	31	31	19	21	70	70	1.7	1.7	27	28	38	38	12	12	19.2	19.3
Summary motoring offences																				
1992	163	*	79	*	42	*	41	*	53	*	2.0	*	41	*	61	*	12	*	18.8	*
1993[3]	152	*	80	*	38	*	33	*	52	*	2.0	*	33	*	59	*	11	*	17.0	*
1994[3]	158	*	84	*	40	*	34	*	53	*	2.0	*	32	*	59	*	11	*	16.2	*
1995[3]	153	*	82	*	37	*	32	*	54	*	2.0	*	31	*	55	*	10	*	16.8	*
1996[3]	146	*	76	*	40	*	30	*	54	*	2.0	*	29	*	57	*	9	*	15.3	*
1997[3]	152	*	83	*	40	*	29	*	57	*	2.0	*	29	*	57	*	9	*	15.3	*
1998[3]	153	*	88	*	38	*	27	*	57	*	1.9	*	28	*	59	*	8	*	14.4	*
1999[4]	145	158	83	90	37	38	24	28	59	59	1.9	1.9	28	32	58	58	8	8	14.6	14.7
2000[4]	150	154	89	89	37	38	24	28	61	61	1.8	1.9	28	32	55	55	8	8	27.5	27.6
2001[4]	151	156	91	91	37	38	23	27	62	62	1.8	1.9	28	31	54	54	8	8	26.8	27.0
2002[4]	155	160	93	93	38	38	24	29	60	59	1.9	1.9	27	31	53	53	8	9	28.3	28.5

Source: Time Intervals Surveys for Criminal Proceedings in magistrates' courts — conducted by Lord Chancellor's Department
(1) Results for 2000 based on proceedings in one sample week in February, June, September and December for indictable offences and February and September only for summary offences. Results for 1999 and earlier years based on proceedings in one sample week in each February, June, September and December for indictable offences, and June and October for summary offences, and June only for summary offences.
(2) Defendants pleading (/not guilty) at a summary trial, as a proportion of those proceeded against in the sample weeks.
(3) Changes in recording procedures have led to small discrepancies with earlier years. From 1993, cases adjourned sine die are not counted until finally disposed of. In addition, cases are excluded which took more than one year to complete (either charge to first listing, or first listing to completion) for reasons which appear to be beyond the control of the court, for example, where the defendant absconded. It is estimated that this change reduced the average interval from first listing to completion by 2 days for indictable offences. Further more from February 1994 survey onwards, cases where the defendant was charged or summonsed over 10 years after the offence occurred have been excluded.
(4) From February 1999 survey onwards results are on a new basis (as the rules which previously excluded longer cases are no longer applied). This means that some intervals in 1999 — especially those including first listing to completion — are slightly longer than they would have been on the old basis. Results on the old basis should be used for comparisons with 1998 and earlier years.

Figure 3.1 Defendants proceeded against at magistrates' courts — average time for criminal cases by offence type and stage of proceedings, percentage dealt with on first appearance, average number of times case listed and average length of adjournments[1], 1992–2002.

3.1.2   Remand — bail or custody?

In all of the examples in **3.1.1** above, the case will be adjourned to another day. Whether this adjournment is a remand depends upon whether it falls within any one of several statutory situations. Essentially, the difference between 'remanding' a defendant and simply 'adjourning' the case is that when the court remands a defendant, it is under a duty to decide whether he or she should be released on bail or kept locked up in custody. If a case is simply 'adjourned', then the defendant is put on trust to return to court at the place, date and time that he or she is told to.

3.1.3   Surrendering to custody

If the defendant is remanded, he or she will either:

- be kept in custody — ie stay locked up until produced by the (police, prison or other) authorities for the next court appearance; or
- be freed on bail. Being released on bail imposes a duty on a defendant to return to court at the appointed date, place and time (often called 'surrendering to custody'). Failure to attend the next hearing is itself a crime (BA 1976, s 6; see also **3.14** below).

It appears that a defendant surrenders to custody by:

- turning up at the court where he or she was due to appear;
- on the due date;
- at the appointed time (usually 10 am); and
- reporting to the appropriate person.

See *DPP v Richards* [1988] QB 701.

The defendant is then allowed to remain *apparently* at liberty, by staying in the public areas of the court building. Strictly, though, he or she is in custody until the case comes up in court. It follows that the defendant is under an implied obligation not to leave the building without first obtaining permission to do so. (Permission should be sought from the court or someone acting on its behalf.) If the defendant leaves without consent, the court may issue a warrant for his or her arrest. See BA 1976, s 7(2); *DPP v Richards* above; confirmed in *R v Central Criminal Court, ex p Guney* [1995] 1 WLR 376; but cf *Burgess v Governor of Maidstone Prison* [2000] All ER (D) 1688.

Remember that some defendants are released on police bail subject to a duty to surrender to custody at a police station. This occurs, typically, where enquiries are being pursued and the individual has not been charged with an offence.

3.2   When will a case be remanded?

Whenever magistrates adjourn a case, they may remand the defendant. The MCA 1980 provides several situations where, on an adjournment, a magistrates' court *must* remand a defendant and then consider the alternatives of bail and custody. See **Figure 3.2**, which is based upon MCA 1980, s 10.

> 1. When D first appeared in the court, was he on bail or in custody?
>   If YES — he must now be remanded (on bail or in custody).
>   If NO —
> 2. Has D been remanded at any time during the proceedings for this offence?
>   If YES — he must now be remanded (on bail or in custody).
>   If NO —
> 3. The magistrates have a choice to remand or simply adjourn the case.

Figure 3.2 Will the adjournment be a remand?

3.2.1 Situations where remand is required

(a) *Magistrates dealing with an offence triable either way.* If, before or during the summary trial of such an offence, an adjournment is needed, then usually the defendant must be remanded on bail or in custody. See **Figure 3.2**.

(b) *Magistrates determining which court will try an 'either way' offence.* If the magistrates adjourn a case while determining whether the defendant will be tried by the magistrates or a jury (MCA 1980, ss 19–23), they must usually remand the defendant on bail or in custody (see MCA 1980, s 18(4)). See **Figure 3.2**.

(c) *Magistrates sending a defendant to the Crown Court for trial.* Following a decision to send the defendant to the Crown Court for trial, if the defendant is currently remanded in custody, the magistrates may either order that he or she be kept in custody pending his or her trial or release him or her on bail with a direction that he or she appear before the Crown Court for trial (MCA 1980, s 8(1); CDA 1998, ss 51 and 52).

There are two other situations to be aware of:

(d) *Magistrates dealing with a summary offence.* Prior to deciding whether a defendant is guilty or innocent in such a case, the magistrates may have to adjourn the proceedings. If they do so, they have a choice — either to remand the defendant or simply to adjourn (MCA 1980, s 10(4)). If the defendant fails to appear at court on the next appointed date, the magistrates may proceed to try the case in the absence of the defendant or, in some circumstances, issue a warrant for arrest (MCA 1980, ss 11 and 13). See **Chapter 5**.

(e) *Magistrates deferring sentence.* Where a magistrates' court defers sentence on a convicted defendant (for up to six months) under PCC(S)A 2000, s 1, this is not a remand, and the defendant, although released subject to a duty to return to court, is not on bail. (See *R v Ross* (1988) 86 Cr App R 337.)

3.2.2 The use of remands or adjournments by magistrates

For an analysis of the use of remands or adjournments by magistrates, see **Figure 3.3**.

England and Wales 2002   Thousands of persons and percentages

Outcome	All person charged or summoned			Total		
	Not remanded by magistrates	Bailed by magistrates	Remanded in custody by magistrates[2]	2002	2001	2000
Number of persons (thousands)						
Acquitted or not proceeded with etc	321.8	143.6	16.0	481.4	466.8	468.5
Convicted:						
Discharge	78.5	34.4	2.4	115.2	114.5	119.2
Fine	893.5	76.0	4.0	973.5	931.9	1,014.8
Community sentence[4]	51.7	102.6	11.1	165.4	146.2	136.5
Fully suspended sentence	0.3	0.6	0.0	1.0	1.1	1.2
Immediate custody[5]	22.5	24.3	18.3	65.1	62.2	60.2
Total number sentenced[6]	1,046.7	244.5	38.5	1,347.7	1,282.4	1,355.3
Committed for sentence:						
On bail	1.9	5.6	0.6	8.1	8.3	9.1
In custody	2.1	0.8	7.3	10.1	8.6	8.2
Committed for trial:						
On bail	17.9	36.9	2.0	56.8[3]	55.5	51.9
In custody	11.7	1.8	12.4	25.9[3]	23.5	18.3
Failed to appear to a summons	127.8	*	*	127.8	113.5	103.2
Failed to appear to bail[7]	*	77.1	5.5	82.6	72.3	67.8
Total	1,580.0	510.3	82.1	2,140.4	2,030.9	2,082.2
Of these:						
Persons proceeded against for failing to surrender to bail[8]	*	*	*	52.2	45.0	41.8
Percentage of persons:						
Acquitted or not proceeded with etc	21	28	19	22	23	22
Convicted:						
Discharge	5	7	3	5	6	6
Fine	58	15	5	45	46	49
Community sentence[4]	3	20	14	8	7	7
Fully suspended sentence	0	0	0	0	0	0
Immediate custody[5]	1	5	22	3	3	3
Total number sentenced[6]	69	48	47	63	63	65
Committed for sentence:						
On bail	0	1	1	0	0	0
In custody	0	0	9	0	0	0
Committed for trial:						
On bail	1	7	2	3	3	2
In custody	1	0	15	1	1	1
Failed to appear to a summons	8	*	*	4	6	5
Failed to appear to bail[7]	*	15	7	6	4	3
Total	100	100	100	100	100	100
Of these:						
Persons proceeded against for failing to surrender to bail(8)	*	*	*	2	2	2

(1)   Includes estimates for those offences omitted from data supplied (see paragraphs 7 and 8, Appendix 2).

(2)   Includes those remanded for part of the time in custody and part on bail.

(3)   . . .

(4)   Includes community rehabilitation orders, supervision orders, community punishment orders, attendance centre orders, community punishment and rehabilitation orders, curfew orders, reparation orders (from June 2000), a drug treatment and testing orders (from October 2000) and referral orders (from April 2002).

(5)   Includes detention in a young offender institution, secure training orders (from January 1998 to April 2000), detention and training orders (from April 2000) and unsuspended imprisonment.

(6)   Includes persons otherwise dealt with.

(7)   It is not known whether the persons prosecuted were remanded partly in custody as well as on bail.

(8)   Prosecutions arise from failure to surrender to bail at both magistrates' courts and the Crown Courts; they may not be completed in the same year in which the bail was breached.

Figure 3.3 Persons proceeded against at magistrates' courts by type of court remand and outcome of proceedings[1], 2002.

3.3   Who can remand a case?

3.3.1   Remands in the magistrates' court

It might seem, from what you have just read, that only magistrates can remand a criminal case. This is not the whole story. The vast majority of remands occur in the magistrates' court simply because that is where the bulk of criminal litigation takes place, particularly when you realise that almost all hearings in a case prior to trial occur in the magistrates' court.

3.3.2   Remands in the Crown Court

The question of a simple adjournment never seems to arise in the Crown Court. A defendant who is committed to the Crown Court (whether for trial or sentence) will be remanded either on bail or in custody. Once there, the Crown Court judge has the power to grant bail for the period before the matter is dealt with (see Supreme Court Act 1981, s 81, as amended).

Once a Crown Court trial has started, the judge will remand the defendant either in custody or on bail during any lunch or overnight breaks in the trial. Whether or not to release on bail is usually regarded as a matter solely within the power and discretion of the trial judge; see the observation by Peter Gibson LJ in *R v Central Criminal Court, ex p Guney* [1995] 1 WLR 376 that from 'the commencement of a [Crown Court] trial it is for the court conducting the trial to decide whether the defendant should be in custody or on bail'.

3.3.3   Police bail

This chapter concentrates on bail in court, as that is where barristers will usually be involved in bail decisions. We should, however, note that the police may also release people on bail. This will usually follow detention at a police station, under PACE 1984, s 47 (and see **2.2.9.1**), or away from the police station, using 'street bail' under PACE 1984, s 30A (see further **3.6.4.2** below).

3.4   Duration of remands

3.4.1   General examples

There are various maximum periods for a remand by magistrates in different circumstances.

Before conviction

(a) Three clear days in police custody (MCA 1980, s 128(7)).

(b) Eight clear days in prison custody (MCA 1980, s 128(6)). (Exception: if an 'either way' offence is to be tried by the magistrates but they cannot convene in time, remand to whenever they can convene the court.)

(c) Twenty-eight clear days in prison custody if the defendant is in court, and has previously been remanded in custody for this offence. (See **3.4.2** below.)

(d) Twenty eight clear days in prison custody if the defendant has at least that long still to serve on a current custodial sentence (MCA 1980, s 131(1)).

(e) Any period to which both the prosecution and defence agree on bail (MCA 1980, s 128(6)).

After conviction

(f) Three weeks in custody for inquiries or reports for sentencing.

(g) Four weeks on bail for inquiries, etc.

Each of these periods is the maximum duration for a *single* remand. At its conclusion, the defendant will be produced before the magistrates once more. At that time, and subject to the custody time limits (see **3.6.4** below), the magistrates may again remand him or her either on bail or in custody for a further period. Once a defendant is sent to the Crown Court, either for trial or sentence to be passed, he or she is remanded on bail or in custody until such time as the case is listed for hearing (again, subject to the custody time limits).

3.4.2 Avoiding weekly remands

A very large number of prisoners is held on remand in custody at any time in England and Wales. Typically, the prisoner has been remanded in custody by a court, prior to his or her trial, and is therefore usually subject to eight-day remands (see **3.4.1(b)** above). The need to produce all of these prisoners at court, every week, would impose a tremendous burden on the Prison Service and its subcontractors, in terms of both administration and logistical arrangements. This effort would in large measure be wasted if the only reason for the court appearance was that eight days had passed. In order to minimise wasted costs, magistrates' courts have the power either to remand prisoners in their absence or to extend the remand period beyond the eight-day norm.

A magistrates' court can remand a defendant in custody, in his or her absence, on up to three occasions. To do so, the defendant must have legal representation and have consented to this procedure. (See MCA 1980, s 128(3A).) This can effectively extend the remand period up to four weeks, although the case is still listed every eight days and the defendant is formerly remanded in his or her absence.

An alternative procedure is simply to remand the defendant for up to 28 clear days. Magistrates' courts are able to do this if:

(a) the accused has been remanded in custody already in the case; and

(b) the accused is present in court when the extended remand is ordered; and

(c) the court has fixed a date when the next stage in the proceedings will take place.

The power to do so derives from the MCA 1980, s 128A. Clearly, it is more straightforward than the alternative under the MCA 1980, s 128(3A) and is the usual method of remanding a prisoner in custody for periods exceeding eight days.

In addition to the above powers, there may also be the opportunity to conduct proceedings via a live television link between the magistrates' court and the prison where a defendant is being held. This power derives from the Crime and Disorder Act 1998, s 57, which provides that a court may treat the defendant as being present for pre-trial hearings where he or she is in custody but is able to see and hear the court (and be seen and heard by the court) via a live television link or other means. This procedure has been piloted in certain magistrates' courts and will be applied nationally to both magistrates' and Crown Courts in due course. See *Blackstone's Criminal Practice* (2005 edn), para D4.13.

3.5 What are the alternatives to remanding a case?

Alternatives to remanding a case have been mentioned already but, in brief, the court may:

(a) *Try the case anyway*. If a case is ready for summary trial and the defendant does not appear, the magistrates may go ahead and try the case in his or her absence, having entered a formal plea of not guilty. (See **5.1.1** below and MCA 1980, s 11(1).) This power to try absent defendants does not exist in the Crown Court — the accused must be present at the start of a jury trial to enter a plea to the indictment personally. However, once the plea has been entered, typically at a plea and case management hearing, if the accused chooses to absent himself from subsequent proceedings, the court *may* try him in his absence. See the guidance on this subject given by Lord Bingham in *R v Jones* [2003] AC 1. The power to hold a summary trial in the absence of the accused is used sparingly. One reason for reluctance is the 'statutory declaration' (see MCA 1980, s 14). This refers to the ability of a person convicted in his or her absence to declare that he or she did not know of the proceedings or summons which resulted in his or her conviction. Once the declaration is made, and served on the clerk to the justices, then the summons and all subsequent proceedings (such as a summary trial and guilty verdict) are void (see MCA 1980, s 14(1)(b)). There may also be concerns about ensuring the defendant has a fair trial; see further the Human Rights Act 1998, Sch 1, Art 6.

(b) *Adjourn to another date*. A case may be simply adjourned to another date and the prosecution and accused told to be at court on that date. No penal sanction exists in this situation to compel attendance at the adjourned hearing. The defence may seek an adjournment in order, for example, to instruct an expert witness to appear as a witness for the defendant. (See *R v Sunderland Justices, ex p Dryden* The Times, 18 May 1994.)

(c) *Adjourn indefinitely and issue a warrant for arrest*. If the defendant does not appear at court, the outcome will often be the issue of a warrant for his or her arrest (sometimes called a 'bench' warrant) (see MCA 1980, s 13). When the defendant is arrested on a bench warrant, he or she will usually stay in custody until a court hearing can be arranged. Sometimes, if the magistrates suspect there might be a reasonable excuse for the defendant's non-attendance, they can issue the warrant *and* release the defendant on bail without requiring a court hearing upon arrest. The effect of this combination is that the defendant will be arrested and taken to a police station (this constitutes execution of the warrant); at the police station, he or she is then released on bail to attend the magistrates' court at a later date. Such a warrant is usually described as being 'backed for bail'. Crown Court judges can also issue such warrants if a defendant is absent from court without permission. (See also **2.4** above and **3.14** below.) The warrant may be issued once the court is satisfied that the information against the accused has been supported on oath, that the accused is aware of the hearing and the offence is imprisonable. Warrants may be issued for non-imprisonable offences if the first two criteria are satisfied *and* the court proposes to impose a disqualification on the defendant.

(d) *Dismiss the case*. If the prosecution is not ready to proceed with a summary trial, it is possible that the magistrates will dismiss the charge if there has been a long delay between the commission of the alleged offence and the court hearing. See, for example, *R v Oxford City Justices, ex p Smith* (1982) 75 Cr App R 200; cf *R v Barnet Magistrates' Court, ex p DPP* (1994) 158 JP 1060. See also **2.3.1** above.

3.6 Bail — practice and procedure

3.6.1 'Unconditional' bail

The question of whether to release a defendant on bail or keep him or her in custody arises whenever a case is remanded (see **3.1** above). If a defendant is granted bail, this means that he or she is released from court subject to a primary duty to attend the next court hearing in the case. This is known as the duty to surrender to custody. (See BA 1976, s 3(1).) Failure to appear at the appointed place, time and date is itself a criminal offence leading to a fine or imprisonment (BA 1976, s 6 — see **3.14** below).

The primary duty may be accompanied by secondary duties imposed on the defendant — for example, to keep a curfew within certain hours; to report to the local police station once a week; to surrender one's passport. These secondary duties are often described as 'conditions of bail' (see **3.12** below). A defendant who is released on bail, subject only to the primary duty to surrender to bail at the next court hearing, is often described as being released on 'unconditional' bail.

The text of the BA 1976, s 3(1), is as follows:

Incidents of bail in criminal proceedings

3.—(1) A person granted bail in criminal proceedings shall be under a duty to surrender to custody, and that duty is enforceable in accordance with section 6 of this Act.

3.6.2 Bail Act 1976, s 4 — the general right to bail

4.—(1)   A person to whom this section applies shall be granted bail except as provided in Schedule 1 to this Act.

(2)   This section applies to a person who is accused of an offence when—

(a)   he appears or is brought before a magistrates' court or the Crown Court in the course of or in connection with proceedings for the offence, or

(b)   he applies to a court for bail in connection with the proceedings.

This subsection does not apply as respects proceedings on or against a person's conviction of the offence.

(2A)   This section also applies to a person whose extradition is sought in respect of an offence, when—

(a)   he appears or is brought before a court in the course of or in connection with extradition proceedings in respect of the offence, or

(b)   he applies to a court for bail or for a variation of the conditions of bail in connection with the proceedings.

(2B)   But subsection (2A) above does not apply if the person is alleged to be unlawfully at large after conviction of the offence.

(3)   This section also applies to a person who, having been convicted of an offence, appears or is brought before a magistrates' court or the Crown Court to be dealt with under—

(a)   Part 2 of Schedule 3 to the Powers of Criminal Courts (Sentencing) Act 2000 (breach of certain youth community orders), or

(b)   Part 2 of Schedule 8 to the Criminal Justice Act 2003 (breach of requirement of community order).

(4)   This section also applies to a person who has been convicted of an offence and whose case is adjourned by the court for the purpose of enabling inquiries or a report to be made to assist the court in dealing with him for the offence.

As amended by the Extradition Act 2003 and the CJA 2003.

3.6.3 The right to bail — a human right?

The Bail Act 1976, s 4 gives a 'general right to bail' (sic) for defendants in criminal litigation. However, s 4 does not apply to all defendants in the criminal justice system nor at all stages of the system (see **3.6.2** and **3.6.4** below). Furthermore, even those defendants to whom BA 1976, s 4 applies cannot demand to be released on bail automatically. There is a presumption, but no more, that such a defendant will be released on bail if a case is remanded. Section 4(1) says that a person to whom s 4 applies shall be granted bail (this is the 'right'), *except* as provided in the BA 1976, Sch 1. When Sch 1 applies, bail will be denied, and he or she will be remanded in custody (see **3.9** below). For the views of one experienced practitioner on how the right to bail works in practice and how it might be reformed, see Michael Mansfield QC, *Presumed Guilty*, Mandarin, 1993, ch 12.

In addition to the 'general right' to bail in BA 1976, s 4, Article 5 of the European Convention on Human Rights provides a right to liberty and security. This is clearly relevant to bail.

Relevant provisions in Article 5 include:

1. *Everyone has the right to liberty and security of person. No one shall be deprived of his liberty save in the following cases and in accordance with a procedure prescribed by law:*

. . .

(c) *the lawful arrest or detention of a person effected for the purpose of bringing him before the competent legal authority on reasonable suspicion of having committed an offence or when it is reasonably considered necessary to prevent his committing an offence or fleeing after having done so;*

(d) *the [lawful] detention of a minor . . . for the purpose of bringing him before the competent legal authority;*

. . .

3. *Everyone arrested or detained in accordance with the provisions of paragraph 1.c of this article shall be brought properly before a judge or other officer authorised by law to exercise judicial power and shall be entitled to trial within a reasonable time or to release pending trial. Release may be conditioned by guarantees to appear at trial.*

5. *Everyone who has been the victim of arrest or detention in contravention of the provisions of this article shall have an enforceable right to compensation.*

The significance of human rights generally to bail (and Article 5 in particular) can be seen in the publication by the Law Commission of a report (No 269) in 2001, entitled *Bail and the Human Rights Act 1998*. Following on from its very thorough review of the bail laws and procedures in England and Wales (Consultation Paper No 157, 1999), this report made several recommendations about legislative changes. Both documents are available on the Law Commission's website, www.lawcom.gov.uk.

Article 5 has already been used to assess the legality of an English bail provision — CJPOA 1994, s 25. In its original form, this provision required courts to deny bail to a defendant accused of a serious offence if already convicted of such an offence. In several cases, notably *Caballero v UK* (2000) 30 EHRR 643, the European Commission found s 25 to contravene Article 5. In consequence, s 25 was amended by the Crime and Disorder Act 1998, s 56. Courts are now allowed to release a defendant who is accused of his second serious offence if there are 'exceptional circumstances which justify it'.

In addition, other provisions of the ECHR have been used to attack English bail law in the courts, although not always successfully. For example, Article 6 (right to a fair trial) has been held not relevant to decisions taken under BA 1976, s 7(5) (see **3.14.2**). See *R (on the application of the DPP) v Havering Magistrates' Court* [2001] 3 All ER 997.

3.6.4   **Where there is no right to bail**

3.6.4.1   Generally

It is important to realise that the 'right' to bail under the BA 1976 *usually* applies only prior to conviction. It also only applies when a defendant appears in court (see BA 1976, s 4). So there is no right to bail in the following situations:

(a) When being arrested.

(b) When being charged with an offence.

(c) When a warrant for the arrest of an accused person is issued.

(d) After conviction for an offence **unless:**

    (i)   the case is adjourned so that inquiries or reports can be made to assist the court when passing sentence (BA 1976, s 4(4)); or

    (ii)   the defendant is subsequently brought before a court to be dealt with for breach of certain youth community orders, or breath of a requirement of a community order (BA 1976, s 4(3) as amended).

(e) If the accused is charged with murder, manslaughter, rape (or an attempt, where appropriate to do so), and he or she has a previous conviction for one of these offences (it is immaterial which one), the court may only grant bail if there are 'wholly exceptional circumstances which justify it'. (See the Criminal Justice and Public Order Act 1994 (CJPOA), s 25, as amended). A previous conviction for manslaughter will only qualify if the accused was sentenced to custody for it.

(f) If the accused appears in court charged with an indictable offence, or one triable either way, and it appears to the court that he or she was already on bail at the time of the present offence, the court need not grant bail under the BA 1976, s 4. The court continues to have discretion to release such a 'bail bandit' on bail once more. (See CJPOA 1994, s 26; BA 1976, Sch 1, Pt I, para 2A.)

CJPOA 1994, ss 25 and 26 may require further amendment in light of the HRA 1998. As noted above, s 25 was amended, following decisions of the European Court of Human Rights. In 2001, the Law Commission's report (No 269) concluded that there were no provisions either in BA 1976 or CJPOA 1994 which were incapable of being interpreted and applied compatibly with Convention rights. The Report nevertheless recommended reform of some legislative provisions and subsequent changes to BA 1976, s 3(6), reflect this sort of concern (see CJA 2003, s 13, for example; *Blackstone's Criminal Practice* (2005 edn), para D5.26).

In situations where there is no right to bail, the defendant may still be released on bail. The court, if it remands such a case, usually has a *discretion* to grant bail. This discretion is unfettered by the need to satisfy BA 1976, Sch 1, if bail is to be refused — in other words, the court has more freedom to refuse bail in such circumstances. On the grant of bail at the police station following charge, see PACE 1984, s 38 (see **2.2.12** above).

3.6.4.2   Street bail

As noted in **3.6.4.1**, there is no right to bail on arrest without a warrant. Under PACE 1984, s 30, an arresting officer is required to take the person arrested 'to a police station as soon as practicable after the arrest'. That requirement is now subject to two exceptions.

The first is where, on the way to a police station, the arresting officer is satisfied that there are no grounds for either keeping the person under arrest or releasing him on bail; in this situation (probably quite unlikely), the person must be released.

The second, and much more significant, exception is the introduction of 'street bail', pursuant to CJA 2003, s 4. This introduced a new provision — PACE 1984, s 30A — enabling a police officer to release a person on bail following their arrest but prior to their arrival at a police station. The person so bailed is then under the duty to attend at a police station. The location, date and time of that attendance ought to be specified in a notice given by the officer using street bail to the person released on bail. Failure to attend is enforceable by arrest without warrant. For an interesting critique of 'street bail', see an article by Anthea Hucklesby [2004] Criminal L R 803.

3.6.5 Custody time limits

There are certain limits on the length of time that a defendant can be kept on remand in custody, under the Prosecution of Offences Act 1985. These limits do not apply to summary offences or treason. See the Prosecution of Offences (Custody Time Limits) Regulations 1987, SI 1987/299, as amended. That there should be limits on the time to be spent in custody awaiting trial cannot be doubted. As Lord Bingham CJ declared in *R v Manchester Crown Court, ex p McDonald* [1999] 1 WLR 841, to proceed without time limits:

... would manifestly afford inadequate protection to unconvicted defendants, since a person could, if the Bail Act conditions were satisfied, be held in prison awaiting trial indefinitely, and there would be no obligation on the prosecuting authority to bring him to trial as soon as reasonably possible.

The regulations impose deadlines within which the proceedings must reach a specified stage. For example, a defendant who is kept in custody must be sent for trial within 70 days of his or her first appearance in court. If the deadline is not met, the defendant *must* be released on bail. There are also deadlines which apply generally, regardless of whether or not the defendant is in custody. These are sometimes referred to as *statutory time limits*. They were introduced in the Prosecution of Offences Act 1985, s 22. In their original form, the result of non-compliance was that the defendant was acquitted of the charge. This provision has now been amended so that non-compliance results in the proceedings merely being stayed. In certain circumstances, the case may be re-started later. See also the CDA 1998, ss 43 and 45, on statutory time limits. The prosecution can apply for a deadline to be extended. It must show (on a balance of probabilities) that there is good and sufficient cause for the extension and that it has acted with all due expedition.

When a defendant is freed on bail due to the expiry of a custody time limit, his or her bail should only have conditions attached to it that he or she can comply with *after* his or her release (eg reporting to a police station or a condition to reside at a specified address). Conditions which must be complied with *prior* to release (eg providing a financial surety) cannot be imposed. The significance of this can be seen in *Re Ofili* [1995] Crim LR 880, where O was originally granted bail, subject to providing a surety of £4,000. O could find no one to stand surety in that sum, so he remained in custody. When O challenged this, the Divisional Court held that on the expiry of the custody time limit, he was entitled to be freed on bail, subject only to reporting or residence conditions.

In a magistrates' court the maximum length of time that a defendant should spend in custody is 70 days. This period should be calculated as follows:

- 70 days from first court appearance to the start of summary trial (for either way offences);

- 70 days from first court appearance to a decision on committal for trial (for either way offences and offences which must be tried on indictment).

Note that, in the first point above, if the magistrates take a decision to proceed to summary trial within 56 days of the defendant's first court appearance, the custody time limit becomes 56 (not 70) days. Note further that, in the second point above, if the committal proceedings are held pursuant to MCA 1980, s 6(1) (ie with consideration of the evidence), then the 70-day limit is satisfied if the magistrates start to hear the prosecution's evidence within that period: they need not reach a decision on whether to commit the accused for trial within that period.

Once the case goes to the Crown Court, the maximum length of time that a defendant should spend in custody prior to his or her trial is 112 days, beginning with the date that he or she was sent for trial by the magistrates and expiring with the date of his or her arraignment (ie being asked in Crown Court to plead either guilty or not guilty). This period can be extended, but any use of a 'sham' arraignment simply to defeat the purpose of the custody time limit will be struck down. See, for example, *R v Maidstone Crown Court, ex p Hollstein* [1995] 3 All ER 503 — H was sent for trial on 24 March 1994, his custody time limit should have expired on 14 July 1994 but was extended to 22 July 1994. He should then have been released on bail but was kept in custody and produced in court on 27 July 1994 when he was arraigned on the indictment and further remanded in custody. He was still remanded in custody on 13 October 1994 (some three months after the expiry of the original time limit) when the Queen's Bench Divisional Court granted his application to quash the decision of 27 July 1994 to remand him in custody — no date for his trial had been fixed and the arraignment was an artificially created situation.

If the 112-day period expires, the CPS should either apply for an extension or bring the defendant back to court to be released on bail. The prison governor has no power to release the defendant without an order from the court. If the defendant continues to be detained in the absence of a court order for release, the appropriate remedies are either to apply to the Crown Court for bail or to seek *habeas corpus* or judicial review. No action will lie against the Home Office for false imprisonment, nor will the CPS be liable for breach of statutory duty if it fails to return the defendant to court after expiry of a custody time limit. See *Olotu v Home Office and another* [1997] 1 WLR 328.

The precise length of the custody time limits may need to be reviewed in the light of the HRA 1998 and Article 5(3) of the ECHR (which provides that everyone detained 'shall be entitled to trial within a reasonable time or to release pending trial'). However, the matter was considered by Lord Bingham CJ in *R v Manchester Crown Court, ex p McDonald* [1999] 1 WLR 841. After reviewing the ECHR case law on the subject, he stated that:

We do not . . . find anything in these European cases which in any way throws doubt on the English law . . . It would indeed appear that the term of 112 days prescribed by the regulations imposes what is, by international standards, an exacting standard.

The 112-day limit does not apply to defendants who are awaiting trial for offences of homicide and rape (see BA 1976, s 4(8) (as amended)).

Where an indictable-only case is sent straight to the Crown Court (under the CDA 1998, s 51), the maximum length of the custody time limit is 182 days. Time runs from the date the case is sent up by the magistrates, less any time already spent in custody.

See *Archbold*, 2005 edn, para 3–56; *Blackstone's Criminal Practice*, 2005 edn, paras D5.21 and D11.4.

3.7   Taking a decision on bail — when and how

3.7.1   When is the decision taken?

Usually, the question of bail or custody is decided at the end of each day's proceedings in the case, immediately prior to adjourning it to another day. If a case is being heard in court in the morning, and will continue in the afternoon, the court should determine whether the accused will take lunch in the cells (custody) or in the restaurant of his or her choice (bail), immediately before breaking for lunch. Sometimes, though, the question of bail is the sole reason for a case appearing in court. Examples are:

- The defendant, sent in custody to the Crown Court for trial or sentence, who applies to the Crown Court for bail pending the anticipated appearance in the Crown Court (see **3.16.1** below).
- The defendant who has been refused bail by magistrates and appeals to a Crown Court judge (see **3.16.1** below).

3.7.2   How is the decision taken?

The court must decide for itself whether or not to grant bail. It may be addressed by representatives of both prosecution and defence if the grant of bail is opposed, but the decision is one for the court. Lay magistrates will often retire briefly to consider whether to grant bail if release on bail is opposed by the prosecution. District and Crown Court judges will normally decide in court, straight after counsel have finished their submissions. If the release of the defendant on bail is unopposed by the prosecution (and especially if the defendant is already on bail in the current proceedings), the decision to grant bail is usually a formality.

3.7.3   Records, reasons, certificates and rights

3.7.3.1   Records

There are two common situations when a record must be kept of a decision on bail. Pursuant to the BA 1976, s 5(1), these are:

- whenever bail is granted (either by the police or a court);
- whenever a defendant with the right to bail under the BA 1976, s 4 is remanded in custody by a court.

Also, if an application is made to a court either:

- to attach conditions to a grant of bail which was hitherto unconditional; or
- to vary any extant conditions of bail,

the court must make a record of its decision.

If the defendant asks for a copy of the record, he or she must be given one (BA 1976, s 5). In some of the situations set out below, the defendant must be given a copy of the record even if one is not requested.

3.7.3.2 Reasons

Reasons for refusing to grant bail, etc. If a defendant has a right to bail under BA 1976, s 4, then if a court:

- refuses to grant bail; or
- grants bail subject to conditions; or
- on application for the purpose, imposes or varies conditions in respect of bail,

the court shall give reasons for its decision (BA 1976, s 5(3)).

These reasons shall be entered on the s 5 record and a copy must be given to the defendant (s 5(4)). However, if the decision is taken by the Crown Court, the defendant is legally represented in court, and the representative does not request a copy, a copy need not be given (BA 1976, s 5(5)). The purpose of giving reasons in these situations is to enable the defendant to make an informed decision about applying to another court about bail.

As well as the specific obligations imposed by the BA 1976, s 5(3), there is a more general obligation to provide reasons when refusing bail. Case law decided under the ECHR establishes that a court must:

. . . examine all the facts arguing for or against the existence of a genuine requirement of public interest justifying, with due regard to the principle of the presumption of innocence, a departure from the rule of respect for individual liberty and set them out in their decisions on applications for release.

See *Letellier v France* (1992) 14 EHRR 83.

In its Consultation Paper on Bail and the HRA 1998 (No 157, 1999), the Law Commission proposed that:

. . . magistrates and judges should be provided with appropriate guidance and training on making bail decisions in a way which is compliant with Article 5, and recording those decisions in such a way as to indicate clearly how they have been reached; and that magistrates' courts should be required to use forms which encourage compliant decision-making and the recording of decisions in a compliant way.

Such guidance was subsequently offered by the Law Commission itself. In its Report on Bail and the Human Rights Act 1998 (No 269, 2001), it compiled 'Guidance for bail decision-takers and their advisers'. This is set out in Pt XIII of the Report and also as a separate document on the Law Commission website (see www.lawcom.gov.uk).

Reasons for granting bail If a defendant is charged with any one of five specific offences, then, if a court grants bail notwithstanding that the prosecution has made certain representations, the court must state its reasons for granting bail, and these should be entered on the s 5 record. The offences are: murder (including attempts); manslaughter; and rape (including attempts).

The prosecution must have made representations that, if the defendant was granted bail, he or she would either fail to surrender to custody, or commit an offence whilst on bail; or interfere with witnesses or otherwise obstruct the course of justice.

The requirement to state reasons in this situation is imposed on the court by the BA 1976, Sch 1, Pt I, para 9A (inserted by the CJA 1988, s 153).

3.7.3.3 Certificates of full argument

Under the BA 1976, s 5(6A), if magistrates withhold bail after hearing a fully argued application for bail, they must issue a certificate stating that they heard full argument. After two unsuccessful bail applications in a case, if the magistrates allow the defendant a third application (which is unsuccessful), they should issue a certificate indicating the change in circumstances or new consideration that persuaded them to hear the third application. See BA 1976, s 5(6A) and (6B); also BA 1976, Sch 1, Pt IIA (inserted by CJA 1988, s 154). See further **3.15** and **3.16** below.

3.7.3.4 Right to appeal a refusal of bail

If the magistrates have issued a certificate of 'full argument', they must tell the defendant that he or she may now apply to a Crown Court judge for bail; the position is the same when magistrates send a case to Crown Court for trial. See BA 1976, s 5(6). On appeals generally, see **3.16** below.

3.8 Applying for bail — what happens in court?

The procedure for determining whether a defendant is to be released on bail does not really vary from court to court, either between courts on the same level of the court system or between courts on different levels. Some defendants have a right to bail under the BA 1976, s 4. Others can only seek the exercise of the court's discretion in their favour. In practice it is always incumbent on the defendant to apply for bail notwithstanding the duty of the court to consider it (BA 1976, Sch 1, Pt 11A). See [1988] Crim LR 397 for a contrary view.

3.8.1 The first step — dealing with the opposition

When a court hearing is adjourned and the defendant is to be remanded, the defendant (or defence counsel) is asked whether he or she seeks release on bail. If the answer is yes, the prosecution will be asked if there are any objections to bail (see **3.9** and **3.10** below).

Usually, defence counsel will seek out the prosecution *before* the case is called into court and ask whether there are any objections to bail. If there are none, the application will be unopposed and is likely to succeed (see **3.8.2**). If there are objections, defence counsel may ask what these are and then think about what bail conditions might overcome them. If defence counsel can get the defendant's agreement to such conditions, the approval of the prosecution may then be sought. If this is obtained, the defence can apply to the court for bail and offer the 'agreed' terms. As the application is now unopposed in effect, success (with the agreed conditions) is likely.

3.8.2 The unopposed application for bail

In this situation, the defence having indicated that bail is sought, the prosecution offer no objection. Although the court could try to investigate whether there are reasons why it should withhold bail from the accused, it is unlikely to do so — largely because the prosecution is its normal source of information which is critical of the accused. If prosecuting counsel sees no reason to object, the court is unlikely to discover such a reason from that source for itself.

3.8.3 The bail application which is opposed

If no agreement on bail has been reached between defence and prosecution prior to coming into court (see **3.8.1**) the prosecution objections are set before the court. The strict rules of evidence do not apply to bail applications but the defence is entitled to cross-examine any witness that the prosecution calls. The defendant may also testify. See *R (on the application of DPP) v Havering Magistrates' Court* [2001] 3 All ER 997. Defence counsel then makes oral submissions dealing with the objections to bail. Counsel may suggest that the objections are groundless and/or propose any conditions which might be attached to bail to overcome the objections (see further **3.11** and **3.12.5** below). The defence may call potential sureties into the witness box in an attempt to persuade the court that the defendant is unlikely to abscond. Finally, the court takes its decision to remand either on bail or in custody.

(See further **Chapter 37** in the *Advocacy Manual* for a checklist and flow chart on bail applications.)

3.9   Objections to a release on bail

As mentioned above, the prosecution may object to the defendant being freed on bail. In practice, any objections will correspond to one or more of the reasons for refusing bail to a 's 4' defendant, found in the BA 1976, Sch 1. These will be substantiated with information provided to the court by the prosecutor. Examples are:

(a) 'The accused is likely to fail to surrender to bail': he failed to turn up last time and we had to get a warrant; he has three convictions for this sort of thing already and faces a long spell in prison; he has no permanent address.

(b) 'The accused is likely to commit offences if freed': he was already on bail for an offence when he was arrested for this lot; he's done it in the past; he makes his living from crime.

(c) 'The accused must be remanded in custody for his own protection': he is on 12 charges of burglary, all from houses on the estate where he lives. Some of the residents have told the police that he's a dead man if he shows his face round there.

3.10   Refusing to release a defendant on bail

3.10.1   If the offence is imprisonable

If a defendant has the right to bail under the BA 1976, s 4, and asks to be released, then the court can only withhold bail where the offence is imprisonable if one (or more) of the following criteria is present in the case:

(a) The court is satisfied that there are substantial grounds for believing that the defendant would:
   (i)   fail to surrender to custody;
   (ii) commit an offence whilst on bail;
   (iii) interfere with witnesses or otherwise obstruct the course of justice.

(b) The defendant is charged with an offence triable either way and it appears to the court that he or she was already on bail at the time of the present offence.

(c) The court is satisfied that the accused must be kept in custody for his or her own protection (or welfare, if the accused is a child or young person — see **Chapter 6** for definitions of these terms).

(d) The accused is currently serving a custodial sentence imposed for a previous offence.

(e) If this is the first time that the case has been in the court and the court is satisfied it has not been practicable to obtain all the information necessary for a proper decision on bail to be made.

(f) If the accused has already failed to surrender to bail in the current case (or has broken the conditions attached to the grant of bail) and has been arrested for this.

(g) If, after conviction, the case is adjourned for inquiries or reports and it appears to the court that it would be impracticable to complete the inquiries or report without keeping the accused in custody.

(See BA 1976, Sch 1, Pt I.)

It remains to be seen exactly how the list set out in the BA 1976, Sch 1, is compatible with the HRA 1998 and the ECHR. The ECHR does not explicitly identify the grounds on which bail may be refused prior to trial but the matter has been considered by the European Court and the Commission. Four grounds have been recognised:

- fear of absconding (reflected in Sch 1; see (a)(i) above);
- prevention of crime (see (a)(ii) above);
- interference with the course of justice (see (a)(iii) above);
- preservation of public order (not explicitly within Sch 1; debatable which of grounds (b)–(g) would be covered).

The Law Commission has said that grounds (a)(ii) and (c) above are compatible with the ECHR but those responsible for taking bail decisions may require further guidance on their application. Ground (b) was felt to be highly likely to be applied in a manner incompatible with the ECHR. Similarly, the Law Commission described ground (f) as an automatic inference of a kind not permitted by the ECHR (namely, 'that a person who has done a given thing in the past is likely, given the chance, to do it again'). Grounds (b) and (f) have since been modified by the CJA 2003 — see below; it remains to be seen whether the modifications go far enough.

Ground (b) is modified by the CJA 2003, s 14 (not yet in force save as shown below). It is retained for bail in connection with extradition proceedings (BA 1976, Sch 1, Pt 1, para 2B; in force from 1 January 2004). Otherwise, it is modified for adult defendants so that our so-called 'bail bandit' need not be granted bail unless the court is satisfied that he presents no significant risk of offending whilst on bail (BA 1976, Sch 1, Pt 1, para 2A). For juvenile defendants, this is no longer a ground for denying bail, it is simply a factor to be considered when taking a bail decision (BA 1976, Sch 1, Pt 1, para 9AA).

Ground (f) is modified by CJA 2003, s 15 (not yet in force for these changes). Bail may be denied to an adult defendant who has already failed to surrender to custody without reasonable cause. In other words, he may not be denied bail simply for having been in breach of any secondary conditions attached to the bail. For juvenile defendants, this is now merely a factor to be considered when taking a bail decision (BA 1976, Sch 1, Pt 1, para 9AB).

We should also note that a new ground for refusing bail has been inserted into BA 1976, Sch 1, Pt I (by CJA 2003, s 19, in force 5 April 2004). Under new paras 6A–6C, in certain areas of the country the courts may deny bail to a defendant who is a Class A drug user. It is a little more complicated than that, of course. There are several criteria to consider:

- the defendant must be aged 18 or over; and
- he or she must have tested positive for the presence of Class A drugs in his or her system (such testing is now permitted after arrest, under PACE 1984, s 63B); and

- either:
  - the current proceedings relate to possession or the supply of Class A drugs; or
  - the court believes that the defendant's misuse of a Class A drug caused or contributed to the current offence; or
  - the court believes that the current offence was motivated by the defendant's intended misuse of a Class A drug; and

- either:

  - the defendant has refused to undergo an assessment of his or her dependency on (or propensity to misuse) Class A drugs; or
  - the defendant has had a positive assessment and refused the offer of such further assessment or assistance or treatment as the original assessor considered appropriate.

If, in the case of such a defendant, he or she is willing to undergo an assessment, or have the suggested follow-up, and the court decides to release the defendant on bail, it must make it a condition of bail that the defendant has the assessment or participates in the follow-up.

3.10.2 Considerations for the court

Schedule 1 to the BA 1976 (at Pt I, para 9) says that when a court is considering whether one of the reasons for refusing bail referred to in (a) (in **3.10.1**) exists, it should take account of:

(a) The nature and seriousness of the offence (and probable sentence).

(b) The character, antecedents, associations and community ties of the accused.

(c) The defendant's record of fulfilling bail requirements in the past.

(d) The strength of the case against the accused (unless adjourning for reports or inquiries before passing sentence).

(e) Any other considerations as appear relevant.

With regard to (b), the disclosure of D's *antecedents* means that the magistrates learn of his or her criminal record, if any. There are several points to note about this:

- evidence of any criminal record should be tendered in writing, not orally (*R v Dyson* (1944) 29 Cr App R 104);

- the press *should not* report any convictions which are publicised, at that time (*R v Fletcher* (1949) 113 JP 365) (note that there is no direct power to coerce the media, although note the Contempt of Court Act 1981, s 4(2));

- any magistrate who sits on a bail application hearing and learns of previous convictions is disqualified from subsequently trying D's guilt/innocence in that case (MCA 1980, s 42).

Also on 'associations and community ties', see the suggestions in *Stone's Justices' Manual*, 2004 edn at para 1–433. The phrase covers:

- name, age, nationality and (if applicable) length of residence in the UK;

- family circumstances (married? dependent children? does he or she live with wife/parents/other relatives?);

- residence (type of accommodation; recent addresses and length of stay);

- employment (recent record; present job — location and income);
- possible sureties, any relative, friend, employer in court . . .;
- anything else that the defendant wants to put forward, eg medical problems, difficulties with job or home if remanded in custody.

With regard to (e) above (any other relevant considerations), one should note the BA 1976, s 4(9), which states that a court may have regard to any misuse of controlled drugs by the defendant, where it is relevant to the court's decision on bail. Section 4(9) was inserted by the Criminal Justice and Court Services Act 2000 (CJCSA), s 58; to support this move, the CJCSA 2000 provides that samples of urine or a non-intimate sample may be taken from an adult defendant charged with a 'trigger offence' (as well as in some other circumstances) for the purpose of ascertaining whether he or she has any specified Class A drug in his or her body (see s 57). Failure to provide a sample is an imprisonable offence; information obtained from a sample may be disclosed for the purpose of informing any decision about granting bail in criminal proceedings to that defendant. Trigger offences include typical drug crimes (possession and possession with intent to supply); also most of the offences in the Theft Act 1968 (see CJCSA 2000, Sch 6).

Special considerations will apply to bail decisions concerning *juvenile* defendants, when the relevant provisions of CJA 2003 come into force:

(a) when deciding whether it is satisfied that there are substantial grounds for believing that the defendant would commit offences if released on bail, the court shall give particular weight to the fact that he was already on bail at the date of the present offence (BA 1976, Sch 1, Pt 1, para 9AA, inserted by CJA 2003, s 14(2))

(b) when deciding whether it is satisfied that there are substantial grounds for believing that the defendant would fail to surrender to custody if released, the court shall give particular weight to the fact that, having been released on bail in the present proceedings, he subsequently failed to surrender to custody without reasonable cause (BA 1976, Sch 1, Pt 1, para 9AB, inserted by CJA 2003, s 15(2)).

Finally, remember, if a court withholds bail from a 's 4' defendant, it must give its *reasons* in open court and on the record (BA 1976, s 5(3); see **3.7.3** above).

3.10.3   If the offence is non-imprisonable

The grounds for refusing bail set out in **3.10.1** are applied only to defendants charged with crimes for which they can be sent to prison, if convicted. The Bail Act 1976, Sch 1 also covers bail for non-imprisonable offences and is more liberal in allowing bail. The grounds for withholding bail now are:

- for the protection of the defendant;
- where the defendant is already serving a custodial sentence;
- where the defendant has been arrested for a bail offence in connection with this case (see **3.14** below);
- where the defendant has previously failed to surrender to bail and, in the light of that failure, the court is satisfied he or she would not surrender to bail if released now.

There is no power to remand a defendant in custody for the purpose of preparing medical/psychiatric reports if the offence is non-imprisonable.

The detailed provisions which govern the imposition of bail conditions are to be found in the BA 1976, Sch 1, Pt I, para 8. Part I applies to defendants 'accused or convicted of *imprisonable* offences' (emphasis added). There is no corresponding text in Sch 1, Pt II, which deals with *non-imprisonable* offences. It might be thought, then, that the BA 1976 makes no provision for attaching conditions to a grant of bail where a defendant is accused or convicted of a non-imprisonable offence. In fact, it has been decided that the basic power to attach conditions to a grant of bail (BA 1976, s 3) applies to both imprisonable and non-imprisonable offences (see *R v Bournemouth Magistrates' Court, ex p Cross* (1989) 89 Cr App R 90).

This decision can produce a rather odd result by virtue of the different criteria which now apply to non-imprisonable offences when (a) refusing bail and (b) imposing conditions. The BA 1976, s 3(6) and Sch 1, Pt I, para 8 both allow a court to attach conditions to a grant of bail if it appears necessary to do so in order to ensure that the defendant surrenders to custody; but Sch 1, Pt II, does not allow a court to withhold bail on the grounds that it believes the defendant will not surrender to custody. So if the court fears that a defendant will abscond, it may attach conditions to his or her bail but if there are no conditions that will allay such fears, they must release on bail anyway.

3.11   Overcoming objections to bail — the power of imagination

It was mentioned earlier (in **3.8.3** above) that if the prosecution is objecting to the release of the defendant on bail, defence counsel can suggest that certain conditions be attached to the grant of bail. These suggestions can be made to the prosecutor before going into court or once the prosecutor states the objections in court. Additionally, defence counsel can make (or repeat) these suggestions in his or her final submissions to the court. Apart from some qualifications on the power of the courts to attach conditions to a grant of bail, the conditions which can be used to overcome the fears of the prosecution or court are almost limitless. See, for example, *R (on the application of Ellison) v Teesside Magistrates' Court* [2001] EWHC Admin 12 which records that a defendant charged with attempted rape was released on bail by a Crown Court judge subject to a number of conditions, one of which was that he was not to consume alcohol.

3.11.1   Keeping one's imagination within reasonable bounds

There are some very common conditions (see **3.12** below) which will be suggested by the defence almost as an automatic reaction to certain objections. Nevertheless, one should not be afraid to put forward novel solutions to allay any objections, subject only to two observations. First, that one should always get the defendant's consent before putting a suggestion forward. Apart from the ethical problem of arguing a case with no instructions from the lay client to do so, there is a practical problem — to get your client released on bail, subject to conditions which he or she will not or cannot accept, is effectively not getting bail. Secondly, remember that the everyday bail conditions are used so often because they are workable and answer a particular objection sensibly. Do not invent new ones which fail to satisfy those criteria. One should seek only to improve the commonplace conditions to deal with novel situations when they arise.

3.12   Attaching conditions to release on bail

3.12.1   Generally

As regards a person granted bail, BA 1976, s 3, provides that:

Incidents of bail in criminal proceedings

3. —(1) A person granted bail in criminal proceedings shall be under a duty to surrender to custody, and that duty is enforceable in accordance with section 6 of this Act.

(2)   *No recognizance for his surrender to custody shall be taken from him.*

(3)   *Except as provided by this section—*

    (a)   *no security for his surrender to custody shall be taken from him,*

    (b)   *he shall not be required to provide a surety or sureties for his surrender to custody, and*

    (c)   *no other requirement shall be imposed on him as a condition of bail.*

(4)   *He may be required, before release on bail, to provide a surety or sureties to secure his surrender to custody.*

(5)   *He may be required, before release on bail, to give security for his surrender to custody.*
    The security may be given by him or on his behalf.

(6)   *He may be required to comply, before release on bail or later, with such requirements as appear to the court to be necessary—*

    (a)   *to secure that he surrenders to custody,*

    (b)   *to secure that he does not commit an offence while on bail,*

    (c)   *to secure that he does not interfere with witnesses or otherwise obstruct the course of justice whether in relation to himself or any other person,*

    (ca)   *for his own protection or, if he is a child or young person, for his own welfare or in his own interests,*

    (d)   *to secure that he makes himself available for the purpose of enabling inquiries or a report to be made to assist the court in dealing with him for the offence, and, in any Act, 'the normal powers to impose conditions of bail' means the powers to impose conditions under paragraph (a), (b) (c) or (ca) above,*

    (e)   *to secure that before the time appointed for him to surrender to custody, he attends an interview with an authorised advocate or authorised litigator, as defined by section 119(1) of the Courts and Legal Services Act 1990.*

Note that BA 1976, s 3(6) is shown as amended by CJA 2003, s 13, which came into force on 5 April 2004.

In **3.6.1** above, it was said that any grant of bail was subject to a primary duty — to surrender to bail at the appointed time, date and place — but also that secondary duties (known as 'conditions of bail') could sometimes be imposed on a defendant. The BA 1976 originally specified two forms of bail condition — the surety and security (see BA 1976, s 3(3) and (4)). The police were originally limited to these two conditions (but see now **3.12.7**), while the courts had more choice due to BA 1976, s 3(6), which allowed a court to impose any condition that they thought necessary to secure certain objectives.

3.12.2   The surety

If the court (or police, following an arrest or charge) considers it is necessary to ensure that the defendant surrenders to custody, the defendant may be required to provide sureties to guarantee his or her surrender (BA 1976, s 8). If no sureties are forthcoming, the defendant stays in custody, although technically bail has been granted. A surety is a person — usually a friend, relative or employer — who agrees to ensure that the defendant attends court at the next hearing. The surety acknowledges that, should the defendant fail to surrender, the surety is liable to forfeit a specified sum of money to the court. See also **3.14.6** below on forfeiture. A person may stand as a surety either in the courtroom or in any of the situations covered by the BA 1976, s 8(4) (for example, at the police station after the accused is charged; by the gaoler at court if the surety arrived too late to appear in court; at the prison holding the defendant).

3.12.3   The surety in court

Before starting the final submissions to the court, defence counsel should call any proposed sureties into the witness box. The 'surety' will take an oath and defence counsel should then explain the obligation to ensure the defendant's surrender to bail and the possibility of the surety losing money should this not happen. He or she should then be asked if he or she is still willing to be a surety. If so, counsel will enquire what sum of money he or she is prepared to run the risk of forfeiting and how this will be paid if required by the court to do so. The court will examine the surety's financial resources, character and any criminal record, and relationship to the defendant (kinship, geographical, etc).

If the procedure outlined above is followed, there should be no problems about lack of resources if the surety is subsequently called on to forfeit his or her recognisance. The issue of the surety's ability to pay was considered by the Divisional Court in *R v Birmingham Crown Court, ex p Ali and another* [1999] Crim LR 504. The court declared that a qualified lawyer, or legal executive, should not put someone forward as a possible surety unless he or she has reasonable grounds for believing that the surety would, if necessary, be able to meet the financial undertaking. Failure to observe this requirement is irresponsible and possibly a matter for consideration by a professional disciplinary body. Furthermore, a court should conduct appropriate enquiries with an individual before accepting that person as a surety. It might be necessary to require evidence of the assets that the would-be surety claims to have. How far that enquiry would go depends upon all of the circumstances, the most important of which is the amount of money at stake. (See **3.14.6** below; also the *Advocacy Manual*, **Chapter 37**.)

3.12.4   Security

The defendant may be required to provide security for his or her surrender (BA 1976, s 3(5) as amended by CDA 1998, s 54(1)). This may take the form of money or other valuables (BA 1976, s 5(9)) and may be demanded from the defendant personally, unlike a surety. It will be deposited with the court and, if the defendant fails to surrender to custody, it may be forfeited by court order, either totally or in part.

The obligation to pay a security, if it is held forfeit, is that of the defendant alone. If a third party actually supplies the funds to deposit with the court, he or she should note that the court is under no obligation to ascertain his or her ability to pay the money. Further, the third party's position need not be considered by the court when it imposes (or varies) bail conditions. Such a third party has far less protection here than when standing as a surety for a defendant: see *R v Maidstone Crown Court, ex p Jodka* (1997) 161 JP 638.

3.12.5   Other bail conditions

A court can impose any conditions it (or defence counsel) can think of, but they must be considered to be necessary to ensure that the defendant either:

- surrenders to custody; or
- does not commit offences while on bail; or

- does not interfere with witnesses; or

- does not obstruct the course of justice; or

- is for his own protection (or for his own welfare or in his own interests, if he is a juvenile); or

- is available for inquiries or reports to be completed; or

- attends an interview with a legal representative.

(See BA 1976, s 3(6).)
See *Stone's Justices' Manual*, 2004 edn at para 1–435.

3.12.6 Common conditions

3.12.6.1 Reporting to a police station

A defendant may be ordered to do this in order to ensure that he or she stays within the vicinity. This may be strictly enforced — for example, 'daily at 7 am and 7 pm' — or be a quite loose check — for example, 'every Thursday'. The purpose of this is to ensure the defendant is around to surrender to custody on the appointed date.

Now that the police are able to be more creative in attaching conditions to bail, there is room for confusion here. The police could always release a suspect on bail, subject to a requirement that he attend subsequently at the police station for further inquiries — that was not conditional bail as the attendance was a primary obligation on the accused. Nowadays, the police may also require a suspect to report to the police station if they are concerned that he or she may abscond — this would be a secondary obligation (he or she is not being required to surrender to custody) and if the suspect failed to report as required he or she would only be in breach of a bail condition; he or she would not have committed an offence under the BA 1976, s 6 (see **3.14.1** below).

3.12.6.2 Keeping curfew

Originally a medieval rule requiring fires to be extinguished at a certain hour at night, this now means the obligation to stay indoors between certain hours (usually at night). This condition is often used where a number of crimes have allegedly occurred at roughly the same time of day — for example, five houses have been burgled in the early hours of the morning: curfew to be kept between 11 pm and 6 am. It is commonly used for juvenile defendants.

3.12.6.3 Staying out of/in a certain area

These are separate conditions. The first aims to separate the accused from temptation — the woman who has been charged with shoplifting from four West End stores in London may be ordered not to go within a two-mile radius of Oxford Circus. (As precise measurement of this is virtually impossible for the average citizen, it is wiser not to tempt fate!) The second condition is intended to prevent the defendant either absconding or, occasionally, from contacting prosecution witnesses. Compliance with both conditions may be very difficult to check but, if a breach does come to the attention of a police officer, the defendant may be re-arrested. In a novel twist on this common condition, it was reported in the press in May 1994 that the Marquis of Blandford had a bail condition that he must not use taxi-cabs unless accompanied by his solicitor; at the time, he was charged with, *inter alia*, using taxis and dishonestly not paying the fares.

3.12.6.4 Electronic monitoring

In certain circumstances, a court may require a juvenile defendant to comply with electronic monitoring of his compliance with bail conditions (see Criminal Justice and Police Act 2001, ss 131–132).

3.12.7 Conditional police bail

In 1993, the Royal Commission on Criminal Justice recommended that the police be given greater powers to attach conditions, when deciding whether to release a detainee on bail from a police station. Originally, the police were limited to requiring just a surety or security. Subsequent changes mean that 'the normal powers to impose conditions of bail' are available to a custody officer at a police station (see PACE 1984, s 47(1A)). The main limitations now are that any conditions must appear to be necessary to ensure that the defendant

- surrenders to custody; or
- does not offend whilst on bail; or
- does not interfere with witnesses or otherwise obstruct the course of justice; or
- is for his own protection (or welfare or otherwise in his own interests, if he is a juvenile).

See BA 1976, s 3A(5), as amended by CJA 2003, s 13(2). In addition, the police cannot use some specific bail conditions — residence in a bail hostel (see BA 1976, s 3A(2)) or in connection with medical reports for defendants accused of murder (see BA 1976, s 3A(3)).

When considering the use of bail conditions, the police are unlikely to be influenced by representations from defence counsel since barristers do not usually attend a police station. The ability of either a duty solicitor or the defendant's own choice of solicitor to suggest or influence bail conditions at the police station remains the subject of speculation. See further on this, Ede and Edwards, *Criminal Defence*, (2002 2nd edn) Law Society.

3.13 Changing bail conditions

If circumstances change, so that the original conditions are no longer appropriate, the defence can apply to the court to alter or remove them. In exceptional situations, the prosecution can apply for existing conditions to be altered (presumably to strengthen them), or for conditions to be attached to an unconditional grant of bail.

Such application is made under the BA 1976, s 3(8), either to the magistrates' court which is dealing with the case or, if the case has been sent to the Crown Court, to a Crown Court judge. Where a defendant has been sent to Crown Court for trial but has not yet been required to surrender to custody at the Crown Court, then the magistrates' court which sent him for trial has concurrent jurisdiction with the Crown Court to hear any application for variation of bail conditions (see *R v Lincoln Magistrates' Court, ex p Mawer* [1995] Crim LR 878). Once the defendant has surrendered to custody at the Crown Court, the magistrates cease to have any jurisdiction over the matter. See also BA 1976, s 3(8A) —this extends the Crown Court's jurisdiction to cover applications made in serious fraud cases which go to Crown Court on a notice of transfer. (For notices of transfer, see **Chapter 11**.) See *Blackstone's Criminal Practice*, 2005 edn, para D5.43 for the basic procedure on bail applications to the Crown Court. Note, though, that this section refers to Crown Court Rules rr 19 and 20; these provisions were replaced by Criminal Procedure Rules 2005, r 19.18, from 4 April 2005.

It should be noted that if a defendant is released by the police on conditional bail, he or she may apply to a custody officer to vary those conditions (see BA 1976, s 3A(4)). The custody officer may impose different conditions and may even make them more onerous than before. Counsel is very unlikely to be involved in such an application. However the defendant may choose to apply to the magistrates' court and counsel may then be briefed (see MCA 1980, s 43B).

3.14   What happens if the defendant disobeys?

3.14.1   Failure to surrender to custody

It seems that around 10–14% of all defendants who are remanded on bail by magistrates subsequently fail to surrender to custody. The proportion does not vary much whether one looks at indictable offences or summary offences; see **Figure 3.4.** The court will usually issue a warrant for the arrest of the accused unless, perhaps, defence counsel is able to offer an explanation for the absence. Such warrants are known as *bench warrants*. When the warrant is executed and the accused is brought before the court, the court is very likely to remand the accused into custody. Note that, even though the accused may have had a general right to bail hitherto (under BA 1976, s 4), they have it no longer (BA 1976, Sch 1). If the defence counsel is able to put before the court some prima facie good reason for the absence of their client, the bench warrant may be *backed for bail*. In this situation, the warrant is executed by arresting the defendant and taking them to a police station. The defendant will then be re-released from the police station on (court) bail, subject to whatever conditions have been endorsed on the bench warrant, and will not then be produced in court but be under a duty to surrender to the court on a date to be notified. For obvious reasons, it is unusual for a bench warrant to be backed for bail.

3.14.2   Non-compliance with other conditions

No separate offence is committed in this situation but the accused is at risk of arrest (without warrant) by a police officer who has reasonable grounds for believing that a bail condition has been broken. Indeed, a police officer can arrest a defendant when he or she has reasonable grounds for believing that the defendant is likely to break a bail condition (see BA 1976, s 7(3)). Once arrested, the defendant must be produced in the magistrates' court within 24 hours. The defendant should not be produced in the Crown Court, even if on Crown Court bail, nor may the magistrates commit the defendant to the Crown Court for a decision to be made on bail. See *R v Marshall* (1995) 159 JP 688; *R (on the application of Ellison) v Teesside Magistrates' Court* [2001] EWHC Admin 12.

When the defendant is produced in the magistrates' court, the magistrates have to make a two-stage determination (see BA 1976, s 7(5); *R (on the application of DPP) v Havering Magistrates' Court* [2001] 2 Cr App R 2). The first stage is to decide whether the defendant has broken (or is likely to break) a condition of his or her bail. The hearing is quite

England and Wales		Number of persons (thousands)		
		Outcome		
How directed to appear	Total	Dealt with by magistrates[3]	Committed for trial	Failed to appear[4]
Indictable offences				
Summoned	51	39	3	8
Arrested and bailed	462	334	53	75
Arrested and held in custody	99	63	26	10
Total	611	436	82	93
Summary offences (excluding motoring)				
Summoned	408	400	*(5)	8
Arrested and bailed	253	202	*(5)	30
Arrested and held in custody	24	22	*(5)	2
Total	665	624	*(5)	40
Summary motoring offences				
Summoned	695	634	*(5)	61
Arrested and bailed	152	138	*(5)	14
Arrested and held in custody	18	16	*(5)	1
Total	865	788	*(5)	77
All offences				
Summoned	1,154	1,073	3	78
Arrested and bailed	846	674	53	119
Arrested and held in custody	141	101	26	13
Total	2,141	1,848	83	210

(1) The number of persons directed to appear includes those who failed to appear to a summons or to bail, who are excluded from the proceedings figures given in other chapters of this volume.
(2) Includes estimates for those offences omitted from 2002 data . . .
(3) Including those committed to the Crown Court for sentence.
(4) At any stage before final disposal by magistrates' court.
(5) Not applicable, because summary offences committed for trial will not be counted as principal offences as they must accompany an indictable only or triable either way offence.

Figure 3.4 Persons directed to appear at magistrates' courts[1] by type of offence, how directed to appear and outcome, 2002[2].

informal; usually, a police officer attends the court and states the grounds for his or her belief that a bail condition has been (or was likely to be) broken. In so doing, the officer may rely on hearsay evidence. There is no need to call other witnesses to testify for the prosecution but the defendant may cross-examine any who are called. The defendant is then entitled to give evidence, if he or she wishes to do so. The defendant must be given a full and fair opportunity to comment on, and respond to, the material put forward by the prosecution but where the defendant asserts that a reasonable excuse existed for a breach, that matter is irrelevant at this stage (see *R (on the application of Vickers) v West London Magistrates' Court* [2003] EWHC Admin 1809)

If the magistrates determine that the defendant has broken a bail condition, the second stage is to consider bail for the future of this case. The defendant may be remanded into custody, or released on bail again. Bail may be subject to the same or different conditions. The breach of bail that was established in stage one is one factor relevant to the magistrates' decision now; another relevant factor would be any suggestion by the defendant that there was a reasonable excuse for the breach. See also

R v Liverpool City Magistrates' Court, ex parte DPP [1993] QB 233; and the commentary at [2004] Crim LR 64.

3.14.3 Prosecutions for failure to surrender

Under BA 1976, s 6, it is an offence for a defendant to fail to surrender to custody at the appointed time and place. This offence is often referred to by courts, and counsel, as 'absconding'. It is otherwise commonly referred to, particularly by defendants, as 'doing a runner'. It is punishable by imprisonment or a fine (see **3.14.5**) and any security or sureties will be liable to forfeiture by order of the court (see **3.14.6**). Although BA 1976, s 6, creates a single offence of failure to surrender to custody, there are some distinctions to observe in the commencement of proceedings (this is an area that is currently dealt with in the *Practice Direction (Criminal: Consolidated)* [2002] 3 All ER 904 at section 1.13):

(a) *Where the defendant fails to surrender to court, having been bailed by police*

It is for the police or prosecutor to decide whether to initiate proceedings for the s 6 offence. If proceedings do go ahead, they should be dealt with on the defendant's first court appearance following arrest. The offence is summary and generally there is a six-month time limit on the commencement of proceedings, starting with the date of absence. However, if the defendant remains undiscovered for a longer period, that will not now defeat proceedings under s 6. CJA 2003, s 15(3) (in force 5 April 2004), provides that proceedings may be instituted within three months of the date when the defendant eventually surrenders to custody, is arrested in connection with the offence for which bail was granted, or appears in court in respect of that offence (and you should thus read the *Practice Direction (Criminal: Consolidated)* part 1.13.7, with caution). Proceedings will be commenced by the laying of an information, until the new procedure of written charge and requisition comes into force (CJA 2003, s 29).

(b) *Where the defendant fails to surrender, having been bailed by a court*

It is for the court to initiate proceedings, at the invitation of the prosecutor. If the defendant is arrested in connection with a new offence, committed outside the jurisdiction of the court which granted bail, the Bail Act offence should be dealt with by the court dealing with the new offence, if practicable. Otherwise, the defendant should be produced at the court dealing with the proceedings for which bail was granted previously — that may be the Crown Court, of course, if the defendant had been sent there for trial or sentence.

In either situation, the bail offence should be dealt with as soon as practicable. It should no longer be the practice to postpone its consideration until the conclusion of the proceedings for the main offence.

3.14.4 The hearing of a s 6 offence

The court is entitled to adopt a relatively informal procedure (*R v Hourigan* [2003] EWCA Crim 2306). The hearing usually begins with the court asking the defendant if he admits the breach of bail. The defendant should always be given the opportunity to explain his absence, and defence counsel should be invited to address the court, if appropriate (see *R v Davis (Seaton Roy)* (1986) 8 Cr App R (S) 64; *R v Boyle* [1993] Crim LR 40; *Hourigan*). The defendant bears the burden of proving a reasonable excuse for non-attendance, on the balance of probabilities. A court should be careful not to tie the hands of a later court (which might deal with the s 6 offence) or the Crown Prosecution Service by expressing a premature view of leniency or indicating that no proceedings need be taken — see *France v Dewsbury Magistrates' Court* [1988] Crim LR 295.

3.14.5 Penalties for failure to surrender

Following conviction by magistrates for absconding, there is a maximum penalty of three months' imprisonment and/or a fine of up to £15,000 (when the amendment made by the CJA 2003 to Level 5 on the standard scale of fines takes effect; see BA 1976, s 6(7)). However, the magistrates may instead commit the defendant to the Crown Court for sentence if they think greater punishment is required or if they are sending him to the Crown Court for trial on another offence and feel that it is appropriate for the Crown Court to deal with him for both offences (see BA 1976 s 6(6)). In the Crown Court, the absconder faces a maximum term of twelve months' imprisonment and/or an unlimited fine. The punishment may be severe if it is thought necessary to deter others. Sentences of six or nine months are not unknown (see *Clarke* [2000] 1 Cr App R (S) 224 and *Igbebion* [2004] EWCA Crim 2724 respectively). Indeed, it has been said that the responsibility for their absence is unaffected by whether or not they were eventually acquitted or convicted of the original offence (see *Clarke* again). For example, in *R v Neve* (1986) 8 Cr App R (S) 270, the defendant had been acquitted at his eventual trial for the main offence but was nevertheless sentenced to six months' imprisonment and ordered to forfeit a security of £10,000 for going to Spain in an attempt to avoid trial.

One of the less obvious possible penalties for absconding is when the court proceeds to try the defendant for the original offence, in his absence. This can happen in the magistrates' court (see MCA 1980, s 11 and **5.1.1** below) but it can also happen in the Crown Court once the defendant has been arraigned on the indictment (for guidance on when to proceed in the absence of the defendant, see the speech of Lord Bingham in *R v Jones* [2003] AC 1).

3.14.6 Forfeiture of a surety

If a defendant was granted bail subject to providing a surety, then a failure by the defendant to surrender to custody puts the surety in jeopardy of losing the sum which he or she guaranteed by his or her oath to the court.

In the past, forfeiture was likely to occur, usually for the whole sum. The test was that the whole sum would fall to be paid, unless it was fair and just to forfeit a lesser amount or nothing at all. Forfeiture provisions were tightened by the CDA 1998, s 55. When a defendant fails to surrender, the court is required to declare any surety to be forfeit *automatically*. It shall then require the surety (if present in court) to explain why he or she should not have to pay the whole sum. The court retains its discretion to demand payment of a lesser sum. If the surety is absent from court, or the court allows him or her time to produce evidence of his or her lack of culpability, it will issue a summons requiring his or her appearance at a later date.

There is a heavy onus on the surety to prove why he or she should not forfeit the full amount. This should be done either by showing a lack of means to meet the forfeiture or by establishing that he or she acted responsibly. The surety has a duty to maintain contact with the defendant and to keep informed as to the conditions of bail in order to ensure the defendant's surrender to custody. It has recently been pointed out by the Court of Appeal that any reduction in the amount ordered to be forfeited, following a defendant absconding, 'must be the exception not the rule and be granted only in really deserving cases'.

Hoffmann LJ observed that 'in one sense the system has unfairness built into it. It may result in persons entirely innocent having to suffer on account of the wrongdoing of another'. Lack of culpability by a surety is a factor to consider but in *R v Maidstone Crown Court, ex p Lever* [1995] 1 WLR 928, two sureties who were found to be blameless for the absconding nevertheless were ordered to forfeit 85% of their total surety of £59,000.

If the initial enquiry into the surety's means was conducted properly (see **3.12.4**), the above surety should have no problem finding the money to pay the forfeit. However, where the enquiry was inadequate, or the surety's means have changed, the sum which the surety is ordered to forfeit should be such as is within his or her or actual means. So, in a case where a surety of £25,000 was forfeited but the surety had originally provided an extremely exaggerated account of his assets, the magistrates' court ordered him to pay the forfeit at £12 per fortnight. The matter was then considered by the Divisional Court who observed that it would be correct in any normal case for the court to think of a sum which the surety could be reasonably expected to pay in full within two or three years (not 80 years as here). The matter was remitted to the magistrates for a rehearing. See *R v Bristol Magistrates' Court, ex p Davies* [1999] Crim LR 504.

Usually, the obligation of a surety will end when the defendant is arraigned on the charges as this is when trial normally commences. At this moment, the defendant is understood to have surrendered to the custody of the court and the surety has done all that the court required. This is subject to exceptions, though, and a surety should remain well-informed as to the exact status of the defendant and the view of the court as to whether the surety's obligation is at an end or continues. The penalty for being ill-informed is seen in *R v Central Criminal Court, ex p Guney* [1994] 1 WLR 438, where a surety for Asil Nadir was ordered to forfeit £650,000 following Mr Nadir's departure to Northern Cyprus. It could have been worse, as originally he stood surety for £1 million; in fact, it got even better for Mr Guney, as the Court of Appeal later quashed the forfeiture completely (see [1995] 1 WLR 376 and [1996] AC 616).

See also MCA 1980, s 120; *Archbold*, 2005 edn, para 3–143/145; *Blackstone's Criminal Practice*, 2005 edn, para D5.49.

3.15   Renewing an application for bail (or 'If at first you don't succeed, try again — but only once!')

3.15.1   Obligation to consider bail

See BA 1976, Sch 1, Pt IIA:

1.   If the court decides not to grant the defendant bail, it is the court's duty to consider, at each subsequent hearing while the defendant is a person to whom s 4 above applies and remains in custody, whether he ought to be granted bail.

2.   At the first hearing after that at which the court decided not to grant the defendant bail, he may support an application for bail with any argument as to fact or law that he desires (whether or not advanced previously).

3.   At subsequent hearings the court need not hear arguments as to fact or law which it has heard previously.

According to the BA 1976, Sch 1, Pt IIA (inserted by the CJA 1988, s 154), at every hearing of a case (when the defendant is in custody) the magistrates' court is obliged to consider whether he or she should be released on bail. The defence is allowed to make up to two applications for bail at which the same arguments may be used. If the accused is still in custody after this, the court may consider the matter of bail no longer open to argument from the defence.

Although the court is under a duty (CJA 1988, s 154) to consider bail at subsequent hearings in the case, these will be formalities. The defence may only reopen the issue of bail by raising fresh circumstances or arguments. Section 154 represents the statutory embodiment of a common law rule which was first reported in *R v Nottingham Justices, ex p Davies* [1981] QB 38.

Several cases have considered what constitutes a 'change in circumstances'. It seems to be a question of fact in each case, although the Queen's Bench Divisional Court has stated that the change need not be major. *R v Blyth Juvenile Court, ex p G* [1991] Crim LR 693 offers an illustration. Where there has been no application for bail by a defendant on the first appearance of a case at court and he or she has been remanded in custody, it seems that he or she has a right to apply for bail at a later hearing of the case (see *R v Dover and East Kent Justices, ex p Dean* [1992] Crim LR 33).

It seems possible that, with the advent of the HRA 1998 and the need to comply with decisions already made under the ECHR, a slight amendment to English law may be needed. It has usually been the position in English case law that simple effluxion of time does not give rise to a change in circumstances. However, in *Neumeister v Austria (No 1)* (1979–80) 1 EHRR 91, the European Court declared that a person should be released at the point when it is no longer reasonable to continue his or her detention. So, as time passes, the prisoner who is held in custody on remand should be able to seek review by the court of the decision to detain. This is clearly relevant to a prisoner held on remand under lengthy custody time limits. According to the European Court of Human Rights:

> ...the nature of detention on remand calls for short intervals [between bail reviews]; there is an assumption in the Convention that detention on remand is to be of strictly limited duration...because its raison d'être is essentially related to the requirements of an investigation which is to be conducted with expedition. In the present case an interval of one month is not unreasonable.

See *Bezicheri v Italy* (1989) 12 EHRR 210.

The matter was considered by the Law Commission of England and Wales (in its Consultation Paper No 157, 1999). The Law Commission felt that it was adequate that bail should be reconsidered by magistrates at least every 28 days (see **3.4.2** above) but was concerned that the possibility of a renewed application for bail might be denied by operation of Sch 1, Pt IIA. It pointed out that para 3 only says the court '*need not* hear arguments as to fact or law which it has heard previously' and thus has a discretion to hear such arguments. However, in practice courts seem to be reluctant to do so and also rarely accept that there has been a change in circumstances. The Law Commission noted reports asserting that if the accused found a job, sureties or a fixed address, these were seldom sufficient to show a change in circumstances. The Law Commission suggests that Sch 1, Pt IIA, can be interpreted and applied consistently with the ECHR, Article 5(4), but that guidance should be given to courts to the effect that 'the lapse of 28 days since the last fully-argued bail application should itself be treated as an argument which the court has not previously heard'. In its final Report on the subject (No 269, 2001), the Law Commission modified its position slightly. It maintained that a review of bail at least every 28 days complies with Article 5(4), but felt that courts should only have to consider whether the lapse of time has resulted in a change of circumstances. A defendant should not be able to insist on a full re-hearing of bail arguments every 28 days even though there had been no material change in the circumstances. See paras 12.9–12.24 of the Report.

3.15.2 The magistrates' certificate

Under the BA 1976, s 5(6A), if magistrates withhold bail after hearing a fully argued application for bail, they must issue a certificate stating that they heard full argument. After two unsuccessful bail applications in a case, if the magistrates allow the defendant a third application (which is unsuccessful), they should issue a certificate indicating the change in circumstances or new consideration that persuaded them to hear that third application. See BA 1976, s 5(6A) and (6B); also BA 1976, Sch 1, Pt IIA (inserted by CJA 1988, s 154).

3.16 Appealing against a bail decision

3.16.1 Appeals to a Crown Court judge by a defendant

A defendant can apply to the Crown Court for bail, as provided for in the Supreme Court Act 1981, s 81 (as amended), in particular:

- where a magistrates' court has committed the defendant to the Crown Court in custody on an offence triable either way (either for trial or sentence); or
- where a magistrates' court has sent the defendant to the Crown Court for trial on an indictment-only offence (under CDA 1998, s 51); or
- where the defendant has been convicted by a magistrates' court, given a custodial sentence, and been refused bail pending an appeal to the Crown Court (against either conviction or sentence); or
- where a case is proceeding in a magistrates' court, the magistrates have heard a fully argued application for bail and refused it.

In this last instance, the defendant can appeal against the refusal to release on bail by producing a certificate issued under BA 1976, s 5(6A) (see **3.7.3** and **3.15.2**). This appeal will be heard at the nearest location of the Crown Court dealing with Class 4 (low-grade) crimes. The appeal will usually be heard by a judge sitting 'in chambers'. This means that counsel need not wear a wig or gown, even though the hearing often takes place in a court-room. The defendant will not usually be present at the hearing, although the Crown Court has the power to permit this.

SCA 1981, s 81 only deals with defendants who are in custody. CJA 2003, s 16 makes provision for defendants who wish to appeal against the conditions subject to which they have been released. CJA 2003, s 16 only allows appeals against certain conditions:

- residence (either at a specified address, other than a bail hostel, or *not* at a specified address or area);
- any surety;
- provision of a security;
- curfew;
- electronic tagging;
- not to contact a specific person.

Furthermore, there must already have been a hearing at which the magistrates were asked to vary the bail conditions (see **3.13** above).

3.16.2   Appeal to a High Court judge by a defendant

The powers of the High Court have been significantly amended by the CJA 2003, s 17. This came into effect on 5 April 2004. Previously, the High Court was a significant alternative route of appeal where a magistrates' court withheld bail or attached conditions to it. Furthermore, a defendant had a choice of appealing the magistrates' decision to either the Crown Court or the High Court and, if he did not like the outcome in the first appeal, could renew it in the second forum. Now, however, the High Court is effectively limited to hearing bail appeals where a magistrates' court has stated a case for the opinion of the High Court (under MCA 1980, s 111) or where a defendant has been convicted or sentenced by a magistrates' court and is seeking judicial review of the decision (see CJA 1948, s 37). The High Court's inherent power in relation to bail for proceedings in the magistrates' courts is abolished (CJA 2003, s 17(2)). Once a bail appeal has been determined by the Crown Court, no further right of appeal to the High Court now exists (CJA 2003, s 17(3) and (4)).

The High Court retains the power to hear applications for a writ of *habeas corpus*, from prisoners seeking their release from custody (under RSC Ord 54; see CPR, Sch 1).

3.16.3   Appeals by the Crown Prosecution Service

3.16.3.1   Appeal to the Crown Court

Under the Bail (Amendment) Act 1993, as amended by CJA 2003, s 18, with effect from 4 April 2005, the prosecution has a general right to appeal when a defendant — charged with (or convicted of) any imprisonable offence — is released on bail. This replaces a previous, more limited, right to appeal.

If such a person was granted bail despite objections from the prosecution, and the prosecution is being conducted by the Crown Prosecution Service, an appeal may be made. If the CPS decides to appeal, it must say so (give oral notice of appeal) *before* the defendant is released from custody. Written notice of appeal must follow, within two hours, and must be served on the court and the defendant. Non-compliance with this two-hour period *may* be fatal to the appeal. That was the decision in *R v Middlesex Crown Court, ex parte Okoli* [2000] Crim LR 921 but it has since been held that as long as the prosecutor uses due diligence in service, a few minutes' lateness in serving the defendant may be excused (see *R (on the application of Jeffrey) v Warwick Crown Court* [2002] EWHC 2469).

The appeal must be heard within 48 hours (excluding weekends and bank holidays). The defendant will be kept in custody until the appeal is determined. If the appeal succeeds, the Crown Court judge may remand the defendant in custody or release him or her on bail with conditions.

3.16.3.2   Reconsideration by the magistrates' court

The prosecution now has a limited ability to ask for 'reconsideration' of a decision to release a defendant on bail. The BA 1976, s 5B, enables a prosecutor to apply to a magistrates' court to reconsider such a decision, whether it was originally taken by the court or by a custody officer. Having reconsidered, the magistrates may attach conditions to unconditional bail, vary the current conditions, or withhold bail (BA 1976, s 5B(1)) or, presumably, preserve the status quo. Reconsiderations may only be sought where the defendant is on bail for an offence which must or may be tried on indictment; the application must be based upon information which was not available to the magistrates (or custody officer) when the original decision was taken.

Useful article: David Tucker, 'The Prosecutor on the Starting Block: The Mechanics of the Bail (Amendment) Act 1993' [1998] Crim LR 728.

3.17 Representation for bail applications

On the initial appearance before a magistrates' court, a defendant is likely to be represented by a solicitor, under the duty solicitor scheme. If the case is not concluded on that first appearance, the defendant may need further legal representation. State-funded representation can be provided under provisions in the Access to Justice Act 1999.

An application for a representation order may be made to the court, either orally or on the prescribed application form. When the defendant is granted a right to representation in criminal proceedings, that right covers representation for the purposes of any related bail proceedings. The court must determine whether a right to representation should be granted, according to the interests of justice. Various factors may be relevant but, so far as bail is concerned, one would look in particular at 'whether the individual would, if any matter arising in the proceedings is decided against him, be likely to lose his liberty or livelihood . . .'.

It appears that the decision to grant a right of representation is simply one for the magistrates' judgment. However, under the Access to Justice Act 1999 circumstances may be prescribed where a right to representation shall always be granted. Under the Legal Aid Act 1988, there were several such circumstances. One was where the defendant had previously been remanded in custody by the court; was not legally represented then; was in danger of being remanded in custody again (or committed to Crown Court for trial in custody); and wished to be legally represented (Legal Aid Act 1988, s 21(3)(c)). Secondary legislation under the 1999 Act was thought likely to provide for representation in this situation, but has not yet done so.

As the right to representation includes representation at 'any preliminary or incidental proceedings', it should cover representation at a bail application in the Crown Court, after a case has been committed there by magistrates for trial or sentence; also, when the defendant is appealing against conviction or sentence, or after the magistrates have issued a certificate of full argument. See further the Access to Justice Act 1999, ss 12 to 15 and Sch 3; the Criminal Defence Service (General) (No 2) Regulations 2001; and the Criminal Defence Service (Representation Order Appeals) Regulations 2001.

3.18 Juvenile bail

Present government policy is that juveniles should spend as little time as possible awaiting final disposal of their cases. Overall time limits for specified stages of preliminary proceedings are being introduced for all cases but they will be 'tougher' for juvenile cases, and even more strict in cases involving persistent young offenders (see Prosecution of Offences Act 1985, ss 22 and 22A).

While awaiting disposal of their cases, most juveniles will be on bail. There is concern that, in this period, juveniles may commit further offences. Steps are being taken to discourage such re-offending or 'spree' activity. In particular, the government is encouraging the involvement of the voluntary sector in bail support schemes, eg the 'Youth Bail

Support Scheme' in Manchester, run by Manchester Children's Society. Youngsters on the Manchester scheme have an individual programme of activities; this is designed to create constructive leisure time, to institute weekly meetings with volunteers, and to provide accompaniment on court appearances. The scheme can also provide support in tackling difficulties at home, at school or in the workplace.

Fast-track procedures have been introduced nationally to cope with persistent young offenders. By this, the Home Office means young offenders who have been dealt with by a court on three or more occasions and who re-offend within three years of their previous court appearance (see eg Home Office Research Findings, No 74, 1998). A variety of reasons exist for the fast-track procedures which were devised by different courts around the country but the government has set a target that all courts should aim to complete at least 50 per cent of their persistent young offender cases within 71 days. Fast-track procedures may also be used for other categories of offender, such as those engaged on 'spree' offending. The procedures work by, for example, being tough on adjournments. There will be resistance to granting an adjournment and the first hearing at court should deal with substantive business. Pre-sentence reports may be required within 15 working days; courts may keep copies of these reports and simply have them updated orally if necessary. In addition to these steps, the government has set guidelines for the length of time which each stage in the youth court should take, in a case involving a persistent young offender. So, no more than two days from arrest to charge; seven days from charge to first appearance in court; no more than 28 days from first appearance in a youth court to commencement of a trial there; and no more than 14 days thereafter to reach the stage of verdict and sentence.

The provisions of BA 1976 apply to juveniles in basically the same manner as they do to adult defendants. That is, juveniles may be remanded on bail or in custody when proceedings in court are adjourned. If a young person is not released on bail, he or she may be remanded to local authority accommodation. Such accommodation is not necessarily secure, however.

The government has enabled courts to remand juveniles direct to secure local authority accommodation. See CDA 1998, ss 97–98, although these provisions will be amended when relevant provisions in the Criminal Justice and Court Services Act 2000 come into force. These provisions apply to all children aged 12–14 and girls aged 15 or 16. Boys aged 15 or 16 will continue to be remanded to Prison Service accommodation (either a remand centre or a prison) unless they are considered to be 'vulnerable'. A youth is vulnerable if the court forms the opinion that a remand to Prison Service accommodation would be undesirable due to his 'physical or emotional immaturity or a propensity of his to harm him-self' (see the Children and Young Persons Act 1969, s 23(5A)).

3.19 Final note

Any question of bail being granted which is not governed by s 4 of the BA 1976 or some other statutory provision is at the discretion of the court. See, for example, *Burgess v Governor of Maidstone Prison* [2000] All ER (D) 1688; *Archbold*, 2005 edn, para 3–170; *Practice Direction (Criminal: Consolidated)* [2002] 3 All ER 904, para 25.

4

Mode of trial

4.1 Classification of offences

All offences fall into one of the following categories:

- summary offences, ie those which must be tried in the magistrates' court;
- offences triable only on indictment, ie those which must be tried in the Crown Court;
- offences which are triable either way, ie those which may be tried in either the magistrates' court or the Crown Court.

Note that the term 'indictable offence' means an offence which 'is triable on indictment, whether it is exclusively so triable or triable either way' (Interpretation Act 1978, s 1(a)).

4.1.1 Summary offences

Summary trial, ie trial by magistrates, is a creature of statute, and all summary offences, similarly, are created by statute. The statute usually does this by providing a maximum penalty for summary conviction, with no alternative penalty for conviction on indictment. A huge number of offences are summary. See **Figure 4.1** for examples.

4.1.2 Offences triable only on indictment

All common law offences are triable only on indictment, ie by a judge and jury in the Crown Court, such as murder and manslaughter. Other offences in this category are created by statute which provides for a maximum penalty for conviction on indictment, with no alternative penalty on summary conviction. See **Figure 4.1** for examples.

4.1.3 Offences which are triable either way

Offences which are triable either way are technically indictable but may be tried in the magistrates' court if both the magistrates and the defendant agree. See **4.2** for details. Offences are shown to be triable either way by either:

- the statute which created them providing for alternative penalties on summary conviction or conviction on indictment; or
- re-classification by statute, in particular the Magistrates' Courts Act 1980 (MCA), s 17, which downgrades to triable either way many offences which were formerly triable only on indictment: see the list in Sch 1 to the Act.

Type of Offence	Triable only on Indictment	Triable Either Way	Triable only Summarily
1. Offences against the person	Murder Manslaughter Attempt to procure an abortion Causing grievous bodily harm with intent	Inflicting grievous bodily harm Unlawful wounding Assault occasioning actual bodily harm Assault with intent to resist arrest	Common assault Assault on a police constable in the execution of his duty
2. Sexual offences	Rape: Intercourse with a girl under 13 Buggery Incest	Unlawful sexual intercourse with a girl under 16 Indecent assault Living on the earnings of a prostitute	Soliciting
3. Theft Act offences	Robbery Aggravated burglary Blackmail Assault with intent to rob Burglary comprising commission of, or intention to commit, an offence only triable on indictment Burglary of a dwelling with threats to occupants	All Theft Act offences not being in the other two categories	Taking a motor vehicle without consent Taking a pedal cycle without consent
4. Criminal damage	Damage or arson with intent to endanger life	Damage where the value involved is over £5,000	Damage where the value involved is £5,000 or less
5. Road traffic	Causing death by dangerous driving	Dangerous driving	Most other traffic offences, eg: Speeding Failing to report an accident Driving while disqualified Driving without insurance Drunk in charge of a motor Vehicle Failing to stop at a red traffic light Aggravated TWOC where only damage is caused and of value less than £5,000
6. Miscellaneous	Perjury Attempt to pervert the course of justice Possessing a firearm with intent to endanger life Using a firearm to resist arrest Carrying a firearm to commit an indictable offence Collecting, communicating, etc information intended to be useful to an enemy Riot	Making false statements on oath not being in judicial proceedings Carrying a loaded firearm in a public place Shortening a shot gun Having an offensive weapon in a public place Using, communicating, etc information entrusted in confidence to a person holding office under the Crown Violent disorder Affray Stirring up racial hatred All offences under the Forgery and Counterfeiting Act 1981 Offences under the Misuse of Drugs Act 1971	Interference with vehicles Being drunk and disorderly Obstructing police Using threatening words or behaviour Dropping litter Failure to pay TV licence All offences under the Factories Act 1961

Figure 4.1 Classification of offences.

4.2   Procedure for determining the mode of trial

Where the offence is triable either way, and may be tried in *either* the magistrates' court or the Crown Court, it must first be determined which court should try the case.

The procedure is governed by the MCA 1980, as amended by the Criminal Procedure and Investigations Act 1996 (CPIA) and further amended by the Criminal Justice Act 2003. The amendments were intended to reduce the workload of the Crown Court, by ensuring that cases in which the defendant intends to plead guilty are dealt with summarily unless the case is serious. To achieve this, the defendant is asked, before a mode of trial decision is made, to indicate his or her plea.

4.2.1   Absence of the defendant

MCA 1980, s 18(2) provides that the defendant must be present during the proceedings in which he or she is asked to indicate his or her plea. There are three exceptions to this:

(a) Section 17B provides for the proceedings to continue in the defendant's absence due to his or her unruly behaviour. In order for the proceedings to continue in the defendant's absence, the following conditions must be satisfied:

   (i)   the defendant is legally represented; and

   (ii) the court considers that by reason of the defendant's disorderly conduct before the court it is not practicable for proceedings under s 17A above to be conducted in his or her presence; and

   (iii) the court considers that it should proceed in the absence of the defendant.

   In these circumstances, the procedure contained in s 17A and described in **4.2.2** is followed, except that all the indications as to plea are provided by the defendant's legal representative on the defendant's behalf, rather than by the defendant.

(b) Where the defendant is legally represented and consents to the case continuing in his or her absence (such consent being indicated by the representative), and the court is satisfied that there is a good reason (such as illness) for that absence (MCA 1980, s 23(1)(a) and (b)).

(c) The defendant is in custody and the court has decided to use a live TV link, having been satisfied that appropriate facilities exist (Crime and Disorder Act 1998, s 57).

4.2.2   The standard procedure

MCA 1980, s 17 as amended applies where a defendant who has attained the age of 18 is charged with a triable either way offence whether or not he or she is legally represented. The defendant must be present in court for this stage of the proceedings, unless one of the exceptions set out in **4.2.1** applies.

The procedure may be presided over by a lay justice sitting alone under MCA 1980, s 17E, though it is more usual to have two or more lay magistrates.

The basic procedure is as follows:

(a) The charge is written down, if it has not already been written down, and read to the defendant.

(b) The court explains to the defendant in ordinary language that he or she may indicate whether he or she would plead guilty should the case proceed to trial. The court should further explain to the defendant that if he or she indicates a plea of guilty, the court will:

(i)   proceed as if the proceedings had constituted a summary trial from the outset;

(ii)   proceed as if the defendant had in fact pleaded guilty to the charge;

(iii) warn the defendant of the possibility of committal for sentence under the Powers of Criminal Court (Sentencing) Act 2000, s 3 or s 3A.

The court will then ask the defendant whether, if the case were to proceed to trial, he or she would plead guilty or not guilty.

There is no set form of words to follow and some courts have developed their own. A suggested form of words to be used by the court has been devised by the Judicial Studies Board, however, and is as follows:

For this charge you may be tried in either the magistrates' court or by a jury in the Crown Court. First however this court must ask you whether, if the case proceeds to trial, you would plead guilty or not guilty. Before you answer that, I want to explain what will happen then. If you say that you would plead guilty, the court will hear the prosecution case against you, listen to your mitigation, and formally find you guilty. The court will then decide that sentence it thinks you should receive. Do you understand?

(Unless repeated or further explanation is required, say) then if the charge against you was to go to trial, would you plead guilty or not guilty?

(c) The defendant indicates a plea of guilty, a plea of not guilty or fails to indicate a plea.

(i)   *Indication of a plea of guilty.* This allows the defendant the earliest opportunity to record a plea of guilty, and gain the credit from having done so, and also to ensure that cases which could properly be dealt with in the magistrates' court remain there: *R v Warley Magistrates' Court ex p DPP [1998] 2 Cr App R 307.* It should be noted that this is not the plea itself, but an indication of what the plea would be in the event of a trial. By virtue of MCA 1980, s 17A(6) however, the court proceeds as if the proceedings had constituted a summary trial from the beginning, and treats the indication of plea as if it were, in fact, a plea of guilty. No further pleas are taken. The court proceeds on to the sentencing stage.

(ii)   *Indication of a plea of not guilty.* Where the defendant indicates that he or she will plead not guilty, the court proceeds to determine the mode of trial as set out in (d)–(k) below.

(iii) *No indication of plea.* Where the defendant fails to indicate a plea, he or she is taken to have indicated a plea of not guilty (MCA 1980, s 17B(3) as amended).

(d) The prosecution has the opportunity to inform the court of the accused's previous convictions, if any. Note that the reference to convictions refers to both convictions in the UK and findings of Courts Martial.

(e) The prosecution and defence have the opportunity to make representations as to whether summary trial or trial on indictment would be more suitable.

(f) The court makes the decision as to whether summary trial or trial on indictment is more suitable, taking into account:

(i)   whether the sentence which the magistrate's court would have power to impose for the offence would be adequate; and

(ii)   any representations advanced by the prosecution or the defence; and

(iii) whether the nature and circumstances of the case make it of serious character having regard to the allocation guidelines issued under the CJA 2003 as definitive guidelines. The allocation guidelines refer to the Mode of Trial

Guidelines, which are included at **4.7** for reference. New guidelines are likely, given the increase in the magistrates' sentencing powers under the CJA;

(iv) the defendant's previous convictions (under s 19(2)(a) inserted by the CJA 2003).

(g) if the defendant is charged with more than one offence, such offences being offences that could be tried together, or arise out of the same or connected circumstances, the reference to 'sentence' is to the aggregate sentence which the magistrate's court would have power to impose for all the offences taken together.

Where summary trial appears more suitable

(h) If the court decides that summary trial is more suitable, the court shall explain to the defendant in ordinary language that:

(i)   it appears to the court more suitable for him to be tried summarily; and

(ii) that he can consent to be so tried or, if he wishes, be tried on indictment; and;

(iii) that in the case of a specified offence, that if he is tried in the magistrates' court and convicted, he may be committed to the Crown Court for sentence under PCC(S)A 2000, s 3A.

See **5.3** below.

Indication of sentence

(i)   The defendant may request an indication of sentence, that is, whether a custodial or non-custodial sentence would be more likely to be imposed if he were to be tried summarily. Such an indication may but need not be given. The statute refers to this as an 'indication' and whether the custodial or non-custodial sentence would be 'more likely'. This is not quite the same as saying that the indicated sentence will inevitably be given, but the section does have that effect. Section 20A of the MCA 1980 says that where a plea has been taken following a sentence indication '*no court may impose a custodial sentence for the offence unless such a sentence was indicated.*'

(j)   If an indication of sentence is given, the court must ask the defendant whether he or she wishes, on the basis of the indication, to reconsider the plea given or taken to have been given. If he or she does wish to reconsider, the question shall be put to him again. If he or she indicates that he would plead guilty, the court proceeds as if the proceedings had constituted a summary trial from the beginning, and he had pleaded guilty.

(k)   Where the court does not give an indication of sentence (either because it has declined to do so or because it was not asked) and the defendant does not wish to reconsider the indication of plea, and does not indicate that he or she would plead guilty:

(i)   the defendant is asked if he consents to be tried summarily, and, if he consents, the court proceeds to summary trial; or

(ii) if he does not consent, the court proceeds to send him to Crown Court for trial, under Crime and Disorder Act 1998 s 51(1).

Where trial on indictment appears more suitable

(l)   If the court decides, under s 19, that the offence appears more suitable for trial on indictment, nothing is explained to, or asked of, the defendant as described above.

The court simply tells the defendant of its decision and proceeds in accordance with Crime and Disorder Act 1998, s 51(1). The defendant's consent is not required.

4.2.3   Failure to comply with the procedure

The procedure outlined above is obligatory, and any deviation from it is likely to render the whole proceedings null and void. The defendant then has the option of applying for judicial review to quash any eventual conviction. For example, in *R v Kent Justices, ex p Machin* [1952] 2 QB 355, under the pre-CJA law, the magistrates failed to tell the defendant of the possibility of a committal for sentence, and the conviction and subsequent committal were quashed.

It is open to the prosecution to seek judicial review of the magistrates' decision, although such proceedings are rare, and are unlikely to be successful. However, for a case where the Divisional Court did overrule the magistrates, see *R v Northampton Magistrates' Court, ex p CCE* [1991] Crim LR 598.

4.2.4   Changing the mode of trial

4.2.4.1   The defendant

The defendant may change his or her election from summary trial to trial on indictment, or vice versa, if the magistrates consent. The typical situation is that the defendant has elected summary trial without taking proper advice and then sought legal representation for the purposes of trial or sentence. In these circumstances the magistrates are likely to allow the change, but it is a matter within their discretion. The test is whether the defendant understood the nature and significance of the choice which he or she was being asked to make (*R v Birmingham Justices, ex p Hodgson* [1985] QB 1131).

According to *R v Bourne Justices, ex p Cope* (1989) 153 JP 161, the essential issue is whether the defendant realised that by his or her election he or she was depriving himself or herself of the right to a jury. The fact that the prosecution witnesses were present and ready to give evidence, and that it would not be desirable to delay the case further was not relevant to the defendant's understanding. However, once it was established that he or she did understand the decision he or she was being asked to make, these matters were ones which the justices could take into account in exercising their discretion to allow a change of election.

If the magistrates allow a change of election, they should also allow a change of plea, if one has been given, as the plea has a major influence on where the defendant should be tried (*R v Birmingham Justices, ex p Hodgson* [1985] QB 1131).

The principles outlined above pre-date the CPIA 1996, but do not appear to be affected by the passing of that Act.

4.2.4.2   The magistrates

At present, the magistrates may change their mode of trial decision from summary trial to trial on indictment and vice versa. They have the power to do this under MCA 1980, s 25. However, once the CJA 2003, Sch 3, comes into effect, it will amend MCA 1980, s 25 and the magistrates will be limited to just the following possibility — where the magistrates have accepted jurisdiction and the accused has consented to summary trial, the prosecution may apply to the court for the offence to be tried on indictment instead. That application must be made before the start of the summary trial. It may be granted but only if the magistrates are satisfied that the sentence which they would have the power to impose for the offence would be inadequate. If the accused faces two or more offences in the same proceedings, and the magistrates consider they form a series of offences of the same or a similar character, they may consider the maximum aggregate sentence which they would have the power to impose if the accused were convicted of all the offences.

4.3 Criminal damage

Under the MCA 1980, s 22, where the defendant is charged with criminal damage (other than where the damage was caused by fire) the magistrates must proceed as if the offence were summary only when the value of the damage is less than £5,000. The court is only proceeding *as if* the offence is summary, but it is not summary for all purposes (*R v Considine* (1980) 70 Cr App R 239 and *R v Fennell* [2000] 1 WLR 2011).

See also *R v Alden* (2002) 2 Cr App R (S) 326, which confirmed that if the Crown Court is dealing with criminal damage (other than under a provision such as CJA 1988, s 40), the maximum sentence of 10 years is available.

4.3.1 Special procedure in criminal damage cases

Under s 22, before embarking on the normal procedure for determining the mode of trial as set out in **4.2** above, the procedure set out below must be followed:

(a) The court shall, having regard to any representations made by the prosecution or defence, consider the value of the thing involved. There is no appeal on the basis that the value was mistaken (s 22(8)).

When determining the value of the damage where the property is damaged beyond repair, the value is the market value of the property at the material time. The court is not concerned with determining consequential loss. See *R v Colchester Justices, ex p Abbott* The Times, 13 March 2001, where the value of damaged genetically modified crops was the market value, and not the consequential loss of lost research.

(b) If the value is:
   (i)   £5,000 or less, the court proceeds to summary trial. The defendant has no right to trial on indictment, nor may he or she be committed for sentence under PCC(S)A 2000, s 3. Under the CJA 2003, the maximum penalty is increased from three months' imprisonment to 51 weeks or a fine up to Level 4 on the Standard Scale (currently £2,500).
   (ii) more than £5,000, the offence is triable either way, and the court follows the procedure to determine the mode of trial set out in **4.2** above. If the offence is tried summarily the maximum penalty is six months' imprisonment and a £5,000 fine;
   (iii) uncertain, the court will ask the defendant if he or she consents to summary trial, after the lower penalty and absence of any power to commit for sentence have been explained. If consent is given then the court proceeds to summary trial. If not, the court will follow the procedure for determining the mode of trial set out in **4.2** above. See s 22(4)–(6). See, for example, *R v Prestatyn Magistrates' Court* [2002] EWCA 1177, where the defendants were charged with criminal damage to an experimental crop of genetically modified maize, which had been grown as a development measure with significant investment.

It was grown for research rather than sale. The court held that to view it as an ordinary crop was artificial. In the circumstances, the value of the crop was uncertain. This appears to conflict with *Ex p Abbott* (above).

4.3.2   A series of offences

If the defendant is charged with two or more offences which appear to the court to be a series of offences of the same or a similar character, then the court has regard to the aggregate value in determining the mode of trial. Thus, if the value of all items damaged totals £5,000 or less, then the magistrates proceed as if the offences are all summary, regardless of the number of offences. See s 22(11), inserted by the CJA 1988, s 38. For an example of the operation of s 22(11), see *R v Braden* (1988) 87 Cr App R 289.

4.4   Linked summary and indictable offences

The CJA 1988, ss 40 and 41, introduced two exceptions to the otherwise inflexible rule that summary offences are only triable summarily. The two sections are similar, but contain important distinctions, and should be analysed with care.

Note: If the defendant is dealt with by the Crown Court under either section, the powers of the Crown Court with regard to sentence are limited to those of the magistrates.

4.4.1   Trial of a summary offence on indictment: s 40

If the defendant has been sent for trial in respect of an indictable offence, the prosecution may include in the indictment a count for a summary offence if:

- the summary offence is common assault, taking a motor vehicle without consent, driving whilst disqualified, criminal damage within the MCA 1980, s 22, assaulting a prison custody officer or secure training officer, or is punishable by imprisonment or disqualification and is specified by the Home Secretary as being suitable for inclusion; and

- the summary offence is either founded on the same facts as the indictable offence or is, or forms part of, a series of offences of the same or similar character. See for example *R v Smith* [1997] QB 836, where the defendant was charged on indictment with dangerous driving. Counts for taking a motor vehicle without authority and driving whilst disqualified were added under s 40. The Court of Appeal held that, as the latter two offences were not founded on the same facts as the first, they were improperly joined and the convictions in relation to them were quashed; and

- the evidence before the court discloses a summary offence.

The magistrates simply send the defendant for trial on the indictable offence. The initiative for including the summary offence must come from the prosecution. Once the summary offence is included in the indictment, then, if the defendant pleads not guilty to both the indictable and summary offences, or even just the summary offence, the defendant will be tried by jury, following the procedure set out in **Chapter 11**. If he or she is convicted, the Crown Court powers of sentence in respect of the summary offence are limited to those of the magistrates.

The effect of s 40, taken together with the Criminal Law Act 1967 (CLA), s 6(3), is that if a person is indicted on a count charging assault occasioning actual bodily harm, he or she can only be found guilty of common assault if that offence is specifically included in the indictment. This also applies to other offences included in s 40 (*R v Mearns* [1991] 1 QB 82). See also **Chapter 10** for the CLA 1967, s 6(3).

In *R v Smith* [1997] QB 836, the Court of Appeal decided that the misjoinder of a summary offence under s 40 does not render the counts alleging indictable offences invalid.

4.4.2   Committal for plea: s 41

The CJA 2003, Sch 3 Part 2, para 60(8), repeals CJA 1988, s 41, but is not yet in force. Until then, s 41 provides that when magistrates send a defendant for trial on an either way offence, they may also send any summary offence which

- is punishable with imprisonment or disqualification, and
- arises out of circumstances which are the same as, or are connected with, those giving rise to the either way offence.

The idea behind s 41 is that it is good sentencing practice for one court to deal with all outstanding sentencing issues for a single defendant. The effect of s 41 is therefore delayed until such time as the defendant stands convicted of the either way offence in the Crown Court. At that moment, the judge will need to impose a sentence for that offence, so it is then sensible to determine if the defendant is also guilty of the summary offence(s), sent up to the Crown Court using s 41.

Under changes to s 41 made by the Courts Act 2003 (which came into effect on 1 April 2005), the defendant will then be asked how he pleads to the summary offence(s). If he pleads guilty, he will be sentenced for that offence by the Crown Court judge. If he pleads not guilty, then the Crown Court judge will be able to sit as a magistrate and conduct a summary trial. If that trial concludes with a conviction, again the judge will pass sentence for the summary offence. In each instance, the Crown Court judge would be limited to the sentencing powers of a magistrates' court when dealing with the summary offences. The CJA 2003 will repeal s 41 because of other procedural changes that it makes. Under CDA 1998, s 51(3) (as amended), when a defendant is sent for trial to the Crown Court, the magistrates will also send any related offence with it. That will include summary offences if punishable with imprisonment or disqualification from driving.

4.5   Advantages and disadvantages of each mode of trial

There are many matters to be taken into account in advising on the most appropriate forum:

(a) *Speed*. Whether a case in the magistrates' court is likely to be heard more quickly than if it had been listed for hearing in the Crown Court depends on local waiting lists. However, the case itself is likely to take less time in the magistrates' court.

(b) *Expense*. Proceedings in the magistrates' court are much less expensive than in the Crown Court — a very important consideration if the defendant is not legally aided.

(c) *Informality*. Proceedings in the magistrates' court are much more informal than in the Crown Court, as fewer people are involved, and counsel do not wear wig and gown. The Crown Court can be daunting to someone who has little experience of criminal courts.

(d) *Sentence*. The magistrates' powers of sentence are very much less than those of the Crown Court, though they do have the power to commit to the Crown Court for sentence. However, if the defendant intends to plead guilty, he or she is likely to opt for a hearing in the magistrates' court in the hope that the magistrates do not commit him or her to Crown Court for sentence. See **Chapters 15–16** for details of the magistrates' powers of sentence.

(e) *Division between the tribunals of fact and law*. In the magistrates' court, the tribunals of fact and law are the same, so that they will first have to hear evidence before deciding on any question of admissibility, and then, if inadmissible, endeavour to forget it. In the Crown Court this problem simply does not arise. The judge alone will decide on admissibility, and evidence will only go before the jury if it is admissible.

(f) *Legal submissions*. Despite the fact that lay magistrates are advised by a clerk, any submissions on the law are made to laymen. (The case may be heard by a stipendiary magistrate, but this would not be known when determining the mode of trial.) In the Crown Court, the same submission would be made to a professional lawyer.

(g) *Appeals*. Appeals from the magistrates' court may be made without leave, (see **Chapter 8**). Appeals from the Crown Court always require leave, and the procedure generally is much more complicated (see **Chapter 12**).

(h) *The benefit of the doubt*. It is generally assumed that a jury is more likely to give the defendant the benefit of the doubt than magistrates. In any event, if the case involves a substantial attack on the police evidence, the defendant is likely to find a jury more sympathetic than magistrates.

You are referred to Home Office Research Study No 125, entitled *Magistrates' Courts or the Crown Court? Mode of Trial Decisions and Sentencing* (London: HMSO, 1992).

4.6 Advance information

The prosecution has a duty to provide the defence with the evidence upon which it will rely at trial on indictment, and with undisclosed material in certain circumstances. See Chapter 9 for a full discussion of the rules relating to disclosure.

The Criminal Procedure Rules 2005, r 21, provides that where the accused is charged with a triable either way offence, the prosecution must provide the defence with copies of its witness statements, *or* a summary of the evidence upon which it proposes to rely, on receiving a request for such information. The purpose of obtaining advance information is to facilitate a mode of trial decision.

The prosecution is entitled to refuse a request, but, under r 21.4 only where it thinks that compliance would lead to the intimidation of witnesses or some other interference with the course of justice. Failure to comply for any other reason will lead to an adjournment, unless the court considers that the defendant has not been prejudiced. See generally r 21.6.

The request for information should be made *before* mode of trial proceedings have been held, and the information should be provided as soon as practicable. Thus, the defendant is able to make his or her decision as to the mode of trial with full knowledge of all the circumstances. It is the duty of the court, under r 21.5 to satisfy itself that the defendant is aware of his or her right to advance information.

Obtaining advance information is now very common, but the defence may decide against a request if clearly one mode of trial is preferable. However, it is the duty of the court under r 21.5 to satisfy itself that the defendant is aware of his or her rights.

Note that the magistrates have no power to *order* disclosure under these rules (*R v Dunmow Justices, ex p Nash* (1993) 157 JP 1153, DC).

Further reading: David Sunman, 'Advancing disclosure. Can the rules for advance information in the magistrates' courts be improved?' [1998] Crim LR 798.

4.7 Allocation Guidelines

The following Mode of Trial Guidelines were introduced in order to assist magistrates make a mode of trial decision prior to CJA 2003. They are to be replaced by allocation guidelines to be known as definitive guidelines. Such guidelines have not been formulated at the time of writing, so the pre-existing guidelines have been reproduced here to illustrate what the definitive guidelines are likely to be.

Practice Direction (criminal: consolidated) [2002] 3 All ER 904, para 51, *Mode of Trial*

51.1   The purpose of these guidelines is to help magistrates decide whether or not to commit 'either way' offences for trial in the Crown Court. Their object is to provide guidance not direction. They are not intended to impinge upon a magistrate's duty to consider each case individually and on its own particular facts. These guidelines apply to all defendants aged 18 and above.

General mode of trial considerations
51.2   Section 19 of the Magistrates' Courts Act 1980 requires magistrates to have regard to the following matters in deciding whether an offence is more suitable for summary trial or trial on indictment:

(a)   *the nature of the case;*

(b)   *whether the circumstances make the offence one of a serious character;*

(c)   *whether the punishment which a magistrates' court would have power to inflict for it would be adequate;*

(d)   *any other circumstances which appear to the court to make it more suitable for the offence to be tried in one way rather than the other;*

(e)   *any representations made by the prosecution or the defence.*

51.3   Certain general observations can be made:

(a)   *the court should never make its decision on the grounds of convenience or expedition;*

(b)   *the court should assume for the purpose of deciding mode of trial that the prosecution version of the facts is correct;*

(c)   *the fact that the offences are alleged to be specimens is a relevant consideration (although, it has to be borne in mind that difficulties can arise in sentencing in relation to specimen counts, see Clark [1996] 2 Cr App R (S) 351 and Kidd [1998] 1 Cr App R (S) 243); the fact that the defendant will be asking for other offences to be taken into consideration, if convicted, is not;*

(d)   *where cases involve complex questions of fact or difficult questions of law, including difficult issues of disclosure of sensitive material the court should consider committal for trial;*

(e)   *where two or more defendants are jointly charged with an offence each has an individual right to elect his mode of trial;*

(f)   *in general, except where otherwise stated, either-way offences should be tried summarily unless the court considers that the particular case has one or more of the features set out in paras 51.4–51.18 and that its sentencing powers are insufficient;*

(g)   *the court should also consider its powers to commit an offender for sentence, under [PCC(S)A 2000, ss 3 and 4], if information emerges during the course of the hearing which leads them to conclude that the offence is so serious, or the offender such a risk to the public, that their powers to sentence him are inadequate. This means that committal for sentence is no longer determined by reference to the character and antecedents of the defendant.*

Features relevant to the individual offences

51.4   Where reference is made in these guidelines to property or damage of 'high value' it means a figure equal to at least twice the amount of the limit (currently £5,000) imposed by statute on a magistrates' court when making a compensation order.

[**Note:** Each of the guidelines in respect of the individual offences set out below (except those relating to drugs offences) are prefaced by a reminder in the following terms 'Cases should be tried summarily unless the court considers that one or more of the following features is present in the case *and* that its sentencing powers are insufficient. Magistrates should take account of their powers under [PCC(S)A 2000, ss 3 and 4] to commit for sentence', see para 51.3(g).]

51.5   *Burglary: dwelling-house*

   (a)   *Entry in the daytime when the occupier (or another) is present.*

   (b)   *Entry at night of a house which is normally occupied, whether or not the occupier (or another) is present.*

   (c)   *The offence is alleged to be one of a series of similar offences.*

   (d)   *When soiling, ransacking, damage or vandalism occurs.*

   (e)   *The offence has professional hallmarks.*

   (f)   *The unrecovered property is of high value: see para 51.4 for definition of 'high value'.*

   (g)   *The offence is racially motivated.*

Note: Attention is drawn to para 28(c) of schedule 1 to the [MCA 1980], by which offences of burglary in a dwelling *cannot* be tried summarily if any person in the dwelling was subjected to violence or the threat of violence.

51.6   *Burglary: non-dwellings*

   (a)   *Entry of a pharmacy or doctor's surgery.*

   (b)   *Fear is caused or violence is done to anyone lawfully on the premises (eg nightwatchman, security guard).*

   (c)   *The offence has professional hallmarks.*

   (d)   *Vandalism on a substantial scale.*

   (e)   *The unrecovered property is of high value: see para 51.4 for definition of 'high value'.*

   (f)   *The offence is racially motivated.*

51.7   *Theft and fraud*

   (a)   *Breach of trust by a person in a position of substantial authority, or in whom a high degree of trust is placed.*

   (b)   *Theft or fraud which has been committed or disguised in a sophisticated manner.*

   (c)   *Theft or fraud committed by an organised gang.*

   (d)   *The victim is particularly vulnerable to theft or fraud (eg the elderly or infirm).*

   (e)   *The unrecovered property is of high value: see para 51.4 for definition of 'high value'.*

51.8   *Handling*

   (a)   *Dishonest handling of stolen property by a receiver who has commissioned the theft.*

   (b)   *The offence has professional hallmarks.*

   (c)   *The property is of high value: see para 51.4 for definition of 'high value'.*

51.9   *Social security frauds*

   (a)   *Organised fraud on a large scale.*

   (b)   *The frauds are substantial and carried out over a long period of time.*

51.10   *Violence (ss 20 and 47 of the Offences against the Person Act 1861)*

   (a)   *The use of a weapon of a kind likely to cause serious injury.*

   (b)   *A weapon is used and serious injury is caused.*

    (c)   *More than minor injury is caused by kicking or head-butting.*

    (d)   *Serious violence is caused to those whose work has to be done in contact with the public or who are likely to face violence in the course of their work.*

    (e)   *Violence to vulnerable people (eg the elderly and infirm).*

    (f)   *The offence has clear racial motivation.*

Note: The same considerations apply to cases of domestic violence.

51.11   *Public Order Act offences*

    (a)   *Cases of violent disorder should generally be committed for trial.*

    (b)   *Affray.*

        (i)   *Organised violence or use of weapons.*

        (ii)   *Significant injury or substantial damage.*

        (iii)   *The offence has clear racial motivation.*

        (iv)   *An attack on police officers, ambulance staff, fire-fighters and the like.*

51.12   *Violence to and neglect of children*

    (a)   *Substantial injury.*

    (b)   *Repeated violence or serious neglect, even if the physical harm is slight.*

    (c)   *Sadistic violence (eg deliberate burning or scalding).*

51.13   *Indecent assault*

    (a)   *Substantial disparity in age between victim and defendant, and a more serious assault.*

    (b)   *Violence or threats of violence.*

    (c)   *Relationship of trust or responsibility between defendant and victim.*

    (d)   *Several more serious similar offences.*

    (e)   *The victim is particularly vulnerable.*

    (f)   *Serious nature of the assault.*

51.14   *Unlawful sexual intercourse*

    (a)   *Wide disparity of age.*

    (b)   *Breach of position of trust.*

    (c)   *The victim is particularly vulnerable.*

Note: Unlawful sexual intercourse with a girl under 13 is triable only on indictment.

Drugs

51.15   Class A

    (a)   *Supply; possession with intent to supply: these cases should be committed for trial.*

    (b)   *Possession: should be committed for trial unless the amount is consistent only with personal use.*

51.16   Class B

    (a)   *Supply; possession with intent to supply: should be committed for trial unless there is only small scale supply for no payment.*

    (b)   *Possession: should be committed for trial when the quantity is substantial and not consistent only with personal use.*

51.17   *Dangerous driving and aggravated vehicle taking*

    (a)   *Alcohol or drugs contributing to dangerousness.*

    (b)   *Grossly excessive speed.*

    (c)   *Racing.*

    (d)   *Prolonged course of dangerous driving.*

(e) *Other related offences.*

(f) *Significant injury or damage sustained.*

51.18 *Criminal damage*

(a) *Deliberate fire-raising.*

(b) *Committed by a group.*

(c) *Damage of a high value.*

(d) *The offence has clear racial motivation.*

Note: Offences set out in Sch 2 to the MCA 1980 (which includes offences of criminal damage which do not amount to arson) must be tried summarily if the value of the property damaged or destroyed is £5,000 or less.

Summary trial

5.1 Procedure at trial

Some 96% of all criminal cases are tried in magistrates' courts. The procedure is the same, whether the offence is triable only summarily, or triable either way, though if the offence is triable either way, the magistrates must first determine the mode of trial (see **Chapter 4**).

See generally *Stone's Justices' Manual* (2004 edn) at para 1–461 et seq and *Blackstone's Criminal Practice* (2005 edn), at paras D19 and D20.

5.1.1 The absence of the defendant

Although the defendant will in fact often be present in court for the hearing, the magistrates have the power to proceed in his absence. There are three situations in which this may arise. ↳ the defendant.

5.1.1.1 Where the defendant fails to attend

Under the Magistrates' Courts Act 1980 (MCA), s 11(1), the magistrates have a discretion to hear the case in the defendant's absence if he or she fails to attend court in answer to a summons. If the offence is triable either way, the prosecution must first establish that the defendant actually knew of the summons, for example, through attending an earlier hearing.

Summarily – as long as prosecution prove summons sent to last known address does not matter if not received by defendant

If the offence is triable only summarily, then the prosecution may prove that the summons was served simply by establishing that, for example, it was sent by registered post to the defendant's last known address, but the prosecution does not have to prove that the defendant received it.

Once service of the summons has been proved, a plea of not guilty will be entered on the defendant's behalf and the prosecution evidence will be called. Such hearings often end in the conviction of the defendant, as none of the prosecution evidence will have been tested by cross-examination, and the magistrates will not have heard the defence case.

Statutory declaration within 21 days of finding out about conviction. – Void so prosecution start again.

If the defendant did not, in fact, know of the proceedings, he or she may make a 'statutory declaration' of this under the MCA 1980, s 14, within 21 days of finding out about them. If the declaration is made, the summons, trial and conviction are rendered void. However, the information remains valid, so that the prosecution can start again.

The discretion to proceed in the absence of the defendant should be exercised judicially. This includes giving the defendant a fair opportunity to be present, and to give or call evidence. See *R v Bolton Magistrates' Court, ex p Merna* [1991] Crim LR 848, where the court proceeded in the absence of the defendant, despite a letter from his doctor saying that he was unfit to attend court.

Whether the defendant's absence should lead to a rehearing of the case was a matter within the justices' discretion, and as long as this was based on facts the justices were entitled to find, the divisional court would not overturn it (*R v North Shields Justices, ex p Darroll* [1991] COD 317).

The s 11 procedure tends to be used only for the less serious offences. In any event, if the defendant is charged with a triable either way offence, the defendant normally has to be present during mode of trial proceedings.

Note that the court ought to be reluctant to try, in his absence, an offender who is young, has not been placed on bail and/or has no record of failing to appear (*R v Dewsbury Magistrates' Court, ex p K* The Times, 16 March 1994).

5.1.1.2   Pleading guilty by post

Under the MCA 1980, s 12 as substituted by Sch 5 to the Criminal Justice and Public Order Act 1994 (CJPOA), a defendant may plead guilty by sending a letter to court. This can be done if:

- the offence is summary; and

- proceedings have been started by the service of a summons.

In such circumstances the procedure is as follows:

(a) The prosecution serves on the defendant:

   (i)   the summons;

   (ii) a brief statement of the facts upon which the prosecution proposes to rely or a copy of such written statements as comply with the Criminal Justice Act 1967 (CJA), s 9(2)(a) and (b);

   (iii) any information relating to the accused which will or may be placed before the court; and

   (iv) a notice explaining the procedure.

(b) If he or she wishes to plead guilty, the defendant notifies the court and may enclose a statement of his or her mitigation. Subsequently, the defendant may withdraw this plea, and the case then proceeds as if it were a not guilty plea.

(c) Neither the prosecution nor the defence is represented or appears at court, and the court proceeds on the basis of the statements which are read out in court. Failure to do so will lead to the conviction being quashed, as in *R v Epping and Ongar Justices, ex p Breach* [1987] RTR 233 where the defendant's statement in mitigation was not read out. The magistrates may refuse to accept the plea of guilty if the statement in mitigation discloses information which amounts to a defence.

[handwritten margin note: The magistrates may refuse a guilty plea if mitigation amounts to a defence]

(d) The magistrates, if content to accept the plea, may sentence, or adjourn for the accused to be present. The magistrates may only sentence the defendant in his or her absence if he or she is to be fined, absolutely discharged, or have his or her driving licence endorsed.

Section 12A of the MCA 1980 deals with the situation where the defendant actually appears in court. Two situations may occur:

- The defendant has informed the court that he or she wishes the case to proceed under s 12, but he or she nevertheless appears in court at the appointed time. The court may proceed to deal with the matter as if he or she were absent, if he or she consents to such a course: s 12A(1).

- The defendant has not notified the court that he or she wishes the case to proceed under s 12, and appears at the appointed time. If he or she indicates that he or she wishes to plead guilty, and consents, the court may proceed to deal with the matter as if he or she were absent (s 12A(2)).

[handwritten margin note: but- in either case the court must allow the defendant to make oral submissions with a view to mitigating the sentence s12.A(c)]

In either case, the court must afford the defendant an opportunity to make oral submissions with a view to mitigation of sentence (s 12(5)(c)).

5.1.1.3 The disorderly defendant

If the defendant's behaviour is so disruptive that the proceedings cannot continue, he or she may be removed, and the court may proceed in his or her absence under MCA 1980, s 11.

Note: If the defendant is represented, he or she is deemed to be present unless his or her presence is expressly required by statute (MCA 1980, s 122(2)).

5.1.2 Absence of the prosecution

Under the MCA 1980, s 15, if the prosecution fails to appear at the time and place fixed for the summary trial, the magistrates may adjourn the case or dismiss the information. Where the magistrates act unreasonably in dismissing a case, their decision is a nullity, and a mandatory order would issue (*R v Hendon Justices, ex p DPP* [1994] QB 167) (see **8.3**).

If the case is adjourned part-heard, then the magistrates may proceed in the absence of the prosecution, the evidence given on the earlier occasion being treated as the entirety of the prosecution case. In these circumstances, the defendant will not face cross-examination of his or her evidence by the prosecution.

5.1.3 Representations in private

[handwritten margin note: all parties must be notified of hearing and must be present with a contemporaneous note being taken usually by the clerk.]

A decision to hear representations in private is within the magistrates' discretion, but careful consideration should always be given to whether such a step is appropriate, given the magistrates' role as fact-finder. In order to guard against injustice, steps must be taken to ensure that all parties are notified of the hearing and are represented, with a contemporaneous note being taken, normally by the clerk (see *R v Nottingham Magistrates' Court, ex p Furnell* (1996) 160 JP 201).

5.1.4 Taking the plea

The defendant must plead unequivocally guilty or not guilty. In practice, this often throws up two separate problems:

[handwritten margin note: A guilty plea may be changed at any time before sentence but this is entirely within the discretion of the Magistrates.]

(a) *The defendant who wishes to change his plea.* The court may consider an application made by a defendant who has unequivocally pleaded guilty to change his or her plea, at any time before sentence (see *S (an infant) v Recorder of Manchester* [1971] AC 481). Whether he or she will be allowed to change the plea is entirely within the discretion of the magistrates. If they take the view that the defendant understood the charge, the consequence of his or her plea, and had intended to make it, they will be unlikely to allow a change. See generally, *R v McNally* [1954] 1 WLR 933.

Where the magistrates have allowed the defendant to change his plea from guilty to not guilty, they should also allow him to reconsider his consent to summary trial (*R v Bow Street Magistrates' Court, ex p Welcome* (1992) 156 JP 609).

[handwritten margin note: A not guilty plea may be changed to guilty with the leave of the court any time before the verdict.]

Where the defendant has pleaded not guilty, and wishes to change his or her plea to guilty, he or she may do so with leave of the court (which for obvious reasons is likely to be granted) any time before the court retires to consider the verdict.

(b) *The defendant's plea is equivocal.* This covers three situations:

(i) The defendant, when pleading guilty, explains his or her plea in words amounting to a defence. See *R v Emery* (1943) 29 Cr App R 47, where the defendant said

= not guilty for trial

'Plead guilty in self-defence'. The magistrates should then explain the law and the defendant is asked to plead again. If the plea is still equivocal, the magistrates must record a plea of not guilty and proceed to trial. If they make no enquiry into the plea, the defendant may later challenge the validity of the plea on appeal.

new information

(ii) The defendant unequivocally pleads guilty, but the plea is rendered equivocal by information given to the magistrates before sentence (see *R v Durham Justices, ex p Virgo* [1952] 2 QB 1 contrasted with *R v Birmingham Crown Court, ex p Sharma* [1988] Crim LR 741). In *P Foster (Haulage) Ltd v Roberts* [1978] 2 All ER 751, it was said that this should not be termed an equivocal plea, and is merely a situation in which the magistrates have a discretion to allow a change of plea.

duress

(iii) The defendant unequivocally pleads guilty and no further information is given to the court casting doubt on the correctness of the plea. However, if the defendant argues that the plea was made under duress, the Crown Court may treat it as an equivocal plea. See *R v Huntingdon Crown Court, ex p Jordan* [1981] QB 857.

In any event, the magistrates should always ensure that the defendant, particularly an unrepresented defendant, understands the offence, the consequences of the plea, and intends to make that plea. The proper forum for any dispute is the Crown Court, which may review the case, and, if it decides that the plea was equivocal, it should remit it to the magistrates with an order that they enter a plea of not guilty and proceed to trial. Before making any such order, the Crown Court should read affidavits from the magistrates and the clerk as to what happened, and magistrates and clerks should cooperate by swearing such affidavits. See *R v Plymouth Justices, ex p Hart* [1986] QB 950.

5.1.5   The prosecution opening speech

Magistrates will be familiar with the cases that frequently come before them, so that, although the prosecution has the right to an opening speech, it is usually brief and is often not made.

In *L and B v DPP* [1998] 2 Cr App R 69, the case was adjourned for a month after hearing the prosecution witnesses. The defendants appealed against their convictions as the prosecution had made a second speech on the resumed hearing, at the magistrates' request, to remind them of the evidence given at the earlier hearing. It was held that there was nothing unfair in that, subject to the safeguard that the defence should always be asked to address the court in reply to correct any errors or draw attention in differences of recollection.

5.1.6   The prosecution evidence

The prosecution calls the evidence upon which it relies. This will take the form of witnesses and written statements, if admissible and appropriate.

As to the defence knowledge of the prosecution case, see **4.6** and **Chapter 9**.

In the Crown Court, the trial judge is the tribunal of law whereas the jury is the tribunal of fact. In the magistrates' court, however, the magistrates are both tribunal of law and tribunal of fact. The question as to whether the magistrates, having heard evidence and decided that it is inadmissible, should then recuse itself was discussed in *R (on the application of Ratra) v DPP* [2004] EWHC 87. Whether it should do so would depend on the principles derived from previous authority, namely, first, whether all the circumstances that had a bearing on the suggestion that the judge was biased would lead a fair-minded and informed observer to conclude that there was a real possibility, or a real danger, the two being the same, that the tribunal was biased; secondly interlocutory rulings did not in the ordinary way (unless there was special reason) deprive the district judge or the justices from continuing with the hearing; and thirdly, even when justices had ruled evidence inadmissible there could, in exceptional cases, be circumstances in which the inadmissible evidence was so highly prejudicial that, as a matter of fairness and appearance of fairness, a differently constituted bench ought properly to conduct the trial.

5.1.7 The submission of no case to answer

At the end of the prosecution evidence, the defence may make a submission of no case to answer. According to Lord Parker CJ, in *Practice Direction (Submission of No Case)* [1962] 1 WLR 227, a submission that there is no case to answer may properly be made and upheld:

- when there has been no evidence to prove an essential element in the alleged offence; or

- when the evidence adduced by the prosecution has been so discredited as a result of cross-examination or is so manifestly unreliable that no reasonable tribunal could safely convict on it.

The Practice Direction was revoked by *Practice Direction (criminal: consolidated)* [2002] 3 All ER 904. No alternative direction was given, however, leaving justices with no revised guidance as to the test to be applied.

Until such guidance is given, except as discussed in the following paragraph, it is likely that justices will decide the issue by asking whether the evidence is such that a reasonable tribunal might convict. There is a case to answer if they decide a reasonable tribunal might convict on the evidence so far laid before it.

In the Crown Court, the test which the trial judge will apply, in deciding on a submission of no case to answer, is set out in *R v Galbraith* [1981] 1 WLR 1039 (see **11.6**). In applying the test, the trial judge does not consider the credibility of the witnesses, as this is a matter for the jury. Similarly, when deciding the issue in the magistrates' court, the magistrates will not normally take into account the credibility of the witnesses (*R v Barking and Dagenham Justices, ex p DPP* (1995) 159 JP 373).

Note that, though it is now usual for magistrates to give reasons following a finding of guilt, Article 6 of the European Convention on Human Rights imposes no obligation to provide reasons for refusing to accede to a submission of no case to answer. Given the highly specific nature of summary procedure, the interests of justice would not be served by imposing such a requirement (*Moran v DPP* [2002] EWHC 89).

5.1.8 The defence case

Assuming no submission of no case to answer is made, or is made and fails, the defence may present its case. The right of the defence to make an opening speech is rarely exercised (see **5.1.9**) and the defence usually begins to call its evidence straight away. The defendant should give evidence before any other witnesses he intends to call (PACE 1984, s 79).

5.1.9 Closing speeches

The defence has the right to either an opening or a closing speech, and invariably elects a closing speech, thus having the benefit of the last word.

Note that the prosecution does not have the right to a closing speech. However, if either party wishes to make a second speech, they may do so with the leave of the court; but if the court is going to allow one party to make a second speech, it must allow the other party a second speech also. If both parties are allowed a second speech, the prosecution must go first, thus allowing the defence the benefit of the last word.

Students are referred to the Criminal Procedure Rules 2005, r 37.1 for the rules relating to speeches in summary trial.

5.1.10   The verdict

Lay magistrates usually retire to consider their verdict, and no one must retire with them as this may create the impression that they have somehow influenced the decision. As to the position of the clerk to the justices, see **5.2** below. The verdict is a majority decision, and the chairman has no casting vote. Therefore, if an evenly numbered court is equally divided, it must adjourn for a fresh hearing before a new bench (*R v Redbridge Justices, ex p Ram* [1992] QB 384).

District judges rarely retire, and usually announce their decision immediately after the defence's closing speech.

In reaching their decision, the magistrates may rely on any local knowledge that they have, but both prosecution and defence should have been informed of this during the trial so that they might be afforded an opportunity to comment upon that knowledge (*Norbrook Laboratories (GB) Ltd v Health and Safety Executive* The Times, 23 February 1998).

See also *Gibbons v DPP* (2001) 165 JP 812, where the district judge hearing a trial visited the place of the offence after closing speeches and checked, inter alia, whether an eye-witness's view could have been obstructed. The Divisional Court held that, given the importance of such matters, the district judge should, at the very least, have informed the parties beforehand so that they could make submissions, if they chose, as to the witness's actual position. The convictions were quashed and a retrial ordered.

Traditionally magistrates have not given reasons for their decisions. They should indicate the basis of their decision, but not in any form of judgment or elaborate form. Following the Human Rights Act 1998, they must show that they have considered the ingredients of the offence so that the accused knows he has been found guilty. This can be done in a few sentences. See generally *R (McGowan) v Brent Justices* (2002) 166 JP 29 and *McKerry v Teesdale and Wear Valley Justices* (2000) 164 JP 355.

It should be noted that the provisions of the Criminal Law Act 1967 (CLA), s 6(3), do not apply in magistrates' courts. Thus the magistrates have no power to find the defendant guilty of an alternative offence not specifically charged (except under s 24(3) and (4) of the Road Traffic Offenders Act 1988, under which a defendant charged with dangerous driving may be found guilty of careless driving). See generally *Lawrence v Same* [1968] 2 QB 93. However, it would be open to the magistrates to ask for a summons for the alternative offence to be preferred immediately and proceed to deal with it at once. As to where the magistrates convict on a more serious charge and dismiss others because further convictions would be oppressive, see *DPP v Gane* [1991] Crim LR 711, DC.

For a discussion of the CLA 1967, s 6(3), see **Chapter 11**.

5.1.11   Sentence

If the magistrates find the case proved, they will proceed to sentence, after an adjournment if necessary. A detailed analysis of the procedure prior to sentence is found in **Chapter 13**, but in brief is as follows:

- the prosecution gives details of the defendant's character and antecedents;
- any pre-sentence or other reports are placed before the court;

- the defence enters a plea in mitigation;
- the court passes sentence.

The magistrates' sentencing powers are discussed in full in **Chapters 15** and **16**. However, in brief, the magistrates may sentence a person over the age of 21 to a maximum period of twelve months' imprisonment on each offence, or the statutory maximum, whichever is the less. Where the person is convicted of two or more offences, the sentences may be made to run consecutively to a maximum of 65 weeks see CJA 2003, ss 154–155, Schs 25 and 26. In addition to any period of imprisonment the magistrates may fine an offender up to £5,000 per offence. See generally the Powers of Criminal Courts (Sentencing) Act 2000 (PCC(S)A), s 78 and the MCA 1980, ss 32 and 133.

5.1.12 Power to rectify mistakes

Under the MCA 1980, s 142 as amended by the Criminal Appeal Act 1995, a magistrates' court may vary or rescind a sentence or other order imposed or made by it, if it appears to the court to be in the interests of justice to do so. The purpose of this provision is to prevent the judicial review of proceedings which clearly should be re-heard.

The following points should be noted:

(a) The magistrates may re-open the case regardless of whether the defendant pleaded guilty or not guilty.

(b) There is no time limit to the re-opening of the case. The original 28-day time limit (abolished in 1995) is still a useful guideline, but delay is not the only factor to be taken into account by the magistrates in exercising their discretion under s 142 (*R v Ealing Magistrates' Court, ex p Sahota* (1998) 162 JP 73).

(c) The magistrates re-opening the case need not be the same magistrates who dealt with the case originally.

These three points were introduced by the Criminal Appeal Act 1995, and considerably widen the magistrates' powers under s 142. It may be that many matters which could previously have been dealt with only by way of appeal may now be dealt with under s 142. For this reason, students should always consider s 142 when dealing with any error made by the magistrates.

In exercising their discretion, the magistrates were entitled to consider the inconvenience to witnesses if defendants did not appear for their trial through their own fault. They were also able to take into account the apparent strength of the prosecution case, though they should attach little weight to that factor (*R v Newport Justices, ex p Carey* (1996) 160 JP 613).

Three further points should be made:

(a) The power to rescind under s 142 only applies where the defendant has been found guilty. See, for example, *Coles v DPP* (1998) 162 JP 687.

(b) When a person is convicted by a magistrates' court, and it appears in the interest of justice that the case should be re-heard by a different bench, the court may so direct (s 142(2), as amended). In this situation the case is treated as if it has simply been adjourned.

(c) The court's right to exercise its powers under s 142 are lost after the case has been appealed to the Crown Court or the High Court by way of case stated, and the court has determined the appeal (s 142(1A) and (2A) inserted by the Criminal Appeal Act 1995, s 2B(3) and (5)).

5.2 The clerk to the justices and court legal adviser

The clerk to the justices is a barrister or solicitor of at least five years' standing. He or she is usually supported by assistant clerks who often are, but need not be, legally qualified.

The clerk has a wide administrative function. This derives from the magistrates' jurisdiction over both domestic and licensing matters in addition to their criminal jurisdiction. Here the clerk is involved in a number of areas, such as the taking of informations and the grant of public funding for defence representation.

During a trial, the clerk has several duties. The most important are:

(a) To speak on behalf of the court, if required to do so. This includes reading the charge to the defendant, putting the election as to the mode of trial to him or her, and taking the plea.

(b) To advise the justices on any question of law and procedure. This advice should be given in open court, so that all parties know the advice given, and the basis upon which the magistrates made their decision.

   Where the justices wish their clerk to advise them on matters of law, it is essential that the clerk is present in court during the submissions of the parties (*R v Chichester Magistrates' Court, ex p DPP* (1993) 157 JP 1049). For example, where the clerk wishes to refer the justices to an authority not previously cited, the advocates in the case should be informed and given the opportunity to comment (*W v W* The Times, 4 June 1993).

   The clerk plays no part in deciding either the facts or the defendant's guilt, but may advise the justices on the law, after they have retired to consider their verdict, and should accompany them only if specifically requested to do so. As soon as he or she has given the advice the clerk should withdraw, unless the case is so complex that his or her advice is required throughout the decision-making process. (See *R v Consett Justices, ex p Postal Bingo Ltd* [1967] 2 QB 9.) For recent examples of where the decision-making process was interfered with, see *R v Eccles Justices, ex p Farrelly* (1992) 157 JP 77 and *R v Birmingham Justices Court, ex p Ahmed* [1994] COD 461.

   It is the duty of the clerk to advise the court. The court is under no obligation to follow that advice although, in practice, the court invariably does. If the clerk thinks that the justices have reached a wrong decision, he or she may not ignore their decision, but should put the matter before the same court with his or her new advice before a different sitting of the court, or arrange for consideration of the matter by a superior court. See *R v Liverpool Magistrates' Court, ex p Abiaka* (1999) 163 JP 497.

(c) To take a note of the evidence. The clerk may refresh the magistrates' memories, and draw their attention to any issues involved in the matters before the court.

(d) To intervene in the case to assist the course of justice when the court is dealing with an unrepresented defendant. But it should be noted that the clerk is there to assist the court by ensuring that the parties present their case clearly and unambiguously, and that he or she is not there to assist one party as against the other.

(e) To advise the magistrates on the range of sentences available. As reaching a decision on sentence can be a very involved process, it is rarely done in open court to avoid an unseemly debate as to the appropriate sentence taking place in front of the defendant.

The role of the clerk has recently been set out in detail in *Practice Direction (criminal: consolidated)* [2002] 3 All ER 904, para 55 as follows:

55.1   A justices' clerk is responsible for:

(a)   *the legal advice tendered to the justices within the area;*

(b)   *the performance of any of the functions set out below by any member of his/her staff acting as legal adviser;*

(c)   *ensuring that competent advice is available to justices when the justices' clerk is not personally present in court; and*

(d)   *the effective delivery of case management and the reduction of unnecessary delay.*

55.2   Where a person other than the justices' clerk (a 'legal adviser'), who is authorised to do so, performs any of the functions referred to in this direction he will have the same responsibilities as the justices' clerk. The legal adviser may consult the justices' clerk or other person authorised by the justices' clerk for that purpose before tendering advice to the bench. If the justices' clerk or that person gives any advice directly to the bench, he should give the parties or their advocates an opportunity of repeating any relevant submissions prior to the advice being given.

55.3   It shall be the responsibility of the legal adviser to provide the justices with any advice they require to properly perform their functions whether or not the justices have requested that advice, on:

(a)   *questions of law (including ECHR jurisprudence and those matters set out in s 2(1) of the Human Rights Act 1998);*

(b)   *questions of mixed law and fact;*

(c)   *matters of practice and procedure;*

(d)   *the range of penalties available;*

(e)   *any relevant decisions of the superior courts or other guidelines;*

(f)   *other issues relevant to the matter before the court; and*

(g)   *the appropriate decision making structure to be applied in any given case.*

In addition to advising the justices it shall be the legal adviser's responsibility to assist the court, where appropriate, as to the formulation of reasons and the recording of those reasons.

55.4   A justices' clerk or legal adviser must not play any part in making findings of fact, but may assist the bench by reminding them of the evidence, using any notes of the proceedings for this purpose.

55.5   A justices' clerk or legal adviser may ask questions of witnesses and the parties in order to clarify the evidence and any issues in the case. A legal adviser has a duty to ensure that every case is conducted fairly.

55.6   When advising the justices, the justices' clerk or legal adviser, whether or not previously in court, should:

(a)   *ensure that he is aware of the relevant facts; and*

(b)   *provide the parties with the information necessary to enable the parties to make any representations they wish as to the advice before it is given.*

55.7   At any time justices are entitled to receive advice to assist them in discharging their responsibilities. If they are in any doubt as to the evidence which has been given, they should seek the aid of their legal adviser, referring to his notes as appropriate. This should ordinarily be done in open court. Where the justices request their adviser to join them in the retiring room, this request should be made in the presence of the parties in court. Any legal advice given to the justices other than in open court should be clearly stated to be provisional and the adviser should subsequently repeat the substance of the advice in open court and give the parties an opportunity to make any representations they wish on that provisional advice. The legal adviser should then state in open court whether the provisional advice is confirmed or if it is varied the nature of the variation.

55.8   [Appraisal of performance.]

55.9   The legal adviser is under a duty to assist unrepresented parties to present their case, but must do so without appearing to become an advocate for the party concerned.

55.10   The role of legal advisers in fine default proceedings or any other proceedings for the enforcement of financial orders, obligations or penalties is to assist the court. They must not act in an adversarial or partisan manner. With the agreement of the justices a legal adviser may ask questions of the defaulter to elicit information which the justices will require to make an adjudication, for example to facilitate his explanation for the default. A legal adviser may also advise the justices in the normal way as to the options open to them in dealing with the case. It would be inappropriate for the legal adviser to set out to establish wilful refusal or neglect or any other type of culpable behaviour, to offer an opinion on the facts, or to urge a particular course of action upon the justices. The duty of impartiality is the paramount consideration for the legal adviser at all times, and this takes precedence over any role he or she may have as a collecting officer. The appointment of other staff to 'prosecute' the case for the collecting officer is not essential to ensure compliance with the law, including the Human Rights Act 1998. Whether to make such appointments is a matter for the justices' chief executive.

5.3   Committal to the Crown Court for sentence

In certain circumstances the magistrates, having found the defendant guilty of an offence or if the defendant pleads guilty, may commit the defendant to the Crown Court for sentence. The most important powers of committal are as follows.

5.3.1   Committal for sentence

Where an adult defendant enters a guilty plea at the plea before venue stage, the magistrates' court must decide if their sentencing powers are sufficient, or whether the defendant should be committed to the Crown Court for sentence. If the court decides that their powers are sufficient, they may not subsequently commit the case for sentence in the Crown Court, except in the case of dangerous offenders or where a case is committed to the Crown Court because the offender is already being sent there for other matters.

See s 3 of the Powers of Criminal Courts (Sentencing) Act 2000, as amended by CJA 2003, Sch 3, which provides as follows:

(1)   *Subject to subsection 4 below, this section applies where—*

(a)   *a person aged 18 or over appears or is brought before a magistrates' court ('the court') on an information charging him with an offence triable either way ('the offence');*

(b)   *he or his representative indicates under section 17A or (as the case may be) 17B of the Magistrates' Courts Act 1980 (initial procedure: accused to indicate intention as to plea), but not section 20(7) of the Act, that he would plead guilty if the offence were to proceed to trial; and*

(c)   *proceeding as if section 9(1) of the Act were complied with and he pleaded guilty under it, the court convicts him of the offence,*

(2)   *If the court is of the opinion that—*

(a)   *the offence; or*

(b)   *the combination of the offence and one or more offences associated with it,*

was so serious that the Crown Court should, in the court's opinion, have the power to deal with the offender in any way it could deal with him if he had been convicted on indictment, the court may commit him in custody or on bail to the Crown Court for sentence in accordance with section 5(1) below.

(3) *Where the court commits a person under subsection (2) above, section 6 below (which enables a magistrates' court, where it commits a person under this section in respect of an offence, also to commit him to the Crown Court to be dealt with in respect of certain other offences) shall apply accordingly.*

(4) *This section does not apply in relation to an offence as regards which this section is excluded by section 17D of the Magistrates Courts Act 1980 (certain offences where value involved is small).*

Under PCC(S)A 2000, s 3A as inserted by CJA 2003, Sch 2, where the court is dealing with a dangerous adult defendant, and the court is of the opinion that the criteria are met for imposition of a sentence under s 225(3) (where the court considers that the offence is such as to justify the imposition of imprisonment for life) or CJA 2003, s 227(2) (the imposition of an extended sentence), the court may commit the defendant to the Crown Court for sentence. In these circumstances, the court is not bound by any indication of sentence that may have been given, and no appeal may be brought on that basis. See generally PCC(S)A 2000, s 3 as amended by CJA 2003, Sch 3.

Where the defendant is committed under s 3 or s 3A, the Crown Court may 'inquire into the circumstances of the case and may deal with the offender in any way in which it could deal with him if he had just been convicted of the offence on indictment before the court': PCC(S)A 2000, s 5 as inserted by CJA 2003, Sch 3.

5.3.2 Committal for sentence on indication of guilty plea by child or young person

Where a child or young person commits one of a number of grave crimes, as defined by PCC(S)A 2000, s 91, he or she may be committed to the Crown Court for sentence under PCC(S)A 2000, s 3B as inserted by CJA 2003, Sch 3. These offences are any offence which is punishable with 14 years or more imprisonment for adult offenders, and various offences under the Sexual Offences Act 2003.

The committal may be made, under s 3B(2):

'If the court is of the opinion that—

(a) the offence; or

(b) the combination of the offence and one or more offences associated with it,

was such that the Crown Court should, in the court's opinion, have power to deal with the offender as if the provisions of section 91(3) below applied . . .'

Where the defendant is committed under s 3B, the Crown Court may 'inquire into the circumstances of the case and may deal with the offender in any way in which it could deal with him if he had just been convicted of the offence on indictment before the court' PCC(S)A 2000, s 5A as inserted by CJA 2003, Sch 3.

Where the defendant is under 18 and is tried summarily for a *specified offence* in the magistrates' court he may be committed for sentence as described above under PCC(S)A 2000, s 3C as inserted by CJA 2003. A *specified offence* is defined in CJA 2003, s 224 and Sch 15. Specified violent offences are set out in Part 1 of Sch 15 and comprise 65 separate offences, including manslaughter, kidnapping, false imprisonment, and grievous bodily harm. Specified sexual offences are set out in Part 2 of Sch 15 and comprise a further 88 offences being many of those under the Sexual Offences Acts 1956 and 2003.

Section 3C provides that the young offender must be committed for sentence to the Crown Court where 'it appears to the court that the criteria for the imposition of a sentence under section 226(3) [a sentence of detention for public protection] or section 228(2) (an extended sentence of detention) would be met.'

5.3.3 Committal for sentence of a child or young person on the indication of a guilty plea

Under PCC(S)A 2000, s 4 as amended by CJA 2003, Sch 3, where a child or young person indicates that he or she would plead guilty to one of the offences mentioned above, the court may commit him to the Crown Court for sentence. The Crown Court 'shall inquire into the circumstances of the offence and may deal with the offender in any way in which it could deal with him if he had just been convicted of the offence on indictment before the court' under PCC(S)A 2000, s 5A as inserted by CJA 2003, Sch 3.

See generally **Chapter 6**.

5.3.4 Committal under the Powers of Criminal Courts (Sentencing) Act 2000, s 6

Section 6 provides that where the magistrates are committing a defendant to the Crown Court in any of the circumstances outlined in **5.3.1** or **5.3.5**, they may also commit for any other offences of which the defendant has been convicted.

The effect is that the magistrates may commit to the Crown Court summary offences which could not otherwise be committed. Thus, a single court can deal with the defendant for all outstanding offences, and this avoids the otherwise inconvenient result of the magistrates' court dealing with the summary offences and the Crown Court dealing with everything else.

The purpose of the section is convenience, and to ensure consistency of sentencing. In these circumstances it would be unfair to the defendant if he or she incurred any greater penalty as regards the summary offences, and therefore the powers of the Crown Court when dealing with a defendant on a committal under s 6 are limited to those of the magistrates. For example, see *R v Whitlock* (1992) 13 Cr App R (S) 157, CA.

Note the power to commit a defendant under the Proceeds of Crime Act 2002 s 6 for a confiscation order to be made.

5.3.5 Breach of a Crown Court order

Where the defendant is convicted of an offence which constitutes a breach of a Crown Court order, the magistrates may commit the offender to the Crown Court (see **19.3** for further details). The most important orders are:

(a) A suspended sentence. If the defendant is convicted of an imprisonable offence committed while subject to a suspended sentence, the magistrates may either commit for sentence or simply notify the Crown Court of the breach (PCC(S)A 2000, s 120).

(b) A community order or conditional discharge. If the defendant is in breach of either order, the magistrates may commit him or her in custody or on bail or deal with him or her themselves. If it is a breach of a conditional discharge, the committal is likely to be on bail.

5.3.6 Appeals

If the defendant wishes to appeal against committal, he or she must apply for judicial review (see **8.3**). He or she cannot appeal to the Crown Court as a committal is neither a conviction nor a sentence (see **8.1**). Nor can he or she appeal by way of case stated as the case has not yet finished (see **8.2.1**).

Similarly, the prosecution may apply for judicial review of the magistrates' refusal to commit. For an example, see *R v Derby Magistrates' Court, ex p DPP* The Times, 17 August 1999, where the defendant assaulted his partner by banging her head against a glass door, causing permanent scarring. The prosecution argued that the decision to accept jurisdiction to sentence in these circumstances was irrational, and further argued that the door constituted a 'weapon' within the National Mode of Trial Guidelines (see **4.7**). The High Court rejected this argument, saying that to describe a door as a weapon was an abuse of language. The court accepted that the maximum sentence which the magistrates could impose would be a lenient one, but it could not be characterised as one that no reasonable bench could properly impose. The application was rejected.

Youth court trials

6.1 Introduction

The youth justice system of England and Wales has been subjected to considerable scrutiny over recent years. The system has recently undergone major changes. It may be helpful to review, briefly, some of the history and objectives that lay behind the root and branch reforms that began in 1998 and have continued up to the present. The Audit Commission observed in its report — *2004 Youth Justice* — that 'given the scope of the reforms and the relatively short space of time in which they have been up and running, it would be unwise to embark on further wholesale change' (see www.audit-commission.gov.uk). For a longer-term look back, one can refer to *Youth justice? Half a century of responses to youth offending* by Caroline Ball [2004] Crim LR 167.

Since Parliament passed the Children and Young Persons Act 1933 (CYPA), courts have been under a statutory duty to have regard to the welfare of juveniles when dealing with them. In a 1996 report, *Misspent Youth*, the Audit Commission said that:

The current system for dealing with youth crime is inefficient and expensive, while little is done to deal effectively with juvenile nuisance. The present arrangements are failing the young people who are not being guided away from offending to constructive activities. They are also failing victims . . . and they lead to waste in a variety of forms, including lost time, as public servants process the same young offenders through the courts time and again . . .

Prior to this, in 1997, the Home Office had published a seminal White Paper on youth justice — *No More Excuses — A New Approach to Tackling Youth Crime in England and Wales*. It expressed concern that too much effort went into merely 'processing' juveniles and very little was directed to the prevention of crime or providing a service to victims, offenders and witnesses. Earlier intervention — nipping crime in the bud — was the preferred option. A 'fundamental change of approach' was required for the youth courts, looking beyond simple questions of 'guilt or innocence'. Courts were to enquire more widely into the circumstances of the offending behaviour, leading on to action being taken to change that behaviour.

One apparent problem was the confusion caused by the conflict between the statutory duty to look to the welfare of a juvenile offender and the aims of protecting the public and preventing offending. An attempt to clarify the correct approach came in the Crime and Disorder Act 1998, s 37:

(a) *It shall be the principal aim of the youth justice system to prevent offending by children and young persons.*

(b) *In addition to any other duty to which they are subject, it shall be the duty of all persons and bodies carrying out functions in relation to the youth justice system to have regard to that aim.*

Research quoted in the White Paper identified the following key factors as relevant to youth criminality:

- being male;
- being brought up by a criminal parent or parents;

- living in a family with multiple problems;
- experiencing poor parenting and lack of supervision;
- poor discipline in the family and at school;
- playing truant or being excluded from school;
- associating with delinquent friends; and
- having siblings who offend.

The 'single most important factor in explaining criminality is the quality of a young person's home life, including parental supervision' (White Paper, ch 1). So, youth courts now have the power to refer first-time offenders, who show contrition, to youth offender panels who will draw up a contract, regulating the juvenile's future behaviour. The police now have the power to give a warning to a juvenile (ie rather than prosecute) and to refer the juvenile to rehabilitation programmes, run by youth offending teams (YOTs). YOTs are multi-agency bodies, created by local authorities, in cooperation with the local chief officer of police, probation service and health authority, under powers given by the CDA 1998, s 39. The Home Office says that these teams are at the cutting edge of the government's reforms for youth justice. Amongst their tasks, they are to:

tackle the issues — from poor parental supervision and domestic violence or abuse to peer group pressure, from truancy and school exclusion to substance misuse or mental health problems — which can place young people at risk of becoming involved in crime.

Sentences introduced in 1998 as part of the reform programme include reparation orders, detention and training orders, action plan orders and parenting orders. Juvenile offenders may be confronted by the victims of their crimes and required to make a direct apology (reparation orders); children and parents may have to attend family counselling sessions (parenting orders). In an attempt to stop offending before it starts ('nipping crime in the bud') powers were given to courts and local authorities to make child safety orders and impose local child curfews on children under ten years. The former are targeted at individual children who are seen to be at risk of being drawn into crime; a court can require a child to be at home at specific times or stay away from specific places or people, and specific conduct may be forbidden (for example, truanting from school). The latter aim to minimise the risk that peer pressure and the absence of responsible adult role models in a community will foster anti-social behaviour; local authorities are empowered to bar all children under ten years from a specified public area after a certain time (not to be earlier than 9 pm).

As noted above, the Audit Commission's 1996 report was very useful in encouraging the recent changes. In 2004, the Commission reviewed the results (see *2004 Youth Justice*). Its bottom line conclusion was that 'the new system is a considerable improvement on the old one.' For example, young offenders were being dealt with faster (on average, twice as quickly compared to 1997). Young offenders were more likely to make amends for their actions (in 2002–03, nearly one in three young offenders received either a referral order or reparation order as their sentence). Reconviction rates, where the young offender had received a final warning or reprimand, were between seven and ten per cent lower than had been predicted. Nevertheless, the report identified some continuing problems — for example, low public confidence in the youth justice system (apparently, three out of four people had not heard of YOTs); also, young offenders from black and ethnic minority backgrounds were much more likely to be remanded in custody or receive a custodial sentence than those from white backgrounds (1 in 12 and 1 in 10 given custodial sentences, compared to 1 in 40). Perhaps the most significant observation in the Report is this:

Many young offenders who end up in custody have a history of professionals failing to listen, assessments not being followed by action and nobody being in charge. If effective early intervention had been provided for just one-in-ten of these young people, annual savings in excess of £100 million could have been made . . . [E]arly intervention programmes can be effective if they are properly co-ordinated . . . [B]etter still, mainstream agencies, such as schools and health services, should take full responsibility for preventing offending by young people.

The Government responded to the Audit Commission's report in December 2004. The response indicated that the Government aims to make much greater use of Final Warnings and reprimands (revised guidelines on the Final Warning Scheme were published in March 2005). This would allow courts to focus on the more serious offences and persistent young offenders. The Government also plans to introduce a 'generic juvenile community sentence' — the Juvenile Rehabilitation Order. This will have a 'menu of interventions', presumably operating in a similar fashion to the adult community order which was introduced in the CJA 2003, s 177, and will replace the eight existing community sentences for juveniles. The Government also plans to introduce an entirely new sentence: the Intensive Supervision and Surveillance Order. This will be 'a robust alternative to custody', tailored to the individual offender. Finally, the Government accepted the point about early and effective intervention, noting that it aims to establish 2,500 Children's Centres by 2008 and highlighting its reforms evolving from its 2003 Green Paper *Every Child Matters* and the Children Act 2004 (further information is available on the website www.everychildmatters.gov.uk; a report relating specifically to children in the criminal justice system was published in December 2004).

6.2   Why distinguish the juvenile from other defendants?

6.2.1   Different court, different system

For most people charged with a criminal offence, there are only two courts to worry about. These are the magistrates' court and Crown Court. (Although remember that cases can go *on appeal* to the Divisional Court or Court of Appeal and then to the House of Lords.)

For juveniles there is another separate court — the youth court. This court is a special type of magistrates' court (see **6.5** below). To avoid confusion, the ordinary magistrates' court will be referred to in this chapter as the *adult* magistrates' court.

The usual method of classifying offences (ie in terms of which court can or must try the offence; see **4.1**) does not apply to juveniles. Apart from homicide offences, there are no offences for which a juvenile *must* be tried on indictment. The concept of offences triable either way is inapplicable to juveniles — the mode of trial procedure (set out in the Magistrates' Courts Act 1980 (MCA), ss 17A–21) is not used and juveniles cannot elect trial by jury. (See further **6.6.1** below.) The general principle is that juveniles should be tried summarily and that such trials will usually be in the youth court. See for example, *R (H) v Southampton Youth Court* [2004] EWHC 2912 (Admin); also MCA 1980, s 24(1) as substituted by CJA 2003, Sch 3, para 9.

6.2.2   What do we mean by 'juvenile'?

A juvenile is basically anyone under the age of 18 (Criminal Justice Act 1991 (CJA), s 68). Once an individual has reached his or her eighteenth birthday, he or she must be treated like any other adult defendant. This could lead to problems if the defendant's eighteenth birthday occurs while a case is pending at court (see **6.7** below). Thus, while for the layman the term 'juvenile' generally means a youth or young person, for the criminal justice system one's youth ends on the eighteenth birthday.

6.2.3   Two subcategories: 'children' and 'young persons'

Juveniles between the ages of 10 and 13 inclusive are often described in criminal law statutes as 'children', but this is not a universal usage. Those aged between 14 and 17 years inclusive are usually described as 'young persons'. See CJA 1991, s 68 and Sch 8. Historically, these two groups have been distinguished for two reasons — sentencing powers, and the presumption of innocence.

6.2.3.1   Sentencing powers for 'children' and 'young persons'

Sentencing powers for young offenders are dealt with at length in **Chapters 17** and **18**. In summary, the range of sentences available to courts when dealing with juveniles differs significantly from those available for adult offenders. Again, different types of sentence (or different maxima) apply to juveniles of different ages. However, the trend in recent years has been to toughen the sentences available, even when dealing with the youngest offenders. One example is the power to sentence defendants as young as 10 to long-term detention for various grave offences (eg burglary of a house, certain types of arson and criminal damage, and robbery). Another example is the power to make detention and training orders (DTOs). A DTO may be used for 15–17-year-olds who are convicted of any imprisonable offence which is sufficiently serious to cross the custody threshold in the CJA 1991. Twelve to 14-year-olds would be at risk of a DTO when convicted of an imprisonable offence if they have a record of persistent offending.

6.2.3.2   The presumption of innocence

A second, historical, reason to distinguish between 'children' and older juvenile defendants was the presumption of innocence (or 'incapacity'), which was applied to juveniles aged 10–13 years. This presumption stated that children were presumed not to know that they were doing wrong, even though they had done an act which constituted a crime. The onus was on the prosecution to rebut this presumption by calling evidence intended to show that the child in question knew that what he or she had done was 'seriously wrong'. The presumption was abolished in 1998 (see CDA 1998, s 34). The rationale for abolition was a concern that the need to call evidence to rebut the presumption 'could lead to real practical difficulties, delaying cases or even making it impossible for the prosecution to proceed' (*No More Excuses*, chapter 4; for a contrary perspective, see *Protecting the Rights of Children*, a report by the Howard League for Penal Reform, 1999).

Many other European countries consider their youngsters incapable of bearing criminal responsibility before their fourteenth birthday. The issue of a minimum age was considered by the European Court of Human Rights in *T v UK* (2000) 30 EHRR 121. The Court considered whether the attribution of criminal responsibility for acts done when the defendant was aged 10 might amount to inhuman or degrading treatment, contrary to the European Convention on Human Rights, Article 3. The Court said that:

it did not find that there was any clear common standard amongst the member States of the Council of Europe as to the minimum age of criminal responsibility. While most had adopted an age-limit which was higher than that in force in England and Wales, other States, such as Cyprus, Ireland, Liechtenstein and Switzerland, attributed criminal responsibility from a younger age, and no clear tendency could be ascertained from examination of the relevant international texts and instruments, for example, the United Nations Convention on the Rights of the Child. Even if

England and Wales was among the few European jurisdictions to retain a low age of criminal responsibility, the age of ten could not be said to be so young as to differ disproportionately to the age limit followed by other European States. The attribution of criminal responsibility to the applicants did not, therefore, in itself give rise to a breach of Article 3.

6.2.3.3 The under-tens

Currently, children aged under 10 years are irrebuttably presumed to be incapable of committing any crime. Therefore, they do not fall within the criminal jurisdiction of any court (CYPA 1933, s 50). The abolition of the presumption of innocence for children aged 10–13, coupled with the introduction of child safety orders and local child curfews for the under-tens, has led to concern in some places that some under-tens may soon feel criminalized, even if they are not strictly covered by the criminal justice system. Finally, it should be noted that older children and adults sometimes use children under 10 to carry out crimes, knowing that no criminal action will be taken against such innocent pawns. This is not new (see, for example, the relationship between Oliver Twist and Fagin, described by Charles Dickens). It may result in the conviction of the 'manipulator', usually as the principal offender, with the child being regarded as merely an innocent agent of the other. See also *Archbold*, 2005 edn, paras 1–90/91 and 18–7; *Blackstone's Criminal Practice*, 2005 edn, para A5.6.

6.3 Juveniles who could be prosecuted but are not

6.3.1 The final warning scheme

It has sometimes been thought that juveniles may be damaged by contact with the criminal justice system. Consequently, an alternative method (or diversion) developed where a juvenile was given a *caution*, instead of being prosecuted for an offence. The effect of a caution was believed to be less traumatic for the juvenile since no court appearance was involved. It might be considered that cautions were quite successful in nipping nascent criminal careers in the bud because statistics show that between 70–80% of offenders who were cautioned did not re-offend within the next two years. However, there was also a small core of persistent juvenile offenders to whom a caution clearly meant nothing (3% of young offenders were said to be responsible for 25% of crimes, according to a Home Office report published in 1997, *Aspects of Crime Young Offenders 1995*).

Thorough reform of the system took place in 1998, when the CDA 1998 introduced a *final warning scheme* (see ss 65–66). Under these provisions, each offence committed by a young offender is met with a progressive response, designed to prevent further offending. The scheme came into effect nationwide in 2000. In summary, the scheme sets up three levels of response to a first-time offender. He or she may receive a reprimand, or a *final warning*, or be charged with the offence and appear in court. When dealt with by a final warning, the juvenile will be referred to a youth offending team (set up under the CDA 1998, s 39). The youth offending team will assess the juvenile to determine if it is appropriate to use a rehabilitation programme, aimed at preventing re-offending. Referral under the final warning scheme is carried out by the police. A similar power enables youth courts to make a *referral order*, where a first-time offender appears for sentence. The juvenile is referred to a youth offender panel which will decide upon the terms of a programme for behaviour, to be adhered to by the juvenile for a maximum of one year (see PCC(S)A 2000, Part III). For an interesting article on the difficulties caused in practice by the use of referral orders, see Jos Greenhow, *Referral orders: Problems in practice* [2003] Crim LR 266.

6.3.2   Deciding upon the appropriate action

The responsibility for taking decisions under the final warning scheme rests with the police. In exceptional circumstances it will still be possible for the police to take informal action but otherwise the police must choose between a reprimand, a warning or a charge.

In order to impose a reprimand or a warning, the following four criteria must be satisfied:

- there is sufficient admissible, reliable evidence to provide a realistic prospect of conviction, if the juvenile were prosecuted;
- the juvenile admits committing the offence;
- the juvenile has no previous convictions;
- a prosecution is not in the public interest.

Once those criteria are satisfied, the juvenile may be given a *reprimand* if:

- he or she has not previously been reprimanded or warned; *and*
- the offence is not so serious as to require a warning.

The juvenile may receive a *warning* if:

- he or she has not been warned before; or
- there has been one previous warning but it was given more than two years before the date of the present offence; *and*
- the offence is not so serious as to require a charge against the juvenile.

In addition to these criteria, the juvenile must give *informed consent* to the conclusion of the proceedings by way of a final warning or reprimand. If this is not done, the procedure will fall foul of the ECHR, Article 6. Informed consent means that the juvenile must be told of the consequences of this action (cp. **6.3.3** below). In the case of two juveniles involved in alleged indecent asaults, a failure to warn them of the requirement to be placed on the sex offenders register meant that they had not given the requisite informed consent; see *R (on the application of U) v Commissioner of Police for the Metropolis* [2003] 1 Cr App R 29.

Reprimands are thought to be appropriate for most first-time offenders. There can be no repeat reprimands, so a second-time offender should normally expect a warning, unless he or she was previously warned in which case the police officer will normally decide to charge the juvenile. The usual decision for third-time offenders will be to charge them with the offence. Fourth-time (and subsequent) offenders cannot be reprimanded or given a warning in any circumstances; the only decision can be to charge the juvenile with the offence. It must be emphasised that if a juvenile does not make a clear and reliable admission to all elements of the offence, the only choice facing the police officer is whether or not to charge the juvenile with the offence.

It is most unlikely that reprimands and warnings will be used for a very serious, indictable-only offence (eg murder, rape). Other offences may be too serious to be dealt with by a reprimand or warning, depending on their circumstances. It can be seen that the key factors in making a decision under the final warning scheme are therefore:

- the seriousness of the offence; and
- the offending history of the juvenile.

Important factors, when determining the seriousness of an offence, include its impact on the victim. Victims will normally be asked for their views on the offence, information on any loss or harm suffered and the impact of the offence in the light of their circumstances. An important aggravating factor will be if an offence was racially motivated. A general list of aggravating and mitigating factors has been devised by the Association of Chief Police Officers and this is likely to be relied on by police officers when assessing the seriousness of an offence (and whether a prosecution is in the public interest). This list, known as the ACPO Gravity Factors, endeavours to attach a numerical value to many offences. That numerical value may change, depending on the presence of aggravating or mitigating factors. Essentially, what the Gravity Factors do is to rank crimes in an abstract hierarchy of seriousness, and then allow aggravating or mitigating factors to 'fine tune' that ranking to accord with the circumstances of the actual offence which the juvenile committed. This exercise should produce a 'Final Gravity Score' which will work like this:

Final Score	Action
4	Always charge.
3	Normally warn for a first offence. If offender does not qualify for a warning then charge. Only in exceptional circumstances should a reprimand be given. Decision-maker needs to justify reprimand.
2	Normally reprimand for first offence. If offender does not qualify for a reprimand but qualifies for a warning then give warning. If offender does not qualify for a warning then charge.
1	Always the minimum response applicable to the individual offender, ie reprimand, warning or charge.

If the police decision is to charge, rather than to reprimand or issue a final warning, the matter passes into the hands of the Crown Prosecution Service. What action the CPS take is governed by the Code for Crown Prosecutors. The relevant provisions are paras 8.8 and 8.9:

8.8 Crown Prosecutors must consider the interests of a youth when deciding whether it is in the public interest to prosecute. However Crown Prosecutors should not avoid prosecuting simply because of the defendant's age. The seriousness of the offence or the youth's past behaviour is very important.

8.9 Cases involving youths are usually only referred to the Crown Prosecution Service for prosecution if the youth has already received a reprimand and final warning, unless the offence is so serious that neither of these were appropriate or the youth does not admit committing the offence. Reprimands and final warnings are intended to prevent re-offending and the fact that a further offence has occurred indicates that attempts to divert the youth from the court system have not been effective. So the public interest will usually require a prosecution in such cases, unless there are clear public interest factors against prosecution.

See further *Final Warning Scheme — Guidance for the Police and Youth Offending Teams* on http://www.homeoffice.gov.uk/docs/final_warning_scheme.pdf.

6.3.3   What happens when a juvenile offender is reprimanded or warned?

A reprimand or warning must be given orally by a police officer in a police station. The officer should normally be in uniform, and should be of inspector rank, although specially-trained sergeants and constables may be used. Unless the juvenile is aged 17, an appropriate adult must be present when the reprimand or warning is given (defined in PACE

Code of Practice, Code C). The oral action will be supported by written advice, usually in a standard form.

The officer should always specify the offence or offences which have resulted in the reprimand or warning. When giving a reprimand, the officer should also explain that:

- the reprimand is a serious matter;
- any further offences will result in a final warning or prosecution in all but the most exceptional circumstances;
- (if one or more of the offences is recordable) the reprimand constitutes a criminal record and will be cited in any future criminal proceedings.

When giving a warning, the officer should explain that:

- the warning is a serious matter;
- any further offences will result in charges being brought in all but the most exceptional circumstances;
- (if one or more of the offences is recordable) the warning constitutes a criminal record;
- the warning may be cited in any future criminal proceedings;
- in the event of a conviction within the next two years, the sentence of a conditional discharge will only be used in exceptional circumstances; in most cases, the juvenile should expect a more severe sentence (CDA 1998, s 66(4));
- the juvenile will be referred to a local youth offending team;
- the referral will result in contact by the youth offending team within two working days and, in general terms, what will happen thereafter.

A member of the youth offending team may be present to help explain to the juvenile what are the implications of the warning and the nature of the rehabilitation programme that he or she is likely to be placed on.

All reprimands and warnings will be recorded. The record will be kept, in the case of 10 and 11 year olds, until they are 18; in the case of other juveniles, records will be kept for at least five years. Reprimands and warnings may be cited in court, in the same circumstances as convictions.

6.4   Who will be in court?

6.4.1   Who will try the case?

In a youth court, the court will usually consist of three lay magistrates (or 'justices of the peace'). They will have been selected from a 'youth court panel' of magistrates who are specially qualified to deal with juveniles and who have also had some additional training for this purpose. Normally, there should be at least one male and one female magistrate present for a hearing in the youth court. If all the magistrates in court are of the same sex, they may only hear cases if:

- this situation could not have been foreseen; and
- having heard representations from the parties in open court, the magistrates do not consider it is expedient to adjourn proceedings to see if a mixed gender bench might be formed.

6.4.2 District judges (magistrates' courts)

District judges are professional judges (formerly known as stipendiary magistrates). They usually sit in the adult magistrates' court but are also members of the youth court panel by virtue of their office and may deal with cases in the youth court. If they do so, they will usually sit unaccompanied by lay magistrates. In 1997, a Home Office report (*Review of Delay in the Criminal Justice System*, often known as the Narey Report after its author) recommended that district judges should specialise in the management of particularly complex cases which, when they involve children and young persons, 'can be particularly difficult'.

6.4.3 The parents of the juvenile

When a juvenile appears in court, accused of a crime, it is understandable that his or her parents may want to be present to support their child. This is not always the attitude of parents, however, and the trial courts possess the power to compel parents to attend court. If a juvenile is aged 15 or under, the court must order a parent to attend, unless it would be unreasonable to do so. If the juvenile is aged 16 or 17, the court *may* make such an order (see CYPA 1933, s 34A, inserted by CJA 1991, s 56). When parents attend court, they usually sit next to their child.

Part of the reason for requiring a juvenile's parents to be present in court may be that although '[p]arents of young offenders may not directly be to blame for the crimes of their children, [they] have to be responsible for providing their children with proper care and control' (*No More Excuses*, 1997). Home Office research has shown that inadequate parental supervision is strongly associated with offending; also that the quality of the parent– child relationship is crucial. Bringing the parents to court may bring home to them the need to modify their behaviour as well as that of their child. However, *No More Excuses* also reported that parental firmness was not necessarily the answer: 'We know that parents who are harsh or erratic in disciplining their children are twice as likely to have children who offend.'

Parents may need to be present in court anyway, to represent their own interests. For example — courts are able to make a *parenting order* (see CDA 1998, s 8). This order obliges parents to attend counselling or guidance sessions for a maximum of three months and to comply with any additional requirements for up to one year (for example, ensuring full school attendance by their child). Non-compliance, without reasonable excuse, may result in a conviction and a fine of up to £1,000. In 2004, the Court of Appeal considered the appeal of a man against a compensation order for £1,000. The man had been ordered by a judge to pay this sum to the victim of a robbery committed by the man's 16-year-old son. The judge had the power to make the order but it was set aside by the Court of Appeal as the judge had failed to give the man the chance to be heard on the matter and had not considered whether it would be reasonable to order the man to pay compensation. See *R v JJB* [2004] EWCA Crim 14; PCC(S)A 2000, s 137.

6.4.4 Public access to the courts

Public access can arise in two ways. First, through actual attendance at court. Secondly, through access to media reports of proceedings in court. These need to be considered separately.

6.4.4.1 Public attendance at court

A distinction must be drawn between public attendance at youth courts and at the two other trial courts — adult magistrates' courts and the Crown Court.

Youth courts

Youth courts operate rather differently from the other courts, in that there is no general right to enter a youth courtroom. Attendance is governed by the CYPA 1933, s 47(2), as amended, so that no person shall be present at any sitting of a youth court except:

- the juvenile, his or her parents, the parties' legal representatives and the magistrate(s);
- court officers (the clerk, ushers);
- bona fide media reporters (but not to take photographs or to film);
- witnesses (both during and after giving their evidence);
- anyone else directly concerned in that case (probation officers, social workers, etc);
- such other persons as the court may specially authorise to be present.

In the past, these restrictions on access have usually been enforced strictly. The reason for this limited access was, in part, a desire to protect the juvenile from being (or feeling) stigmatised as a criminal. The effect was to exclude the general public and, not infrequently, the victim of the offence. The victim would enter the courtroom only when and if needed as a witness, where the juvenile pleaded not guilty. In the late 1990s this led to criticism of the youth court system as a 'secret garden', where proceedings took place in private and young offenders were not encouraged to face the consequences of their actions and take steps to change their behaviour. It was suggested that the practice placed too great an emphasis on protecting the identity of young offenders at the expense of victims and the community. In 1998, the former Home Office Minister Alun Michael observed that youth courts:

. . . have wide discretion about who can attend [their] proceedings . . . We believe that justice is best served in an open court where the criminal process can be scrutinised and the offender cannot hide behind a cloak of anonymity.

Subsequently, the Home Office and Lord Chancellor's Department issued a joint circular which included the following recommendations:

- all victims of juvenile crime should have the opportunity to attend the youth court (for the trial or preceding hearings) unless to do so would not be in the interests of justice;
- greater access should be allowed for the public to attend proceedings in the youth court (an example being a case where the offender's conduct has had an impact on the local community generally).

Adult magistrates' courts and the Crown Court

Both these trial courts operate their usual policy of being open to the general public when hearing a case, whether or not the case involves a juvenile (either as a witness or defendant). These courts have the power to order the public to be cleared from the courtroom if a juvenile witness is to testify in a trial involving offences of indecency or immorality. The possibility also exists for the court to order that a vulnerable witness may, in certain circumstances, give his or her evidence from behind a screen, or through a live television link, or in the form of a pre-recorded video (see further **6.4.5**).

6.4.4.2   Media reporting of juvenile proceedings

Youth court

Currently there is a ban on the media reporting any details which may identify any child or young person involved in a case in the youth court (whether as a defendant or as a witness; see CYPA 1933, s 49 as substituted by CJPOA 1994, s 49). Thus, no report shall be published which reveals the name, address or school of any child or young person concerned in the proceedings or includes any particulars likely to lead to the identification of [such a person]; [further] no picture shall be published [of any such person].

This ban may be lifted in three situations.

(a) The defence may apply to lift the ban. Publicity must be appropriate for the avoidance of injustice to the juvenile accused (for example, publicising details of the incident to attract the attention of potential defence witnesses).

(b) The prosecution may apply to lift the ban. Publicity may be necessary here if the juvenile accused is 'unlawfully at large' and publicity may assist in his or her recapture. The offence must be either:

(i) serious (in that it carries a maximum punishment of 14 years' or more imprisonment for an adult offender); or

(ii) violent or sexual (as defined in CJA 1991; see **Chapter 20** and *Blackstone's Criminal Practice*, 2005 edn, section E1.10).

(c) After the juvenile has been convicted, the youth court itself may consider it to be in the public interest to remove the reporting restrictions. Before doing so, the court should allow the parties to make representations on the matter. The aims here are to disclose the outcome of the case, to show that justice has been done and, perhaps, to shame the individual offender.

The CYPA 1933, s 49 has been amended by the Youth Justice and Criminal Evidence Act 1999 (YJCEA), Sch 2 but that provision is not yet in force. When it is brought into force, the prohibition will read:

No matter relating to any child or young person concerned in proceedings to which this section applies shall while he is under the age of 18 be included in any publication if it is likely to lead members of the public to identify him as someone concerned in the proceedings.

The CYPA 1933, s 49 applies mainly to proceedings in the youth court. A complementary, discretionary, power to prohibit reports on information which may lead to the identification of a defendant, victim or witness under the age of 18 in any other criminal court proceedings now exists but is not yet in force (see YJCEA 1999, s45). Once this new discretionary power comes into effect, the CYPA 1933, s 39 will continue in force only for non-criminal proceedings.

Adult magistrates' court and the Crown Court

The general principle here is that the media can report proceedings unless ordered not to. Under the CYPA 1933, s 39 any court may direct that no newspaper report of its proceedings shall reveal the name, address, school or any particular calculated to lead to the identification of a child or young person in the proceedings, whether involved as accused, witness or victim. Similar powers exist to censor broadcasts in the sound, television and cable media.

One example of the Crown Court using s 39 was at the murder trial at Preston Crown Court of Robert Thompson and Jon Venables in November 1993. The victim was a toddler, James Bulger, who had been abducted and the case had attracted nationwide publicity. The trial judge ordered that the two accused be known simply as 'child A' and 'child B'. The fact that the identities of these children were published subsequently illustrates the fact that such a ban may be temporary. Typically, it will last until the end of the trial. If the verdict is not guilty, the juvenile is acquitted and the ban will continue in force. If the juvenile is convicted, the ban may be removed. It is thought that the public interest served by naming the juvenile offender may outweigh the consequences of publicity for him or her. However, the court should consider the age of the juvenile and the potential damage that he or she may suffer by being publicly identified as a criminal, before lifting the ban. See further *R v Lee (Anthony William) (A Minor)* [1993] 1 WLR 103; *R v Inner London Crown Court, ex p Barnes (Anthony)* [1996] COD 17.

6.4.5   Protecting young witnesses

6.4.5.1   Special measures under the YJCEA 1999

The YJCEA 1999 established a coherent set of provisions to deal with all of the so-called 'special measures' which may be used by courts to protect vulnerable (or intimidated) witnesses. In summary, these are:

- the power to clear the public from the courtroom while the witness gives evidence (in trials involving sexual offences or when it appears that someone is trying to intimidate the witness);
- that the lawyers and the judge may remove their wigs and gowns;
- that a screen may be used in court, to shield the witness from the accused;
- that a pre-recorded video may serve as part or all of the evidence of the witness;
- that the witness may give evidence at the trial from a separate room via a live link.

Some of these provisions existed already, either in statute or more informally. The intention of the YJCEA 1999 appears to be to clarify and strengthen the facilities which are available to aid children (and other vulnerable witnesses). Also, the process of making decisions on which special measures to adopt is put onto a rational basis. In principle, the special measures are available for proceedings in all criminal trial courts. In practice, a specific court will need notice from the Home Secretary that appropriate facilities are available to it, either permanently or temporarily, before it can consider making a special measures order.

6.4.5.2   Three categories of child witness

Special measures are not available for defendants of any age. Any other witness will be eligible for help if he or she is found to be vulnerable or intimidated. Children under the age of 17 at the time of the trial are presumed to be in need of such help. The procedure for determining which special measure to use for a child witness will depend upon which of three categories the witness falls into:

- children testifying in a case involving a sexual offence;
- children testifying in a case involving an offence of violence, abduction or neglect;
- children giving evidence in all other cases.

For most child witnesses, the YJCEA 1999, s 21, creates a presumption that their evidence will be given by pre-recorded video (for evidence-in-chief) and live link (for all other evidence). The appropriate orders for special measures should be made unless the court decides that the measures would not be likely to maximise the quality of the witness's evidence as far as practicable.

A child testifying in a trial for a sexual offence will give evidence-in-chief through a pre- recorded video. Any cross-examination should also take place at a pre-trial hearing and be recorded for playback at the trial unless the witness tells the court that he or she does not want that protection. Video evidence may be excluded in certain circumstances; in particular if the court is of the opinion, having regard to all the circumstances of the case, that it is not in the interests of justice that the recording be used in evidence (YJCEA 1999, s 27(2)). The special measures provisions of the YJCEA 1999 were brought into force in July 2002 (except for ss 28 and 29). In an earlier decision on 'the interests of justice' the Divisional Court held that:

> Orders . . . are appropriate where there is a real risk that the quality of the evidence given by that child would [not be a full and proper account due to upset, intimidation or trauma caused by appearing in court] or that it might even be impossible to obtain any evidence from that child . . . [Under s 32A] the court must bear in mind that Parliament has determined that the primary method by which a child witness's evidence should be given to a court is by means of the video interview. It . . . is for a defendant to establish that any prejudice to him displaces this parliamentary intention.

See *R (on the application of the DPP) v Redbridge Youth Court; R (on the application of L) v Bicester Youth Court* [2001] 4 All ER 209. Where the Youth Court had found that the child witnesses would suffer only embarrassment if required to testify in court (to an insignificant degree if the court sat in private), and that their evidence would not be more reliable if given by way of video link, the defendant had 'discharged the burden of establishing that the legislative purpose would not be compromised by not making an order'. In a commentary on this case, in [2001] Crim LR 475, Professor Diane Birch suggests that the Divisional Court may have been motivated by a desire to promote 'equality of arms' as between a child prosecution witness and a child defendant. It should be remembered that the juvenile defendant is deliberately excluded from the ambit of a special measures direction under the YJCEA 1999. See also *R (on the application of DPP) v Acton Youth Court* [2002] Crim LR 75, and Professor Birch's commentary on the 'almost spiteful' exclusion of juvenile defendants from special measures.

A child witness in a trial for an offence involving violence, abduction or neglect will have his or her examination-in-chief recorded on video for playback at the trial. Any further evidence (including cross-examination and re-examination) will normally be via a live link. The court is not required to take a decision on whether the special measures are likely to maximise the quality of the evidence.

It should also be noted that a child witness must not be cross-examined by an unrepresented defendant where the trial involves sexual offences. In such cases, the defendant will be given an opportunity to appoint a lawyer specifically to cross-examine the witness. If he or she does not take that opportunity, the court must decide whether it should appoint a cross-examiner in the interests of justice (YJCEA 1999, s 38).

See also, Jenny McEwan, 'In the Box or on the Box? The Pigot Report and Child Witnesses' [1990] Crim LR 363; Glaser and Spencer, 'Sentencing, Children's Evidence and Children's Trauma' [1990] Crim LR 371; Birch, 'Children's Evidence' [1992] Crim LR 262.

6.5 How does the youth court work?

6.5.1 Where does the youth court sit?

Youth courts often sit in the same buildings and rooms that are used by the local adult magistrates' court. However, courts are required to make arrangements so 'that young defendants do not associate with adult defendants whilst awaiting hearing' (see CYPA 1933, s 31).

In some places, mainly inner city areas where the scale of juvenile proceedings justifies the cost, special youth courts have been built to deal with the workload. Adult defendants never appear in these courtrooms.

6.5.2   Where does everyone sit?

There will not usually be seating provided for members of the public in dedicated youth courtrooms (see also **6.4.4.1**). These courtrooms usually provide seating only for those people who are specifically allowed to be present during the proceedings (see CYPA 1933, s 47(2)). The magistrates do not sit up on a raised platform, but often are on ordinary chairs behind plain tables. Since the court clerk, lawyers, probation officers and social workers also sit on ordinary chairs behind desks, it is not as obvious as in other courtrooms where one should sit.

As a rule of thumb, the chairs in the centre of the room will be reserved for the juvenile defendant(s) and parents. These chairs will face the desk where the magistrates sit (and the Royal Coat of Arms may be on the wall behind the magistrates). The clerk's desk will be at the side of the one used by the magistrates and, usually, the lawyers' seats and desks will be on the same side of the room as the clerk. These dedicated youth courtrooms do not contain docks to hold a prisoner.

In adult magistrates' courts and the Crown Court, public seating is always provided. When an adult courtroom is used as a youth court, typically the public seating will be left empty. Everyone will sit where they normally would, except that no dock will be used even if there is one. In such cases, the juvenile defendant will sit in front of the dock.

6.5.3   Procedure at the hearing

As the youth court is a special type of magistrates' court, most of what happens in a hearing is the same as for adults in the adult magistrates' court. In particular, a juvenile can be tried summarily, sentenced if found guilty and remanded if a case is adjourned for any reason by the youth court. The youth court can issue a warrant for the arrest of a juvenile defendant who fails to attend the hearing (see BA 1976, s 7; MCA 1980, s 13). There are some differences, however, which are largely semantic. See **Figure 6.1**.

Name
Juveniles (both defendants and witnesses) are addressed by their first names.

Oath
Juveniles promise to tell the truth. The usual form of oath requires a witness to swear to do so. (Those aged under 14 give evidence *unsworn*: YJCEA 1999, s 55.)

Guilt
A juvenile is never 'convicted' of an offence; the court will simply record a finding of guilt.
The difference is largely cosmetic, presumably to avoid the trauma of conviction.

Sentence
A juvenile is not sentenced to a punishment after the case has been proved, rather the court makes an order upon a finding of guilt. Again, the distinction is semantic.

Figure 6.1

6.6   In which courts can a juvenile defendant appear?

6.6.1   The usual system for classification of offences does not apply to juveniles

A juvenile *never* has the right to elect trial in the Crown Court, and the usual distinction between offences which must be tried summarily, those which must be tried on indictment, and those which are triable either way has no relevance when determining where a juvenile will be tried.

6.6.2   The usual forum — youth court

By a combination of statutory provisions, the court in which the juvenile makes his or her first appearance when being prosecuted for any offence is normally the youth court (CYPA 1933, s 46; CYPA 1963, s 18). The juvenile may be the sole defendant or may be charged with others. If the juvenile is charged alone or with other juveniles, then he or she will appear in the youth court. This court will hear all the proceedings in the case, from the first occasion when the juvenile comes before a court up to the final disposal of the case. There is an exception to this — if the youth court decides that the juvenile should be sent to the Crown Court. This can happen for various reasons and is considered below at 6.6.5.

6.6.3   When will a juvenile appear in an adult magistrates' court?

Exceptionally, a juvenile defendant may make his or her first court appearance, after being charged, in an adult magistrates' court. This will occur in any of the following four situations:

- the juvenile is on a joint charge with an adult defendant;
- the court mistakenly believes the juvenile to be aged 18 or over;
- the juvenile is charged with aiding and abetting an adult to commit a crime (or vice versa);
- the juvenile is charged with a crime which arises out of circumstances which are the same as, connected with, those which resulted in a charge against an adult defendant.

It should be noted that in three of these situations the appearance of the juvenile in an adult magistrates' court is the consequence of being allegedly involved with an adult defendant.

6.6.4   A juvenile charged together with an adult defendant

Adult and juvenile defendants will appear together in the adult magistrates' court when they are jointly charged with committing a single offence. Alternatively, they may be separately charged with related offences — for example, one defendant aiding and abetting the other, or where one charge arises out of the same circumstances as the other. Any such charge may, of course, be for either a summary or an indictable offence.

If the offence is summary, then both defendants will be asked to enter a plea. If both plead not guilty, then they must be tried together in the adult magistrates' court if they face a joint charge. If the adult pleads guilty and the juvenile not guilty, then the juvenile may face summary trial in the adult magistrates' court or (which is more likely) will be remitted to the youth court for trial. See MCA 1980, s 29. If the juvenile pleads guilty in the adult court, the adult's plea is irrelevant. The adult court may now proceed to sentence the juvenile only if it is of the opinion that the proper order is one of the following:

- Absolute or conditional discharge.
- Fine.
- Parental recognisance to take proper care and exercise proper control over the juvenile.
- Referral order to a youth offender panel.

If none of these applies, then the adult court must remit the juvenile to the youth court. See PCC(S)A 2000, s 8.

If the offence is indictable, then CDA 1998, s 51 applies. Under s 51(7), the adult magistrates' court will first consider the adult defendant. The adult may be sent forthwith to Crown Court for trial (either because the offence is one which is triable only on indictment, or because it is triable either way and that is the mode of trial outcome). If so, then the juvenile will go through a plea before venue procedure, under MCA 1980, s 24A (inserted by CJA 2003, Sch 3). The court will explain to the juvenile that if he pleads guilty, the court will proceed as if this was a summary trial and he has pleaded guilty. It will also explain that, if he pleads guilty and the offence is one mentioned in PCC(S)A 2000, s 91 (1) (long-term detention), he may be committed to the Crown Court for sentence. If the juvenile then indicates a not guilty plea, he shall be sent forthwith to Crown Court for trial, if the court considers it is necessary in the interests of justice to do so; see CDA 1998, s 51(7) as amended by CJA 2003, Sch 3. This procedure will also apply where the charge is not a joint one but the juvenile appears in court charged with a related indictable offence. Finally, the procedure applies whether the juvenile appears on the same occasion as the adult defendant, or subsequently. Where a juvenile is sent for trial pursuant to s 51(7), the adult magistrates' court may also send for trial any related indictable or summary offence with which the juvenile is charged.

6.6.5   A juvenile charged with a serious offence

In certain circumstances, a juvenile may be sent to the Crown Court for trial, regardless of the involvement of any adult defendant. Where the offence charged is homicide, then the juvenile must be sent forthwith to Crown Court for trial; CDA 1998, s 51A (inserted by CJA 2003, Sch 3). The same result will occur if either:

- a notice of transfer has been given (cases of serious or complex fraud, or certain cases involving child witnesses) under CDA 1998, ss 51B or 51C; or
- the offence charged is a serious sexual or violent offence and the court considers that, if convicted, the juvenile could face a sentence of detention for life or an extended sentence; or
- the offence charged is a serious offence within PCC(S)A 2000, s 91(1) and the court considers that, if he is convicted of that offence, it ought to be possible to sentence him to long-term detention under s 91(3). Offences falling within s 91(1) are:
  - those which, in the case of an adult offender, are punishable with imprisonment for 14 years or more; or
  - a number of offences under the Sexual Offences Act 2003.

We need to consider that final situation involving s 91 offences in more detail. Before a court sends such an offence for trial, it must go through a plea before venue process, under MCA 1980, s 24A. The court will explain to the juvenile:

  (a) that he may now indicate his plea and that, if it is guilty, he will be regarded as having pleaded guilty and will be sentenced for the offence;

(b) that, as the offence is a serious one, falling within PCC(S)A 2000, s 91(1), the court may commit him to Crown Court for sentence under PCC(S)A 2000, s 3B or 3C, if the court forms the opinion that it ought to be possible to sentence him to long-term detention under s 91(3).

If the juvenile then indicates a guilty plea, the court will consider whether a community order or a detention and training order (where applicable) is suitable as the sentence. If not, it may then commit him to the Crown Court for sentence, under PCC(S)A 2000, s 3B (or s 3C if he is a dangerous offender). If the juvenile indicates a not guilty plea (or gives no indication), then the magistrates will consider whether, if eventually convicted, it ought to be possible to sentence him to long-term detention under s 91(3). If they decide it need not be a sentencing option, then s 51A will cease to apply. Conversely, if they decide that long-term detention should be a sentence available to the sentencer, they will send the juvenile forthwith to Crown Court for trial. That begs the question of what factors will influence the magistrates on this issue. Guidance appears in many cases; a recent example is *R (H) v Southampton Youth Court* [2004] EWHC 2912 (Admin). The court said that Crown Court trial ought to be limited to the most serious cases; also, that magistrates should recognise the policy that, usually, first-time offenders aged 12–14 and all offenders aged under 12 should not be detained in custody. Offenders aged under 15 would rarely require a sentence of detention, and such a sentence would be even more exceptional for offenders aged under 12. Magistrates should ask — taking account of the juvenile's age — is there a real prospect that this defendant will require a sentence of two or more years' detention? If the defendant was aged under 15 and would not qualify for a detention and training order, the court might ask if there was a real prospect that a sentence of less than two years' detention was required but the case would need to contain some unusual feature to justify that conclusion.

At the same time that a court sends a juvenile to Crown Court for trial using CDA 1998, s 51A, it may also send him for trial on any charge involving a related indictable offence (or a related summary offence if it is imprisonable or involves disqualification from driving); CDA 1998, s 51A(4). If the juvenile subsequently appears before a magistrates' court charged with such a related offence, the court may send him forthwith to Crown Court for trial on that charge; CDA 1998, s 51A(5).

6.7 Can the youth court deal with an adult defendant?

6.7.1 Defendants aged 18 or over at the start of proceedings

The youth court has no jurisdiction over such defendants. If a defendant was aged under 18 when charged with an offence, but is 18 when the case first comes to court, he or she should appear in the adult magistrates' court. Parents may be charged with offences such as not sending their child to school. This will be a matter for an adult magistrates' court to hear and to determine the appropriate steps to take to ensure the well-being of the juvenile.

6.7.2 Defendants who reach their eighteenth birthday after their case has begun in the youth court

This situation is governed by the CDA 1998, s 47(1)–(4). This provides a youth court with the discretionary power to remit a defendant to an adult magistrates' court either for trial or for sentence. The power is exercisable if the defendant, having appeared initially before the youth court as a juvenile, subsequently has his or her eighteenth birthday. In that situation, the youth court may remit the defendant either:

- before the start of the trial; or
- after conviction and before sentence.

The defendant has no right of appeal against a decision to remit. The adult magistrates' court may proceed as if all previous proceedings relating to the offence had taken place in that court. The intention behind s 47(1) appears to be to enable the courts to deal with young people in the most appropriate way, taking into account their maturity, attitude and offending history.

The youth court has no power to remit a defendant to the Crown Court for trial or sentence, simply because he or she is now aged 18. Some of the defendants who are remitted to the adult magistrates' court will have been awaiting trial for an offence which, for adults, is triable either way (see **4.1**). It is possible that when such defendants appear in the adult magistrates' court, they will now have the opportunity to opt for trial in the Crown Court; case law on the subject prior to s 47 is unhelpful. It is also possible that a remitted defendant will have only a brief stay in the adult magistrates' court. He or she may be charged with an offence which must be tried on indictment, in the case of an adult. That classification was inapplicable only whilst the case was in the youth court. Now that the defendant is appearing in the adult magistrates' court, the magistrates should send the defendant to Crown Court for trial (and see CDA 1998, s 51).

If a defendant reaches the age of 18 before sentence is passed, he or she may be remitted to the adult magistrates' court for sentence (PCC(S)A 2000, s 9). One effect might be to take the offender out of the detention and training order scheme, and make him or her eligible for detention in a young offender institution. Also, if the offence is triable either way, the offender may be remitted from the youth court into the adult magistrates' court and may then even be committed to the Crown Court for sentence (pursuant to the PCC(S)A 2000, s 3). Alternatively, it appears that the youth court can decide to retain jurisdiction over the 18-year-old and sentence him or her as if still a juvenile (CYPA 1963, s 29).

The Court of Appeal has stated that, where a defendant crosses a relevant age threshold between the date of commission of an offence and the date of conviction, the starting point for the court's sentencing powers is the sentence which the defendant would have been likely to receive if sentenced at the date of commission. In practice, this will mean that a juvenile aged 15, who is not a persistent offender, should not receive a custodial sentence (whether of DTO or under PCC(S)A 2000, s 91), if aged 14 at the time of the offence. Likewise, a defendant aged 17 at the time of the offence but 18 when sentenced may expect to receive a custodial sentence of no more than two years, as this is the maximum term of DTO that could have been imposed. See *R v LM* [2002] EWCA Crim 3047, [2003] Crim LR 205; *R v Ghafoor (Imran)* [2003] 1 Cr App R (S) 84, respectively.

Sending cases to the Crown Court

7.1 Background

The majority of cases which are dealt with in the Crown Court are dealt with initially by the magistrates' court. That being so, a mechanism of some sort is necessary to remove the matter from the jurisdiction of the magistrates into that of the Crown Court.

For many years a procedure known as Committal Proceedings was used. This procedure has been under considerable scrutiny in recent years, and was replaced by s 51 of the Crime and Disorder Act 1998 (CDA) in relation to indictable only offences. Section 51 has now been extended to deal with **all** offences, by the CJA 2003, and the CJA 2003 abolishes committal proceedings altogether.

coming into force September 2006.

7.2 Procedure under s 51

Since 15 January 2001, all indictable only offences are sent to the Crown Court for trial, without spending any time in the magistrates' court other than the first hearing. This is designed to reduce delay in the criminal justice process and is consistent with the close management of the case, through the Plea and Case Management Hearings that the Crown Court now has.

This procedure has now been extended to cover all cases which are to be heard in the Crown Court, and s 51 has been amended and extended by CJA 2003, Sch 3.

Under s 51, an adult who appears before a magistrates' court must have the case sent to the Crown Court in the following cases:

(a) The offence is triable only on indictment. This reflects the position before the CJA 2003.

(b) The offence is triable either way, but the court is required to send it to the Crown Court because either:

    (i) the defendant has elected trial on indictment; or

    (ii) the court has decided the case is not suitable for summary trial; or

    (iii) the court has decided to send a case to the Crown Court from a summary trial that has already commenced.

(c) The offence is one for which a notice has been given under CDA 1998, s 51B (notices in serious or complex fraud) or s 51C (notices in certain cases involving children). This is broadly similar to the position before the CJA 2003.

(d) The offence is an either way offence, and the adult is jointly charged with a youth who has been sent (or will be sent) to the Crown Court in respect of that matter or that matter is related to an offence already sent in respect to the youth under CDA 1998, s 51A (sending cases to the Crown Court: children and young persons).

(e) The offence is a related summary (punishable by imprisonment or disqualification) or either-way offence. If another adult is jointly charged or is charged with a related offence, he shall also be sent to the Crown Court.

Section 51, as amended, provides as follows:

(1)   Where an adult appears or is brought before a magistrates' court ('the court') charged with an offence and any of the conditions mentioned in subsection (2) below is satisfied, the court shall send him forthwith to the Crown Court for trial for the offence.

(2)   Those conditions are—

(a)   that the offence is an offence triable only on indictment other than one in respect of which notice has been given under section 51B or 51C below;

(b)   that the offence is an either-way offence and the court is required under section 20(9)(b), 21, 23(4)(b) or (5) or 25(2D) of the Magistrates Courts Act 1980 to proceed in relation to the offence in accordance with subsection (1) above;

(c)   that notice is given to the court under section 51B or 51C below in respect of the offence.

(3)   Where the court sends an adult for trial under subsection (1) above, it shall at the same time send him to the Crown Court for trial for any either-way or summary offence with which he is charged and which—

(a)   (if it is an either-way offence) appears to the court to be related to the offence mentioned in subsection (1) above; or

(b)   (if it is a summary offence) appears to the court to be related to the offence mentioned in subsection (1) above or to the either-way offence, and which fulfils the requisite condition (as defined in subsection (11) below).

(4)   Where an adult who has been sent for trial under subsection (1) above subsequently appears or is brought before a magistrates' court charged with an either-way or summary offence which—

(a)   appears to the court to be related to the offence mentioned in subsection (1) above; and

(b)   (in the case of a summary offence) fulfils the requisite condition, the court may send him forthwith to the Crown Court for trial for the either-way or summary offence.

(5)   Where—

(a)   the court sends an adult ('A') for trial under subsection (1) or (3) above;

(b)   another adult appears or is brought before the court on the same or a subsequent occasion charged jointly with A with an either-way offence; and

(c)   that offence appears to the court to be related to an offence for which A was sent for trial under subsection (1) or (3) above,

the court shall where it is the same occasion, and may where it is a subsequent occasion, send the other adult forthwith to the Crown Court for trial for the either-way offence.

(6)   Where the court sends an adult for trial under subsection (5) above, it shall at the same time send him to the Crown Court for trial for any either-way or summary offence with which he is charged and which—

(a)   (if it is an either-way offence) appears to the court to be related to the offence for which he is sent for trial; and

(b)   (if it is a summary offence) appears to the court to be related to the offence for which he is sent for trial or to the either-way offence, and which fulfils the requisite condition.

(7)   Where—

(a)   the court sends an adult ('A') for trial under subsection (1), (3) or (5) above; and

(b)   a child or young person appears or is brought before the court on the same or a subsequent occasion charged jointly with A with an indictable offence for which A is sent for trial under subsection (1), (3) or (5) above, or an indictable offence which appears to the Court to be related to that offence,

the court shall, if it considers it necessary in the interests of justice to do so, send the child or young person forthwith to the Crown Court for trial for the indictable offence.

(8)   Where the court sends a child or young person for trial under subsection (7) above, it may at the same time send him to the Crown Court for trial for any indictable or summary offence with which he is charged and which—

    (a)   (if it is an indictable offence) appears to the court to be related to the offence for which he is sent for trial: and

    (b)   (if it is a summary offence) appears to the court to be related to the offence for which he is sent for trial or to the indictable offence, and which fulfils the requisite condition.

(9)   Subsections (7) and (8) above are subject to sections 24A and 24B of the Magistrates' Courts Act 1980 (which provide for certain cases involving children and young persons to be tried summarily).

(10)   The trial of the information charging any summary offence for which a person is sent for trial under this section shall be treated as if the court had adjourned it under section 10 of the 1980 Act and had not fixed the time and place for its resumption.

(11)   A summary offence fulfils the requisite condition if it is punishable with imprisonment or involves obligatory or discretionary disqualification from driving.

(12)   In the case of an adult charged with an offence—

    (a)   if the offence satisfies paragraph (c) of subsection (2) above, the offence shall be dealt with under subsection (1) above and not under any other provision of this section or section 51A below;

    (b)   subject to paragraph (a) above, if the offence is one in respect of which the court is required to, or would decide to, send the adult to the Crown Court under—

        (i)   subsection (5) above; or

        (ii)   subsection (6) of section 51A below,

the offence shall be dealt with under that subsection and not under any other provision of this section or section 51A below.

(13)   The functions of a magistrates' court under this section, and its related functions under section 51D below, may be discharged by a single justice.

7.3   Restrictions on reporting

CDA 1998, s 52A provides for restrictions on the reporting of allocation or sending proceedings, in certain circumstances and with certain exceptions. These restrictions are similar to the restrictions that had been in place in relation to committal proceedings. Essentially, under CDA 1998, s 52A(1), publishing any written or broadcast report of the allocation or sending proceedings is unlawful, subject to the following exceptions:

(a) the magistrates' court may order that s 51A does not apply (s 51A(2)).

(b) the following matters may be published without an order of the court:

    (i)   the identity of the court and the name of the justice or the justices;

    (ii)   the name, age, home address, and occupation of the accused;

    (iii)   in the case of an accused who has been charged with an offence in relation to which a notice has been issued under s 51B (serious or complex fraud) any relevant business information. This includes the name and address of the business, and similar information;

    (iv)   the offence or offences, or a summary of them, with which the accused is charged;

    (v)   the names of counsel and solicitors engaged in the proceedings;

    (vi)   the date and place of adjournment, if adjourned;

    (vii)   any arrangements as to bail;

    (viii)   whether the accused is funded by the Criminal Defence Service.

Reporting or publishing a matter in contravention of s 52A is an offence punishable with a fine at level 5 in the standard scale. See s 52B for details of these offences.

7.4 Voluntary bills of indictment

Under the Administration of Justice (Miscellaneous Provisions) Act 1933, s 2, as amended by CJA 2003, a High Court judge may direct a prosecutor to prefer a voluntary bill of indictment, that is, he or she may order that the accused be tried on indictment. In making such an order, the case is not sent to the Crown Court in the usual way.

The preferment of a voluntary bill is exceptional, and consent to the preferment should only be given where 'good reason to depart from the normal procedure is clearly shown, and only where the interests of justice, rather than considerations of administrative convenience, require it': Practice Direction (Criminal: Consolidated) [2002] 3 All ER 904, para 35.3.

Traditionally, voluntary bills have been sought in two situations:

(a) Where committal proceedings have resulted in the discharge of an accused. (Committal proceedings are abolished by CJA 2003, and this situation will no longer apply.)

(b) Where the prosecution case is that an offence was committed jointly by two or more persons, and at least one of them has already been sent for trial, and an indictment signed against him or her. In these circumstances, the prosecution will wish to try all the accused together, but may only do so if a second indictment is signed against all the accused. A voluntary bill of indictment will achieve the desired result.

Under para 35.2 of the Practice Direction, applications for a voluntary bill must not only comply with the 1933 Act and the Indictments (Procedure) Rules 1971, but must also be accompanied by:

(a) A copy of any charges on which the defendant has been sent for trial.

(b) A copy of any existing indictment which has been preferred in consequence of his sending.

(c) A summary of the evidence or other document which:
(i)   identifies the counts in the proposed indictment on which he has been sent for trial (or which are substantially the same as charges on which he has been so sent); and
(ii) in relation to each other count in the proposed indictment, identifies the pages in the accompanying statements and exhibits where the essential evidence said to support that count is to be found.

(d) Marginal markings of the relevant passages on the pages of the statements and exhibits identified under (c) (ii) above.

The judge will consider the application and any written submission from the defendant and may seek amplification if necessary. He or she may invite oral submissions from either party or accede to a request for the opportunity to make such oral submissions if he or she considers it necessary or desirable in order to make a sound and fair decision. Any such oral submission should be made on notice to the other party. (Paragraph 35.6 of the *Practice Direction*.)

There is no requirement under either the Act or the Rules that a defendant be notified of the application for a voluntary bill. Paragraph 35.5 of the *Practice Direction*, however, gives guidance to prosecutors on procedures to be adopted in seeking judicial consent, directing prosecutors:

- on the making of the application, to notify the defendant;
- at about the same time, to serve on the defendant a copy of all the documents delivered to the judge;
- inform the defendant of his or her right to make written submissions to the judge within nine working days of giving the notice. *within 9 days.*

These procedures should be followed unless there are good reasons for not doing so, in which case the prosecutor must inform the judge, and ask for leave to dispense with all or any of them. The judge will only give leave if good grounds are shown.

A High Court judge's decision to issue a voluntary bill is subject to review, according to *R v IRC ex p Dhesi* The Independent, 14 August 1995, despite other authority to the contrary *(R v Manchester Crown Court, ex p Williams* (1990) 7 54 JP 589). However, given the nature of the voluntary bill, where the application is made *ex parte* and therefore against the rules of natural justice, the courts' jurisdiction in respect of judicial review is limited and could only be exercised in the case of alleged malice on the part of the prosecutor.

Once the bill of indictment has been preferred, it is an indictment like any other, and capable of amendment under the Indictments Act 1915, s 5 *(R v Wells* (1995) 159 JP 243).

8

Appeals from decisions of magistrates

There are three ways of appealing against the decision of the magistrates:

- appeal to the Crown Court;
- appeal to the High Court by way of case stated;
- application for judicial review.

Students should also be aware of the power of the magistrates to rectify mistakes under the Magistrates' Courts Act 1980 (MCA), s 142, discussed at **5.1.12**. This may often prove to be a quick and simple way to correct an error.

8.1 Appeal to the Crown Court

The defendant may appeal against conviction and/or sentence to the Crown Court. If the defendant has pleaded guilty, he or she may only appeal against sentence (MCA 1980, s 108) unless he or she can argue that the plea was equivocal (see **5.1.4**).

Note that if the Criminal Cases Review Commission refers a conviction in the magistrates' court to the Crown Court, such a reference is treated as if it had been made by the person under s 108, whether or not he or she pleaded guilty.

8.1.1 Procedure for appealing

See generally on appeals under MCA 1980, s 108, the Criminal Procedure Rules 2005, Part 63.

(a) Notice of appeal is given in writing to the clerk of the magistrates' court and to the prosecution within 21 days of sentence. The 21 days run from the date of sentence, even if the appeal is against conviction and the appellant was convicted and sentenced on different days.

(b) The notice of appeal must state the grounds of appeal (see CPR 2005, r 63.2(4)). *but don't need to say by law* (This represents an apparent change from the previous rule (Crown Court Rules 1982, r 7), which required the notice to specify whether the appeal was against conviction or sentence or both, but did not require any grounds to be given.)

(c) All documents are forwarded to the Crown Court, where the listing officer will place the appeal on the list, and send notice of the time and place to the appellant, the prosecution and the magistrates' court.

(d) The appellant may appeal out of time by applying for leave in writing from the Crown Court. Leave is not otherwise required.

8.1.2   Bail

If the appellant is in custody and gives notice of appeal, the magistrates may grant him or her bail, with a duty to appear at the hearing of the appeal (MCA 1980, s 113). If bail is refused, or unacceptable conditions are imposed, the appellant may appeal against the decision to the Crown Court under the Supreme Court Act 1981 (SCA), s 81. (See further **3.17**.)

The appellant does not have the right to bail, but bail may well be granted if the sentence is likely to have been served before the appeal is heard.

8.1.3   The hearing

At the hearing, the judge (usually a circuit judge or recorder) sits usually with two lay magistrates who have not been concerned with the case in the magistrates' court.

Where the appeal is an appeal against conviction, the hearing itself is a complete re-hearing of the whole case. It is not a review of what happened before the magistrates. Thus, either party may call evidence not called before the magistrates, or omit evidence that was called before the magistrates.

The lay magistrates must accept the law from the judge, but the decision on the appeal itself is a majority decision. Thus, the lay magistrates may outvote the judge. However, if an evenly numbered court is equally divided, the judge has a casting vote.

A Crown Court judge giving the decision of the court must give reasons for its decision, and a refusal to do so might amount to a breach of natural justice. The reasoning required would depend on the circumstances of each case, but should be enough to demonstrate that the court had identified the main contentious issues, and how it had resolved them. An appellant is entitled to know the basis upon which the prosecution case has been accepted by the court. See *R v Harrow Crown Court, ex p Dave* [1994] 1 WLR 98, DC.

Reasons should be given whether the Crown Court accepts or rejects the appeal (*R v Inner London Crown Court, ex p London Borough of Lambeth Council* [2000] Crim LR 303). Failure to do so will usually, but not necessarily, invalidate the decision of the Crown Court. The decision will not be invalidated, for example, if the reasons are obvious as in *R v Kingston Crown Court, ex p Bell* (2000) 164 JP 633.

The reasons should enable the defendant: (i) to see the nature of the criminality found to exist by the court; and (ii) to consider properly whether there are grounds for a further appeal to the Divisional Court by way of case stated (*R v Snaresbrook Crown Court, ex p Input Management Ltd* (1999) 163 JP 533).

8.1.4   Powers of the Crown Court

Under the SCA 1981, s 48, as amended by the CJA 1988, s 156, the Crown Court may:

(a) Confirm, reverse or vary any part of the decision appealed against. Thus, if the defendant has appealed against only part of the magistrates' decision, the Crown Court is not restricted to reviewing just that part, but may review the whole decision.

(b) Remit the case to the magistrates with its opinion. This will usually be a direction to enter a plea of not guilty and hear the case, if it thinks the plea was equivocal.

(c) Make any such order as it thinks just. This includes a power to increase sentence up to the maximum sentence which was available to the magistrates. This power is rarely exercised, but its existence is a means of discouraging frivolous appeals, bearing in mind that no leave to appeal is required.

8.1.5   Appeal against sentence

The appropriate court to deal with an appeal against sentence is normally the Crown Court, where the case may be appealed by way of rehearing (see **8.2.1(d)**).

8.1.6   Appeals against orders made under the Crime and Disorder Act 1998

The Crown Court has additional powers when dealing with an appeal against the making of an anti-social behaviour order or a sex offender order, created by ss 1 and 2 of the Crime and Disorder Act 1998 respectively. In determining the appeal, the Crown Court may, under s 4(2):

- make such orders as may be necessary to give effect to its determination of the appeal; and

- also make such incidental or consequential orders as appear to it to be just.

Any order so made is treated as if it were an order of the magistrates' court from which the appeal was brought and not an order of the Crown Court.

Note that there is no appeal to the Crown Court against the refusal of the magistrates to make either sort of order.

8.2   Appeals to the High Court by way of case stated

Under the MCA 1980, s 111(1):

any person who was a party to any proceeding before a magistrates' court or is aggrieved by the conviction, order, determination or other proceeding of the court may question the proceeding on the ground that it is wrong in law or in excess of jurisdiction by applying to the justices to state case for the opinion of the High Court on the question of law or jurisdiction involved . . .

Appeals by way of case stated go to the Administrative Court in the High Court (formerly the Divisional Court of the Queen's Bench Division). The procedure is set down in the Criminal Procedure Rules 2005, Part 64; see also the Civil Procedure Rules, Part 52 and PD 52 (in particular, paragraphs 18.1–18.20).

8.2.1   Subsidiary points on appeals by way of case stated

(a) The magistrates have no power to state a case until they have reached a final determination on the matter. Thus, they have no power to state a case during the hearing and must wait until the end. Similarly, it is not an appropriate method of challenging a committal for trial or sentence.

(b) Both the defence and the prosecution have the right to apply for a case to be stated, and so may a third party whose legal rights have been affected. This means that effectively the prosecution can appeal against the defendant's acquittal, and if it is successful the acquittal will be reversed.

(c) The appellant must show that the decision of the magistrates was either wrong in law or in excess of jurisdiction. Questions raised will therefore be questions of jurisdiction, admissibility of evidence and so on. If the appeal is based on the facts of the case, then generally speaking it will be refused, unless the magistrates have made a finding of fact which is totally unsupported by the evidence, or is one which no reasonable tribunal, properly directing itself, could have reached, in which case the High Court may treat it as an error of law. As to where the magistrates are entitled to draw inferences from facts, see *Plowden v DPP* [1991] Crim LR 850.

Where the applicant sought to raise new matters of fact and law, which were not included in the case stated by the justices, in his appeal by way of case stated, the appeal would be dismissed: *Campbell v DPP* [2003] All ER (D) 412.

Appeal by case stated or judicial review is not appropriate unless there are clear and substantial reasons for believing that disposal in such a way is in the interests of the defendant. See *Allen v West Yorkshire Probation Service Community Service Organisation* [2001] EWHC Admin 2.

(d) The statement itself is usually drafted by the clerk of the magistrates' court, and exceptionally by the magistrates themselves. If parties at trial are represented by advocates, the court may invite the advocates to submit a first draft indicating any areas of disagreement, as long as, by the time the case is stated, it is in satisfactory form: *Vehicle and Operator Services Agency v George Jenkins Transport Ltd and others* [2003] EWHC 2879.

(e) Once an application to state a case to the High Court is made, the right to appeal to the Crown Court is lost (MCA 1980, s 111(4)).

(f) If the same point arises in several cases on the same day, the appellants may apply for a collective case to be stated.

8.2.2 Procedure

(a) The application must be made in writing within 21 days of the sentence, and should state the point of law upon which the opinion of the High Court is sought.

(b) The application is sent to the clerk of the convicting magistrates' court.

(c) The magistrates may refuse to state a case, but this decision is reviewable by the High Court on an application for judicial review. For an example of such an application, see *R v Huntingdon Magistrates' Court, ex p Percy* [1994] COD 323. Magistrates may legitimately refuse to state a case in two situations:

   (i) They may refuse to state the case if they consider that the application is frivolous. The test is whether the application raises an arguable point of law (*R v City of London Justices, ex p Ocansey* (1995) and *R v East Cambridgeshire Justices, ex p Stephenson* (1995). The magistrates must give the appellant a certificate to that effect, enabling him or her to seek judicial review of the decision not to state a case.

   (ii) They may refuse to state the case unless the appellant enters into a recognisance to prosecute the appeal without delay, and to pay such costs as the High Court may award. Such a condition would be imposed if the magistrates think the appellant is likely to abandon the appeal halfway through, having incurred expense and wasted time.

   Where the magistrates refuse to state a case, the appellant should immediately apply for permission to bring judicial review. If the magistrates have already given a reasoned judgment, the single judge should give permission for judicial review of the original order, assuming there is an arguable point, thus avoiding case stated entirely. In any event, the Divisional Court will adopt the shortest, least expensive and swiftest course of action. The same principles apply to the Crown Court when it refuses to state a case. See generally *R v Blackfriars Crown Court, ex p Sunworld Ltd* [2000] 1 WLR 2102.

(d) The statement itself is usually drafted by the clerk of the magistrates' court, and exceptionally by the magistrates themselves. If parties at trial are represented by advocates, the court may invite the advocates to submit a first draft indicating any areas of disagreement, as long as, by the time the case is stated, it is in satisfactory form: *Vehicle and Operator Services Agency v George Jenkins Transport Ltd and others* [2003] EWHC 2879.

Note: It is a part of the procedure for stating a case that if a properly drafted question is to be altered, the party which framed the original question must be allowed to comment on the changes (*Waldie v DPP* (1995) 159 JP 514).

(e) The draft statement is submitted to the parties for their comments, which must be lodged with the court within 21 days. The statement may be adjusted in response. Where it is adjusted, the court will consider only the final statement, and not any earlier variations.

(f) The contents of the statement are:

  (i)   The names of the parties and of the court.

  (ii) The charges.

  (iii) The findings of fact, but not the evidence upon which those findings were made, unless the appellant's argument is that, on that evidence, the magistrates could not have come to the conclusion that they did (see *Crompton and Crompton v North Tyneside Metropolitan Borough Council* [1991] COD 52).

  (iv) The points of law involved, and the authorities relied on. This should include the arguments heard by the justices (*DPP v Kirk* [1993] COD 99).

  (v)   The decision of the magistrates.

  (vi) A request for the opinion of the High Court, posing the question which the appellant wishes the High Court to answer.

(g) Once the final draft is completed, the magistrates sign it and send it to the appellant.

(h) The appellant then has 10 days in which to lodge the statement at the Crown Office of the High Court, and a further four days to serve notice on the respondent.

Note: All the time limits set out above may be extended except the first limit of 21 days, which is statutory and cannot be varied (see s 111(2), *Michael v Gowland* [1977] 1 WLR 296 and *Reid v DPP* [1993] COD 111, DC, where 'pressure of work' on the part of the solicitor was insufficient reason for extending time).

8.2.3 Bail

Under the MCA 1980, s 113, the appellant may be granted bail pending the outcome of the hearing in the High Court. Bail will be granted on the basis that the appellant returns to the magistrates' court within 10 days of the High Court hearing, unless the conviction is quashed.

8.2.4 The hearing

Under the SCA 1981, s 66(3), the court must consist of at least two judges, though there are usually three. The court acts entirely on the basis of the facts as set out in the case, and no new evidence is adduced. The hearing therefore consists solely of legal argument by counsel.

If only two judges are sitting, and cannot agree, the decision of the judge who agrees with the court below prevails, and thus the appeal will fail.

Note: In considering the matter, the judge should not act as prosecutor in the absence of the prosecution advocate. This amounts to a procedural irregularity, as the judge is not sufficiently removed from the proceedings to meet the requirement of justice (*R v Wood Green Crown Court, ex p Taylor* [1995] Crim LR 879).

8.2.5 Powers of the High Court

Under the Summary Jurisdiction Act 1857, s 6, the High Court may affirm, reverse or vary the decision of the court below, make any other order it thinks fit, or remit it back to the original court with its opinion. The High Court decision is enforced as if it were the decision of the court below. Thus, if the High Court thinks that the acquittal is incorrect, it can remit it back to the magistrates with a direction to convict and sentence. Generally speaking, the High Court does not deal with sentence itself, taking the view that it is not the appropriate forum. However, it may deal with sentence if it is obvious what the sentence should be.

The power of the High Court under s 6 includes a power to order a rehearing of the case before the same or a different bench of justices whenever such a course is appropriate (see *Griffith v Jenkins* [1992] AC 76; *R v Farrand and Galland* [1989] Crim LR 573).

8.2.6 Case stated from the Crown Court

Appeal lies to the High Court from the Crown Court on matters not related to a trial on indictment, by way of case stated. Thus, if the defendant has appealed to the Crown Court against conviction or has been committed to the Crown Court for sentence, either party may appeal to the High Court by way of case stated, under the SCA 1981, s 28, on the basis that the final decision was wrong in law or in excess of jurisdiction.

The procedure is much the same as for applications from the magistrates' court, except that it is usually the appellant who drafts the statement. The respondent also has the right to submit a draft. The judge, who was the judge at the hearing of the appeal or the committal, will read the drafts submitted to him and state a case on that basis.

For a recent example of the High Court hearing cases by way of case stated from the Crown Court, see *R (on the application of Westminster City Council) v Middlesex Crown Court* [2002] EWHC 1104.

Useful article: J Backhouse, 'Rights of appeal by way of case stated — should it be satisfied?' 156 JPN 310.

8.3 Application for judicial review

Judicial review is the method by which the High Court controls the activities of inferior tribunals, that is, magistrates' courts and the Crown Court, in matters not relating to trial on indictment. The existence of a right of appeal to the Crown Court does not preclude a person convicted by magistrates from seeking relief by way of judicial review where the complaint was of procedural impropriety, unfairness or bias. Application for judicial review is made to the Queen's Bench Division of the High Court, specifically the Administrative Court (older case reports refer to the Divisional Court of the QBD). The Court's permission to proceed is required whenever a claim is made for judicial review. Permission, however, should only be granted where the applicant has an apparently plausible complaint, and immaterial and minor deviations from the rules will not have this effect (*R v Hereford Magistrates' Court, ex p Rowlands* [1998] QB 110). In reaching this decision, the Divisional Court considered *R v Peterborough Justices, ex p Dowler* [1996] 2 Cr App R 561, which held that it was unnecessary to grant the defendant judicial review because, on the facts of the case, the procedural irregularity complained of could be rectified on appeal to the Crown Court. The court in *Ex parte Rowlands* did not doubt the correctness of the decision in *Ex parte Dowler* on the facts, but held that it was not authority for the proposition that parties complaining of procedural irregularity or unfairness in the magistrates' court should be denied permission to apply for judicial review. To hold otherwise would be to deprive a defendant of the right to a proper trial before the magistrates with a right of appeal to the Crown Court, and would emasculate the supervisory jurisdiction of the Divisional Court over the decisions of the magistrates.

Note that the right to apply to the Administrative Court from the Crown Court on matters not relating to a trial on indictment includes the right to apply for reviews of the decision of the Crown Court after an appeal to it from a decision of the magistrates. See, for example, *R v Aylesbury Crown Court, ex p Lait* [1998] Crim LR 264.

8.3.1   Prerogative orders

The High Court exercises its control by the use of prerogative orders, namely quashing, mandatory and prohibiting orders (previously *certiorari, mandamus* and prohibition).

8.3.1.1   Quashing orders

A quashing order has the effect of quashing the decision appealed against. In addition, the High Court may:

- remit the case to the court concerned with a direction to reconsider it and reach a decision in accordance with the finding of the High Court (SCA 1981, s 31(5)).

- substitute for an unlawful sentence one which the court had the power to pass (SCA 1981, s 43(1)).

It is usually said that a quashing order 'will go' (ie be issued) in three situations:

(a) There is an error on the face of the record. However in a magistrates' court, the record is brief, and in any event magistrates rarely give reasons for their decisions. If the magistrates in fact give reasons, or include them in any affidavit they are swearing for consideration of the High Court, the High Court will treat them as part of the record.

(b) The court acts in excess of jurisdiction. See, for example, *R v Tunbridge Wells Justices, ex p Tunbridge Wells Borough Council* [1996] 160 JP 574, where the justices adjourned the case, part heard, after a submission of no case to answer was made. The High Court set aside the decision to accept the submission, which was subsequently pronounced in open court by a different bench of magistrates, as *ultra vires*. See also *R v Parker and the Barnet Magistrates' Court, ex p DPP* (1994) 158 JP 1061. The High Court may also set aside a sentence if it is one which the magistrates have no power to pass, but such an error is rare. However, in very limited circumstances, the High Court will treat a sentence which is so harsh and oppressive that no reasonable tribunal could have passed it as being in excess of jurisdiction, and quash it accordingly, even though it was in fact within the court's powers (see *R v St Albans Crown Court, ex p Cinnamond* [1981] QB 480). But such a course is exceptional, and should only be followed when an appeal against sentence to the Crown Court has failed (*R v Battle Justices, ex p Shepherd* (1983) 5 Cr App R (S) 124). But see also on this point, *R v Bradford Justices, ex p Wilkinson* [1990] 1 WLR 692 and *R v Truro Crown Court, ex p Adair* [1997] COD 296. The appropriate test for interfering with sentence was set out in *Ex parte Adair* as follows:

> It would perhaps seem more helpful to ask the question whether the sentence or order in question falls clearly outside the broad area of the lower court's sentencing discretion.

(c) Where the court acts in breach of the rules of natural justice. The court is under a duty to act fairly, there being two aspects of this duty:

   (i)   No person may be a judge in his or her own cause. See, for example, *Dimes v Grand Junction Canal* (1852) 3 HLC 759 and *R v Altrincham Justices, ex p Pennington* [1975] 1 QB 549.

   (ii) The court must hear both sides of the case. The rule will be relied on where there has been some procedural irregularity which has prejudiced the appellant. The test laid down in *R v Gough* [1993] AC 646, 'Was there a real danger that the appellant did not receive a fair trial?' was considered in *Re Medicaments and Related Cases of Goods (No 2)* [2001] 1 WLR 700. The Court of Appeal reviewed *R v Gough* and all the authorities in the light of the Human Rights Act, and concluded that, once European Convention case law had been taken into account, 'a modest adjustment' to *R v Gough* was required. The approach should be as follows. The court must ascertain all the circumstances having a bearing on the suggestion of bias. It must then ask whether those circumstances would lead a fair-minded and informed observer to conclude that there was a real possibility or a real danger (which were the same thing) of bias. One circumstance will be any explanation offered by the judge. If this explanation is not accepted by one party, it becomes something for the court to take account of from the point of view of a fair-minded observer, thereby avoiding the necessity of the court ruling on whether the explanation should be accepted or rejected.

   There are many and varied examples of the application of this principle to be found in the law reports, and the following are included merely by way of example:

   —*R v Thames Magistrates' Court, ex p Polemis* [1974] 1 WLR 1371 (where the defendant was not given sufficient time to prepare his case);

   —*R v Marylebone Justices, ex p Farrag* [1981] Crim LR 182 (where a verdict of guilty was announced before defence counsel's closing speech);

   —*R v Romsey Justices, ex p Gale* [1992] Crim LR 451 (where one of the magistrates, during the prosecution case, prepared a note of what he proposed the bench should say if it were to convict);

   —*R v Ely Justices, ex p Burgess* [1992] Crim LR 888 (where the justices travelled to view the *locus in quo* with the prosecutor, and did not allow the defendant to be present — either or both of these factors would allow the conviction to be quashed);

—*R v Hendon Justices, ex p DPP* [1994] QB 167 (where the magistrates announced an acquittal without hearing prosecution evidence and without having a good reason to refuse to hear witnesses);

—*Vincent v The Queen* [1993] 1 WLR 862, PC (where the fact that the defendant, following normal practice, was not given detailed notice of the evidence against him was not sufficient to establish that he had been denied a fair hearing);

—*R v Newbury Justices, ex p Drake* [1993] COD 24 (where the allegedly partisan demeanour of the clerk was held not to have affected the magistrates' decision);

—*R v Nottingham Justices, ex p Fraser* (1995) 159 JP 612 (where the magistrates took into account the adequacy of the defendant's representation);

—*R v Worcester Justices, ex p Daniels* (1997) 161 JP 121 (where a member of the bench failed to give full attention to the defendant's evidence, and had been reading material unconnected with the trial);

—*Johnson v Leicestershire Constabulary* The Times, 7 October 1998 (where a magistrate recognised the defendant from his role as a prison visitor, thereby apprising the bench that the defendant had spent some time in prison).

The High Court has on occasion issued a quashing order even though the failure to provide the defence with the necessary information lay with the prosecuting authority and not with the court itself. Consider the following examples:

- *R v Leyland Justices, ex p Hawthorn* [1979] QB 283 (where the defence were not informed of witnesses who could assist their case);

- *R v Knightsbridge Crown Court, ex p Goonatilleke* [1986] QB 1 (where the store detective failed to tell the police that he had a conviction for wasting police time);

- *R v Liverpool Crown Court, ex p Roberts* [1986] Crim LR 622 (where the police did not inform the defence of an additional statement made by the victim which was inconsistent with another statement and with his testimony);

- *R v Bolton Justices, ex p Scally* [1991] 1 QB 537 (where a lack of care meant that medical kits used for testing the level of alcohol in the blood were themselves contaminated with alcohol).

Note: A quashing order to quash an acquittal on the ground that it had been procured by fraud or perjury should seldom if ever be made (*R v Portsmouth Crown Court, ex p DPP* [1994] COD 13, DC).

8.3.1.2 Mandatory orders

A mandatory order compels an inferior tribunal to carry out its duties. It will be ordered when the court refuses to act when it should; not when it has acted and made a mistake. The appropriate remedy in the latter case would be a quashing order. See, for example, *R v Hendon Justices, ex p DPP* [1994] QB 167.

8.3.1.3 Prohibiting orders

A prohibiting order will be made to stop the court acting in excess of its powers. Parties do not have to wait for the final outcome of the hearing, and if there is genuine doubt as to the court's powers, the court will adjourn, so that the opinion of the High Court can be sought.

8.3.2 Discretion

The power to award any of the prerogative orders is entirely discretionary, and even though the appellant has established a prima facie case, the order may still be refused. See, again, *R v Battle Justices, ex p Shepherd* (1983) 5 Cr App R (S) 124.

8.3.3 Procedure

Under the SCA 1981, s 31, the Civil Procedure Rules, Part 54 and PD54, the procedure is as follows:

(a) Within three months of the decision, the applicant must file an application for leave to apply for judicial review, setting out his or her name and address and that of his or her solicitor, the relief sought and the grounds. This application must be supported by affidavit evidence.

(b) The application for leave is heard *ex parte* (ie in the absence of the other side), usually without a hearing. If there is no hearing, the judge will simply read the papers in chambers. If the applicant specifically applies for a hearing, one may be held, and this may be in court.

(c) If leave is refused, the applicant has 10 days in which to renew his or her application before the Divisional Court.

(d) If leave is granted, the application is made by originating motion. Notice of motion must be served on the other side, and on the court below.

(e) The hearing itself consists of affidavit evidence and argument from counsel. Evidence is not usually called, though it may be necessary to establish the error of the court below.

(f) The court will reach a decision, and make any appropriate orders.

8.3.4 Bail

Magistrates have no power to grant bail for an application for judicial review. The application for bail must be made to the High Court judge in chambers under the Criminal Justice Act 1967, s 22. However, if the application is from the Crown Court on a matter not relating to trial on indictment, the Crown Court may grant bail.

Further reading: Inigo Bing, 'Curing bias in criminal trials — the consequences of *R v Gough*' [1998] Crim LR 148.

8.3.5 Case stated and judicial review compared

In many situations, the appellant could apply for either a case to be stated or judicial review, and in some respects the two are similar. However, by appealing by way of case stated, the appellant is challenging the actual decision of the court, alleging, for example, that a statute has been misapplied. In some circumstances this may be said of judicial review, but judicial review tends to be directed, not at the decision itself, but more at the decision-making process. It is the legality of the process which is under review, not whether the decision is right or wrong.

If both remedies do apply, the appellant should appeal by way of case stated, as all the facts can then be placed before the High Court (*R v Ipswich Crown Court, ex p Baldwin* [1981] 1 All ER 596 and *R v Oldbury Justices, ex p Smith* (1995) 159 JP 316). See also *R v Ipswich Justices, ex p D* (5 December 1994) and *R v Gloucester Crown Court, ex p Chester* [1998] COD 365.

8.4 Appeal to the House of Lords

A decision of the High Court in a criminal cause or matter is appealed directly to the House of Lords, and there is no right of appeal to the Court of Appeal (Administration of Justice Act 1960, s 1). The appeal will lie if the following conditions are satisfied:

- the High Court certifies that the case involves a point of law of general public importance; and
- leave is granted by either the High Court or the House of Lords.

9

Disclosure

We have already seen that the prosecution has to disclose the evidence that it will be adducing against the defendant (under the Advance Information Rules in cases tried in the magistrates' court or through the process of committal or transfer in Crown Court cases).

The Criminal Procedure and Investigations Act 1996 (CPIA) creates additional duties of disclosure. This Act is considered in section D6 of *Blackstone's Criminal Practice*. The Act is supplemented by a Code of Practice issued under CPIA 1996 and by Attorney-General's Guidelines: Disclosure of Information in Criminal Proceedings, both of which are set out in full in Appendix 6 of *Blackstone's Criminal Practice*.

9.1 The duty of the investigating officer

The investigating officer is under a duty to retain material obtained in a criminal investigation which may be relevant to that investigation. Paragraph 5.4 of the Code of Practice issued under s 23 of the CPIA 1996 provides a non-exhaustive list of the material that should be retained:

(a) Crime reports (including crime report forms, relevant parts of incident report books or police officers' notebooks).

(b) Custody records.

(c) Records derived from tapes of telephone messages (eg 999 calls) containing descriptions of the alleged offence or offender.

(d) Final versions of witness statements (and draft versions where their content differs from the final version).

(e) Interview records.

(f) Communications between police and experts (eg forensic scientists) and reports of work carried out by experts.

(g) Any material casting doubt on the reliability of a confession.

(h) Any material casting doubt on the reliability of a witness.

(i) Any other material that would fall within the test for primary prosecution disclosure (see below).

9.2 Prosecution disclosure

Section 3 of the CPIA 1996 (as amended by the CJA 2003) requires the prosecutor to:

. . . disclose to the accused any prosecution material which might reasonably be considered capable of undermining the case for the prosecution against the accused or of assisting the case for the accused.

This is an objective test, covering a very wide range of material. The Attorney-General's Guidelines on Disclosure of Information in Criminal Proceedings were based on the CPIA 1996 before its amendment by the CJA 2003; however, much of that guidance remains valid. According to the Guidelines, the prosecution should disclose any material which:

- casts doubt upon the accuracy of any prosecution evidence;
- may point to another person, whether charged or not (including a co-accused) having involvement in the commission of the offence;
- may cast doubt upon the reliability of a confession;
- might go to the credibility of a prosecution witness;
- might support a defence that is either raised by the defence or apparent from the prosecution papers (if the material might undermine the prosecution case it should be disclosed at this stage even though it suggests a defence inconsistent with or alternative to one already advanced by the accused or his solicitor);
- may have a bearing on the admissibility of any prosecution evidence.

A useful rule-of-thumb test is that material ought to be disclosed if it might give the defence a useful basis for cross-examination of prosecution witnesses or if it would support defence arguments that prosecution evidence is inadmissible or that the proceedings ought to be stayed.

It follows, for example, that the prosecution should inform the defence if any prosecution witnesses have previous convictions (see *R v Vasiliou* [2000] Crim LR 845).

Under s 7A of the 1996 Act (inserted by the CJA 2003), there is a continuing duty on the prosecution to disclose unused material that falls within the ambit of s 3. Section 7A provides as follows:

Continuing duty of prosecutor to disclose

(1) *This section applies at all times—*
  (a) *after the prosecutor has complied with section 3 or purported to comply with it, and*
  (b) *before the accused is acquitted or convicted or the prosecutor decides not to proceed with the case concerned.*
(2) *The prosecutor must keep under review the question whether at any given time (and, in particular, following the giving of a defence statement) there is prosecution material which—*
  (a) *might reasonably be considered capable of undermining the case for the prosecution against the accused or of assisting the case for the accused, and*
  (b) *has not been disclosed to the accused.*
(3) *If at any time there is any such material as is mentioned in subsection (2) the prosecutor must disclose it to the accused as soon as is reasonably practicable . . .*
(4) *In applying subsection (2) by reference to any given time the state of affairs at that time (including the case for the prosecution as it stands at that time) must be taken into account.*
(5) *Where the accused gives a defence statement [or an updated defence statement],*
  (a) *if as a result of that statement the prosecutor is required by this section to make any disclosure, or further disclosure, he must do so . . .*
  (b) *if the prosecutor considers that he is not so required, he must . . . give to the accused a written statement to that effect.*
(6) *For the purposes of this section prosecution material is material—*
  (a) *which is in the prosecutor's possession and came into his possession in connection with the case for the prosecution against the accused, or*
  (b) *which . . . he has inspected in connection with the case for the prosecution against the accused.*

. . .

(8)   *Material must not be disclosed under this section to the extent that the court, on an application by the prosecutor, concludes it is not in the public interest to disclose it and orders accordingly.*

...

9.3   Defence disclosure

Where the case is to be tried in the Crown Court, the defence *must* supply a 'defence statement' to the prosecution (see s 5 of the CPIA 1996); where the case is to be tried in the magistrates' court, the defence *may* supply such a statement (see s 6 of the CPIA 1996).

The content of the defence statement is governed by s 6A of the CPIA 1996. This requires the accused to set out the nature of his defence, including any particular defences on which he intends to rely, and indicate any points of law he wishes to take. Section 6A provides:

6A Contents of defence statement

(1)   *For the purposes of this Part a defence statement is a written statement —*
   (a)   *setting out the nature of the accused's defence, including any particular defences on which he intends to rely,*
   (b)   *indicating the matters of fact on which he takes issue with the prosecution,*
   (c)   *setting out, in the case of each such matter, why he takes issue with the prosecution, and*
   (d)   *indicating any point of law (including any point as to the admissibility of evidence or an abuse of process) which he wishes to take, and any authority on which he intends to rely for that purpose.*
(2)   *A defence statement that discloses an alibi must give particulars of it, including —*
   (a)   *the name, address and date of birth of any witness the accused believes is able to give evidence in support of the alibi, or as many of those details as are known to the accused when the statement is given;*
   (b)   *any information in the accused's possession which might be of material assistance in identifying or finding any such witness in whose case any of the details mentioned in paragraph (a) are not known to the accused when the statement is given.*
(3)   *For the purposes of this section evidence in support of an alibi is evidence tending to show that by reason of the presence of the accused at a particular place or in a particular area at a particular time he was not, or was unlikely to have been, at the place where the offence is alleged to have been committed at the time of its alleged commission.*

...

Under s 6B of CPIA 1996, the accused, prior to the trial, must provide an updated defence statement, or else a written statement that there are no changes to be made to the defence statement previously served.

Section 6C of the CPIA 1996 requires the defence to identify any witnesses they propose to call. It provides:

6C Notification of intention to call defence witnesses

(1)   *The accused must give to the court and the prosecutor a notice indicating whether he intends to call any persons (other than himself) as witnesses at his trial and, if so —*
   (a)   *giving the name, address and date of birth of each such proposed witness, or as many of those details as are known to the accused when the notice is given;*
   (b)   *providing any information in the accused's possession which might be of material assistance in identifying or finding any such proposed witness in whose case any of the details mentioned in paragraph (a) are not known to the accused when the notice is given.*

...

(4)   If, following the giving of a notice under this section, the accused —

    (a)   decides to call a person (other than himself) who is not included in the notice as a proposed witness, or decides not to call a person who is so included, or

    (b)   discovers any information which, under subsection (1), he would have had to include in the notice if he had been aware of it when giving the notice, he must give an appropriately amended notice to the court and the prosecutor.

This was a very controversial proposal. In an attempt to allay fears that people might be put off testifying as defence witnesses, or encouraged to change their evidence, s 21A of the CPIA 1996 requires the Secretary of State to publish a Code of Practice giving guidance to police officers (and others charged with the duty of investigating offences) in relation to the arranging and conducting of interviews of people whose particulars are given to the prosecution because they are alibi witnesses or because they fall within s 6C. Section 21A(2) requires that:

The code must include (in particular) guidance in relation to —

    (a)   information that should be provided to the interviewee and the accused in relation to such an interview;

    (b)   the notification of the accused's solicitor of such an interview;

    (c)   the attendance of the interviewee's solicitor at such an interview;

    (d)   the attendance of the accused's solicitor at such an interview;

    (e)   the attendance of any other appropriate person at such an interview taking into account the interviewee's age or any disability of the interviewee.

Because of the potentially damaging effects of failure to comply with the obligations imposed by these provisions, s 6E(2) of the CPIA states that:

If it appears to the judge at a pre-trial hearing that an accused has failed to comply fully with section 5, 6B or 6C, so that there is a possibility of comment being made or inferences drawn under section 11(5), he shall warn the accused accordingly.

The obligations of the defence extend beyond witnesses they propose to call in the case of experts, where there is an obligation to reveal the identity of experts who have been instructed on behalf of the defence, whether or not they are to be called as defence witnesses. This obligation is contained in s 6D of the 1996 Act, which provides:

6D Notification of names of experts instructed by accused

(1)   If the accused instructs a person with a view to his providing any expert opinion for possible use as evidence at the trial of the accused, he must give to the court and the prosecutor a notice specifying the person's name and address.

. . .

Section 5 of the CPIA 1996 makes provision for the service of defence statements on co-defendants, if the court so orders. It provides:

(5A) Where there are other accused in the proceedings and the court so orders, the accused must also give a defence statement to each other accused specified by the court.

(5B) The court may make an order under subsection (5A) either of its own motion or on the application of any party.

. . .

This essentially gives statutory effect of the decision of the Court of Appeal in *R v Cairns* [2003] 1 WLR 796, that the prosecution would sometimes have to disclose the statement of one co-defendant to the other where it might assist the defence of that other defendant.

The defence statement is important because of the adverse inferences that can be drawn under s 11 of the CPIA 1996 (see below). However, s 6E makes it important to take great care in the drafting of defence statements for another reason: it makes provision for the jury to be shown the defence statement (or updated defence statement if there is one). Section 6E provides as follows:

(4) *The judge in a trial before a judge and jury —*

    (a) *may direct that the jury be given a copy of any defence statement, and*

    (b) *if he does so, may direct that it be edited so as not to include references to matters evidence of which would be inadmissible.*

(5) *A direction under subsection (4) —*

    (a) *may be made either of the judge's own motion or on the application of any party;*

    (b) *may be made only if the judge is of the opinion that seeing a copy of the defence statement would help the jury to understand the case or to resolve any issue in the case.*

. . .

The defence statement has be served within 14 days of the date on which the prosecution comply (or purport to comply) with their duty of disclosure under s 3 of the Act (see para 2 of the Criminal Procedure and Investigations Act 1996 (Defence Disclosure Time Limits) Regulations 1997 (SI 1997/684).

To remove any doubt as to whether a defence statement served by the defendant's solicitor is to be regarded as being given on behalf of the defendant, s 6E(1) of the CPIA 1996 provides that where the accused's solicitor 'purports to give on behalf of the accused' a defence statement or an updated defence statement, that statement 'shall, unless the contrary is proved, be deemed to be given with the authority of the accused'.

Defence statements are normally drafted by the accused solicitor, but counsel may be instructed to draft the defence statement. In the Code of Conduct (available online on the Bar Council web site), *Section E: Guidance on Preparation of Defence Case Statements* says that where a barrister is instructed to draft a defence statement, he or she must ensure that the accused:

- understands the importance of the accuracy and adequacy of the defence statement, and
- has had the opportunity of carefully considering the statement drafted by counsel and has approved it.

In *R v Wheeler* (2000) 164 JP 565 the defendant was convicted for an offence contrary to s 170(2) of the Customs and Excise Management Act 1979 following his arrest at Gatwick airport when he was found to be concealing drugs internally. At trial, an inconsistency had become apparent between the defence statement which had been served by his solicitors (in which it was said that the accused knew he was carrying the drugs when he arrived in the UK) and his evidence during cross-examination (in which he maintained that he believed he had regurgitated all of the packets before travelling to the UK). The defence statement had not been signed and the defendant alleged that his solicitor had made a mistake in serving an incorrect statement of his case. Although the trial judge referred to the alleged mistake in his summing up, he did not provide the jury with specific guidance. The Court of Appeal held that the judge had erred in failing to give specific directions as to the inconsistency, given that the jury would be affected by it. The court said that it was advisable that defence statements were signed by a defendant rather than served by solicitors on a defendant's behalf without procedures being followed to verify accuracy. It should be noted, however, that the court has no power to order the defence statement to be signed by the accused (*R (Sullivan) v Maidstone Crown Court* [2002] 1 WLR 2747).

Special provisions apply to alibi evidence, defined as:

evidence tending to show that by reason of the presence of the accused at a particular place or in a particular area at a particular time he was not, or was unlikely to have been, at the place where the offence is alleged to have been committed at the time of its alleged commission (s 5(8)).

Where the accused will be relying on an alibi, the defence statement must include the names and addresses of any witnesses the accused believes are able to give evidence in support of the alibi or (if the accused does not know names or addresses) any information which might be of assistance in finding such witnesses.

9.4 Sanctions for non-compliance by the defence

The penalties for non-compliance by the defence with their disclosure obligations under the CPIA 1996 are set out in s 11 (as amended by the CJA 2003). Section 11 applies in three cases:

(a) Where the accused is to be tried in the Crown Court (and so is required by s 5 of the Act to provide a defence statement) and the accused:

    (i) fails to give an initial defence statement under s 5, or

    (ii) provides an initial defence statement but does so late, or

    (iii) fails to provide an updated defence statement (or a statement that there are no changes), or

    (iv) provides an updated statement (or a statement that there are no changes) but does so late, or

    (v) sets out inconsistent defences in the defence statement, or

    (vi) at the trial, puts forward a defence which was not mentioned in his defence statement or which is different from any defence set out in that statement, or

    (vii) at the trial, relies on a matter which was not mentioned in his defence statement but which should have been so mentioned, or

    (viii) at the trial adduces evidence in support of an alibi without having given particulars of the alibi in the defence statement, or

    (ix) at the trial, calls an alibi witness without having given appropriate notice of the alibi, or details of that particular witness, in the defence statement.

(b) Where the accused is to be tried in a magistrates' court and gives an initial defence statement voluntarily but does so late or does any of the things set out in paragraphs (c) to (i) in the preceding paragraph.

(c) Where the accused gives a witness notice (under s 6C) but does so late or, at the trial, calls a witness who was not included, or not adequately identified, in a witness notice.

Under s 11(5), where s 11 applies:

(a) the court or any other party may make such comment as appears appropriate;

(b) the court or jury may draw such inferences as appear proper in deciding whether the accused is guilty of the offence concerned.

Section 11(6) provides that where adverse inferences could be drawn for failure to mention a point of law (including any point as to the admissibility of evidence or an abuse of process) or an authority used to support legal argument, comment by another party may be made only with the leave of the court. Similarly, s 11(7) provides that where the failure in question is a failure to comply with the witness notice requirements, comment by another party may only be made with the leave of the court.

Section 11(9) stipulates that where the accused calls a witness whom he has failed to include, or to identify adequately, in a witness notice, the court must have regard to whether there is any justification for the failure. Under s 11(8), where the accused puts forward a defence which is different from any defence set out in his defence statement, the court must have regard (a) to the extent of the differences in the defences, and (b) to whether there is any justification for it.

Section 11(10), importantly, confirms that 'a person shall not be convicted of an offence solely on an inference drawn under subsection (5)'.

9.5 Public Interest Immunity

Public Interest Immunity ('PII') enables the prosecution to withhold material that would otherwise have to be disclosed under the CPIA. Material can only be withheld on the basis of PII with the permission of the court. Common examples of cases where PII is raised are where the prosecution wish to protect the identity of an informant whom the prosecutor does not intend to call as a witness at the trial (as in *R v Turner* [1995] 1 WLR 264) or where the police wish to keep secret the location of an observation post from which they were watching the movements of the accused (as in *R v Johnson* [1988] 1 WLR 1377).

The Attorney-General's Guidelines on Disclosure, dealing with applications for non-disclosure in the public interest, state that:

41. Before making an application to the court to withhold material which would otherwise fail to be disclosed, on the basis that to disclose would not be in the public interest, a prosecutor should aim to disclose as much of the material as he properly can (by giving the defence redacted or edited copies of summaries).

42. Prior to or at the hearing, the court must be provided with full and accurate information. The prosecution advocate must examine all material which is the subject matter of the application and make any necessary enquiries of the prosecutor and/or investigator. The prosecutor (or representative) and/or investigator should attend such applications.

In *Rowe and Davis v United Kingdom* (2000) 30 EHRR 1, the European Court held that there is a:

fundamental aspect of the right to a fair trial that criminal proceedings, including the elements of such proceedings which relate to procedure, should be adversarial and that there should be equality of arms between the prosecution and defence. The right to an adversarial trial means, in a criminal case, that both prosecution and defence must be given the opportunity to have knowledge of and comment on the observations filed and the evidence adduced by the other party. In addition Article 6(1) requires, as indeed does English law, that the prosecution authorities should disclose to the defence all material evidence in their possession for or against the accused (para 61).

However, the Court went on to hold that:

the entitlement to disclosure of relevant evidence is not an absolute right. In any criminal proceedings there may be competing interests, such as national security or the need to protect witnesses at risk of reprisals or keep secret police methods of investigation of crime, which must be weighed against the rights of the accused. In some cases it may be necessary to withhold certain evidence from the defence so as to preserve the fundamental rights of another individual or to safeguard an important public interest. However, only such measures restricting the rights of the defence which are strictly necessary are permissible under Article 6(1). Moreover, in order to ensure that the accused receives a fair trial, any difficulties caused to the defence by a limitation on its rights must be sufficiently counterbalanced by the procedures followed by the judicial authorities (para 61).

In *Jasper v United Kingdom* (2000) 30 EHRR 441, where the European Court held that (by a bare majority of nine votes to eight) there was no violation of Article 6, the defence had been informed that a PII application was to be made by the prosecution (although they were not told which category the material being withheld was said to fall); the defence had thus had the opportunity to make submissions and to participate (albeit to a comparatively limited extent) in the decision-making process. The defence had been notified that an application to withhold material was to be made, but were not told of the category of material which the prosecution sought to withhold. They were given the opportunity to outline the defence case to the trial judge and to ask the judge to order disclosure of any evidence relevant to that case. On this basis, the Court (at para 55) said that it was:

satisfied that the defence were kept informed and permitted to make submissions and participate in the above decision-making process as far as was possible without revealing to them the material which the prosecution sought to keep secret on public interest grounds.

At para 56, the Court said that:

The fact that the need for disclosure was at all times under assessment by the trial judge provided a further, important, safeguard in that it was his duty to monitor throughout the trial the fairness or otherwise of the evidence being withheld . . . He was fully versed in all the evidence and issues in the case and in a position to monitor the relevance to the defence of the withheld information both before and during the trial

In some cases involving PII, however, the defendant will not have the information that the defence had in *Jasper*. In *R v H; R v C* [2004] UKHL 3, [2004] 2 WLR 335, the House of Lords considered the question of public interest immunity and the potential role for 'special independent counsel' in PII hearings. The Court of Appeal had certified two points of law of general public importance were involved in its decision:

(1) Are the procedures for dealing with claims for public interest immunity made on behalf of the prosecution in criminal proceedings compliant with article 6 of the European Convention for the Protection of Human Rights and Fundamental Freedoms?

(2) If not, in what way are the procedures deficient and how might the deficiency be remedied?

The procedure for determining claims of PII was set out in *R v Ward* [1993] 1 WLR 619 and *R v Davis* [1993] 1 WLR 613 at 617–618. The Court of Appeal identified three classes of case, which Lord Bingham (in *R v H*) summarised in the following terms:

In the first, comprising most of the cases in which a PII issue arises, the prosecution must give notice to the defence that they are applying for a ruling of the court, and must indicate to the defence at least the category of the material they hold (that is, the broad ground upon which PII is claimed), and the defence must have the opportunity to make representations to the court. There is thus an *inter partes* hearing conducted in open court with reference to at least the category of the material in question. The second class comprises cases in which the prosecution contend that the public interest would be injured if disclosure were made even of the category of the material. In such cases the prosecution must still notify the defence that an application to the court is to be made, but the category of the material need not be specified: the defence will still have an opportunity to address the court on the procedure to be adopted but the application will be made to the court in the absence of the defendant or anyone representing him. If the court considers that the application falls within the first class, it will order that procedure to be followed. Otherwise it will rule. The third class, described as 'highly exceptional', comprises cases where the public interest would be injured even by disclosure that an *ex parte* application is to be made. In such cases application to the court would be made without notice to the defence. But if the court considers that the case should be treated as falling within the second or the first class, it will so order (para 20).

The procedural regime established by *R v Ward* and *R v Davis* was given statutory effect in the Crown Court (Criminal Procedure and Investigations Act 1996) (Disclosure) Rules 1997 (SI 1997/698) and by the Magistrates' Courts (Criminal Procedure and Investigations Act 1996) (Disclosure) Rules 1997 (SI 1997/703). These Rules will eventually be replaced by Part 23 of the Criminal Procedure Rules.

The House of Lords in *R v H* goes on to give guidance on how the courts should approach PII hearings (para 36):

When any issue of derogation from the golden rule of full disclosure comes before it, the court must address a series of questions:

(1)   What is the material which the prosecution seek to withhold? This must be considered by the court in detail.

(2)   Is the material such as may weaken the prosecution case or strengthen that of the defence? If No, disclosure should not be ordered. If Yes, full disclosure should (subject to (3), (4) and (5) below, be ordered.

(3)   Is there a real risk of serious prejudice to an important public interest (and, if so, what) if full disclosure of the material is ordered? If No, full disclosure should be ordered.

(4)   If the answer to (2) and (3) is Yes, can the defendant's interest be protected without disclosure or disclosure be ordered to an extent or in a way which will give adequate protection to the public interest in question and also afford adequate protection to the interests of the de-fence?

This question requires the court to consider, with specific reference to the material which the prosecution seek to withhold and the facts of the case and the defence as disclosed, whether the prosecution should formally admit what the defence seek to establish or whether disclosure short of full disclosure may be ordered. This may be done in appropriate cases by the preparation of summaries or extracts of evidence, or the provision of documents in an edited or anonymised form, provided the documents supplied are in each instance approved by the judge. In appropriate cases the appointment of special counsel may be a necessary step to ensure that the contentions of the prosecution are tested and the interests of the defendant protected (see paragraph 22 above). In cases of exceptional difficulty the court may require the appointment of special counsel to ensure a correct answer to questions (2) and (3) as well as (4).

(5)   Do the measures proposed in answer to (4) represent the minimum derogation necessary to protect the public interest in question? If No, the court should order such greater disclosure as will represent the minimum derogation from the golden rule of full disclosure.

(6)   If limited disclosure is ordered pursuant to (4) or (5), may the effect be to render the trial process, viewed as a whole, unfair to the defendant? If Yes, then fuller disclosure should be ordered even if this leads or may lead the prosecution to discontinue the proceedings so as to avoid having to make disclosure.

(7)   If the answer to (6) when first given is No, does that remain the correct answer as the trial un-folds, evidence is adduced and the defence advanced?

It is important that the answer to (6) should not be treated as a final, once-and-for-all, answer but as a provisional answer which the court must keep under review.

37. Throughout his or her consideration of any disclosure issue the trial judge must bear constantly in mind the overriding principles referred to in this opinion. In applying them, the judge should involve the defence to the maximum extent possible without disclosing that which the general interest requires to be protected but taking full account of the specific defence which is relied on. There will be very few cases indeed in which some measure of disclosure to the defence will not be possible, even if this is confined to the fact that an ex parte application is to be made. If even that information is withheld and if the material to be withheld is of significant help to the defendant, there must be a very serious question whether the prosecution should proceed, since special counsel, even if appointed, cannot then receive any instructions from the defence at all.

Lord Bingham concludes that:

Provided the existing procedures for dealing with claims for public interest immunity made on behalf of the prosecution in criminal proceedings are operated with scrupulous attention to the governing principles referred to and continuing regard to the proper interests of the defendant, there should be no violation of Article 6 of the Convention.

The main focus of the case was the appointment of special independent counsel to protect the interests of the defendant but who may not disclose to the defendant the secret material that is disclosed to him in order to make representations on behalf of the defendant and who is not, in the ordinary sense, professionally responsible to the defendant. Such special counsel may be appointed where the interests of justice are shown to require it. However, the House of Lords said that the need must be shown; such an appointment will always be exceptional, never automatic; a course of last and never first resort. It should not be ordered unless and until the trial judge is satisfied that no other course will adequately meet the overriding requirement of fairness to the defendant.

The House of Lords also gave general guidance on PII hearings in magistrates' courts. Lord Bingham affirmed the approach taken in *R (DPP) v Acton Youth Court* [2001] EWHC Admin 402, [2001] 1 WLR 1828.

If PII applications are confined, as they should be, to material which undermines the prosecution case or strengthens that of the defence, the bench will not be alerted to material damaging to the defendant. If it is, the principles which should govern the court's decision whether to recuse itself are the same as in the case of any other tribunal of fact, but the court's duty of continuing review ordinarily militates in favour of continuing the proceedings before the court which determines the PII application. If a case raises complex and contentious PII issues, and the court has discretion to send the case to the Crown Court for trial, the magistrates' court should carefully consider whether those issues are best resolved in the Crown Court. The occasions on which it will be appropriate to appoint special counsel in the magistrates' court will be even rarer than in the Crown Court (para 44).

Indictments

10.1 What is an indictment?

The indictment is the formal document which sets out the charge(s) to be tried in the Crown Court. Detailed information on indictments can be found in section D10 of *Blackstone's Criminal Practice*. The key legislative provisions governing the form and content of indictments are to be found in ss 3 and 5 of the Indictments Act 1915, s 2 of the Administration of Justice (Miscellaneous Provisions) Act 1933, and in rr 4 to 9 of the Indictment Rules 1971 (SI 1971/1253).

10.1.1 What does an indictment contain?

The indictment begins with a heading, which contains a unique reference number for the case, identifies the location of the Crown Court and the name of the defendant(s).

Each charge faced by the defendant is contained in a separate 'count'.

10.1.2 What does a count contain?

Section 3(1) of the Indictments Act 1915 provides that the indictment must contain 'a statement of the specific offence or offences with which the accused person is charged, together with such particulars as may be necessary for giving reasonable information as to the nature of the charge'. Rule 5 of the Indictment Rules 1971 requires that, 'every indictment shall contain . . . a statement of the specific offence with which the accused person is charged describing the offence shortly, together with such particulars as may be necessary for giving reasonable information as to the nature of the charge'.

There may be a single count in the indictment or there may be more than one. Rule 6 of the Indictment Rules 1971 sets out what each count must contain.

Each count is divided into two parts:

- the 'Statement of Offence', which sets out the name of the offence (for example, 'theft') and, where the offence is a statutory one, the statutory provision which creates the offence (for example, s 1 of the Theft Act 1968).
- the 'Particulars of Offence', giving factual information about the charge; this must disclose the essential elements of the offence.

Further guidance on drafting indictments can be found in **Chapter 24** of the *Drafting Manual*. Guidance on how to draft counts in respect of particular offences is given in the commentary relating to individual offences in Part B of *Blackstone's Criminal Practice*.

Rule 4 of the Indictment Rules applies where more than one offence is alleged. It provides that, 'Where more than one offence is charged in an indictment, the statement and particulars of each offence shall be set out in a separate paragraph called a count . . .'. It follows that a single count must only allege one offence. If a count alleges more than one offence, it is 'duplicitous' or 'bad for duplicity', and the defence can ask the court to quash the count. For example, a count which alleges that the defendant 'on 16 August 2003 assaulted John Smith and on 17 August 2003 assaulted Peter Jones' is alleging two separate offences and so will be quashed.

It is possible, however, for several acts to constitute a single offence. In *DPP v Merriman* [1973] AC 584, it was said that a number of acts may properly be said to amount to a single offence if they form part of the 'same transaction'. For example, in *R v Wilson* (1979) 69 Cr App R 83, the defendant was charged in one count with stealing a number of different items from Debenhams (three jumpers, a pair of shorts, two pairs of trousers, four dimmer switches and a cassette tape) and in another count with stealing a number of different items from Boots (eight records and a bottle of aftershave). The defence sought to argue that each count was duplicitous, on the basis that the goods had been stolen from different departments of the stores in question and so there should have been separate counts relating to each department. The Court of Appeal held that where counts in an indictment each charge theft of a number of separate items from different departments of the same store, those counts are not bad for duplicity, since it is legitimate to charge in a single count one activity even though that activity may involve more than one act. The various acts of theft in each store had amounted to a single course of conduct, and so those acts could legitimately be regarded as amounting to a single offence of theft.

Similarly, in *DPP v McCabe* [1992] Crim LR 885, it was held that an allegation that the defendant stole 76 library books between two specified dates was a single offence and so a count alleging this theft was not bad for duplicity. However, a count which alleged that the defendant stole £200 from A one day and £200 from B the next would be duplicitous because there are two separate acts of theft.

Rule 7 of the Indictment Rules provides that if a section of a statute creates one offence which may be committed in a number of ways, the alternatives may be charged in a single count. If, however, the section creates more than one offence, each offence the prosecution wish the jury to consider must be put in a separate count. A good example of the operation of r 7 (in practice, if not in strict legal theory) may be seen in the offence of handling stolen goods (s 22 of the Theft Act 1968). Handling effectively comprises two offences. The first is that of dishonestly receiving stolen goods; the second comprises all the other ways of handling and these ways are all different ways of committing a single offence. The various ways of committing the second form of handling can, and usually will, be charged in a single count. However, a count which charged receiving and the other forms of handling together would be regarded as defective.

Thus, there are two basic handling counts; either:

- AB on [date] dishonestly received stolen goods, namely [description of goods], knowing or believing the same to be stolen goods; or

- AB on [date] dishonestly undertook or assisted in the retention, removal, disposal or realisation of stolen goods, namely [description of goods], by or for the benefit of another, or dishonestly arranged to do so, knowing or believing the same to be stolen goods.

If a count is bad for duplicity (in that it charges more than one offence), the defence may make an application to quash the indictment. However, the prosecution may counter this application by asking for leave to amend the indictment under s 5(1) of the Indictments Act 1915, thus splitting the duplicitous count into two separate counts. In *R v Levantiz* [1999] 1 Cr App R 465, several discrete acts of supplying a controlled drug were alleged in a single count in the indictment. The Court of Appeal held that, where a count in an indictment is duplicitous, that count is not void and the conviction is not necessarily unsafe. It follows that an appeal against conviction on that count can be dismissed if the Court of Appeal decides that the conviction is safe despite the irregularity in the indictment. In deciding whether a conviction based on a duplicitous count is safe, it is submitted that the Court should ask itself whether the accused was prejudiced by the duplicitous nature of the count. If it is the case that the defendant must have been guilty of everything alleged in the count — or nothing alleged in the count — it is unlikely that he would have been prejudiced by the duplicity.

Each count in an indictment is a separate entity. In *R v O'Neill* [2003] EWCA Crim 411 (unreported), the defendant was charged in a indictment which included a count that was defective, in that it was based on a statutory provision which had not been in force at the relevant time. The Court of Appeal confirmed that even if one count charges an offence not known to the law, any other counts in the same indictment can stand and need not be quashed.

EXAMPLE 10.1

This is an example of an indictment containing two counts.

No. 04/12345

INDICTMENT

THE CROWN COURT AT CROYDON

THE QUEEN *v* ANDREW JAMES CLARKE

ANDREW JAMES CLARKE is charged as follows:

COUNT 1

Statement of Offence

Burglary, contrary to s 9(1)(b) of the Theft Act 1968

Particulars of Offence

ANDREW JAMES CLARKE, on 3 August 2004, having entered a dwelling, namely 27 Acacia Avenue Croydon, as a trespasser, stole therein a television set and video recorder belonging to John Mark Richardson.

COUNT 2

Statement of Offence

Unlawful wounding, contrary to s 20 of the Offences Against the Person Act 1861

Particulars of Offence

ANDREW JAMES CLARKE, on 3 August 2004, unlawfully and maliciously wounded John Mark Richardson.

10.1.3   Who draws up the indictment?

The indictment is normally drafted by the Crown Prosecution Service. In complex cases, however, counsel may be instructed to advise on evidence and to draft the indictment. The document is then sent to the Crown Court, where it is signed by an officer of the court. Strictly speaking, the document is known as a 'bill of indictment' until it has been signed by the officer of the Crown Court. After signature, it becomes an indictment.

Although the drafting of the indictment is the responsibility of the prosecution, an indictment is only valid if it has been signed by a proper officer of the Crown Court (Administration of Justice (Miscellaneous Provisions) Act 1933, s 2(1)).

The bill of indictment should be 'preferred' (ie delivered to the Crown Court — see rule 14.1 of the Criminal Procedure Rules 2005) within 28 days of the service of the documents on the defendant when the case is sent for trial under s 51 of the Crime and Disorder Act 1998 (see rule 14.2(1)of the Criminal Procedure Rules). This period may, however, be extended by an appropriate officer of the Crown Court for 28 days, or by a Crown Court judge for any period (rule 14.2(2) and 14.2(3)).

Where there is more than one defendant, the order in which the names of defendants are placed on an indictment is the responsibility of the prosecutor, who has a discretion as to that order. The mere fact that a co-defendant named later on the indictment might give evidence adverse to a defendant after that defendant has given evidence, provides no basis for regarding the prosecution's exercise of its discretion in drafting the indictment as improper. Nor does it provide grounds for severing the indictment and ordering a separate trial since, in principle, defendants jointly charged should be tried in a single trial: *R v Cairns* [2002] EWCA Crim 2838; [2003] 1 WLR 796.

10.2   Joinder of counts

Under r 9 of the Indictment Rules 1971, counts may be joined in the same indictment if the charges are either:

- founded on the same facts; or
- form, or are part of, a series of offences of the same or a similar character.

10.2.1   Founded on the same facts

Two offences are founded on the same facts if they arise from a single incident or are part of the same 'transaction' (eg assaulting the householder in the course of a burglary).

One offence can also arise from the same facts as another if one would not have been committed but for the other. For example in *R v Barrell and Wilson* (1979) 69 Cr App R 250, the indictment charged assault and affray (arising out of a single incident) and attempting to pervert the course of justice (based on attempts to prevent prosecution witnesses from testifying). The defence objected to the joinder of the latter charge. However, it was held by the Court of Appeal that the phrase 'founded on the same facts' does not mean that for charges to be properly joined in the same indictment, the facts in relation to the respective charges must be identical in substance or virtually contemporaneous; rather, the test is whether the charges have 'a common factual origin'. That test was satisfied in *Barrell and Wilson*: the allegation of attempting to pervert the course of justice would not have arisen but for the allegations of assault and affray, and so it could legitimately be said that the charges had a common factual origin.

10.2.2   Series of similar offences

For two offences to belong to a series of similar offences, there must be a 'nexus' between them. For a nexus to exist, the offences must be similar both legally and factually. See *Ludlow v Metropolitan Police Commissioner* [1971] AC 29, in which the House of Lords upheld the joinder of a count alleging attempted theft at a public house in Acton on 20 August 1968 and a count alleging robbery at a public house in Acton on 5 September 1968.

It should be noted that two offences do not form a series merely because evidence relating to one offence is uncovered during the investigation into the other (see *R v Harward* (1981) 73 Cr App R 168).

Several examples of the operation of the second limb of r 9 of the Indictment Rules 1971 can be found in para D10.26 of *Blackstone's Criminal Practice*.

10.3   Joinder of defendants

A count in an indictment can name more than one defendant if it is alleged that there was more than one participant (*DPP v Merriman* [1973] AC 584). Where one person aided and abetted the other, he or she can either be charged specifically with aiding and abetting the offence or as a principal. In practice, secondary participants are usually charged as principal offenders. So, if it is alleged that John Smith carried out a burglary and Jane Jones acted as look-out, the usual practice would be to charge them jointly (in the same count) with burglary.

It is also permissible to join defendants in an indictment even if the defendants are not charged with the same offence, provided that the offences are sufficiently linked so that they can properly be joined under r 9 (*R v Assim* [1966] 2 QB 249). In that case, there were two defendants. The charges arose out of a fracas at a nightclub. A receptionist at a nightclub (D1) had tried to prevent a customer from leaving without paying and was alleged to have wounded the customer; another customer had intervened and was alleged assaulted by a doorman (D2). Given the fact that this was effectively a single incident with a number of participants, it was held that there was sufficient nexus for the two separate counts (one against D1 and the other against D2) to be joined in the same indictment.

10.4   Discretion to order separate trials

Section 5(3) of the Indictments Act 1915 provides that where (either before the trial or at any stage of a trial) the court is of the opinion that the defendant may be:

prejudiced or embarrassed in his defence by reason of being charged with more than one offence in the same indictment, or that for any other reason it is desirable to direct that the person should be tried separately for any one or more offences charged in an indictment, the court may order a separate trial of any count or counts of such indictment.

This power to order separate trials of offences on an indictment is technically known as 'severing the indictment'. It applies both to a defendant who seeks separate trials for a number of offences and to co-defendants seeking separate trials from each other.

This power can only be exercised where joinder of the offences is proper under r 9 of the Indictment Rules 1971, and so this power cannot be used to cure the defect where counts are joined improperly (see *R v Newland* [1988] QB 402).

The power to order separate trials applies where a single trial would prejudice or embarrass the defendant(s) or if there is some other good reason (s 5(3)). In *Ludlow*, the House of Lords said that where counts are properly joined under r 9, they should normally be tried together unless the defendant can show a 'special feature' justifying separate trials. In other words, the burden rests on the defendant to show that exceptional circumstances merit separate trials.

Relevant considerations include the following:

(a) How easy or difficult will it be for the jury to disentangle the evidence relating to the different counts?

(b) Is one of the counts likely to arouse hostility in the minds of the jurors, creating a risk that they will not approach the other counts with open minds?

(c) Is the strength of the evidence relating to the counts disproportionate, with the risk that the jury will think that if the defendant is guilty of the charge supported by the stronger evidence, he must also be guilty of the charge in respect of which the evidence is weaker?

(d) Is the evidence on all the counts weak, creating a risk that the jury may convict on the basis of an overview of the case rather than considering the evidence in respect of each count separately?

It has to be borne in mind that the effect of these risks can be minimised, if not removed altogether, by appropriately worded directions from the judge on how to approach the task of analysing the evidence.

Where there are two defendants and they seek separate trials, it has to be shown that a fair trial cannot be achieved without severance. Judges are reluctant to order separate trials of defendants charged with the same offence. If there are separate trials, the cost of the proceedings will be doubled, the witnesses will have to testify twice, and there is a risk of inconsistent verdicts.

In *R v Lake* (1976) 64 Cr App R 172, the prosecution evidence included material which was admissible against D1 but inadmissible against D2. D2 argued that he should be tried separately, since the jury would otherwise hear the inadmissible evidence. The Court of Appeal upheld the judge's refusal to order separate trials, on the basis that the judge's direction to the jury was sufficient to ensure that the jury would disregard evidence that was inadmissible against D2 when considering the case against that defendant even if the same evidence was admissible against D1. Similarly, separate trials were not thought necessary in *R v Grondkowsik and Malinowski* [1946] KB 369, even though the defendants were blaming each other (running so-called 'cut-throat' defences).

The result was the same in *R v Kennedy* [1992] Crim LR 37, where two defendants were charged with affray and D1 indicated that he would be referring to the previous convictions of D2 in the hope of persuading the jury that he had been acting in self-defence (a permissible course of action according to the House of Lords in *R v Randall* [2003] UKHL 69; [2004] 1 WLR 56); even though this was evidence which the prosecution would not have been able to adduce, and was clearly prejudicial to the other defendant, the judge's decision not to order separate trials was upheld.

If a defendant is charged in an indictment containing more than one count, he or she may apply for that indictment to be severed, so that particular counts are tried separately. An example of where severance would have been appropriate is *R v Laycock* [2003] EWCA Crim 1477; [2003] Crim LR 803, where the defendant was charged with a number of offences, including possession of a firearm when a prohibited person, namely having been sentenced to imprisonment for more than three years (an offence under the Firearms

Act 1968). The very nature of this offence revealed the fact that he had previously been convicted of a serious offence. The Court criticised the number of counts, saying that in formulating an indictment an excessive number of counts should not be included, since this overloads the indictment. Furthermore, the Court went on to say that prosecutors should be careful not to charge counts that would prejudice a defendant unless there is a real purpose to be served. In the present case, the firearms offence should not have been joined in the indictment since it did not give the judge any additional sentencing powers. If the prosecution were determined to seek a conviction for the offence in question, a separate trial of that count would have been fairer.

10.5 Misjoinder

If an indictment contains counts which should not be joined together, because the rules for joinder are not satisfied, there is no power to sever the indictment (ie order separate trials). See *R v Newland* [1988] QB 402, where the defendant was charged with a drugs offence and three counts alleging assault which were wholly unconnected with the drugs charge. The trial judge simply ordered separate trials (purporting to 'sever' the indictment under Indictments Act 1915, s 5(3)), so that the drugs offence and the assault charges were tried separately. The Court of Appeal held that the judge had no power to 'sever' the indictment under s 5(3), since this power applies only to a valid indictment, and the indictment in the present case was invalid because it failed to comply with r 9 of the Indictment Rules. The court went on to say that the trial judge should have deleted from the indictment either the drugs charge or the assault charges, and proceeded with the trial on that indictment. The allegations deleted from the indictment could only be proceeded with if the prosecution brought fresh committal proceedings in respect of them or else sought a voluntary bill of indictment.

In *R v Follett* [1989] QB 338, a differently constituted Court of Appeal accepted a rather simpler solution. In this case, the indictment was invalid because it contained counts which were not sufficiently linked. The Court of Appeal upheld the decision of the trial judge to stay proceedings on the indictment as drafted and to give the prosecution leave to prefer fresh indictments (each complying with r 9) out of time. The effect of this is that the invalid indictment remains in existence but becomes irrelevant. Two or more trials then follow, based on the new indictments, without the need for fresh committal proceedings or a voluntary bill of indictment.

It follows that, where there has been misjoinder, the situation can be remedied in either of two ways:

- delete one or more counts from the indictment, leaving only counts which can properly be joined under r 9 (the course of action taken in *Newland*); or

- stay the existing indictment and allow the prosecution to prefer fresh indictments out of time, each indictment containing only counts which can properly be joined under r 9 (the course of action taken in *R v Follett* [1989] QB 338).

There was authority to the effect that an indictment containing improperly joined counts was invalid (and so if a defendant was to be convicted on such an indictment, all the convictions would have to be quashed). That line of authority was based on a misreading of *Newland*.

In *R v Smith* [1997] 2 WLR 588, three summary offences were added to an indictment under CJA 1988, s 40; joinder of two of those summary offences was improper because there was no sufficient link with the indictable offence which was also on the indictment. The Court of Appeal held that convictions for offences which are correctly joined are valid convictions. Accordingly, the convictions on the indictable offence and the correctly joined summary offence stood; only the convictions for the two improperly joined summary offences were quashed. Similarly, in *R v Lockley and Sainsbury* [1997] Crim LR 455, the appellants were charged with conspiracy to commit burglary and dangerous driving (on the basis that the car they used in connection with the burglary was dangerously defective). Both offences are indictable offences and so only r 9 of the Indictment Rules had to be considered. The Court of Appeal held that the dangerous driving charge was improperly joined. The court confirmed that CJA 1988, s 40 and r 9 of the Indictment Rules are in all material respects in the same terms, and so the same principles regarding misjoinder and the consequences thereof must apply to both. The court went on to hold that misjoinder does not nullify the whole indictment. It followed that only the conviction(s) on the wrongly joined count(s) should be quashed.

It is thus clear that misjoinder of counts does not render the entire indictment invalid.

10.6 Deciding the contents of the indictment

In most cases, the counts on the indictment are the same as the committal charges (or charges which were transferred under s 51 of the Crime and Disorder Act 1998). However, it is possible for the indictment to contain different charges to the original ones. Under s 2(2) of the Administration of Justice (Miscellaneous Provisions) Act 1933 the indictment may contain, as well or instead of the original charges, any counts which are disclosed in the prosecution witness statements and which can properly be joined in the same indictment. In other words, the resulting indictment may contain only:

- the original charge or a substitute for the original charge;
- other offences disclosed in the prosecution witness statements which can properly be joined to the original charge (or its substitute) under r 9.

In *R v Lombardi* [1989] 1 WLR 73, the Court of Appeal emphasised that counts for which there is evidence in the prosecution papers, but in respect of which there was no committal, can only be added later to the indictment if they are in substitution for offences which were the subject of the committal, or could lawfully be joined in the indictment resulting from the committal (on the basis that they arise from the same facts as, or form a series of offences of the same or similar character to, the original charge).

Some examples may help to illustrate the effect of s 2(2) of the 1933 Act.

Example 1
The defendant is sent for trial on a charge of burglary. When the prosecution drafts the bill of indictment it believes that, although there is ample evidence of theft, the evidence relating to the element of trespass is very weak. The prosecutor could draft a count for theft in place of the burglary charge on which the defendant was sent for trial.

Example 2
The magistrates send the defendant for trial on a charge of theft but the prosecution subsequently decide that there is sufficient evidence to prove that the theft was committed in the course of a burglary. The prosecution could indict the defendant for burglary instead of theft.

Example 3

The defendant is sent for trial on a single charge of robbery. The prosecution witness statements include evidence that the defendant was brandishing a gun. The allegation of possession of a firearm arises from the same facts as the robbery, so the prosecutor could add a charge alleging a firearms offence even though the defendant was not sent for trial in respect of that offence.

Example 4

The defendant is charged with handling stolen goods. In the course of investigating the handling charge, the police search the defendant's home and find a quantity of drugs. The defendant is sent for trial only on the handling offence. The prosecutor cannot add a drugs charge to the handling charge, because the defendant was not sent for trial in respect of it and joinder of the two charges would not be permissible under r 9. The prosecutor cannot put the drugs charge in a separate indictment, because the defendant was not sent for trial in respect of the drugs charge.

In *Lombardi*, Lord Lane CJ said that where the magistrates have sent a defendant to the Crown Court on more than one charge, the prosecution may prefer a number of separate indictments if they feel that it is appropriate to do so.

If the magistrates send two or more defendants for trial at the same time, it is open to the prosecution to draft separate indictments against them if the prosecution feel that it would be appropriate to do so. If defendants are not sent for trial at the same time, it is nevertheless open to the prosecution to join those defendants in the same indictment (assuming r 9 is satisfied). This is so even if an indictment in respect of a defendant who has been sent for trial has already been signed (see *Practice Direction (Criminal Proceedings: Consolidation)* [2002] 1 WLR 2870, para 34.2).

10.7   Alternative counts

It is possible for counts to appear on an indictment in the alternative. For example, the indictment might contain one count alleging wounding with intent (s 18 of the Offences Against the Person Act 1861) and a separate count alleging unlawful wounding (s 20 of the 1861 Act). This is appropriate where the prosecution is unsure whether there is sufficient evidence to prove the more serious offence.

10.8   Amending the indictment

Under s 5(1) of the Indictments Act 1915, where, either before the trial or at any stage during the trial, it appears to the court that the indictment is defective, the court is empowered to make such order for the amendment of the indictment as it thinks necessary to meet the circumstances of the case, unless, having regard to the merits of the case, the required amendments cannot be made without injustice.

In *R v Pople* [1951] 1 KB 53 it was held that it is not necessary that an indictment, in order to be 'defective' within the meaning of s 5(1) of the Indictments Act 1915, does not have to be bad on its face. On the contrary, said the court, any alteration in matters of description may be made in order to meet the evidence in the case so long as the amendment causes no injustice to the accused. In that case, the Court of Appeal upheld the decision of the trial judge to allow the indictment to be amended at the close of the prosecution case to allege the obtaining by deception of a cheque rather than alleging the obtaining of a sum of money for which the cheque was drawn. The court held that the defendant was not prejudiced, since the substance of the allegation was unaltered.

In *R v Collison* (1980) 71 Cr App R 249, the defendant was charged with one count of wounding with intent (s 18 of the Offences Against the Person Act 1861). The jury was unable to reach either a unanimous or a majority verdict on this count. The judge allowed the prosecution to add a further count of unlawful wounding (contrary to s 20 of the 1861 Act). The Court of Appeal held that no injustice to the defendant had resulted from the amendment since the lesser s 20 offence was already before the jury. The jury could have acquitted the defendant of the s 18 offence and convicted him of the s 20 offence under s 6(3) of the Criminal Law Act 1967.

In *R v Harris* The Times, 22 March 1993, a charge of attempted rape was substituted for one of rape after the defendant's case was closed but before closing speeches. The Court of Appeal held that a judge exercising his discretion to allow an alternative offence to be put to the jury had to take into account the timing of the application because it was important that a defendant should have the opportunity to deal with the revised case against him. Where a judge allowed an alternative charge, and defence counsel might otherwise have conducted the case differently, the defendant's conviction would be unsafe.

The term 'defective' in s 5(1) of the Indictments Act 1971 includes the concept of 'lack' or 'want'. It follows that, where there is no suggestion of injustice, an indictment can be amended under s 5(1) so as to add a new defendant (*R v Palmer* [2002] EWCA Crim 892).

Crown Court trial

11.1 Preliminary Hearings

Part 3 of the Criminal Procedure Rules contains general case management powers. Part 3 is supplemented by Part IV.41 of the Consolidated Criminal Practice Direction (amended with effect from April 2005). Para IV.41.3 of the Practice Direction states that a preliminary hearing ('PH') is not required in every case sent for trial; a PH should be ordered by the magistrates' court or by the Crown Court only where such a hearing is considered necessary. Where a PH is necessary, it should be held approximately 14 days after sending. A Case Progression Preliminary Hearing Form has to be completed by the parties, providing an agenda for the PH; the form envisages three possible outcomes, namely a guilty plea (at the PH or a subsequent hearing), directions for a 'plea and case management hearing' (PCMH), or fixing of the trial date.

11.1.1 Plea and Case Management Hearings

Whether or not the magistrates' court orders a PH, it must order a PCMH to be held within approximately 14 weeks after the case has been sent for trial where the defendant is in custody (within approximately 17 weeks where the defendant is on bail) (para IV.41.5). In a case where the defendant intends to plea not guilty, it is clear that the effectiveness of the PCMH is dependent on the presence of the trial advocate or of an advocate who is able to make decisions and give the court the assistance which the trial advocate could be expected to give (para IV.41.8). Additional pre-trial hearings should be held only for some compelling reason; where necessary, the power to give, vary or revoke a direction without a hearing should be used (para IV.41.12).

Annex E to the Consolidated Criminal Practice Direction contains a standard form to be completed for PCMHs. It includes questions such as

- Has the defendant been advised about credit for pleading guilty?
- Has the defendant been warned that if he is on bail and fails to attend, the proceedings may continue in his absence?
- Might the case against a defendant be resolved by a plea of guilty to some counts on the indictment or to a lesser offence?
- In the case of a guilty plea, is there a written basis of plea? Is the basis of plea acceptable to the prosecution?
- Are there any other matters which should be dealt with at the same time as these proceedings (other offences/TICs)?
- What is the estimated length of the prosecution, defence cases?
- Should the defendant's interview(s) be edited before the trial?

[Handwritten margin note: 14 wks if D in custody. 17 wks if D on bail.]

- Has a defence statement been served (under the CPIA 1996)? Is there an issue as to its adequacy? Is the defence alleging that the prosecution has not complied with its obligation to disclose material?
- Have the parties considered formal admissions?
- Is expert evidence likely to be called by either side? Does the court approve of the need for the identified expert evidence? Should the expert evidence be presented in a particular way in order to be more easily understood by the jury? Would it be helpful if the experts produced a written note of points of agreement or disagreement with a summary of reasons?
- Are there any outstanding issues about special measures or live links?
- Are any special arrangements needed for a child defendant?
- Will a defendant be unrepresented at trial?
- Will there be applications regarding hearsay evidence or bad character evidence?
- What are the legal or factual issues which should be resolved before the trial? Do the parties wish to call witnesses to give evidence orally to enable the court to resolve the issues?

The PCMH guidance notes state that the parties must use their best endeavours to reduce the amount of oral evidence given to a minimum, in particular by reducing the number of witnesses who give similar evidence, or by the deletion of challenged passages the omission of which will not materially affect the case for the party calling that witness, or by the use of admissions which make the calling of the witness in person unnecessary.

Under s 40 of the CPIA 1996, the court may make rulings, which have binding effect, as to: (a) any question as to the admissibility of evidence; (b) any other question of law relating to the case concerned. The extent to which courts exercise the power to make these rulings at this hearing is a matter for the court, after considering representations. Such rulings can be varied or discharged but only if there has been a material change of circumstance since the order was made and if the judge is satisfied that it is in the interests of justice to do so.

To encourage pre-trial resolution of issues, PCMH guidance notes say that the parties should, before the PCMH, agree or try to agree what legal issues are likely to be raised (for example, joinder, severance, admissibility of evidence, abuse of process, issues of substantive law etc) and at what stage they should properly be resolved. Applications to stay an indictment on the ground of abuse of process should be considered at the PCMH.

11.1.2   Preparatory hearings

Under the CPIA 1996, s 29 (as amended by CJA 2003, s 309), a Crown Court judge may, 'on an application by one of the parties or of his own motion', order a preparatory hearing to take place if it appears to the judge that the indictment 'reveals a case of such complexity, *a case of such seriousness* or a case whose trial is likely to be of such length, that substantial benefits are likely to accrue from a hearing . . . ' (words in italics added by CJA 2003). See also Rule 15 of the Criminal Procedure Rules.

Thus a preparatory hearing can be held on the basis that the case appears to be:

- complex, or;
- serious, or;
- lengthy.

Section 29(2) sets out the purposes of the preparatory hearing:

(a)   *identifying issues which are likely to be material to the verdict of the jury;*
(b)   *assisting their comprehension of any such issues;*

(c)   expediting the proceedings before the jury;

(d)   assisting the judge's management of the trial;

(e)   considering questions as to the severance or joinder of charges [(e) was added by CJA 2003, s 310(4)].

Section 31(3) empowers the judge to make rulings as to:

(a)   any question as to the admissibility of evidence;

(b)   any other question of law relating to the case;

(c)   any question as to the severance or joinder of charges [(c) was added by s 310(5) of the Criminal Justice Act 2003].

In *R v Claydon* [2004] 1 Cr App R 36, the Court of Appeal ruled that applications to exclude evidence (eg under PACE 1984, s 78) should be regarded as being for the purpose of 'expediting the proceedings before the jury', as within s 29(2)(c).

There are provisions for appeals from rulings made by the judge at a preparatory hearing to the Court of Appeal and, ultimately, the House of Lords. Where leave to appeal has been granted, the preparatory hearing may continue, but the jury trial cannot begin until the appeal has been determined or abandoned.

The judge may also order the prosecutor to:

- supply to the court and to the accused a written case statement (setting out the principal facts of the case for the prosecution, the witnesses who will give evidence of those facts, any exhibits relevant to those facts, and any proposition of law on which the prosecutor proposes to rely);

- prepare the prosecution evidence and any explanatory material in such a form as appears to the judge to be likely to aid comprehension by the jury;

- give the court and the accused written notice of documents, the truth of the contents of which ought in the prosecutor's view to be admitted, and any other matters which in his view ought to be agreed.

Where a judge has ordered the prosecutor to give a case statement and the prosecutor has complied with the order, the judge may order the accused to:

- provide a written statement setting out (in general terms) the nature of his defence and indicating the principal matters on which he takes issue with the prosecution;

- give the court and the prosecutor written notice of any objections that he has to the case statement;

- give the court and the prosecutor written notice of any point of law (including any point as to the admissibility of evidence) which he wishes to take, and any authority on which he intends to rely for that purpose.

In *Kanaris v Governor of Pentonville Prison* [2003] 1 All ER 593, [2003] UKHL 2, the House of Lords held that a Crown Court judge is entitled to hold separate preparatory hearings (under s 29 of the CPIA 1996) in respect of defendants who are charged jointly in the same indictment.

11.1.3   Adjournments

The existence of the various forms of pre-trial hearing should mean that the trial can go ahead on the date that is fixed. However, there may still be occasions when an adjournment is sought. In *R v Chaaban* [2003] EWCA Crim 1012; *The Times*, 8 May 2003, the Court of Appeal said that adjournments must be justified and, if at all possible, should be avoided. However, the Court noted that the decision whether or not to adjourn is preeminently a matter for the trial judge, and so the Court of Appeal will not interfere with that decision unless it can be demonstrated that the decision to refuse an adjournment was wholly unreasonable and caused real (as opposed to fanciful) prejudice to the defendant, undermining the safety of the conviction.

11.2 The arraignment

At the arraignment (which should take place at the preliminary hearing), the indictment is 'put' to the defendant, in that he or she is asked to plead guilty or not guilty. The proceedings will go something like this:

Clerk of the Court: 'Are you Michael Smith?'
Smith: 'Yes.'
Clerk: 'Michael Smith, you are charged in an indictment containing one count of robbery contrary to s 8 of the Theft Act 1968. The particulars of the offence are that on 8 May 2003 you robbed Alice Jones of £45 in cash. Michael Smith, to this indictment do you plead guilty or not guilty?'

If the indictment contains more than one count, each count will be put to the defendant separately, so that a plea is entered on each. The defendant must enter his or her plea personally (not through counsel or solicitor).

The defendant must be present at the arraignment in order to enter a plea. If the defendant fails to attend court on the date fixed for the trial, a bench warrant for the defendant's arrest will be issued. The court also has a discretion to proceed with the trial in the absence of the defendant. In *R v Jones* [2002] 2 WLR 524, the defendants had pleaded not guilty on arraignment but absconded before the date fixed for the trial. The judge (after a number of adjournments) decided to try them in their absence. It was held by the House of Lords that the discretion to commence a trial in the absence of the defendant should be exercised with the utmost care and caution, and if the absence is attributable to involuntary illness or incapacity it will very rarely, if ever, be right to do so, at any rate unless the defendant is represented and has asked that the trial should begin. The House of Lords went on to say that it is generally desirable that a defendant be represented even if he has voluntarily absconded. Trial judges should therefore ask counsel to continue to represent a defendant who has absconded and counsel should normally accede to such an invitation and defend their absent client as best they properly can in the circumstances.

If the defendant pleads guilty to some charges but not guilty to others, the sentencing on the offences to which there was a guilty plea will usually be postponed until the trial of the charges on which there was a not guilty plea has been concluded.

11.2.1 Procedure on a plea of guilty

If the defendant pleads guilty to all the counts on the indictment, the prosecution will summarise the facts of the offence(s) and tell the court about the defendant's antecedents, that is basic details about his or her life (education, employment, income, etc) based on what the defendant has told the police, together with details of any relevant previous convictions. The court will in fact have a complete list of the defendant's previous convictions, but will invite the prosecution to read out only those that are relevant, which will usually mean fairly recent ones. See para 28 of the Consolidating Practice Direction [2001] 1 WLR 2870.

11.2.2 The *Newton* hearing

In some cases, the defendant may plead guilty to an offence but on a factual basis that is less serious than the version of events put forward by the prosecution. The procedure to be adopted by the court in such a case was laid down in *R v Newton* (1982) 77 Cr App R 13 (dealt with extensively in para D18.2 of *Blackstone's Criminal Practice*).

According to *Newton*, where the defendant pleads guilty but there is a significant difference between prosecution version and defence version (significant in the sense of being likely to have an effect on the sentence imposed by the court), the court must either accept the defence version of events or else hear evidence (in a *Newton* hearing) about what happened and then make a finding of fact. In other words, in a case where there is a significant factual dispute, the court cannot accept the prosecution version of events without having first heard evidence to support that version.

For example, in *R v McFarlane* (1995) 16 Cr App R (S) 315, the defendant was charged with assault occasioning actual bodily harm. He pleaded guilty. The prosecution alleged that he had jabbed his wife in the face with a fork and had repeatedly punched her about the face. He admitted assaulting her but claimed that he had not jabbed her in the face with a fork and said that he had slapped her (and not punched her).

The course of action set out in *Newton* should be followed unless the defence story may fairly be described as 'incredible' (*R v Hawkins* (1985) 7 Cr App R (S) 351).

Where a *Newton* hearing takes place, the judge must be satisfied beyond reasonable doubt before accepting the prosecution version of events (*R v Kerrigan* (1993) 14 Cr App R (S) 179).

Where the judge does hold a *Newton* hearing, the Court of Appeal will not interfere with the judge's findings of fact unless no reasonable judge could reach those findings based on the evidence heard (*R v Ahmed* (1984) 80 Cr App R 295; *R v Wood* [1991] Crim LR 926).

If the judge wrongly accepts the prosecution version of events without having held a *Newton* hearing, the Court of Appeal will give the defendant the benefit of the doubt and will replace the sentence imposed by the judge with the sentence that would have been appropriate on the basis of the version of events put forward by the defendant (*R v Mohun* (1993) 14 Cr App R (S) 5).

In *R v Tolera* [1999] 1 Cr App R 29 the Court of Appeal emphasised the responsibility of defence counsel to make sure that the court is alerted to any significant difference between prosecution and defence versions of the facts.

In *Newton*, the Court of Appeal suggested an alternative way of resolving a dispute of fact on a guilty plea — by empanelling a jury to decide the issue. That method is only appropriate where the difference between the prosecution version and the defence version amounts (in effect) to an allegation by the prosecution that the defendant committed an additional offence. For example, in *R v Gandy* (1989) 11 Cr App R (S) 564 the defendant was charged with violent disorder. The prosecution alleged that he had thrown a glass at someone (who lost an eye as a result). The defendant denied throwing the glass. The Court of Appeal noted that this dispute could (indeed should) have been resolved by adding a count alleging wounding with intent (Offences Against the Person Act 1861, s 18) or a count alleging unlawful wounding (s 20 of the 1861 Act). Another example is *R v Eubank* [2002] 1 Cr App R (S) 4, [2001] EWCA Crim 891. In that case, the defendant was charged with robbery. The prosecution alleged that the accused had brandished a firearm, but he denied this fact. The judge held a *Newton* hearing to resolve the dispute about whether or not the accused had been in possession of a gun at the time of the robbery. The Court of Appeal held that this dispute should have been resolved by adding a firearms charge to the indictment and empanelling a jury to try that count. Indeed, the failure to do so meant that the accused had been deprived of his right to jury trial in respect of that allegation. An example of a case where it was wrong to empanel a jury is *R v Dowdall* (1992) 13 Cr App R (S) 441. The dispute in that case was whether the theft of a pension book (which the defendant admitted) was theft by finding or theft by taking the book from the victim's bag. The judge resolved the dispute by amending the indictment to contain one count alleging theft by finding and a second count alleging theft from the victim's bag. The Court of Appeal held that this was inappropriate, as both allegations were in law the same, namely theft.

11.2.3   Prosecution offering no evidence; leaving counts on the file

If the defendant pleads not guilty to some or all of the counts on the indictment, the next stage (which will take place some time after the hearing) is to empanel a jury. However, it may be that new evidence has come to light showing that the wrong person has been charged or considerably weakening the case against this defendant, or it may be that a vital witness has refused to testify (and although a person can be compelled to give evidence, a reluctant witness nearly always does more harm than good). In that case the prosecution will offer no evidence against the defendant, in which case a finding of not guilty is entered under the Criminal Justice Act 1967, s 17. An alternative to offering no evidence is for the prosecution to ask the judge to direct that one or more counts be left on the file marked 'not to be proceeded with without the leave of the Crown Court or the Court of Appeal'. The advantage of this is that if the prosecution obtain a conviction on another count but the defendant successfully appeals against that conviction, the prosecution could (with leave) proceed on the other counts. Leaving a count on the file is not an acquittal, whereas if the prosecution offers no evidence this does result in an acquittal. The prosecution may adopt this course where the defendant pleads guilty to some counts but not guilty to others, and the prosecution is content for the defendant to be dealt with solely on the basis of the counts to which he has pleaded guilty. The counts which have been left on the file would not be reactivated save in very unusual circumstances (for example, where the Court of Appeal sets aside the guilty pleas because the pleas were entered under duress).

11.2.4   Plea of guilty to an alternative offence: 'plea bargaining'

If there are several counts on the indictment, the defendant might be willing to plead guilty to some but not to others. If that is acceptable to the prosecution, the counts to which the defendant pleads not guilty are either 'left on the file' or else the prosecution offers no evidence in respect of those counts. Furthermore, the Criminal Law Act 1967 (CLA), s 6(1)(b) provides that the defendant may plead not guilty to the offence on the indictment but guilty to a lesser offence of which the jury would be able to convict him or her under the CLA 1967, s 6(3). For example, the offence of robbery is committed by a person who commits theft together with actual or threatened violence. If the accused admits the theft but denies the use or threat of violence, a plea of 'not guilty to robbery but guilty to theft' could be offered. In *R v Yeardley* [2000] 1 QB 374 it was held that where the defendant pleads not guilty to the offence on the indictment but guilty to a lesser offence, the guilty plea becomes a nullity if the prosecution choose to proceed with the offence on the indictment. The obvious solution is to add the lesser offence to the indictment.

11.2.5   Different pleas from different defendants

If there is more than one defendant and one pleads guilty and the others not guilty, it is a matter for the judge whether to sentence the one who has pleaded guilty immediately or at the end of the trial of the others. The argument in favour of postponing sentence is that, at the end of the trial, the judge will have a much better idea of who did what. However, it is a little more difficult if the defendant who pleads guilty also indicates a willingness to 'turn Queen's evidence', giving evidence against his or her co-defendants. This will attract a very substantial discount in sentence, well beyond the one-third normally credited to those who simply plead guilty. Such a person becomes a competent witness for the Crown after pleading guilty. However, if sentence is postponed, it may seem that the sentence imposed after the defendant has given evidence depends more on the quality of the evidence given than on the defendant's guilt; on the other hand if the defendant is sentenced before giving evidence, then he or she may have a change of mind and the lenient sentence given on the basis of the promised testimony cannot be altered (see *R v Stone* [1970] 1 WLR 1112). The Court of Appeal in *R v Weekes* (1980) 74 Cr App R 161 said that sentence should normally be postponed until after the trial of the other defendant. However, in *R v Clement* The Times, 12 December 1991 the court observed that it is a matter for the judge whether the defendant is sentenced sooner or later.

If one defendant pleads guilty but another pleads not guilty, the jury should not be told about the guilty plea of the other defendant (unless, of course, that defendant gives evidence for the prosecution). For example, in *R v Manzur and Mahmood* [1997] 1 Cr App R 414, three people had been charged with rape. One defendant pleaded guilty, the other two pleaded not guilty, saying that the victim had consented to sexual intercourse. The judge allowed the jury to be told of the third defendant's plea of guilty. The Court of Appeal accepted the argument that the jury might have taken the view, on the basis of the third defendant's guilty plea, that the two appellants must have known that the victim was not consenting and so might not have given proper consideration to the evidence of the two appellants that they believed the woman to be consenting to intercourse. The admission of the evidence of the plea of the third defendant was therefore unduly prejudicial to the appellants and so a retrial was ordered.

11.2.6 The ambiguous plea

If the defendant pleads guilty but then advances mitigation which amounts to a defence, then the plea is ambiguous (eg the defendant was guilty of theft but thought that the property was his or her own). In those circumstances, the law will be explained to the defendant, who will then be asked to plead again. If the plea remains ambiguous, a plea of not guilty will be entered on behalf of the defendant and a trial will take place in the usual way.

Sometimes a defendant will say to counsel, 'I didn't do it but I want to plead guilty to get things over and done with quickly'. In such a case, counsel should try to dissuade the client from pleading guilty to an offence that he or she denies. In particular, it should be pointed out that nothing can be said in mitigation which suggests innocence (since that would render the plea ambiguous) or even remorse (one cannot be remorseful for something one denies doing).

11.2.7 Seeing the judge in chambers

Paragraph 45 of *Practice Direction (criminal: consolidated)* [2002] 3 All ER 904 states that any discussion with the judge must involve the advocates on both sides. If counsel is instructed by a solicitor who is in court, the solicitor should also be allowed to attend the discussion. These sort of discussions may be appropriate where counsel wishes to communicate matters which, in the interests of the defendant, ought not to be mentioned in open court. The *Practice Direction* gives the example of when an advocate, by way of mitigation, wishes to tell the judge that the accused has not got long to live because he is suffering from cancer, a fact of which he is and should remain ignorant. An example more likely to be encountered is when the advocates wish to discuss with the judge whether it would be proper, in the particular case, for the prosecution to accept a plea to a lesser offence.

The *Practice Direction* goes on to make it clear that the judge should, subject to one exception, never indicate the sentence he is minded to impose. The only exception is that it is permissible for a judge to say (where appropriate) that, whether the accused pleads guilty or not guilty, the sentence will or will not take a particular form. Where any such discussion on sentence has taken place, the advocate for the defence should disclose it to the accused and inform him of what took place.

Such discussions with the judge should be recorded either by a tape recorder or a shorthand writer.

These principles flow from *R v Turner* [1970] 2 QB 321. The Court of Appeal has regularly repeated the importance of complying with these guidelines (see, for example, *R v Ryan* (1999) 163 JP 849 and *R v Dosseter* [1999] 2 Cr App R (S) 248). These cases make it clear that visits to the judge should only occur in exceptional circumstances. It should also be noted that if the judge does give an indication as to likely sentence, that indication will be binding on the judge who passes sentence even if that is not the same judge who gave the original indication. If a defendant does change his or her plea in light of an indication as to likely sentence, and the sentence imposed is more severe than indicated, the Court of Appeal will often (though not invariably) feel constrained to reduce the sentence to that indicated, even if the indicated sentence was lower than that merited by the offence.

The same issues arose yet again in *R v Nazham* [2004] EWCA Crim 491. The appeal in that case related to a conversation which took place, between counsel and the judge, in the judge's chambers before the defendants changed their pleas to guilty. The defendants argued that their convictions were unsafe because, when the conversation was relayed to them by their respective counsel, it fettered their freedom of choice as to their plea. The judge had said to counsel that, 'this has got plea written all over it and bags of credit'; that even though the case was listed for trial, a plea would still attract credit; that a plea would make for a shorter term of imprisonment, ie a term of less than four years; he added that, 'At the end of the day they know whether they are guilty or not you know and they have got an eye for a deal, I would have thought'. The Court of Appeal held that the judge should not have said what he did in his room, but the indication which he gave as to the sentence he was minded to impose in the event of a plea of guilty (which was all that was conveyed to the appellants by their counsel) did not improperly inhibit their freedom of choice, or give rise to any injustice, apparent or real. The Court added that nothing in the judgement was intended to detract from the advice given in *R v Turner* and in paragraph 45.4 of the *Practice Direction*. However, proof of such an irregularity on the part of the trial judge is not necessarily sufficient for the conviction to be quashed on appeal. The Court of Appeal seemed to be taking a very strict line in this case. It should perhaps be borne in mind that the most important things for the trial judge to avoid are (a) giving an indication that the sentence will take a different form depending on whether the defendant pleads guilty or is found guilty (eg a custodial sentence if found guilty, a community sentence if a plea of guilty), or (b) indicating that the defendants are likely to be found guilty by a jury. Merely saying that the sentence will be shorter is simply confirming what counsel will already know (and will doubtless have told the client), that a guilty plea attracts a discount (usually of about one-third). See also *R v Nazham* [2004] EWCA Crim 491.

11.3   The jury

11.3.1   Who can serve?

Prior to the amendment of the Juries Act 1974 by the CJA 2003, some people were ineligible to serve on a jury. This category included the judiciary (including lay magistrates), lawyers, those concerned in the administration of justice (for example, police officers, prison officers, probation officers), the clergy, and the mentally disordered. Other people had the right to be excused from jury service if they so wished. This category included those aged 65 or over, those who have served on a jury within the last two years, members of Parliament, full time serving members of the armed forces, and medical personnel (such as doctors, dentists, nurses and vets). CJA 2003, Sch 33 amends the Juries Act 1974, s 1 and s 9, and abolishes (except in the case of mentally disordered persons) the categories of people who are ineligible for, or entitled to be excused as of right from, jury service. Thus, the bar on the judiciary, those concerned with the administration of justice, and the clergy, is lifted; similarly, the entitlement to refuse to serve as jurors enjoyed by people over 65, members of Parliament, medical professionals and members of certain religious bodies, is removed. Under the amended version of s 1, 'every person shall be qualified to serve as a juror in the Crown Court . . . and be liable accordingly to attend for jury service when summoned under this Act' if on the electoral roll and neither mentally disordered or disqualified from jury service because of previous convictions.

New rules

Disqualification as a result of previous convictions is dealt with by the Juries Act 1974, Sch 1, Part 2 (as amended by CJA 2003). The following people are disqualified from jury service:

- a person who is on bail in criminal proceedings at the relevant time;
- a person who has at any time been sentenced in the United Kingdom to imprisonment or detention for life, to detention during her Majesty's pleasure, to imprisonment or detention for public protection, to an extended sentence under CJA 2003, s 227 or s 228, or to a term of imprisonment or detention of five years or more;
- a person who at any time in the last ten years has, in the United Kingdom, served any part of a sentence of imprisonment or detention, or has had passed on him a suspended sentence of imprisonment or detention;
- a person who at any time in the last ten years has, in England and Wales, had made in respect of him a community order under CJA 2003, s 177, a community rehabilitation order, a community punishment order, a community punishment and rehabilitation order, a drug treatment and testing order or a drug abstinence order.

The CJA 2003 repeals Juries Act 1974, s 9(1), which enabled some people to be 'excused as of right' from jury service. The effect of this is that no-one is entitled to refuse to do jury service. However:

- s 9(2) of the Juries Act 1974 provides that a person who has been summoned for jury service may seek excusal if they can show a 'good reason' for this; and
- s 9A(1) enables a person summoned for jury service to seek deferral of the summons (and so, if the dates specified in the summons clash with the person's holiday arrangements or business commitments, attendance can be deferred to a later date).

The discretion to excuse or defer is exercised by the Jury Central Summoning Bureau (JCSB) (part of the Lord Chancellor's Department) which administers the jury summoning system on behalf of the Crown Court in England and Wales. The JCSB works on the basis that deferral is always preferable to excusal.

Section 9B of the Juries Act 1974 enables a person to be excused from jury service because he or she is not capable of acting effectively as a juror because of a physical disability. Para 42 of *Practice Direction (Criminal Proceedings: Consolidation)* [2002] 1 WLR 2870 states:

42.1   Jury service is an important public duty which individual members of the public are chosen at random to undertake. The normal presumption is that . . . he or she will be required to serve when summoned to do so. There will, however, be circumstances where a juror should be excused, for

[handwritten: may be excused if]

instance where he is personally concerned in the facts of the particular case or is closely connected with a party or prospective witness.

42.2   He may also be excused on grounds of personal hardship or conscientious objection to jury service. Each such application should be dealt with sensitively and sympathetically.

42.3   Any person who appeals to the court against a refusal by the appropriate officer to excuse him from jury service must be given an opportunity to make representations in support of his appeal.

It is likely this part of the *Practice Direction* will have to be amended to reflect the changes made by the Criminal Justice Act 2003 and the change in ethos, whereby deferral is to be regarded as preferable to excusal.

11.3.2   Empanelling the jury

[handwritten: defendant has the right to challenge jurors before they are sworn.]

A number of potential jurors come into the courtroom. The clerk reads out the names of 12 of them, selected randomly from the list of those present. The 12 go into the jury box. The clerk will also explain to the defendant that the list of names about to be called out will form the jury which will try him or her but that he or she has the right to challenge jurors before they are sworn.

11.3.3   Challenging potential jurors

There are two main types of challenge.

11.3.3.1   Stand by   *[handwritten: Prosecution only - does not have to give a reason]*

The first type of challenge is the right of the prosecution to stand a juror by. Just as the juror starts to take the oath, the prosecuting counsel says 'Stand by'. The judge will then explain to that juror that he or she cannot sit on this jury but may be required to sit on another one. This challenge is confined to the prosecution, and prosecuting counsel does not have to give any reasons for the challenge. The fact that the prosecution would seem to have an advantage over the defence (who no longer have any right of peremptory challenge) led the Attorney-General to issue guidelines on the related issues of use of the stand by and jury vetting (see Appendix 4 to *Blackstone's Criminal Practice* for the full text). In many cases there will be no check at all on potential jurors. However, in ordinary cases the names of the potential jurors may be put through the Police National Computer to see if any have previous convictions which mean that they are disqualified from jury service or are unsuitable to serve on this particular jury. In cases involving national security and terrorism, however, a more thorough check is carried out, with use being made of Special Branch files. Unsuitable jurors can then simply be stood by. Another case where use of the stand by is appropriate, according to the Guidelines, is where the person is manifestly unsuitable to sit on this jury, and the defence agrees that he or she should not sit. An example might be the person who is clearly unable to read the words on the card which contains the jury oath and so is unsuitable for a case which involves perusal of documentary evidence.

It should be noted that the judge also has power to stand a juror by, but this power is exercised only very rarely. Some judges had used it (at the request of the defence) to try to secure a racially balanced jury so that some members shared the defendant's ethnic origin. However, in *R v Ford* [1989] QB 868 the Court of Appeal ruled that this practice was unlawful. *Ford* was followed in *R v Smith* [2003] EWCA Crim 283, [2003] 1 WLR 2229 where a black defendant was tried by an all white jury with causing serious injury to a white victim. It was held that the jury-summoning procedure in the Juries Act 1974 is not inconsistent with Article 6 of the European Convention on Human Rights. The court said that it is neither unfair that a black defendant is tried by a randomly selected all white jury, nor would a fair-minded and informed observer consider it unfair. The court added that consideration of the evidence in the present case did not require knowledge of the traditions or social circumstances of a particular racial group (even though there was a racial element to the offence); rather it was a common situation of violence outside a club. Similarly, in *R v Tarrant* [1998] Crim LR 342, it was held that the judge cannot use his discretion to discharge individual jurors so as to interfere with the composition of the jury panel by selecting jurors from outside the court's catchment area, in order to minimise the risk of intimidation.

11.3.3.2   Challenge for cause

The other important form of challenge (and the only one open to the defence) is the challenge for cause. This challenge is used in cases where it is suspected that a potential juror might be biased. It should be remembered that although the names of potential jurors are available for inspection by the prosecution and defence, it is unlikely that any checks will have been carried out apart from the check for previous convictions carried out by the prosecution. The defence is unlikely to have information to show that a particular juror is biased (unless the defendant happens to recognise the person in question). Further (and this is different from the position in the United States) no questions may be asked of a potential juror unless the challenging party has already established a prima facie case that the person is likely to be biased (see *R v Chandler* [1964] 2 QB 322). An example of how this operates may be seen in the trial of the Kray brothers, presided over by Lawton J. A national newspaper had published a colourful account of the allegations against the Krays. The judge was persuaded that anyone who had read this material might well be biased against the defendants. He therefore allowed the defence to ask each juror whether he or she had read the material in question. If the juror said yes, that person was then successfully challenged. However, a more restrictive view was taken by the Court of Appeal in *R v Andrews* [1999] Crim LR 156. The appellant claimed that her conviction for murder was unsafe because of adverse pre-trial publicity. It was argued on her behalf that potential jurors should have been asked whether they had read or heard the reports in question. It was held that such questioning of jurors (whether done orally or by means of a questionnaire) is of doubtful efficacy and may even be counter-productive (by reminding the jurors of the publicity); it should therefore only be done in the most exceptional circumstances. In *Montgomery v HM Advocate; Coulter v HM Advocate* [2001] 2 WLR 779, the Privy Council (hearing a Scottish appeal) held that where there has been prejudicial pre-trial publicity, the court is entitled to expect the jury to follow the directions which they receive from the trial judge and to return a true verdict based only on the evidence they have heard in court. On that basis, a defendant may be regarded as having received a fair trial even if there has been adverse pre-trial publicity. The Court of Appeal took the same view in *R v Stone* [2001] Crim LR 465.

To challenge for cause, counsel merely says 'challenge' before the juror takes the oath. If it is a straightforward case (eg the juror knows the defendant), counsel will simply state that this is the case and the judge will ask that person to leave the jury box. If it is more complicated, the jurors who have already been sworn and the rest of the potential jurors (the 'jury in waiting') will be asked to leave court and counsel will have to explain the basis of the challenge and (if the judge so directs) question the challenged juror.

In *R v Gough* [1993] AC 646 the House of Lords held that the test where bias is alleged is whether there is a 'real danger' that the juror is biased. In *Porter v Magill* [2002] 2 AC 357, the House of Lords said that the test is whether a fair-minded and informed observer

[handwritten margin note: wife of a prison officer as juror]

would conclude that there was a real possibility of bias on the part of the tribunal. See also *R v Wilson* [1995] Crim LR 952, where convictions were quashed (and retrials ordered) because one of the jurors was the wife of a prison officer serving at the prison where the appellants had been held on remand. The Court of Appeal said that the test is one of *possibility* of bias rather than *probability* of bias and so it was not necessary to inquire into the juror's actual state of mind. There was a real danger that, consciously or not, she may have been biased against the appellants.

11.3.3.3   Replacement of juror after successful challenge

When a juror has been stood by or successfully challenged, he or she is replaced by another member of the jury in waiting.

11.3.4   Discharge of jurors

11.3.4.1   Discharge of individual jurors during the trial

A jury always starts off with 12 jurors. However, under the Juries Act 1974, s 16, up to three jurors may be discharged during the course of the trial in case of illness or other necessity (eg bereavement).

What constitutes necessity is a matter for the trial judge. In *R v Hanberry* [1977] QB 924 a juror was discharged because the trial went on longer than expected and she would otherwise have had to cancel a holiday.

If more than three jurors can no longer serve the trial has to be abandoned; a fresh trial will take place later.

11.3.4.2   Discharge of entire jury

The entire jury may be discharged if, for example:

(a) The jury hears evidence that is inadmissible and prejudicial to the defendant; where evidence that is prejudicial to the defendant has inadvertently been adduced, it is not automatically the case that the jury should be discharged, since in some instances a direction to the jury to ignore the inadmissible evidence might be sufficient (*R v Weaver* [1968] 1 QB 353). Whether or not the jury should be discharged is a matter for the discretion of the trial judge. The test to be applied is the test for bias, namely whether there is a real danger of injustice occurring because the jury, having heard the prejudicial matter, may be biased (*R v Docherty* [1999] 1 Cr App R 274).

(b) The jury cannot agree on a verdict (see **11.13.5** below).

(c) An individual juror has to be discharged and there is a risk that he or she may have contaminated the rest of the jury (eg, because he or she knows that the defendant has previous convictions or is facing further trials for other offences — see, for example, *R v Hutton* (1990) Crim LR 875). Where a juror has specialised knowledge of something relevant to the case against the defendant, and has communicated that knowledge to the rest of the jury, who have then come to a verdict, the judge is obliged to discharge the jury since the defendant has had no opportunity to challenge what amounts to new evidence or to put forward his or her own explanation (*R v Fricker* The Times, 13 July 1999).

If members of the jury misbehave during the course of the trial, the jury should be discharged if there is a 'real danger of prejudice' to the accused (*R v Spencer* [1987] AC 128).

In *R v Sawyer* (1980) 71 Cr App R 283, for example, some jurors were seen in conversation with prosecution witnesses during an adjournment. The trial judge questioned them and it transpired that the conversation had been on subjects unconnected with the trial. The decision of the judge not to discharge the jury was upheld by the Court of Appeal.

Where the jury is discharged from giving a verdict, the defendant can be retried, as he or she is not regarded as having been acquitted.

11.3.5 Start of the trial

Once the jury has been empanelled, the trial begins with the clerk reading out the indictment and telling the jury that the defendant has pleaded not guilty. The jury is then told, 'It is your charge to say, having heard the evidence, whether he [or she] be guilty or not'.

11.4 Change of plea

The defendant may change his or her plea from not guilty to guilty at any stage of the trial before the jury has returned a verdict. The defence simply asks for the indictment to be put again and the defendant pleads guilty. The jury usually returns a formal verdict of guilty; however, in *R v Poole* [2002] 1 WLR 1528, the Court of Appeal held that where a defendant pleads not guilty but then changes the plea to guilty during the course of the trial, there is no requirement that the judge should ask the jury for a formal verdict of guilty. It is permissible for the judge to discharge the jury and proceed to sentencing (though many judges will doubtless continue to ask the jury for a formal verdict).

The defendant can change his or her plea from guilty to not guilty at any stage of the trial prior to the passing of sentence, but only at the discretion of the judge. The judge will want some explanation for the change of heart and may take into account matters such as the legal advice the accused has received, his or her age and level of intellect, and experience of criminal proceedings. See *R v Dodd* (1981) 74 Cr App R 50; *S v Recorder of Manchester* [1971] AC 481. Permission to withdraw the guilty plea is unlikely to be given unless the defendant did not realise that he had a defence when he pleaded guilty (*R v McNally* [1954] 1 WLR 933). In *R v Sheikh* [2004] EWCA Crim 492; [2004] 2 Cr App R 13, the defendants applied to withdraw their pleas of guilty. The basis of their application was that they had not been informed that they could be made the subject of confiscation proceedings in the event of conviction. The trial judge refused to allow a change of plea, and the Court of Appeal upheld the refusal. The Court said that it is well accepted that, quite apart from cases where the plea of guilty is equivocal or ambiguous, the court retains a residual discretion to allow the withdrawal of a guilty plea where not to do so might work an injustice. Examples might be where a defendant has been misinformed about the nature of the charge or the availability of a defence or where he has been put under pressure to plead guilty in circumstances where he is not truly admitting guilt. Commonly, however, it is reserved for cases where there is doubt that the plea represents a genuine acknowledgement of guilt. The possibility of confiscation proceedings taking place could not, of itself, have any bearing upon their acceptance of guilt. In *R v Drew* [1985] 1 WLR 914, Lord Lane CJ (at 923c) said that it would be appropriate in only rare cases to allow a defendant to change an unequivocal plea of guilty to one of not guilty. Particularly this is so in cases where the accused has been advised by experienced counsel.

11.5   The prosecution case

After the indictment has been read to the jury, counsel for the prosecution opens the Crown's case:

May it please your Honour [or your Lordship, if a High Court judge or sitting at the Old Bailey], members of the jury, I appear to prosecute and my learned friend Miss Green appears for the accused.

11.5.1   The opening speech

The purpose of the prosecution opening speech is to give the jury an overview of the prosecution case. The jury will be reminded of the charge(s) which the defendant faces, which should be explained in everyday language. Counsel will probably tell the jury what witnesses will be called by the prosecution and what it is hoped they will establish. Counsel will also mention the burden of proof and the standard of proof, and make it clear that anything said about the law is subject to what the judge will say in the summing-up.

If counsel for the defence takes the view that an objection should be taken to the admissibility of some of the evidence which the prosecution will be calling (as disclosed to the defence in the bundle of committal statements, together with any notice of additional evidence), but no ruling on admissibility was sought at the preliminary hearing, then he or she should inform counsel for the prosecution. The prosecutor will then omit any reference to the disputed material from the opening speech. The judge will then be asked to rule on the admissibility of the evidence at the appropriate moment (see **11.5.2.4**). It may be, however, that the disputed evidence is such an important part of the prosecution case that an opening speech would make no sense if no reference were to be made to that evidence; for example, the only evidence against the defendant is a confession, the admissibility of which is disputed. In that case, once the jury has been empanelled, the judge will be informed (either by the prosecution or the defence) that a ruling on a matter of law is needed at the outset. The jury will be sent out of the court and counsel will then seek the judge's ruling on the admissibility of the evidence. If the judge rules the evidence inadmissible, the prosecution will almost certainly have little option but to offer no evidence (see **11.2.3** above), in which case the jury will be called back into court and directed to acquit the defendant.

11.5.2   The prosecution evidence

At the conclusion of the opening speech, prosecuting counsel calls the evidence. It is the rule that the prosecution must call all the witnesses whose evidence was included in the bundle of statements sent to the magistrates' court in the committal proceedings (or as part of the transfer procedure applicable to indictable-only offences). If one witness is expected to duplicate the evidence of another (eg the second police officer present at an interview with the accused), the prosecution may 'tender' that second witness for cross-examination. This means that the witness is called into the witness box by counsel for the prosecution and having been identified and his or her relevance to the case established, he or she will be told to stay there in case the defence has any questions. The only exceptions to the rule that the prosecution must call (or tender for cross-examination) all the witnesses whose evidence was used in the committal proceedings are those set out in *R v Armstrong* [1995] 3 All ER 831:

- the defence has consented to the written statement of that witness being read to the court;

- counsel for the prosecution takes the view that the evidence of that witness is no longer credible; or
- counsel for the prosecution takes the view that the witness would so fundamentally contradict the prosecution case that it would make more sense for that person to be called as a witness by the defence.

The other side of the coin is that the prosecution can *only* call as witnesses people whose evidence was used at committal proceedings (or the equivalent under the transfer procedure for indictable-only offences) or whose statements have been disclosed to the defence by way of notice of additional evidence. The notice of additional evidence procedure is used wherever the prosecution wants to use evidence which was not before the examining justices (or not available when indictable-only offences are transferred to the Crown Court). A copy of the witness statement is served on the defence along with a notice saying that the prosecution will be adducing the evidence of this witness at trial. The statement can be tendered in evidence (ie read to the court) unless the defence objects within seven days of the service of the notice, in which case the prosecution must either abandon that evidence or call the maker of the statement as a witness at the trial. There is no time limit within which a notice of additional evidence must be served, but if it is served just before the trial, so that the defence has had insufficient time to adjust its preparation in the light of the new evidence, then the judge should grant an adjournment. (For the position on disclosure of *unused* material, see **Chapter 9**.)

11.5.2.1 Taking evidence from the witnesses

Each witness called by the prosecution, having taken the oath (or affirmed) to 'tell the truth, the whole truth and nothing but the truth', is examined in chief by counsel for the prosecution (unless that witness is only being tendered for cross-examination) and may produce (ie identify) items of real evidence which then become exhibits in the case. Counsel must take great care not to lead the witness on matters which are contentious — if in doubt, ask your opponent if he or she will let you lead on specified matters.

Each witness is then subject to cross-examination by the defence. Cross-examination is not limited to matters arising from the examination-in-chief, but must be relevant to the issues arising in the case. The cross-examination is followed by re-examination by the prosecution; the rule against leading questions applies to re-examination and the questions must arise out of the cross-examination.

For the position on memory-refreshing documents, see the ***Evidence Manual***.

In summary, under CJA 2003, s 139(1), witnesses may, whilst giving evidence, refresh their memory from documents made or verified by them at an earlier time if they testify that the document records their recollection of the matter at that earlier time, and that their recollection of the matter is likely to have been significantly better at that time than it is at the time of the oral evidence. CJA 2003, s 139(2), allows a witness to refresh their memory from the transcript of a sound recording in the same circumstances.

11.5.2.2 Formal admissions

If the defendant pleads not guilty, that puts the prosecution to proof of each and every element of the offence(s) on the indictment to which a plea of not guilty has been entered. The only exception to this is where the defence has made a formal admission under the Criminal Justice Act 1967, s 10. This provides that either party in a criminal case (though it is usually the defence) may admit any fact which would otherwise be in issue and this admission is conclusive evidence of the fact admitted. This admission may be made orally in court (by counsel) or in writing signed by the person making it, in which case the document will be read to the jury (but note that in the magistrates' court the formal admission must be in writing).

11.5.2.3   Reading witness statements

Formal admissions are not in fact very common. Usually, where evidence is not disputed by the defence, it will consent to the prosecution reading out the written statement of the witness who provides the uncontroversial evidence (eg the loser of stolen property where the defence case is not that the property was not stolen but rather that the defendant was not the thief). If a witness says some things which are not disputed by the defence but others which are, that witness will have to give oral evidence (since it would not be appropriate for the written statement to be read to the court) and it will no doubt become apparent from the cross-examination by the defence which parts of that witness's evidence are disputed by the defence.

When the written statement of a witness is read to the court with the consent of the defence, the judge should explain to the jury that the contents of the witness statement are not in dispute and so the defence has consented to the statement being read to the jury without the maker having to attend court, thus saving time and money. The jury should be told that the evidence is just as good as evidence given 'live'. Counsel, in reading the statement, must read out the declaration signed by the maker of the statement, that it is true to the best of that person's knowledge and belief and is made knowing that a prosecution may be brought if the statement contains anything which the maker knows or believes to be false.

The main instances where a statement may be read to the jury without the consent of the defence are those set out in the Criminal Justice Act 1988, s 23 (see the *Evidence Manual*). In summary, this applies where a witness does not testify because of fear. In order to satisfy the requirements of s 23, the court must hear oral evidence (for example, from a police officer) as to the fear of the witness (*R v Belmarsh Magistrates' Court, ex p Gilligan* [1998] 1 Cr App R 14, following *Neill v North Antrim Magistrates' Court* [1992] 4 All ER 846).

Where a statement has been read to the jury without the consent of the defence, the jury must be warned to use particular care when considering that witness statement, since the maker of the statement was not in court to be cross-examined as to its contents. Where the witness statement is vital to the prosecution case, failure to give such a direction will render any subsequent conviction unsafe (*R v Curry* The Times, 23 March 1998).

11.5.2.4   Defence objections to prosecution evidence

If counsel for the prosecution agrees with the defence suggestion made before the start of the trial that certain evidence is inadmissible, the prosecutor should (via the Crown Prosecution Service representative or the police officer in charge of the case) warn the relevant witness not to give that particular evidence. If this involves evidence which will come into the possession of the jury (eg interview notes which count as real evidence and may be exhibited and so handed to the jury), this evidence may well have to be edited. In accordance with *Practice Direction (criminal: consolidated)* [2002] 3 All ER 904, para 24, this should be done after consultation between both counsel and the judge.

If, however, the prosecution does not accept that the evidence in question is inadmissible, the question of admissibility may be dealt with at the pre-trial hearing, at which the judge is empowered to give binding rulings on the admissibility of evidence. Otherwise, the objection is made (in the absence of the jury) during the course of the trial. If the objection is made during the course of the trial, the prosecution evidence is called in the usual way until the part of the evidence to which there is objection is reached. At that point the jury is invited to retire to the jury room.

Although s 82 of PACE 1984 expressly preserves the common law rules on the admissibility of evidence, objections to prosecution evidence are usually made under PACE 1984, s76 (which applies only to confessions) or s 78 (which applies to all prosecution evidence).

Where the defence invokes s 76 and alleges that a confession has been obtained by oppression or in circumstances likely to render it unreliable, the prosecution must prove beyond reasonable doubt that the confession was not so obtained. The requirement for the prosecution to prove this means that they must call evidence on the point and so a *voir dire* ('trial within a trial') takes place.

Unless the witness is in the middle of giving (or has already given) evidence in the course of the trial, a witness giving evidence on a *voir dire* takes a special form of oath: 'I swear by almighty God that I will answer truthfully all such questions as the court may ask.'

Each prosecution witness called in the *voir dire* may be cross-examined by the defence. When the relevant prosecution witnesses have given evidence, the defence may call evidence (including the evidence of the defendant himself); each defence witness may be cross-examined by the prosecution.

After the evidence has been called, both counsel may address the judge and the judge then rules on the admissibility of the confession. In *Mitchell v The Queen* [1998] AC 695, it was held by the Privy Council that where a judge conducts a *voir dire* and holds that a confession is admissible, the judge should not tell the jury of the ruling (the trial should simply continue with the prosecution leading evidence of the confession). If the judge indicates that he has ruled against the accused, this might lead the jury to think that the judge does not believe the accused.

The only question to be determined under s 76 is *how* the confession was obtained. It is wholly irrelevant whether the confession was true or not.

If the defence case is simply that the police have fabricated the confession, this is a matter for the jury to decide and not a question of admissibility. However, there are cases where the defence alleges that the confession has been fabricated but also argues that, even if that was not so, the confession is inadmissible anyway. In *Thongjai v The Queen* [1997] 3 WLR 667, the Privy Council (following *Ajodha v The State* [1982] AC 204) said that if the defendant denies making an oral admission and also alleges that he was ill-treated by the police before or at the time of the alleged admission, the two issues are not mutually exclusive. The judge has to assume that the admission was made and decide whether it is admissible. If (and only if) the judge decides that the evidence is admissible, it is then for the jury to decide whether the admission was in fact made.

If the objection to the prosecution evidence is brought *solely* on the basis of s 78, that it would be unfair to the defence for the evidence to be admitted, the judge may hold a *voir dire* but is not obliged to do so. Such applications can be dealt with on the basis of submissions by counsel if the factual basis for the submissions is agreed between prosecution and defence; for example, the custody record discloses breaches of the Codes of Practice under PACE 1984 and the only question to be determined is whether the evidence thereby obtained should be excluded under s 78. These submissions will, of course, be heard in the absence of the jury. The judge gives a ruling and the trial then proceeds, either with or without the disputed evidence.

It should be noted that if inadmissible evidence is heard by the jury, the judge has to consider whether the prejudicial effect can be cured by an appropriate direction in the summing-up or whether the entire jury should be discharged and a new trial take place.

11.5.3   Special Measures

Sections 16–33 of the Youth Justice and Criminal Evidence Act 1999 contain provision for various 'special measures' which the court can direct in respect of certain witnesses:

- screening the witness from the accused (s 23);
- giving evidence by live link (s 24) [this provision will become less relevant, as s 51 of the Criminal Justice Act 2003 enables a court to authorise witnesses, other than the defendant, to give evidence through a live link in criminal proceedings];
- ordering the removal of wigs and gowns while the witness gives evidence (s 25);
- giving evidence in private, in a sexual case or where there is a fear that the witness may be intimidated (s 26);
- video recording of evidence-in-chief (s 27) [again, this provision is made less relevant, as s 137 of the Criminal Justice Act 2003 extends the circumstances in which evidence-in-chief can take the form of a video-recorded statement];
- video recording of cross-examination and re-examination where the evidence-in-chief of the witness has been video recorded (s 28);
- examination through an intermediary in the case of a young or incapacitated witness (s 29);
- provision of aids to communication for a young or incapacitated witness (s 30).

The procedure for making an application for special measures is contained in the Crown Court (Special Measures Directions and Directions Prohibiting Cross-examination) Rules 2002 (SI 2002/1688). Applications in the magistrates' court are dealt with by the Magistrates Courts (Special Measures Directions) Rules 2002 (SI 2002/1687).

Such applications have to be made in the prescribed form (set out in the Schedule to the Rules). The other parties to the proceedings may then serve notice of opposition to the application. There will then be a hearing to determine the application. The rules also contain provision for applications to vary or discharge a special measures direction (see s 20 of the 1999 Act); such applications must be based on a material change of circumstances since the direction was made. Also, where an application for a special measures direction has been refused by the court, the application may be renewed if there is a material change of circumstances since the court refused the application.

Rule 7 in each set of Rules deals with applications for special measures directions for witnesses to give evidence by means of a live television link. A party who seeks to oppose an application for a child witness to give evidence by means of a live link must state why, in his view, the giving of a special measures direction would not be likely to maximise the quality of the witness's evidence (unless the application relates to a child witness in need of special protection within the meaning of s 21(1)(b) of the 1999 Act, in which case this provision does not apply). Rule 7 goes on to state that, where a special measures direction is made enabling a witness to give evidence by means of a live link, the witness must be accompanied at the live link only by persons acceptable to the court.

Rule 8 in each set of rules deals with video recording of testimony from witnesses. Where an application is made for a special measures direction enabling a video recording of an interview of a witness to be admitted as evidence-in-chief of the witness, the application must be accompanied by the video recording which it is proposed to tender in evidence and must include full details of the circumstances in which the recording was made. Where a party opposes the use of the video recording, he must lodge a notice giving reasons why it would not be in the interests of justice for the recording (or part of it) to be admitted.

s29.
People with
communication
difficulties.

Section 29 of the Youth Justice and Criminal Evidence Act 1999 allows, as part of the special measures provision, for the use of intermediaries to facilitate communication with witnesses with special communication difficulties. Section 29, which was brought into force in February 2004, states that the function of an intermediary is to communicate (a) to the witness, questions put to the witness, (b) to any persons asking such questions, the answers given by the witness in reply to them, and to explain such questions and answers so far as necessary to enable them to be understood by the witness or person in question. Such intermediaries have to be professionally experienced in their own specialist area of communication, and are subject to a Code of Practice and a Code of Ethics. The Crown Court (Special Measures Directions and Directions Prohibiting Cross-examination) (Amendment) Rules 2004 (SI 2004/185) and the Magistrates' Courts (Special Measures Directions) (Amendment) Rules 2004 (SI 2004/184) contain details of the procedural rules for the use of intermediaries.

Part 8 livelink

Part 8 of the Criminal Justice Act 2003 extends the circumstances where live links can be used. A 'live link' (defined in s 56(2)) will usually mean a closed circuit television link, but could apply to any technology with the same effect, such as video conferencing facilities or the internet. Under CJA 2003, s 51(4), a direction that a witness may give evidence through a live link may be given if the court is satisfied that it is in the interests of the efficient or effective administration of justice for the person concerned to give evidence in the proceedings through a live link. Under s 51(6), (7), in deciding whether to give a direction under this section the court must consider all the circumstances of the case, and in particular: the availability of the witness; the need for the witness to attend in person; the importance of the witness's evidence to the proceedings; the views of the witness; the suitability of the facilities at the place where the witness would give evidence through a live link; whether a direction might tend to inhibit any party to the proceedings from effectively testing the witness's evidence. CJA 2003, s 54, empowers the judge to give the jury 'such direction as he thinks necessary to ensure that the jury gives the same weight to the evidence as if it had been given by the witness in the courtroom or other place where the proceedings are held'.

CJA 2003, s 137(1), extends the cases where evidence can be given by means of a video recording. It empowers the court to allow a video recording of an interview with a witness (other than the defendant), or a part of such a recording, to be admitted as evidence in chief of the witness (ie to replace live evidence-in-chief of that witness) provided that the person is called as a witness in proceedings for an offence which is triable only on indictment, or for an either way offence prescribed in regulations made under the section; and the person claims to have witnessed (whether visually or in any other way) events alleged by the prosecution to include conduct constituting the offence or part of the offence, or events that were closely connected with such events; and that person has previously given an account of the events in question; and that account was given at a time when those events were fresh in the person's memory; and a video recording was made of the account.

s137(3) not
in relation to a
defendant

Under s 137(3), such a direction may not be made in relation to a recorded account given by the defendant. In respect of any other person, a direction may be made only if it appears to the court that the witness's recollection of the events in question is likely to have been significantly better when they gave the recorded account than it will be when they give oral evidence, and it is in the interests of justice for the recording to be admitted. In deciding whether it is in the interests of justice, the court must have regard (under s 137(4) to the interval between the time of the events in question and the time when the recorded account was made; any other factors that might affect the reliability of what the witness said in that account; the quality of the recording; and any views of the witness as to whether their evidence-in-chief should be given orally or by means of the recording.

Reporting Directions for youths [handwritten margin note]

The *Crown Court (Reports Relating to Adult Witnesses) Rules 2004* (SI 2004/2420) and the *Magistrates' Courts (Reports Relating to Adult Witnesses) Rules 2004* (SI 2004/2419), both in force from 7 October 2004, make provision for the making of orders under s 46 of the Youth Justice and Criminal Evidence Act 1999, which empowers the court to impose 'reporting directions'. The effect of such directions is that no matter relating to the witness is to be included in any publication during the lifetime of the witness, if that matter is likely to lead members of the public to identify that person as a witness in the proceedings. The application may be made in writing (using the standard form contained in the Schedule to the Rules) or orally (rule 2).

11.6 Submission of no case to answer

When the prosecution has called all its witnesses, counsel will say, 'That is the case for the prosecution'. At the close of the prosecution case the defence may, if it wishes, make a submission that there is no case to answer (colloquially called 'a half-time submission').

This submission is made in the absence of the jury. Counsel for the defence makes the submission and counsel for the prosecution has the right to reply.

The submission is governed by the principles laid down in *R v Galbraith* [1981] 1 WLR 1039 at 1042 (*per* Lord Lane CJ):

(a) The submission should succeed if the judge comes to the conclusion that the prosecution evidence, taken at its highest, is such that a jury, properly directed, could not properly convict on it. In this case the judge should direct the jury to acquit on the count(s) in respect of which the submission has succeeded. If there are other counts on the indictment and either no submission was made in respect of them or a submission was made but failed, the trial proceeds on those counts.

(b) The submission should fail if the strength or weakness of the prosecution case depends on the view to be taken of the reliability of a witness and, on one possible view, there is evidence on which a reasonable jury, properly directed, could convict. In this case, the matter should be left to the jury and the trial should be allowed to take its course with the jury being left in ignorance about what has happened.

The basis for this distinction is that questions of the credibility of witnesses are matters of fact which are within the exclusive province of the jury. However, the words of Lord Lane must not be taken too literally. Regard should be had to the ruling of Turner J in *R v Shippey* [1988] Crim LR 767. His Lordship found no case to answer because of 'really significant inherent inconsistencies' in the complainant's evidence, which he found to be 'frankly incredible'. In other words, the judge can have regard to the sheer improbability of what the witness says and to internal inconsistencies in the evidence. If no reasonable jury could believe the witness whose evidence is central to the prosecution case, then the submission of no case to answer should succeed.

Note that where the only evidence against the accused is identification evidence, the special considerations highlighted in *R v Turnbull* [1977] QB 224 should be borne in mind and the case withdrawn from the jury if the evidence is weak.

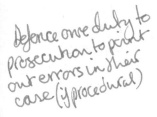

defence owe duty to prosecution to point out errors in their case (if procedural) [handwritten margin note]

If defence counsel notices a procedural error on the part of the prosecution, he or she should take the point at the outset, and not wait until the close of the prosecution case. For example, in *R v Gleeson* [2003] EWCA Crim 3357; [2004] 1 Cr App R 29, the defendant was charged with common law conspiracy. The charge was inappropriate and the trial judge accepted a submission of no case to answer. However, the judge also gave the prosecution leave to amend the indictment to allege statutory conspiracy. The Court of Appeal held that, just as a defendant should not be penalised or unfairly prejudiced by faults or errors on the part of his legal representatives in the conduct of his defence, so also the prosecution should not be frustrated by errors on the part of the prosecutor, unless such errors have irremediably rendered a fair trial for the defendant impossible. It is, said the Court, contrary to defence counsel's professional duty, and not in the legitimate interests of the defendant, to take advantage of procedural errors by the prosecution by delaying in identifying those errors as issues in the case until the last possible moment. Auld LJ said that a criminal trial is not a game; its object is to ensure that the guilty are convicted and the innocent acquitted.

If the judge wrongly refuses to uphold a submission of no case to answer this constitutes an error of law. Any evidence called afterwards (that is by the defence) is irrelevant on appeal as no evidence would have been called by the defence if the submission had been upheld. So if in the course of giving evidence the accused makes damaging admissions, those admissions will have to be ignored by the Court of Appeal. See *R v Smith* [2000] 1 All ER 263.

In *Attorney-General's Reference (No 2 of 2000)* (2001) 165 JP 195, the Court of Appeal held that, where a prosecution has been properly brought (ie it is not an abuse of process), a trial judge has no power to prevent the prosecution from calling evidence, nor to direct the jury to acquit, on the basis that he or she thinks a conviction unlikely. However, if the judge, at the conclusion of all the evidence (that is, both the prosecution case and the defence case), is of the view that no reasonable jury could convict, he should raise that view for discussion with counsel (in the absence of the jury), whether or not a submission of no case to answer was made at the close of the prosecution case. If, having heard submissions, the judge remains of the view that there is no case to answer, he should withdraw the case from the jury. However, this power is to be used very sparingly (*R v Brown* [2002] 1 Cr App R 5).

It should be borne in mind that the Criminal Justice and Public Order Act 1994 (CJPOA), s 34(2)(c) provides that adverse inferences can be drawn from failure to answer police questions when the court is considering a submission of no case to answer. However, s 34(2)(c) can only be relied upon to take the case past half-time if a fact has been relied on by the defence which brings s 34 into play. This would be the case where, for example, the defence cross-examine prosecution witnesses on the basis of facts that were not mentioned by the defendant when he or she was questioned.

Not to be confused with the right of the defence to seek a ruling from the judge that there is no case to answer, the jury themselves have the power to stop the case and acquit the defendant at any time after the close of the prosecution case. In *R v Kemp* [1995] 1 Cr App R 151, the Court of Appeal said that where the judge informs the jury that they may acquit the defendant without hearing further evidence, the direction should not to do anything other than merely inform them of their right to stop the case. Thus, the judge should not in effect invite the jury to acquit the defendant. If the judge considers that the case against the defendant is too weak to be left to the jury, then the judge should simply stop the case. In *R v Speechley* [2004] EWCA Crim 3067; The Times, December 1 2004, the Court of Appeal held that the common law right of the jury to acquit a defendant after the conclusion of the prosecution case is exercisable only where they have been invited to do so by the trial judge. It follows that, if a jury is invited by counsel (or seeks of its own motion) to return a verdict before being asked by the judge to do so, the judge should direct the jury that it is not open to them to return a verdict until the judge has invited them to do so.

[handwritten margin note: s34(c) CJPOA '94 adverse inferences when failing to answer police questions]

11.7   The defence case

The defence is under no obligation to call any evidence and so it would be possible for counsel for the defence to address the jury on the basis that the prosecution evidence has failed to show beyond reasonable doubt that the defendant is guilty. This may be appropriate where there is only just a case to answer. However, the CJPOA 1994, s 35, enables adverse inferences to be drawn by the jury if the accused either fails to give evidence or fails without good cause to answer questions put by the prosecution. It follows that the accused should, in the vast majority of cases, be advised to give evidence. If a defendant decides not to give evidence, despite the advice to the contrary of counsel, that defendant should be asked to endorse a note on counsel's brief confirming that he or she has chosen not to give evidence (see *R v Bevan* (1993) 98 Cr App R 354). *Practice Direction (criminal: consolidated)* [2002] 3 All ER 904, para 44, requires the judge to ensure that the defendant is aware of the possible consequences of not testifying.

The defence case may start with an opening speech outlining the evidence the defence will be calling and showing how it will rebut the evidence called by the prosecution. In fact, opening speeches are rarely made by the defence (unless the case is a complex one). In any event, the defence is not allowed to make an opening speech unless it will be calling at least one witness to the facts of the case, in addition to the evidence of the defendant. So, if the only defence evidence is from the accused and/or character witnesses, there can be no opening speech.

11.7.1   The defence evidence

If the defendant does give evidence, then he or she must be called as the first defence witness (unless the judge gives leave to the contrary) (PACE 1984, s 79).

Each defence witness (including the defendant, if he or she gives evidence) takes the oath (or affirms) and is then examined in chief on behalf of the defendant, cross-examined by the prosecution and (if necessary) re-examined on behalf of the defence.

For the position in relation to the loss of shield by the defendant, see the *Evidence Manual*.

11.7.1.1   Alibi evidence

If the defendant wishes to adduce evidence in support of an alibi, he or she must give particulars of that alibi to the prosecution (CPIA 1996, s 5). Subsection 5(8) defines alibi evidence as:

evidence tending to show that by reason of the presence of the defendant at a particular place or in a particular area at a particular time he was not, or was unlikely to have been, at the place where the offence is alleged to have been committed at the time of its alleged commission.

Thus, alibi evidence must show where the defendant was at the time of the offence: evidence which merely shows that the defendant was not present at the scene of the crime does not amount to alibi evidence (*R v Johnson* [1994] Crim LR 949).

Section 5(7) requires the defence to supply the prosecution with the name and address of any witness the accused believes is able to give evidence in support of the alibi or (where the defendant does not know the name or address) information which may help the prosecution to find the witness. The defence must give notice of the intention to adduce alibi evidence even if evidence in support of that alibi will come only from the defendant himself or herself.

If the defendant fails to give particulars of the alibi in the defence statement, or calls a witness without having giving particulars of that witness to the prosecution, the jury may draw 'adverse inferences' against the defendant (see **9.6**).

11.7.1.2 Expert evidence

The defence may not call any expert witness without leave of the judge if it has not disclosed the expert's written report to the prosecution before the trial. See the Crown Court (Advance Notice of Expert Evidence) Rules 1997 (SI 1987/716).

11.8 Closing speeches

At the close of the defence case the prosecution may make a closing speech. However, the prosecution has no right to make a closing speech if the defendant is unrepresented and has called no witnesses as to the facts of the case apart from his or her own testimony. In a fairly straightforward case the prosecution will usually forgo a closing speech.

The defence always has the right to make a closing speech and this right should never be waived. It is a vital speech, giving counsel the chance to show how reasonable doubt has been cast on the prosecution case.

11.9 Two or more defendants

Where two or more defendants are charged in the same indictment (and remember that joinder must satisfy the requirements of r 9 of the Indictment Rules 1971), and those defendants are separately represented, their cases will be presented in the order in which their names appear on the indictment. So if the indictment is against D1, D2 and D3, the order is:

D1 opening speech
D1's witnesses (including D1 if he or she wants to give evidence)
   Examination-in-chief by D1's counsel
   Cross-examination on behalf of D2
   Cross-examination on behalf of D3
   Cross-examination by prosecution
   Re-examination by D1's counsel (if necessary)
D2 opening speech
D2's witnesses (including D2 if he or she wants to give evidence)
   Examination-in-chief by D2's counsel
   Cross-examination on behalf of D1
   Cross-examination on behalf of D3
   Cross-examination by prosecution
   Re-examination by D2's counsel (if necessary) and so on.
Closing speeches are in the order: prosecution, D1, D2, D3.

If the defendants are jointly represented, they are regarded as putting forward a joint defence. Their counsel may make an opening speech. Then D1 may give evidence, followed by D2, then D3, then any other witnesses the defence wish to call.

11.10 Unrepresented defendants

Where the defendant is unrepresented:

- the trial judge should ask such questions as he or she sees fit to test the reliability of the prosecution witnesses and may ask the defendant whether there are certain matters he or she wishes to be put to the witnesses;
- the jury should be instructed (at the start of the trial and in the summing-up) that the defendant is entitled to represent himself or herself and the defendant should also be warned of the difficulty of doing so properly;
- the judge should prevent repetitious questioning of prosecution witnesses by the defendant.

It should be borne in mind that the Youth Justice and Criminal Evidence Act 1999, s 34, provides that no person charged with a sexual offence may cross-examine the complainant, either in connection with that offence, or in connection with any other offence (of whatever nature) with which that person is charged in the proceedings. Under s 35, unrepresented defendants are not allowed to cross-examine in person a child who is either the complainant of, or a witness to the commission of, an offence of kidnapping, false imprisonment or abduction. Section 36 gives courts the power to prohibit unrepresented defendants from cross-examining witnesses in cases where a mandatory ban does not apply under ss 34 and 35, but where the court is satisfied that the circumstances of the witness and the case merit a prohibition, and that it would not be contrary to the interests of justice.

11.11 The summing up

After the prosecution and defence counsel have made their closing speeches, the judge sums the case up to the jury. The judge must do this in all cases, however simple the case may seem. Although traditionally the judge produces the summing up without reference to counsel, in *R v Taylor* [2003] EWCA Crim 2447; The Times, 8 October 2003, the Court of Appeal said that, where complex directions are to be given to the jury, counsel in the case should be permitted to consider and comment upon the draft directions before the judge addresses the jury. A summing up should contain the following elements:

(a) *The respective functions of judge and jury*. Questions of law are for the judge and questions of fact are for the jury. The judge is entitled to express a view on the facts but should always make it very clear that if he or she should seem to be expressing a view on the facts then the jury must feel free to disregard what he or she has said. In *R v Jackson* [1992] Crim LR 214, the Court of Appeal approved a direction in these terms:

> It is my job to tell you what the law is and how to apply it to the issues of fact that you have to decide and to remind you of the important evidence on these issues. As to the law, you must accept what I tell you. As to the facts, you alone are the judges. It is for you to decide what evidence you accept and what evidence you reject or of which you are unsure. If I appear to have a view of the evidence or of the facts with which you do not agree, reject my view. If I mention or emphasise evidence that you regard as unimportant, disregard that evidence. If I do not mention what you regard as important, follow your own view and take that evidence into account.

(b) *Burden and standard of proof.*   The prosecution has brought the case and it is for the prosecution to prove it, not for the accused to prove his or her innocence. Before convicting, the jury must be satisfied so that they are sure (a preferred formulation to the time-honoured 'beyond reasonable doubt'). The judge should not expand on what is meant by 'sure', as this is likely to generate confusion. However, if the jury later seeks further guidance, the judge can tell the jurors that they need to be as sure as they would be to make a decision which is very important in their own lives. If the case (exceptionally) involves a burden on the defendant (eg to show lawful authority or reasonable excuse for possession of an offensive weapon: Prevention of Crime Act 1957, s 1) then the jury must be told that the standard is to the balance of probabilities, more likely than not. See *Ferguson v The Queen* [1979] 1 WLR 94 and *R v McVey* [1988] Crim LR 127. In *R v Stephens* [2002] EWCA Crim 1529 (a case in which the jury sought additional guidance on how sure they had to be before convicting), the Court of Appeal stated that the Judicial Studies Board guideline to direct a jury to be satisfied so that it was sure of guilt is a well-established direction. It is not helpful for a judge to direct a jury to distinguish between being sure and being certain and a judge should avoid doing so. If necessary, a judge should direct a jury that his telling it to be sure is the limit of the help that he can give.

(c) *The law and the evidence.*   There should be an explanation of the law involved and how it relates to the facts of the case. The judge should remind the jury of the main features of the prosecution and defence evidence, even if the case is a straightforward one (see *R v McVey* [1988] Crim LR 127 and *R v Gregory* [1993] Crim LR 623). In *R v Bowerman* [2002] 2 Cr App R 189, the Court of Appeal emphasised the importance of the summing up as a means of focusing the jury's attention on the issues to be decided. This involves fitting the evidence that has been heard into the legal framework of the charge(s) so that the jury knows what the prosecution must prove and what (if anything) the defence has said in response. In going through the evidence which has been heard, the judge must be careful to present both the prosecution and defence stories even-handedly (*R v Marr* (1989) 90 Cr App R 154). If there is an appeal, the Court of Appeal will look at the overall effect of the summing-up (*R v Berrada* (1989) 91 Cr App R 131). In *R v Spencer* [1995] Crim LR 235, the defendant's conviction was held to be unsafe as a result of excessive and largely one-sided comments made by the judge when directing the jury. It was said by Henry LJ that some comment is permissible, but not to the extent that the rehearsal of the evidence is interrupted and the jury's task made more difficult. See also *R v Farr* (1999) 163 JP 193 where a conviction was quashed, and a retrial ordered, because the summing-up failed to refer to a number of the key features of the defence case and, instead of being fair and balanced, resembled a speech for the prosecution. Indeed, where the case against the defendant is strong, and his or her defence correspondingly weak, the judge has to be scrupulous to ensure that the defendant's defence is presented to the jury in an even-handed and impartial manner (*R v Reid* The Times, 17 August 1999).

(d) *Identification evidence.*   If the case against the accused depends on identification evidence, there should be a warning about the special need for care when examining identification evidence as a witness may appear convincing yet also be mistaken. The factors which should be taken into account in assessing the quality of the evidence should be set out. See *R v Turnbull* [1977] QB 224.

(e) *More than one count or defendant.*   If there is more than one count or more than one defendant, a warning must be given that each count and each defendant must be considered separately. Where evidence is admissible against one defendant but not the other (eg a police interview in which a defendant implicates himself or herself and a co-accused), the judge must instruct the jury to disregard the evidence in so far as it relates to the other defendant. In a case where there are co-defendants and each defendant says that he or she is not responsible for the alleged crime, the jury should be directed that: (i) the case for and against each defendant should be considered separately; (ii) the case should be decided on all of the evidence, including the evidence of the co-defendant(s) and the defendant whose case they are considering; (iii) when considering a co-defendant's evidence against the particular defendant whose case they are considering, they should bear in mind that he or she may have an interest to serve; (iv) they should assess the evidence of a co-defendant in the same way as any other witness in the case (see *R v Jones and Jenkins* [2003] EWCA Crim 1966; [2004] 1 Cr App R 5).

(f) *Previous convictions.*   If the defendant's previous convictions have been revealed, the judge must tell the jury that they are relevant only to the defendant's credibility as a witness and are not evidence that he or she has committed the present offence(s) (*R v McLeod* [1994] 3 All ER 254).

Where the defendant has no previous convictions, the jury should be directed that this is relevant both to the credibility of the defendant as a witness and to the likelihood that he or she committed the offence (*R v Vye* [1993] 1 WLR 471, *R v Teasdale* [1993] 4 All ER 290 and *R v Aziz* [1996] AC 41) although it should be noted that in *Barrow v The Queen* [1998] 2 WLR 957, it was held by the Privy Council that the judge ought only to direct the jury on the relevance of the good character of the accused if the matter is raised by the defence either calling evidence or questioning prosecution witnesses with a view to establishing the defendant's good character. Where a defendant has previously been cautioned by the police, it is proper for the trial judge to direct the jury as to the relevance of the defendant's lack of previous convictions in relation to his or her credibility as a witness but not to give the second limb of the *Vye* direction in relation to the defendant's lack of propensity to commit the offence charged (*R v Martin* [2000] Cr App R 42). In *R v Gray* [2004] EWCA Crim 1074; [2004] 2 Cr App R 30, the Court considered the law on good character directions. Rix LJ (at para 57) summarises the law as follows:

(i) The primary rule is that a person of previous good character must be given a full direction covering both credibility and propensity. Where there are no further facts to complicate the position, such a direction is mandatory and should be unqualified. (ii) If a defendant has a previous conviction which, either because of its age or its nature, may entitle him to be treated as of effective good character, the trial judge has a discretion so to treat him, and if he does so the defendant is entitled to a *Vye* direction. (iii) Where the previous conviction can only be regarded as irrelevant or of no significance in relation to the offence charged, that discretion ought to be exercised in favour of treating the defendant as of good character. In such a case the defendant is entitled to a *Vye* direction. Where there is room for uncertainty as to how a defendant of effective good character should be treated, a judge is entitled to give an appropriately modified *Vye* direction. (iv) Where a defendant of previous good character, whether absolute or effective, has been shown at trial, whether by admission or otherwise, to be guilty of criminal conduct, the prima facie rule of practice is to deal with this by qualifying a *Vye* direction rather than by withholding it. However, in such a case, there remains a narrowly circumscribed residual discretion to withhold a good character direction in whole, or in part, where it would make no sense, or would be meaningless or absurd or an insult to common sense, to do otherwise. (v) A direction should never be misleading. Therefore, where a defendant has withheld something of his record so that otherwise a trial judge is not in a position to refer to it, the defendant may forfeit the more ample, if qualified, direction which the judge might otherwise have been able to give.

Vye Direction

(g) *Failure by accused to testify.*   In *R v Cowan* [1996] QB 373 the Court of Appeal considered what should be said in the summing-up if the defendant decides not to testify. The judge must remind the jury that the burden of proof remains on the prosecution. The jury must also be directed that:

(i)   an inference from failure to give evidence cannot on its own prove guilt (CJPOA, s 38(3);

(ii)   it must be satisfied (on the basis of the evidence called by the prosecution) that the prosecution has established a case to answer before inferences can be drawn from the accused's silence under the CJPOA 1994, s 35; and

(iii)   it can only draw an adverse inference from the accused's silence if it concludes that the silence can only sensibly be attributed to the accused having no answer to the charge or none that stands up to cross-examination.

In *R v Birchall* [1999] Crim LR 311, the Court of Appeal emphasised that where the defendant fails to testify, the trial judge must tell the jury that it should not start to consider whether to draw adverse inferences from the failure to testify until it has concluded that there is a case to answer, ie that the Crown's case against the defendant is sufficiently compelling to call for an answer by him or her. This is so even if there is plainly sufficient evidence to amount to a prima facie case against the defendant.

Thus, there are two key steps before adverse inferences can be drawn under s 35:

(i)   Is the jury satisfied that the prosecution has established a case to answer against the defendant?

(ii)   Has the jury rejected any explanation put forward by the defendant for his refusal to give evidence?

If the answer to these questions is 'yes', the jury may draw adverse inferences from the defendant's silence.

(h) *Failure to answer police questions.*   In *R v Condron* [1997] 1 WLR 827, the Court of Appeal said that the guidelines set out in *R v Cowan* [1996] QB 373 regarding the drawing of adverse inferences where the accused fails to testify are equally applicable where the accused fails to answer questions when being interviewed by the police. More detailed guidance was given in *R v Argent* [1997] 2 Cr App R 27, where the Court of Appeal set out the conditions which have to be satisfied before adverse inferences can be drawn from a person's failure to answer police questions (CJPOA 1994, s 34). The conditions include:

(i)   the alleged failure must take place before the person has been charged;

(ii)   the alleged failure must occur during questioning under caution;

(iii)   the questioning must be directed at trying to discover whether and by whom the alleged offence has been committed;

(iv)   the alleged failure must be a failure to mention a fact relied on by the defendant in his or her defence;

(v)   the fact must be one which this particular defendant (not some hypothetical reasonable accused) could reasonably be expected to have mentioned when being questioned, taking account of all the circumstances existing at that time (for example, the time of day, the defendant's age, experience, mental capacity, state of health, sobriety, personality and access to legal advice).

It should be borne in mind that a defendant may rely on a fact even if that defendant does not give evidence of that fact. In *R v Webber* [2004] UKHL 1; [2004] 1 WLR 404 (following *R v Bowers* (1999) 163 JP 33), the House of Lords confirmed that s 34 might apply if a defendant fails to mention when questioned by the police a significant matter on which he seeks to rely in his defence at trial (a) by giving evidence of it, (b) by adducing evidence of it from another witness, or (c) by putting it to a prosecution witness. Thus, adverse inferences can be drawn under s 34 even if the accused does not testify at the trial. Where the judge decides that it is not appropriate for the jury to draw adverse inferences from the defendant's silence, the jury should be specifically directed not to draw adverse inferences (*R v McGarry* [1999] 1 Cr App R 377). In *R v Betts and Hall* [2001] 2 Cr App R 257, the Court of Appeal considered the effect of the Human Rights Act 1998. The defendants had elected to remain silent in interviews with the police following legal advice. The judge directed the jury that it was entitled to draw adverse inference from the defendants' silence. The Court of Appeal held that any direction that left the jury at liberty to draw an adverse inference from a defendant's failure to answer questions in police interview, notwithstanding that it might have been satisfied as to the plausibility of the explanation for not so doing, amounts to a breach of the right to a fair trial under Article 6(1) of the European Convention on Human Rights. If it was a plausible explanation that the reason for not mentioning facts when interviewed was that the particular defendant had acted on the advice of his or her solicitor, and not because the defendant had no satisfactory answer to give, then no inference could be drawn. It must be made clear to the jury that it can only draw inferences against a particular defendant if it is sure that he or she had no explanation to offer, or none that he or she believed would stand up to questioning or investigating.

In *R v Gowland-Wynn* [2002] 1 Cr App R 41, the Court of Appeal commended the specimen direction prepared in July 2001 by the Judicial Studies Board (quoted in *Archbold* (2002 edn), para 15–334).

In *R v Beckles* [2004] EWCA Crim 2766; [2005] 1 All ER 705, the Court of Appeal re-visited the effect of legal advice not to answer questions, holding that where a defendant relies on a solicitor's advice as an explanation for having failed to mention in interview any fact relied on at trial, the ultimate question for the jury under s 34 remains whether the facts relied on at trial were facts which the defendant could reasonably have been expected to mention when interviewed. If they were not, that is the end of the matter. If the jury consider that the defendant genuinely relied on the advice, that is not necessarily the end of the matter; if it is possible to say that the defendant genuinely acted upon the advice but did so because it suited his purpose, that might mean he was not acting reasonably in failing to mention the facts. His reasonableness in not mentioning the facts remains to be determined by the jury: if they conclude he was acting unreasonably, they can draw an adverse inference from the failure to mention the facts.

(i) *Adverse inferences under CPIA.* Where the defendant fails to provide a defence statement setting out the defence case (CPIA 1996, s 5), or does so late, or sets out inconsistent defences in the defence statement, or presents to the court a defence which is inconsistent with the defence statement, or presents alibi evidence without having given details of the alibi to the prosecution, adverse inferences may be drawn by the jury. The judge must therefore give an appropriate direction to the jury.

(j) *Lies by defendant.* Where there is evidence before the jury that the defendant has lied about something, and there is a risk of the jury thinking that, because the defendant has lied, he or she must therefore be guilty of the offence charged, they should be directed that proof of lying is not proof of guilt (in other words, that an innocent defendant might lie) (*R v Lucas* [1981] 1 QB 720).

(k) *Alibi.* Where the defendant has relied on an alibi and the prosecution has sought to prove that the alibi was false, the judge should direct the jury to the effect that 'even if you conclude that the alibi was false, that does not entitle you to convict the defendant. The Crown must still make you sure of his guilt. An alibi is sometimes invented to bolster a genuine defence'. A failure to give such a direction does not, however, automatically render a conviction unsafe. The Court of Appeal will consider whether the jury might have come to a different conclusion had the direction been given (*R v Harron* [1996] Crim LR 581 and *R v Lesley* [1996] 1 Cr App R 39).

(l) *Corroboration.* Where an accomplice testifies as a prosecution witness against a defendant, there is no duty to warn the jury about the dangers of convicting on the basis of that evidence (CJPOA 1994, s 32). However, the trial judge nevertheless has a discretion to give such a warning (*R v Makanjuola; R v Easton* [1995] 1 WLR 1348). The Court of Appeal will only rarely interfere with the exercise of this discretion. Under the European Convention on Human Rights, admitting evidence of an accomplice may not violate Article 6 provided that the jury is made fully aware of the circumstances. It is open to question whether the removal of the mandatory corroboration warning by s 32 of the 1994 Act accords with this principle.

(m) *Expert witness.* Where there has been evidence from an expert witness, the jury should be directed that it is not bound by the opinion of the expert witness (*R v Stockwell* (1993) 97 Cr App R 260; *R v Fitzpatrick* [1999] Crim LR 832).

(n) *Failure to call defence witness.* It should be noted that it is generally inappropriate for the judge to comment on the failure of the defence to call a particular witness, as such comment can easily detract from what is said about the burden of proof (see *R v Wheeler* [1967] 1 WLR 1531, 1535; *R v Wright* [2000] Crim LR 510).

(o) *Reaching a verdict.* Finally, the judge will tell the jury that at this stage at least a unanimous verdict is acceptable (and that the jury should not at this stage concern itself with the possibility of a majority verdict) and the judge will suggest that the jury elects a foreman to chair its discussions. So that the jury does not get distracted by the possibility of a verdict other than a unanimous verdict, para 46.1 of *Practice Direction (criminal: consolidated)* [2002] 3 All ER 904 suggests that, before the jury retires, the judge should direct them as follows:

> As you may know, the law permits me, in certain circumstances, to accept a verdict which is not the verdict of you all. Those circumstances have not as yet arisen, so that when you retire I must ask you to reach a verdict upon which each one of you is agreed. Should, however, the time come when it is possible for me to accept a majority verdict, I will give you a further direction.

In *R v Hastings* [2003] EWCA Crim 3730; The Times, 12 December 2003, the Court of Appeal reiterated that it is extremely important that the judge warns the jury not to deliberate on their verdict until all jury members are present and after the jury bailiffs have been sworn.

In *R v Mirza* [2004] 2 WLR 201, the House of Lords confirmed that the Court of Appeal is not entitled to enquire what happened in the jury room while the jury was considering its verdict. In an attempt to make sure that any problems come to light before the verdict has been delivered (so that the judge can investigate and take appropriate action), the *Practice Direction (Crown Court: Guidance to Jurors)* The Times, 27 February 2004 makes an amendment to para 42 of the *Practice Direction (Criminal Proceedings: Consolidation)* [2002] 1 WLR 2870 by adding a requirement that trial judges should ensure that the jury is alerted to the need to bring any concerns about fellow jurors to the attention of the judge at the time, and not to wait until the case is concluded. Judges should therefore take the opportunity, when warning the jury of the importance of not discussing the case with anyone outside the jury, to add a further warning, to the effect that it is the duty of jurors to bring to the judge's attention, promptly, any behaviour among the jurors or by others affecting the jurors, that causes concern. The point should be made that, unless that is done while the case is continuing, it may be impossible to put matters right. Particularly in the case of a longer trial, the judge should consider whether a reminder on the lines of the further warning is appropriate prior to the retirement of the jury.

The judge is under a duty to sum up even-handedly. For example, it is important that the defence case is put fully and fairly before the jury (*R v Gaughan* [1990] Crim LR 880). The judge must avoid sarcastic and extravagant language which disparages the defence case (*R v Berrada* (1989) 91 Cr App R 131).

Where the judge fails to direct the jury adequately on a particular point, and that failure appears to provide a ground of appeal, defence counsel should not remain silent but should draw the matter to the attention of the judge. The duty to assist the judge rests upon both the prosecution and the defence (*R v Langford* The Times, 12 January 2001).

In *R v Wang* [2005] UKHL 9; [2005] 1 All ER 782, the House of Lords held that there are no circumstances in which a judge is entitled to direct a jury to return a verdict of guilty.

A very useful resource is the *Criminal Bench Book* published by the Judicial Studies Board. It contains a set of specimen directions which cover all the major matters which have to be covered in a summing-up. These specimen directions are freely available on the web at www.jsboard.co.uk/criminal_law/index.htm.

11.12   Bail

In *R v Central Criminal Court, ex p Guney* [1996] 2 All ER 705 the House of Lords held that when a defendant who has not previously surrendered to the custody of the court is arraigned, he or she thereby surrenders to the custody of the court at that moment. The result is that the Crown Court judge then has to decide whether or not to grant bail; unless the judge grants bail, the defendant will remain in custody pending and during the trial.

In *R v Maidstone Crown Court, ex p Jodka* (1997) 161 JP 638, the Divisional Court went further and held that bail granted by magistrates ceases when the defendant surrenders to the custody of the Crown Court, whether or not the defendant is arraigned at the hearing at which he or she surrenders. Where the magistrates grant bail subject to a surety, the responsibility of that surety under the magistrates' court order ceases once the defendant surrenders to the custody of the Crown Court. If the Crown Court wishes to grant bail subject to the same surety, the court must consider the position of that surety before imposing such a condition.

It follows from this that the question of bail will have to be considered at the pre-trial hearing. In any event, if the defendant is on bail before the trial, this bail effectively expires at the start of the trial. Therefore, once a defendant who was on bail before the trial has surrendered to the custody of the court at the start of the trial, he or she will only be released from custody if the judge grants bail. So a very brief bail application has to be made at the lunchtime adjournment and the end of each day. Such application should be made in the absence of the jury (as refusal might prejudice them against the accused).

Practice Direction on Bail

Some judges will withhold bail at lunchtime (eg where there is a risk that the defendant might come into contact with jurors); others grant bail but forbid the defendant to leave the court building or require the defendant to remain in the company of his or her solicitor. Paragraph 25.3 of *Practice Direction (criminal: consolidated)* [2002] 3 All ER 904 states that an accused who was on bail while on remand should not be refused overnight bail during the trial unless the judge is of the opinion that there are positive reasons to justify this refusal. The *Practice Direction* suggest that such reasons are likely to be: (a) that a point has been reached where there is a real danger that the accused will abscond, either because the case is going badly for him, or for any other reason; (b) that there is a real danger that he may interfere with witnesses or jurors. Paragraph 25.4 goes on to state that there is no universal rule of practice that bail shall not be renewed once the summing-up has begun: it is for the judge to assess the risks involved in granting bail at this stage. Finally, para 25.5 points out that once the jury has returned a verdict, a further renewal of bail should be decided in the light of the gravity of the offence and the likely sentence to be passed in all the circumstances of the case.

11.13 The verdict

11.13.1 The jury's retirement

The jury is put in the charge of a jury bailiff, who takes an oath to take the jurors to a private place and not to allow anyone to speak to them. The jurors then go off to the retiring room to consider their verdict.

Section 13 of the Juries Act 1974 (amended by s 43 of the CJPOA 1994) enables the court to allow the jury to separate after (as well as before) it has been sent out to consider its verdict. Formerly, separation was only permitted before the jury had been sent out to consider its verdict.

In *R v Oliver* [1996] 2 Cr App R 514, the Court of Appeal gave guidance on the directions which should be given to a jury which is allowed to separate before delivering its verdict. The jury must be warned that:

- it may only decide the case on the basis of the evidence it has heard in court; and
- jurors must not talk to anyone about the case except other jurors and even discussions with other jurors may only take place while they are deliberating in the retiring room.

Where a jury is sent to an hotel overnight, it must be told not to continue its deliberations in the hotel but only to discuss the case when it has returned to court the following day (otherwise, discussions might take place without all jurors being present) (*R v Tharakan* [1995] 2 Cr App R 368).

When deliberating, the jury is allowed to have with it any exhibit in the case. In *R v Tonge* (1993) 157 JP 1137 the Court of Appeal considered what should be done if the jury (after it has retired) asks to hear the tape recording of the defendant's interview at the police station. It was said that if the tape recording has not been played in open court during the trial and the jury asks to hear the tape, it should usually be played in open court. However, if the tape has already been played in court, the jury may be allowed to hear it again in the jury room.

Once the jury has retired, any communication between the judge and jury has to take place in open court in the presence of the entire jury, both counsel and the defendant (*R v*

McCluskey (1993) 98 Cr App R 216). Where the judge receives a note from the jury, he or she should follow the procedure laid down in *R v Gorman* [1987] 1 WLR 545: unless the note has nothing to do with the trial, the judge should, in open court (but in the absence of the jury), state the contents of the note and seek submissions from both counsel. The judge should then send for the jury and deal with the query in open court. In *Ramstead v The Queen* [1999] 2 AC 92, the Privy Council reiterated that where the judge receives a note from the jury he or she should follow the procedure laid down in *Gorman* and *McCluskey*.

Once the jury has retired to consider its verdict, no further evidence can be adduced before them. This is an absolute rule, with no exceptions (*R v Owen* [1952] 2 QB 362). In *Owen*, the jury came out of retirement to ask whether the premises where an indecent assault was alleged to have taken place would have been occupied or not at the relevant time. The Court of Appeal held that no further evidence can be called after the jury has retired to consider its verdict.

Each time the jury comes into court, it is asked by the clerk, 'Have you reached a verdict upon which you are all agreed?' If it has come back with a query, the answer will of course be no. If it has come back with a verdict, the answer will be yes. A verdict must be taken on each count of the indictment separately. However, if two counts were in the alternative, if the jury convicts on the first count, it will be discharged from giving a verdict on the second.

11.13.2 Alternative verdicts

It is possible for the jury to acquit the defendant of the count on the indictment but to convict of another offence, a 'lesser included offence'. This is only possible if the Criminal Justice Act 1967, s 6 applies. This provides that where allegations in an indictment amount to or include, whether expressly or by implication, an allegation of another offence which may be tried on indictment, then the jury may acquit of the offence charged and convict of that other offence.

'Express inclusion' means that if certain words are deleted, the allegation of another offence remains: eg the indictment alleges that 'AB on 1st January 2003 entered 4 Gray's Inn Place as a trespasser and stole therein a television set, the property of City University, London'. If the words 'entered 4 Gray's Inn Place as a trespasser and' are deleted, that leaves a valid count alleging theft. So if the jury feels that the prosecution has failed to prove trespass, an essential ingredient of burglary, but none the less find that the defendant stole the goods in question, it can convict of theft.

'Implied inclusion' means that the lesser offence is either a necessary step towards committing the offence charged on the indictment or else is an offence which, in the vast majority of cases, is a step on the road to committing the offence charged. See *Metropolitan Police Commission v Wilson* [1984] AC 242. So, for example, theft is a valid alternative verdict to a charge of robbery (where the jury decides there was no assault); indecent assault is a valid alternative to rape. Section 47 of the Offences Against the Person Act 1861 is a valid alternative to s 20 of that Act (*R v Savage* [1992] 1 AC 714); s 20 is a valid alternative to s 18 of the Act (*R v Mandair* [1995] 1 AC 208).

Section 11 of the Domestic Violence, Crime and Victims Act 2004 amends s 6 of the Criminal Law Act 1967 by adding a subsection (3A), which provides that an offence falls within the jurisdiction of the Crown Court if it is an offence to which s 40 of the CJA 1988 applies even if a count charging the offence is not included in the indictment. This reverses the effect of *R v Mearns* [1991] 1 QB 82 (where it had been held that the jury could only convict of a summary offence to which s 40 applies if such an offence were added to the indictment) and confirms the effect of *R v Fennell* [2000] 1 WLR 2011 (where the Court of Appeal upheld the decision of the trial judge to allow a jury to convict the accused of criminal damage even though he was charged only with racially aggravated criminal damage). Thus, the jury may acquit the accused of the offence on the indictment but convict him of an offence under s 40 of the 1988 Act, even though that offence is a summary offence (provided, of course, that it is expressly or impliedly included in the offence that does appear on the indictment). For example, if the accused is charged with assault occasioning actual bodily harm (s 47 of the Offences Against the Person Act 1861) but the jury find that no actual bodily harm was caused, they may acquit of that charge but convict of common assault (to which s 40 of the 1988 Act applies) even though that charge does not appear on the indictment.

Under s 6(3B), a person convicted of an offence by virtue of s 6(3A) may only be dealt with for it in a manner in which a magistrates' court could have dealt with him.

There are, in any event, some specific statutory provisions which enable the jury to convict the defendant of a summary offence if they acquit the defendant of an indictable offence. The Theft Act 1968, s 12(4) provides that taking a conveyance without the owner's consent is a valid alternative verdict to a charge of theft and the Road Traffic Offenders Act 1988, s 24 provides that careless driving is a valid alternative verdict to a charge of dangerous driving or causing death by dangerous driving.

Of course a jury will only be aware of its power to convict of a lesser included offence if it is told that it can do so; and even if the possibility is raised by counsel, the judge can decide to direct the jury not to consider that possibility. So what attitude should the judge take? In *R v Fairbanks* [1986] 1 WLR 1202 the Court of Appeal said that if there was an alternative and less serious offence to that charged, the judge should put the alternative offence to the jury if it was necessary in the interests of justice to do so. The court seemed to create a presumption in favour of leaving the lesser offence to the jury. The defence might argue that the jury might think that the defendant was innocent of the offence charged but guilty of something and so convict as charged to prevent the defendant getting off scot-free; the prosecution might argue that if the jury took the view that the defendant was guilty of something, albeit not the offence on the indictment, it would be wrong for him or her to be acquitted altogether.

In any event, in *R v Maxwell* [1990] 1 WLR 401 the House of Lords took a more restrictive view. In that case, the defendant was charged with robbery but would have been willing to plead guilty to burglary. The prosecution declined to add a plea of burglary to the indictment and to accept the defendant's plea to that rather than to robbery. Defence counsel asked the judge to leave theft to the jury as an alternative to robbery. The judge refused and his refusal was ultimately upheld by the House of Lords. It was said that, in view of the way the prosecution had presented the case, the essential issue was whether or not violence had been used; the theft was trivial in comparison. To have left theft to the jury would have been to distract it from the main issue in the case. As such it represented an unnecessary and undesirable complication. This decision appears to say that the judge should give great weight to the view of the prosecution before letting the jury consider a lesser offence. Similarly, in *R v Hussain*, The Daily Telegraph, 5 February 2004, where the defendant was charged with causing death by dangerous driving, the trial judge rejected an application to leave the alternative offence of careless driving to the jury. The Court of Appeal confirmed that the test to be applied when considering whether to leave an alternative offence to the jury is: (i) whether there is any sensible basis on which the jury might convict of the more serious offence; (ii) whether leaving an alternative charge might compromise the jury's consideration and lead to an element of confusion; and (iii) in circumstances where the criminality is graver than the alternative offence, whether it is undesirable to leave an alternative to the jury, even if that renders the situation of the defendant overly favourable on the basis that the options are only an acquittal or a conviction. Where an alternative offence is not left to the jury, a conviction might be rendered unsafe, said the Court, if the jury convicted the defendant out of reluctance to see an acquittal where they had found some misconduct. In those circumstances, it is incumbent on the judge properly to direct the jury exactly as to what they have to find in order to convict. On the facts of the present case, it was open to the judge not to leave the alternative to the jury, and the direction to the jury was clearly designed to ensure that the jury only convicted the defendant if the offence on the indictment was made out; the conviction was therefore safe.

In *R v Coutts* [2005] EWCA Crim 52; The Times, January 26 2005, the Court of Appeal reiterated that the judge should only direct the jury on the possibility of an alternative verdict if it is in the interests of justice for that to happen. It is not in the interests of justice for that to happen, said the Court, where it would result in unfairness to a defendant, or where it would make the task of the jury far more difficult without there being any sufficient countervailing benefit which justifies an additional burden being placed upon the jury.

Allowing the jury to consider an alternative verdict will only be in the interests of justice as far as the accused is concerned if he or she has had the opportunity of fully meeting the alternative charge in the course of presenting the defence case. Would the cross-examination of prosecution witnesses have been different? Would the defence have called different witnesses or presented its case differently? In other words, it is the same test as that applied if the court is asked to add a count to an indictment during the course of the trial. See, for example, *R v Piggott and Litwin* [1999] 2 Cr App R 320.

In *R v Salter* [1993] Crim LR 891 a jury sent out to consider an allegation of rape asked if it could convict of attempted rape. The judge allowed them to return a verdict of guilty to attempted rape. It was held by the Court of Appeal that a jury should only be directed after it has retired that it may bring in a verdict on an alternative offence if the judge has first discussed with counsel the precise formulation of the direction to the jury and canvassed the possible need to remind it of any relevant evidence.

Where a judge refuses to leave an alternative offence to the jury, the Court of Appeal will only quash a conviction for the offence charged on the indictment if satisfied that the jury convicted the defendant only because it was reluctant to allow him to get away completely with his misconduct (see *R v O'Hadhmaill* [1996] Crim LR 509 and *R v Bergman and Collins* [1996] 2 Cr App R 399).

It would of course be inappropriate to leave a lesser offence to the jury if it is inappropriate to the way in which the defence has been conducted, eg if the defence is one of alibi.

Note that a verdict on a lesser offence is only possible if the jury acquits of the offence actually on the indictment. In *R v Collison* (1980) 71 Cr App R 249, for example, the jury was unable to agree on an acquittal. To enable it to convict of a lesser offence, that offence had to be added to the indictment as a new count (and the decision to do this even though the jury had been considering its verdict for some time was upheld as the defence would not have been conducted any differently).

11.13.3 Majority verdicts

The Juries Act 1974, s 17, provides that a majority verdict may be accepted after the jury has been out for two hours, or such longer time as the judge thinks appropriate given the nature and complexity of the case. As a matter of practice, the jury is given a further 10 minutes in which to settle into the retiring room and elect a foreman.

Should the jury return before two hours and ten minutes (or such longer time as the judge thinks reasonable) has elapsed since the jury retired to consider its verdict, it should be asked, 'Have you reached a verdict upon which you are all agreed? Please answer "Yes" or "No" '. If it has reached a unanimous verdict, it should be asked, 'What is your verdict?' If the jury has not reached a unanimous verdict, it should be sent out again for further deliberation with a further direction to arrive, if possible, at a unanimous verdict.

When the judge decides that (subject to the two hour, 10 minute minimum) the jury has had long enough to reach a verdict, it will be called back into court and asked if it has reached a unanimous verdict. If it has not, the judge will direct it to retire once more and will tell the jury that it should continue to endeavour to reach a unanimous verdict but that, if it cannot, the judge will accept a majority verdict.

The only permissible majorities (bearing in mind that up to three jurors may be discharged during the course of the trial due to illness or other necessity) are:

12 jurors: 11–1 or 10–2
11 jurors: 10–1
10 jurors: 9–1

If the jury has been reduced to nine jurors, only a unanimous verdict is acceptable.

When the jury returns into court after the majority verdict direction has been given, it will be asked, 'Have at least 10 [or nine as the case may be] of you agreed on your verdict?'. If the answer is 'Yes', it will be asked 'What is your verdict? Please only answer "guilty" or "not guilty" '. If the verdict is 'not guilty', that is the end of the matter. If the verdict is 'guilty', the jury will be asked, 'Is that the verdict of you all or by a majority?' If the answer is that it was a majority verdict, the jury will be asked, 'How many of you agreed to the verdict and how many dissented?'

The reason for this slightly complicated procedure is to prevent it being known that a verdict of 'not guilty' was a majority verdict, and to ensure that a verdict of 'guilty' was that of a permissible majority.

Under s 17(3) of the Juries Act 1974, the foreman must state in open court the number of jurors who respectively agreed to and dissented from the verdict before the judge can accept a majority verdict of guilty. In *R v Austin* [2003] Crim LR 426, the court confirmed that a majority verdict of guilty will be a nullity if the words used by the clerk of the court and the foreman are not such that it would be clear to an ordinary person how the jury was divided.

11.13.4   Reaching a verdict

No pressure should be put on the jury to reach a verdict. An example of the attitude of the Court of Appeal is to be found in *R v Duggan* [1992] Crim LR 513. The judge said to the jury that it was important that the jury should not feel under pressure and that, if necessary, hotel accommodation would be provided for the jurors. The appeal against the conviction which followed soon after the judge's words was allowed because some members of the jury had expressed anxiety about commitments at home and the thought of not being able to go home might have exerted undue pressure on them. Presumably, the judge should simply have sent the jurors to a hotel without giving them advance warning of this possibility.

Another form of pressure was considered in *R v Watson* [1988] QB 690. In that case the Court of Appeal provided a model direction to be given to a jury which is having trouble reaching a verdict. Essentially, the judge may encourage the jurors to listen to each other's views, pooling their wisdom and experience, and engaging in give and take providing that each remains within the scope of his or her oath. However, if the judge gives such a direction, there must be no reference to the cost and inconvenience that would be caused by the need for a retrial if it could not reach a verdict. See also *R v Boyes* [1991] Crim LR 717.

The *Watson* direction was considered in *R v Buono* (1992) 95 Cr App R 338. It was held that there should rarely be any need for a *Watson* direction, but if one had to be given it should be given either during the summing-up (which the present writer thinks unlikely ever to be justified) or after the jury has been given a reasonable time to consider a majority verdict direction. The *Watson* direction should never be given at the same time as a majority verdict direction. Further, the judge should not add to the words of the model direction given by the Court of Appeal in *Watson*. In *R v Atlan* [2004] EWCA Crim 1798; [2005] Crim LR 63, the jury sent a note to the judge saying that they were unanimous on all counts except for one, and that they wanted assistance. The judge gave a modified *Watson* direction, telling the jury that they had to try harder as it was not yet time to allow a majority verdict, but that 'there might have to be a bit of give and take in your deliberations and your thoughts'. Shortly afterwards, the jury convicted the defendant under the count in question. The Court of Appeal said that a *Watson* direction has to make it clear that any 'give and take' should be within the scope of the juror's oath. It is, said the court, just as dangerous to omit words from the *Watson* direction as to add them. Moreover, such a direction should not be given after the jury have retired unless a majority verdict is to be permitted. In the present case, the direction might have put undue pressure on the jury to compromise, and so the subsequent conviction was unsafe.

Where the defendant is charged with a number of offences and the jury indicates that it has agreed on verdicts on some, but not all, of the offences, it is good practice to take the verdicts on those counts upon which the jury is agreed before it carries on to consider the other counts (*R v F* [1994] Crim LR 377).

11.13.5   Discharge of the jury

If the jury cannot reach a verdict within what the judge holds to be a reasonable time, the jury will be discharged. This does not count as an acquittal and there is every chance that there will be a retrial. There is no need for fresh committal proceedings (or transfer, in the case of an indictable-only offence). In the event of the second jury being 'hung', the prosecution is likely to let the matter rest.

11.14   Sentence

If the defendant is convicted of some or all of the counts on the indictment, the judge will proceed to hear the defendant's antecedents (including any relevant previous convictions) from prosecuting counsel, just as on a plea of guilty (see **11.2.1** above). Obviously, there is no need for the prosecution to summarise the facts as the judge has just presided over the trial.

It is possible that a pre-sentence report will have been prepared already, but this is very unlikely. Normally, the case will have to be adjourned (with the presumption in favour of bail created by the Bail Act 1976, s 4 still applying to the defendant) for the preparation of a report, although the court may dispense with a report if it takes the view that a report is unnecessary. If the case is adjourned in this way, prosecuting counsel may ask to be excused from attendance at the subsequent hearing. Once a report is available, counsel for the defence makes a plea in mitigation in the usual way.

11.15 The effect of the European Convention on Human Rights

Article 6 of the Convention guarantees the right to a fair trial. Under Article 6(1) this is a right to a fair and public hearing, within a reasonable time, by an independent and impartial tribunal. Article 6(1) goes on to provide that judgment shall be pronounced publicly but the press and public may be excluded from all or part of the trial in the interest of morals, public order or national security in a democratic society, where the interests of juveniles or the protection of the private life of the parties so require, or to the extent strictly necessary in the opinion of the court in special circumstances where publicity would prejudice the interests of justice.

Article 6(2) enshrines the presumption of innocence.

Article 6(3) confers a number of 'minimum rights', for example, for the accused to examine, or have examined, witnesses against him or her and to obtain the attendance and examination of witnesses on his or her behalf under the same conditions as witnesses against him or her.

It has been held by the European Court of Human Rights that Article 6 does not apply to preliminary hearings concerning trial arrangements (*X v UK* (1978) 5 EHRR 273).

An important aspect of the operation of Article 6 is the principle of 'equality of arms'. This requires that the defendant should have a reasonable opportunity of presenting his or her case to the court under 'conditions which do not place him at a substantial disadvantage vis-à-vis his opponent' (*Foucher v France* (1998) 25 EHRR 234). For example, handcuffing the accused during the trial may violate Article 6 (*Kaj Raninen v Finland* [1998] EHRLR 344).

The trial must take place before an unbiased tribunal. In the case of trial on indictment, that requirement applies to both the judge and the jury. There is a presumption that the court has acted impartially (*Hauschildt v Denmark* (1990) 12 EHRR 266; compare the UK case of *Locabail (UK) Ltd v Bayfield* [2000] QB 451). The test applied by the European Court of Human Rights is whether a legitimate doubt as to the impartiality of the tribunal can be objectively justified (*Hauschildt v Denmark*). This seems very similar to the test applied by UK courts ('a real danger or possibility of bias': see *R v Gough* [1993] AC 646) and *Porter v Magill* [2002] 2 AC 357.

11.16 Less common pleas

Most of this chapter has been devoted to cases which involve straightforward pleas of guilty or not guilty. Other situations are sometimes encountered, for example, where the defendant is unfit to enter a plea, or where he or she seeks to rely on the 'double jeopardy' rule.

11.16.1 Fitness to plead

A person is unfit to plead if he or she is incapable of understanding the proceedings and so cannot put forward any defence, challenge any juror for cause, give proper instructions to defence counsel, or follow the evidence (see *R v Podola* [1960] 1 QB 325). The issue of fitness to plead can be raised by the prosecution or the defence. The procedure to be followed is contained in the Criminal Procedure (Insanity) Act 1964, as amended by the Criminal Procedure (Insanity and Unfitness to Plead) Act 1991. The court may postpone consideration of the question of fitness to plead until any time up to the opening of the defence case if this is in the defendant's interests (s 4(2) of the 1964 Act). This enables a submission of no case to answer to be made before the question of fitness has to be determined.

Section 22 of the Domestic Violence, Crime and Victims Act 2004 amends s 4(5) of the 1964 Act by requiring the question of fitness to be determined 'by the court without a jury'.

If the defendant is found fit to plead, the trial takes its normal course. If, however, the defendant is found unfit to plead, a jury has to decide whether the defendant committed the *actus reus* of the offence. If the question of fitness was determined at the start of the trial, a jury must be empanelled to determine whether the defendant committed the *actus reus*. If determination of the question was postponed and the defendant is found unfit to plead, the jury trying the substantive offence must determine whether the defendant committed the *actus reus* (s 4A(5)). If it is found that the defendant did not commit the *actus reus*, he or she is acquitted. If it is found that the defendant is not fit to plead, a hospital order (with or without a restriction order) or a supervision order may be made or the court may grant an absolute discharge (s 5).

In *R v H* [2003] UKHL 1; [2003] 1 All ER 497 the House of Lords held that the procedure laid down by s 4A of the Criminal Procedure (Insanity) Act 1964 for determining whether the accused has done the act charged against him does not involve the determination of a criminal charge but is, in any event, compatible with the rights of the accused under Article 6 of the European Convention on Human Rights.

11.16.2 Double jeopardy: autrefois acquit and autrefois convict

The principle of autrefois acquit and convict, sometimes known as the rule against double jeopardy, comprises the following elements (set out in *Connelly v DPP* [1964] AC 1254):

(a) A person should not be tried for a crime in respect of which he has previously been acquitted or convicted.

(b) A person should not be tried for a crime of which he could on some previous occasion have been convicted by way of an alternative verdict under s 6(3) of the Criminal Law Act 1967. For example, where the defendant was tried for rape, the jury could, if it acquitted him of rape, convict him instead of the lesser offence of indecent assault; it follows that the defendant should not be tried, on a later occasion, for indecent assault arising out of that incident.

(c) A person should not be tried for a crime, proof of which would necessarily entail proof of a crime of which he has previously been acquitted. In *R v Forest of Dean Justices, ex p Farley* [1990] RTR 228 it was said that there is an almost invariable rule that when a person is tried on a lesser offence, he or she is not to be tried again on the same facts for a more serious offence, eg a person acquitted of theft should not be tried for robbery, of which theft is an essential ingredient, arising out of the same incident.

(d) The defendant cannot be tried for a crime which is in effect the same, or substantially the same, as one of which he has previously been acquitted or convicted (or of which he could have been convicted by way of alternative verdict).

In *R v Beedie* [1998] QB 356, the Court of Appeal held that, in all cases except the first, the court has a discretion whether or not to strike out the later prosecution.

In *R v Dabhade* [1993] QB 329, it was held that where a charge is dismissed (without a hearing on the merits) on the ground that it is defective as a matter of law or because the evidence available to the prosecution is insufficient to sustain a conviction on the charge as laid, it cannot properly be said that the defendant was ever in jeopardy of conviction, and so the autrefois principle does not apply. This is particularly the case where the prosecution substitutes a new charge which is regarded as more appropriate to the facts. The consensual dismissal of the original charge does not give rise to the application of the doctrine of autrefois acquit.

However, in *R v G* [2001] 1 WLR 1727 it was held that, where the prosecution offers no evidence against a defendant and a verdict of not guilty is entered, the prosecution cannot then proceed against the defendant on a charge alleging a more serious offence based on the same facts, as the defendant is entitled to rely on the defence of autrefois acquit.

The autrefois principle does not apply where the defendant is re-prosecuted following the quashing of an indictment; where the prosecution serves a notice of discontinuance but reserves the right to institute proceedings at a later date under the Prosecution of Offences Act 1985, s 23(9); where the first jury was discharged from giving a verdict; or where the High Court quashes an acquittal where, under the Criminal Procedure and Investigations Act 1996, ss 54–57, someone has been convicted of interfering with, or intimidating, a juror or witness in the original trial.

Part 10 of CJA 2003 provides, by way of exception to the normal rule against 'double jeopardy', for retrials in certain cases. CJA 2003, s 75, restricts the possibility of re-trial following acquittal to 'qualifying offences' (listed in Part 1 of Sch 5). Under s 76, the prosecution may apply to the Court of Appeal for an order quashing the defendant's acquittal and ordering him to be retried for the qualifying offence. Such an application may only be made with the written consent of the Director of Public Prosecutions. Only one application for an acquittal to be quashed may be made in respect of any acquittal, giving the prosecution only one further 'bite at the cherry'. The Court of Appeal can only order a re-trial where the requirements of ss 78 and 79 are satisfied. Section 78 is satisfied if there is 'new and compelling evidence against the acquitted person in relation to the qualifying offence'. Under s 78(2), evidence is 'new' if it was not adduced in the proceedings in which the person was acquitted; and evidence is 'compelling' if it is 'reliable', 'substantial', and 'appears highly probative of the case against the acquitted person'. Under s 79, an order for re-trial can only be made if, in all the circumstances, it is in the interests of justice for the court to make such an order. Section 79(2) provides that this question is to be determined having regard to whether existing circumstances make a fair trial unlikely (having regard to the length of time since the qualifying offence was allegedly committed); whether it is likely that the new evidence would have been adduced in the earlier proceedings against the acquitted person but for a failure by an officer or by a prosecutor to act with due diligence or expedition; and whether, since those proceedings or, if later, since the commencement of this Part, any officer or prosecutor has failed to act with due diligence or expedition. Thus, s 78 requires the Court to make a decision on the strength of the new evidence and the impact it would have had if it had been adduced at the original trial. In considering the interests of justice, the Court will have regard to factors such as whether a fair trial would be made more difficult because of, for example, adverse publicity about the case or the length of time that has elapsed since the original trial. The Court is specifically required to consider whether the police and prosecution acted with due diligence and expedition in relation to both the original trial and the new evidence that has come to light.

11.17   Trial by judge alone

[handwritten margin note: Complex fraud or danger of jury tampering .]

Part 7 of the CJA 2003 makes provision for trial by judge alone in complex fraud cases and in cases where there is a danger of jury tampering.

Section 43 of the 2003 Act enables an application to be made by the prosecution for certain fraud trials to be conducted without a jury. Such an order can only be made with the approval of the Lord Chief Justice or a judge nominated for this purpose by the Lord Chief Justice (s 43(4)). It only applies where notice has been given under s 51B of the Crime and Disorder Act 1998 (notices in serious or complex fraud cases) in respect of the offence(s) (s 43(1)(b)) and the judge can only accede to the request if:

the complexity of the trial or the length of the trial (or both) is likely to make the trial so burdensome to the members of a jury hearing the trial that the interests of justice require that serious consideration should be given to the question of whether the trial should be conducted without a jury (s 43(5)).

In deciding whether or not he is satisfied that this condition is fulfilled, the judge must have regard to any steps which might reasonably be taken to reduce the complexity or length of the trial (s 43(6)); in other words, a trial without a jury is very much a last resort. However, under s 43(7), 'a step is not to be regarded as reasonable if it would significantly disadvantage the prosecution'.

Section 44 of the Act enables an application to be made by the prosecution for a trial to be conducted without a jury where there is a danger of jury tampering. The judge may only make such an order if two conditions are satisfied: the first condition is that 'there is evidence of a real and present danger that jury tampering would take place' (s 44(4)) and the second condition is that 'notwithstanding any steps (including the provision of police protection) which might reasonably be taken to prevent jury tampering, the likelihood that it would take place would be so substantial as to make it necessary in the interests of justice for the trial to be conducted without a jury' (s 44(5)). Section 44(6) gives some examples of cases where there may be evidence of a real and present danger that jury tampering would take place:

- a case where the trial is a retrial and the jury in the previous trial was discharged because jury tampering had taken place;
- a case where jury tampering has taken place in previous criminal proceedings involving the defendant or any of the defendants;
- a case where there has been intimidation, or attempted intimidation, of any person who is likely to be a witness in the trial.

The word 'examples' indicates that this is not intended to be an exhaustive list of the cases where s 44 may apply.

Under CJA 2003, s 45, an application for an order under s 43 or s 44 must be made at a preparatory hearing; all parties must be given an opportunity to make representations about the application.

Section 46 of the Criminal Justice Act 2003 makes provision for the discharge of a jury because of jury tampering. Before discharging the jury in such a case, the judge must allow the parties an opportunity to make representations. The judge may then make an order that the trial is to continue without a jury if satisfied that jury tampering has taken place, and that to continue the trial without a jury would be fair to the defendant or defendants. Under s 46(4), if the judge considers that it is necessary in the interests of justice for the trial to be terminated, he or she must terminate the trial; in such a case the judge may (under subs (5)) order that any new trial must be conducted without a jury.

Section 17 of the Domestic Violence, Crime and Victims Act 2004 makes further provision for Crown Court trial without a jury (building on the provisions contained in the Criminal Justice Act 2003). It permits a judge, on application by the prosecution, to order such trial of some, but not all, of the counts on the indictment if three conditions are satisfied, namely:

- the number of counts included in the indictment is likely to mean that a trial by jury involving all of those counts would be impracticable.
- each count or group of counts which would be tried with a jury can be regarded as a sample of counts which could be tried without a jury.
- it is in the interests of justice for an order to be made.

In deciding whether or not to make an order, the judge must have regard to any steps which might reasonably be taken to facilitate a trial by jury, but a step is not to be regarded as reasonable if it could lead to the possibility of a defendant receiving a lesser sentence than would be the case if that step were not taken.

Section 19 sets out the effect of an order under s 17(2): where, in the course of the proceedings to which the order relates, a defendant is found guilty by a jury on a count which can be regarded as a sample of other counts to be tried in those proceedings, those other counts may be tried without a jury in those proceedings. Where the defendant is found guilty, the judge must give a judgment which states the reasons for the conviction.

Section 18 requires that applications under s 17 must be determined at a preparatory hearing (under s 29 of the Criminal Procedure and Investigations Act 1996); s 18(5) makes provision for appeal (under s 35 of the 1996 Act) to the Court of Appeal from the determination by a judge of an application under s 17.

Appeals to the Court of Appeal

12.1 The Criminal Division of the Court of Appeal

The Criminal Division of the Court of Appeal entertains appeals from the Crown Court on all matters relating to a trial on indictment, and appeals against any sentence imposed by the Crown Court following a committal for sentence. Appeals on matters not relating to a trial on indictment, such as when the Crown Court hears an appeal from a decision of the magistrates, are heard in the High Court, either on appeal by way of case stated, or on an application for judicial review.

The following have all been held to be matters relating to a trial on indictment, and hence not susceptible to appeal in the High Court:

- a ruling given at a pre-trial hearing (*R v Southwark Crown Court, ex p Johnson* [1992] COD 364, DC);

- an order staying the whole or part of an indictment (*R v Manchester Crown Court, ex p DPP* [1993] 2 WLR 846, HL);

- a decision, after argument, as to the date of the trial (*R v Southwark Crown Court, ex p Ward* [1995] COD 140).

12.1.1 Composition of the court

If the Court of Appeal is hearing an appeal against conviction, the court must comprise at least three judges. Very occasionally, if the court is dealing with a case of exceptional difficulty, the court will consist of five judges. If the court is dealing with an appeal against sentence, it is usual for two judges only to sit. However, it is rare to have more than one judgment delivered, in order to make for certainty of the law.

The Court of Appeal itself consists of 32 Lords Justices of Appeal, and a number of ex-officio judges including the Lord Chief Justice. In addition, the Lord Chief Justice may ask either of the following to sit in the Criminal Division:

- any High Court judge, who may deal with any case that comes before the Court of Appeal, except a case in which he was either the trial judge or passed sentence; or

- in certain circumstances, circuit judges, who may sit in appeals specified as suitable by the Lord Chancellor, except that they may not sit on any appeal from the decision of a High Court judge (s 9(1) of the Supreme Court Act 1981, as amended by s 52 of the Criminal Justice and Public Order Act 1994).

12.1.2 The court's Registrar

The administrative work of the Criminal Division is carried out by the Registrar of Criminal Appeals, who receives all notices and applications, and in turn serves all relevant notices on the parties to the appeal. In addition, the Registrar will obtain necessary transcripts, exhibits or other material. Certain additional powers have been conferred on him by virtue of the Criminal Appeal Act 1995. See **12.7.1** below.

12.1.3 The right of appeal

The statute governing the right to appeal is the Criminal Appeal Act 1968, as amended by the Criminal Appeal Act 1995 referred to in this chapter as the CAA 1968 and the CAA 1995 respectively. The changes effected by the CAA 1995 came into effect on 1 January 1996, unless otherwise indicated.

12.2 The appeal against a ruling

Sections 57–74 of the CJA 2003 permit the prosecution to appeal against certain of the trial judge's rulings, namely a 'termination ruling' or an 'evidentiary ruling. A termination ruling is one that has the effect of stopping the case such as a ruling that there is no case to answer or that the proceedings should be stayed. An evidentiary ruling is one which relates to matters such as the inclusion or exclusion of evidence. Such rulings may have a serious and detrimental effect on the way the prosecution develops its case. It seems inevitable that some evidentiary rulings will form part of an appeal against a termination ruling. However, the provisions on termination rulings came into force on 4 April 2005, whilst the provisions on evidentiary rulings are not yet in force.

An appeal against a ruling only lies with leave of the trial judge or the Court of Appeal (s 57(4)).

12.2.1 The general right of appeal in respect of rulings

The procedure for appeal is fairly complex, but in essence is as follows, under CJA 2003 ss 58–61:

(a) Following the ruling, the prosecution informs the court that it intends to appeal or requests an adjournment to consider whether to appeal. It must also inform the court that it agrees that, if leave to appeal is not granted or the appeal is abandoned, the defendant should be acquitted.

(b) The trial judge may agree to or refuse the request for an adjournment. If an adjournment is granted and the prosecution decide to appeal, it must inform the court at the adjourned hearing. If an adjournment is refused, the prosecution must decide either to continue with the appeal, or lose the right to do so.

(c) Where there are two or more offences, the prosecution must indicate which offence is the subject of the appeal.

(d) Where the trial judge has ruled that there is no case to answer, and the prosecution has informed the court that it intends to appeal, it may also nominate other rulings made in the course of the trial.

(e) The trial judge must decide whether to:
    (i)   adjourn the case and expedite the appeal. The Court of Appeal may reverse the order to expedite.
    (ii)   adjourn the case and not order that the appeal is expedited;
    (iii) discharge the jury and not order that the appeal is expedited.

(f) Once the prosecution has informed the court that it intends to appeal the ruling, the ruling has no effect whilst the appeal is pursued. Any consequences of the ruling equally have no effect, and no steps should be taken in consequence of the ruling. Such a consequence seems to include that a defendant who has been detained in custody prior to and during the trial will continue to be detained, even though the trial judge has decided that there is no case to answer. One can envisage conflict between the application of the defence for bail, which the trial judge is minded to give, and the clear wording of the section.

12.2.2   Power of the Court of Appeal for an appeal under s 58

On hearing an appeal under s 58, the Court of Appeal may either:

(a) Where the challenged ruling is no case to answer and the Court of Appeal confirms the ruling, the defendant is acquitted of that offence.

(b) Where the challenged ruling is no case to answer and the Court of Appeal reverses or varies the ruling, it must consider the following rulings:

   (i)   an order that proceedings are resumed in the Crown Court, if necessary in the interests of justice;

   (ii) an order that a fresh trial should commence in the Crown Court, if necessary in the interests of justice;

   (iii) order that the defendant be acquitted of that offence.

12.2.3   The right of appeal in respect of evidentiary rulings

A separate set of provisions, CJA 2003, s 62 and 63, applies to evidentiary rulings. Nothing in these sections affects the right of the prosecution to appeal under s 58 (s 62(11)). The ruling must be one which significantly weakens the prosecution case (s 63(2)).

In order to come within these sections, the ruling must:

- be made before the close of the prosecution case (s 62(2)); and
- relate to one of the qualifying offences in Sch 4 (s 62(9)). These are the most serious offences and include murder, manslaughter, rape, arson, endangering life, and war crimes.

In order to appeal against the trial judge's evidentiary ruling, the following procedure is followed:

(a) The prosecution inform the court, before the opening of the defence case, that it intends to appeal against the ruling, and specifies to which ruling or rulings the appeal relates.

(b) For the avoidance of doubt, s 62(8) defines the opening of the defence case as the earliest of the following events:

   (i)   evidence begins to be adduced on behalf of the defendant;

   (ii) it is indicated to the court that no evidence will be adduced on behalf of the defendant; or

   (iii) the defence make an opening speech.

(c) Leave of the trial judge or the Court of Appeal must be obtained. This will only be given if the court is satisfied that the ruling significantly weakens the prosecution case (s 63(l)).

12.2.4   Power of the Court of Appeal for an appeal under s 62

On hearing an appeal under s 62, the Court of Appeal may, by virtue of s 66:

(a) Confirm, reverse or vary any ruling to which the appeal relates.

(b) In addition, the Court of Appeal must, in respect of each offence, make one of the following orders:

    (i)   an order that the proceedings be resumed in the Court of Appeal;

    (ii)   an order that a fresh trial take place in the Crown Court;

    (iii) an order that the defendant be acquitted of that offence, if the prosecution indicate that it does not intend to continue with the prosecution of the offence.

Under s 63, the Court of Appeal may not reverse a ruling unless it is satisfied that:

- the ruling is wrong in law; or
- the ruling involved an error of law or principle; or
- the ruling was a ruling that it was not reasonable for the judge to have made.

Section 64 permits a further appeal to the House of Lords.

12.3   The appeal against conviction

By virtue of the CAA 1968, s 2, as substituted by the CAA 1995, s 2, a person convicted on indictment may appeal on the single ground that the conviction is 'unsafe' (see **12.3.2**). Leave to appeal is always required (see **12.3.3**).

12.3.1   Grounds of appeal:the 1968 Act

Prior to 1996, the Court of Appeal would allow an appeal if one of the three grounds of appeal, set out below, were made out. The proviso to this was that the Court of Appeal could dismiss the appeal if no miscarriage of justice had actually occurred. This was known as 'exercising' or 'applying' the proviso. In this situation the Court of Appeal in effect agreed that a ground of appeal had been made out but that the ground was so trivial that the jury would inevitably come to the same conclusion. The grounds were as follows:

(a) *The conviction was unsafe or unsatisfactory*. In deciding whether the conviction was unsafe or unsatisfactory, the Court of Appeal considered the case as a whole and asked itself the subjective question 'whether we are content to let the matter stand as it is, or whether there is not some lurking doubt in our minds which makes us wonder whether an injustice has been done'. See *R v Cooper* [1969] 1 QB 267 *per* Widgery LJ, applied in *R v O'Leary* (1988) 87 Cr App R 387.

(b) *The trial judge made a wrong decision on a question of law*. If an appeal was on the basis of a wrong decision by the trial judge on a question of law, even if this could be demonstrated, the Court of Appeal still had to consider whether the judgment of the trial court should be set aside on that account. In effect, it considered the proviso. See *R v Moghal* (1977) 65 Cr App R 56.

(c) *There was a material irregularity in the course of the trial*. An appeal on the basis that there was a material irregularity succeeded if there had been a procedural error during the trial. But the irregularity had to be major and material, ie serious enough to have affected the course of the trial.

12.3.2   Grounds of appeal: the 1995 Act

The CAA 1995 abolishes the three grounds of appeal and the proviso, replacing them with the single test of the safety of the conviction.

The CAA 1995, s 2 provides as follows:

2.— In section 2 of the 1968 Act (disposal of appeal against conviction), for subsection (1) (grounds on which Court of Appeal are to allow or dismiss appeal including the proviso) substitute—

(1)   Subject to the provisions of this Act, the Court of Appeal—

(a)   shall allow an appeal against conviction if they think that the conviction is unsafe; and

(b)   shall dismiss such an appeal in any other case.

The Act does not contain any definition of the word 'unsafe'. The meaning of the word has, however, been considered by the Court of Appeal in the following cases.

In *R v Chalkley* [1998] QB 848, it was described as 'in essence much the same as the intertwined and overlapping provisions of the old test, as was intended by the Royal Commission in recommending it, the Government in promoting it, the senior judiciary in supporting its parliamentary passage and Parliament in enacting it'.

The 'lurking doubt' test was relied on in some earlier cases, but its use was disapproved of in *R v Farrow* (20 October 1998), where the Court of Appeal described the new test as simple and clear and one upon which it was undesirable to place any gloss, in particular that of 'lurking doubt'.

12.3.3   The Criminal Appeal Act 1968 and the Human Rights Act 1998

The power of the Court of Appeal to uphold a conviction of an appellant if it is 'safe' must now be read in the light of Article 6 of the European Convention on Human Rights, which confers on the defendant the right to a fair trial. The relationship between the safety of the conviction and the fairness of the trial has been the subject of some discussion in the Court of Appeal. On one hand, the Court of Appeal may find that the conviction is safe even though there has been some irregularity or misdirection in the trial that would render it 'unfair', ie the defendant is guilty. On the other hand, a conviction may be quashed because the trial was unfair even though the defendant is clearly guilty, ie the conviction would be 'safe'.

A review of all the cases in which the Court of Appeal has dealt with these different approaches is beyond the scope of this Manual, but the following cases are worthy of note: *Condron v United Kingdom* [2000] Crim LR 679, *R v Francom* [2001] 1 Cr App R 237, *R v Davis* [2001] 1 Cr App R 115 and *R v Togher* [2001] 3 All ER 463.

In *Condron* the European Court of Human Rights stressed the need for the Court of Appeal to examine the fairness of the trial, rather than the safety of conviction, stating: 'The question whether or not the rights of the defence guaranteed to an accused under Article 6 of the Convention were secured in any given case cannot be assimilated to a finding that his conviction was safe in the absence of any enquiry into the issue of fairness.'

In *Francom*, where the trial judge had failed to direct the jury at all, the Court of Appeal accepted that the term 'unfair' in the context of Article 6 had to be given a broad meaning favourable to the accused. It was not limited to the safety of the conviction itself, but encompassed the entire prosecution process. Lord Woolf went on to say:

A misdirection of the jury could result in a breach of Article 6. But it may not do so. In the same way it may not make a conviction unsafe. It all depends on the circumstances of the case. In a case such as the present, we would expect this court to approach the issue of lack of safety in exactly the same way as the [European Court of Human Rights] approaches the lack of fairness. The directions which a judge gives at trial are designed to achieve the very fairness required by Article 6(1). As we understand the jurisprudence of the ECHR, that court does not adopt a technical approach to the question of fairness. The European Court is interested . . . in requiring fairness of the trial in all circumstances.

Later he continued:

The test which we have to apply before upholding the conviction is whether, notwithstanding the non-direction, we are satisfied that no reasonable jury could have come to a different conclusion from that which was reached by the jury, if they were properly directed. That approach not only means there must not be a lack of safety, it also means there must be no unfairness because the non-direction or misdirection must not affect the accused's right to a fair trial.

In *Davis*, the European Court of Human Rights decided that there had been a violation of the appellant's right, which was not cured by the appeal process. Mantell LJ stated that:

The court is concerned with the safety of the conviction. A conviction can never be safe if there is doubt about guilt. However the converse is not true. A conviction may be unsafe even where there is no doubt about guilt, but the trial process has been vitiated by serious unfairness or significant legal misdirection. That being so, there is no tension between s 2(1)(a) of the Criminal Appeal Act 1968 and s 3(1) of the Human Rights Act 1998.

Later he said:

[W]e are satisfied that the two questions (ie safety and fairness) must be kept separate and apart. The European Court of Human Rights is charged with enquiring into whether there has been a breach of a Convention right. This court is concerned with the safety of the conviction. That the first question may intrude upon the second is obvious. To what extent it does so will depend upon the circumstances of the particular case.

In *Togher*, an appeal following a plea of guilty, Lord Woolf CJ said, after discussing *Condron*:

Now that the Convention is part of our domestic law, it would be most unfortunate if the approach identified by the European Court and the approach of this court continued to differ unless this is inevitable because of provisions contained in this country's legislation or the state of our case law.

Moreover, in *Togher* Lord Woolf said, 'We would expect . . . that the approach of this court applying the test of lack of safety would produce the same result as the approach of the European Court applying the test of lack of fairness'.

Note that in the view of the editors of *Blackstone's Criminal Practice*, there is no insuperable problem in interpreting the requirement under the CAA 1968 that the conviction is safe in such a way as to encompass the Convention right that the trial is fair. If this is done, then the two requirements are not incompatible.

12.3.4   Errors commonly before the Court of Appeal

Some errors occur commonly and the following cases are intended to illustrate the way the Court of Appeal approaches such errors. This list includes cases decided both before and after the CAA 1995, and it may be that some of the pre-1995 cases would now be decided differently, particularly in view of the Human Rights Act 1998 (HRA). This list is not intended to be exhaustive.

(a) *The wrongful admission or exclusion of evidence.* If the wrongful admission or exclusion of evidence renders the conviction unsafe, the Court of Appeal will quash the conviction.

(b) *Defects in the indictment.* For example, the indictment is bad for duplicity or falls foul of r 9 of the Indictment Rules 1971, SI 1971/1253. Before 1995, the Court of Appeal would only quash the conviction if the defect was serious. Applying the new test in the light of the HRA 1998, the Court of Appeal may now come to a different conclusion.

(c) *The absence of corroboration.* If there was no corroboration when it was required, the Court of Appeal will usually quash the conviction.

(d) *Failure or misdirection by the trial judge on the burden or standard of proof.* Such a non-direction or misdirection will often lead to the quashing of the conviction, but see *R v Edwards* (1983) 77 Cr App R 5, where the trial judge did not direct the jury as to the standard of proof. The conviction was upheld because the evidence against the defendant was overwhelming and the jury had been reminded of the standard by both counsel in any event.

(e) *A wrong rejection of no case to answer.* Prior to 1995, if the trial judge wrongly rejected a submission of no case to answer, the appeal succeeded and the proviso was not applied. Had the trial judge not erred in law, the defendant would have been acquitted and no matter what evidence was adduced in the trial subsequently, the acquittal would not have been affected (*R v Cockley* (1984) 79 Cr App R 181). In *R v Smith* [1999] 2 Cr App R 238, the Court of Appeal reached the same conclusion applying the new test, even though, in this case, the defendant admitted guilt during cross-examination.

(f) *Interventions by the trial judge.* If there are a large number of interventions by the trial judge, which effectively prevent the proper development of the defence case, then the conviction is likely to be quashed (see *R v Matthews and Matthews* (1984) 78 Cr App R 23, *R v Whybrow* The Times, 14 February 1994 and *R v Ahmed* The Times, 9 March 1995). In *R v Cameron* [2001] Crim LR 587 the Court of Appeal upheld the actions of the trial judge who conducted the cross-examination of the 14-year-old complainant in a rape case after she refused to respond to questions put by defence counsel. For a recent example, see *R v Marsh* [2002] EWCA 1497.

See also *R v Garrett* 2 December 2003, CA, where the conviction was quashed due, *inter alia*, to the cumulative effect of the trial judge's questions to the jury in a short and straightforward case.

(g) *Failure or misdirection by the trial judge on law.* This will usually lead to the quashing of the conviction. See, for example, *R v Jones* [1997] Crim LR 598 where, on a charge of robbery, the trial judge did not direct the jury that the use of force had to be with the intention of stealing. The Court of Appeal quashed the conviction, holding that it was crucial to direct the jury on this element as well as the theft element.

(h) *Failure to deal with the essential thrust of the defence case.* For a recent example, see *R v Osborn* [2002] All ER (D) 320, where the Court of Appeal quashed the conviction of a defendant charged with causing grievous bodily harm where the possibility of accident, raised at the trial, was not mentioned in the summing-up.

In *R v Stephenson* 18 November 2003, CA, the conviction for possession with intent to supply was quashed because the trial judge introduced a new factual basis for the commission of the offence in his summing up to the jury.

(i) *Errors by defence counsel.* The Court of Appeal will not allow an appeal on the basis that defence counsel's actions were mistaken or unwise, though in the case of 'flagrantly incompetent advocacy' it will quash the conviction (*R v Ensor* [1989] 1 WLR 497). In *R v Clinton* [1993] 1 WLR 1181, the appeal was on the basis that the appellant was not advised to give evidence but should have been. The Court of Appeal said that the crucial issue was not counsel's incompetence, but the effect on the trial and the verdict, and quashed the conviction. The test of flagrantly incompetent advocacy has been doubted in subsequent cases, for example *R v Chatterjee* [1996] Crim LR 801 where the conviction was quashed because impressive expert evidence available to defence counsel was not properly put before the jury, and *R v Scollan* [1999] Crim LR 566 where defence counsel did not properly follow the accused's instructions as to crucial details of the defence. In *R v Nangle* [2001] Crim LR 506, and *R v Thakrar* [2001] 1 All ER (D) 103, the Court of Appeal said that if the failures of de- fence counsel mean that the defendant has been deprived of his right to a fair trial, it may be compelled to intervene. In *R v Doherty* [1997] 2 Cr App R 218, the Court of Appeal set out the guidance and procedure to be followed where the appeal involves criticism of trial counsel. Guidance issued in December 1995 by the Bar Council was quoted with approval by the Lord Chief Justice. In particular, an appeal on this basis should not be pursued unless 'it can be demonstrated that in the light of the information available to him at the time, no reasonably competent counsel would sensibly have adopted the course taken by him at the time when he took it'. In *R v Pluck* [2002] All ER (D) 281, where the Court of Appeal held that decisions made by defence counsel in good faith after proper consideration of the arguments, and after discussion with the defendant if appropriate, did not render the conviction unsafe. See also *R v Hobson* [1998] 1 Cr App R 31, *R v Nasser* The Times, 19 February 1998 and *Boodram v Trinidad and Tobago* [2002] 1 Cr App R 12.

The point arose again in slightly unusual contexts in *R v Shatwell and Lea* [2002] EWCA Crim 215 and *R v Hall* [2002] EWCA Crim 1881. In the first case, the defendants' appeal was rejected, as the fact that prosecution were represented by Queen's Counsel did not mean that the defendants had been deprived of their right to a fair trial on the basis of an inequality of arms. What was required was that the chosen advocate had competently presented the defence, and in this case, no valid criticism could be made. In the second case, leading counsel had been diagnosed with a terminal illness just before the trial, and the defendant argued that he had not received a fair trial, as the illness may have affected counsel's ability to make decisions regarding his defence. The Court of Appeal dismissed the appeal, holding that the question was whether the conduct of the case fell below the proper standard so that the defendant did not receive a fair trial. In this case, the decisions made by counsel were within the range of decisions which competent counsel could have made. In *R v Kamar* The Times, 5 November 2002, the Court of Appeal held that, where credibility is an issue of central importance, the failure of defence counsel to raise the issue of the defendant's good character rendered the trial defective.

The test when assessing if the conduct of a legal adviser had been such as to render a defendant's trial unfair was whether the conduct of the legal adviser had been unreasonable in the *Wednesbury* sense and whether as such it had had an actual affect on the fairness of the trial: *R v Bolivar, R v Lee* 14 April 2003, CA.

(j) *A refusal by the trial judge to exercise a discretion in favour of the defence.* The Court of Appeal is generally reluctant to interfere with the exercise of the trial judge's discretion, and will usually do so only if the discretion was exercised on the wrong basis (eg *R v Morris* [1991] Crim LR 385) or if the discretion was not exercised at all (eg *R v Dubarry* (1976) 64 Cr App R 7). Where the trial judge is exercising a discretion under PACE 1984, s 78, however, the Court of Appeal is much more willing to interfere. See the ***Evidence Manual***.

(k) *A failure by the trial judge to direct the jury to ignore his views.* In *R v Dow* 20 November 2003, CA, the trial judge's failure to direct the jury, *inter alia*, that they should ignore his views unless they coincided with the jury's own was not enough to lead to the quashing of the conviction.

(l) *The residual discretion of the CA.* Even where the trial process cannot be faulted, there remains in the Court of Appeal a residual discretion to set aside a conviction where it is felt it would be unsafe or unfair to allow it to stand: *R v B* [2003] All ER (D) 67, where the defendant was put in an impossible position to defend himself, having regard to the 30-year delay, even though the judge had warned the jury fairly and carefully with ample warning of the difficulties faced by the defendant, and the very limited evidence which was available. This was one of the residual cases where, in the interests of justice, the conviction had to be set aside.

(m) *Inconsistencies in the verdicts.* Where the verdict of guilty is inconsistent with the verdict of not guilty, the conviction may be quashed. See for example *R v Loi* [2003] EWCA 801.

Where a trial judge removes a defence from a jury's consideration, the prosecution must still prove an affirmative case and it remains for the jury to return its own voluntary verdict. It is never right for the trial judge to direct the jury to convict in terms: *R v Kelleher* [2003] EWCA 2846 where the defence was self-defence, and on the evidence, the only proper verdict was guilty and the conviction was safe.

The deliberations of the jury are immune from examination, and the Court of Appeal will not intervene where, after an unambiguous verdict, a juror subsequently alleges that the verdict was not unanimous. As a matter of policy, the verdict is final. Further, jurors should be protected from pressure or inducement to alter their views. This position is not altered by the HRA 1998. See *R v Millward* [1999] 1 Cr App R 61, and *R v Lewis* (26 April 2001). Note also *R v Young* [1995] QB 324, where the use, by some members of the jury, of a ouija board during the overnight adjournment to determine the defendant's guilt was held to be outside the course of the jury deliberations and therefore reviewable by the Court of Appeal.

12.3.5 Leave to appeal

By virtue of the CAA 1968, as amended, leave to appeal against conviction is always required. Leave may be given either by the trial judge, or by the Court of Appeal itself.

The CAA1968, s 1 provides as follows:

(2) An appeal under this section lies only —
   (a) with the leave of the Court of Appeal; or
   (b) if the judge of the court of trial grants a certificate that the case is fit for appeal.

The certificate may be granted either:

- on the judge's own initiative, in which case the judge drafts the question which he or she considers ought to be raised (it is then read to counsel for their comment); or

- on counsel's application (in which case counsel normally drafts the question and the application itself is made in chambers with a shorthand writer present).

See generally *Practice Direction (criminal: consolidated)* [2002] 3 All ER 904, para 50.

There must be a particular and cogent ground of appeal on which the appellant will have a substantial chance of succeeding (*R v Bansal* [1999] Crim LR 484). See also *Practice*

Direction (criminal: consolidated), para 50 and, in particular, see para 50.4:

The first question for the judge is then whether there exists a particular and cogent ground of appeal. If there is no such ground there can be no certificate, and if there is no certificate there can be no bail. A judge should not grant a certificate with regard to sentence merely in the light of mitigation to which he has, in his opinion, given due weight, nor in regard to conviction on a ground where he considers the chance of a successful appeal is not substantial. The judge should bear in mind that, where a certificate is refused, application may be made to the Court of Appeal for leave to appeal and for bail.

Under the Proceeds of Crime Act 2002, the person (designated by the statute) who has applied for a restraint order under s 40–41 (prohibiting the person specified in the order from dealing with any 'realisable property'), or the person affected by the order may appeal against the decision of the Crown Court with leave of the Court of Appeal. A further appeal may be made to the House of Lords, but a certificate from the Court of Appeal that the case involves a point of law of general public importance is not required, nor is leave to appeal from either the Court of Appeal or the House of Lords.

12.3.6   Appeals after a plea of guilty

The defendant may appeal against conviction after a plea of guilty but only in exceptional circumstances. These are:

(a) Where the defendant did not appreciate the nature of the charge (*R v Forde* [1923] 2 KB 400).

(b) Where the defendant did not intend to admit that he or she was guilty of the charge (*Forde*). This would include cases where pressure was put on the defendant to plead guilty by either counsel or the trial judge.

(c) Where on the admitted facts the defendant could not in law have been convicted of the offence charged (*Forde*).

(d) In exceptional circumstances where the defendant knew what he was doing when he pleaded guilty, intended to plead guilty and did so unequivocally after having taken legal advice (*R v Lee* [1984] 1 WLR 578).

(e) Where the plea was founded on an incorrect ruling of law on admitted facts which left an accused with no legal escape from a verdict of guilty (*R v Chalkley* [1998] QB 848). If, on the other hand, the defendant pleaded guilty because he realised that as a result of the ruling the evidence against him was so strong that his case was hopeless, no appeal against conviction would apply. In such cases, the accused should plead not guilty and appeal in the normal way. *Chalkley* was followed in *R v Rajcoomar* [1999] Crim LR 728.

   The second, wider, approach was preferred in *R v Togher* [2001] 3 All ER 463, to the effect that a plea of guilty following a material irregularity could also found an appeal. In particular, the word 'unsafe' should be applied in a way compatible with the European Convention on Human Rights. Fairness of the trial and the safety of conviction went together. Denial of a fair trial almost inevitably rendered the conviction unsafe. See **12.3.2**

Note that where the appellant appeals after a plea of guilty, there is no power to substitute a verdict of guilty of an alternative offence under CAA 1968, s 3.

12.3.7   Single right of appeal

Under the CAA 1968, the appellant has the right to bring an appeal before the Court of Appeal. If that appeal is dismissed, he or she has no right to bring a second appeal on the same matter (see *R v Pinfold* [1988] QB 462). Two apparent exceptions were recognised in *Pinfold*:

- where an appellant seeks to revive an abandoned appeal;
- where, owing to some defect in the procedure, the appellant has, on the first appeal being dismissed, suffered an injustice, such as where he or she was not notified of a hearing date.

In *R v Thomas* [2002] EWCA 941, the Court of Appeal held that it was not bound by the rule in *Pinfold* when dealing with a case which had been referred to it by the Criminal Cases Review Commission (see **12.13**). The power to make such a re-determination, however, should be limited to 'exceptional circumstances'. The court found it difficult to envisage such exceptional circumstances, but concluded that they would have to be such as to convince the court that if the case had been argued in that way on the previous occasion, it would, not might, have quashed the conviction. In any event, the court should be very slow to differ from the earlier judgement.

It appears that the appellant has a separate right of appeal on the basis that the proceedings were a nullity, as the powers of the Court of Appeal to issue a *venire de novo* (an order returning the proceedings to the point immediately before the error, so that it can be corrected) exist independently of CAA 1968. See also *R v Lamming* (1989) 90 Cr App R 450.

12.3.8   Appeals in the case of death

Prior to the CAA 1995, there was no procedure whereby the conviction of a deceased person could be challenged on appeal. The CAA 1995, s 7 inserts an entirely new provision into the CAA 1968. Section 44A now gives a person approved by the Court of Appeal the right to begin or continue an appeal after the death of the deceased.

The persons approved by the Court of Appeal under s 44A(3) must be one of the following:

- the widow or widower of the deceased;
- his or her personal representatives;
- any other person who, by family or other similar relationship with the deceased, has a substantial financial or other interest in the determining of the appeal.

The application for approval must be made within one year of death (s 44A(4)).

R v Whelan [1997] Crim LR 659, is believed to be the first application under this section. A widow was held to be entitled to continue her deceased husband's appeal against conviction for assault on his daughter, where only death had prevented him from pursuing the appeal himself.

12.4   Evidence

Under the CAA 1968, as amended by the CAA 1995, s 4, the Court of Appeal may receive any evidence if it considers that it is necessary or expedient in the interest of justice.

The CAA 1968, s 23, as amended, provides as follows:

(1)   For purposes of an appeal under this part of this Act [appeals against conviction and/or sentence and references to the Court of Appeal by the Home Secretary] the Court of Appeal may, if they think it necessary or expedient in the interests of justice —

(a)   order the production of any document, exhibit or other thing connected with the proceedings, the production of which appears to them necessary for the determination of the case;

(b)   order any witness who would have been a compellable witness in the proceedings from which the appeal lies to attend for examination and be examined before the court, whether or not he was called in those proceedings; and

(c)   receive any evidence which was not adduced in the proceedings from which the appeal lies.

(2)   The Court of Appeal shall, in considering whether to receive any evidence, have regard in particular to —

(a)   whether the evidence appears to the Court to be capable of belief;

(b)   whether it appears to the Court that the evidence may afford any ground for allowing the appeal;

(c)   whether the evidence would have been admissible in the proceedings from which the appeal lies on an issue which is the subject of the appeal; and

(d)   whether there is a reasonable explanation for the failure to adduce the evidence in those proceedings.

(3)   Subsection (1)(c) above applies to any evidence of a witness (including the appellant) who is competent but not compellable.

(4)   For purposes of an appeal under this Part of this Act, the Court of Appeal may, if they think it necessary or expedient in the interests of justice, order the examination of any witness whose attendance might be required under subsection (1)(b) above to be conducted, in a manner provided by rules of court, before any judge or offIcer of the Court or other person appointed by the Court for the purpose, and allow the admission of any depositions so taken as evidence before the Court.

In *R v Pendleton* [2002] 1 WLR 72, the House of Lords considered that the correct test to be applied, where fresh evidence was to be admitted, was whether the conviction was safe, and not whether the accused was guilty. This was a matter for the judgment of the Court of Appeal, which should apply the test from the viewpoint of the effect of the fresh evidence on the minds of members of the court, and not the presumed effect on the minds of the trial jury. However, it would usually be appropriate for the court to ask itself the question, to test its provisional view, whether the evidence, if given at the trial, might reasonably have affected the decision of the trial jury to convict. If so, the conviction should be regarded as unsafe.

In *R v Hanratty* [2002] EWCA 1141, the Court of Appeal held that the overriding consideration in deciding whether fresh evidence should be admitted was whether the evidence would assist the Court to achieve justice, which may either be by upholding a conviction which was safe or setting it aside if it was unsafe. Fresh evidence may be admitted where, though not relevant to a specific ground of appeal, it was relevant to the overall question of the guilt or innocence of the appellant. Where the issue before the court was the safety of the conviction, ie the guilt of the appellant, fresh evidence would usually be admitted. Where the issue before the court was the fairness of the proceedings, fresh evidence would not usually be admissible because it did not deal with the defect at the trial, unless it placed the defect in its context. This approach was particularly important where the Court was dealing with old cases where standards have changed over the years. The Court would be expected to enforce standards, but this did not apply where the rule was not in force at the time of the trial.

For recent examples see *R v Winzar* [2002] EWCA 2950, *R v Jacques* [2003] All ER (D) 26 and *R v Mynott* [2003] All ER (D) 39.

The following points may be noted about s 23 of the CAA 1968:

(a)   The test for receiving evidence is that of the interests of justice. See *R v Jones* The Times, 23 July 1996, where the court received fresh medical evidence, even though there was no strong argument to do so, holding that it was expedient in the interests of justice.

(b) The section permits any evidence to be called before the Court of Appeal, whether or not it was called at the trial (*R v Mercer* [2001] All ER (D) 187).

(c) If evidence is to be received, the matters contained in s 23(2) are important. These points, however, are merely matters to which the court should have regard and not conditions for the admissibility of the evidence namely:

   (i)   whether the evidence appears to be capable of belief;

   (ii) whether the evidence affords any ground for allowing the appeal;

   (iii) whether the evidence would have been admissible;

   (iv) where there is a reasonable explanation for not calling the evidence at trial.

(d) Section 23(2)(a) provides that the evidence must be 'capable of belief', replacing the old test of 'likely to be credible'. In *R v Parks* [1961] 1 WLR 1484, it was held that 'likely to be credible' meant whether the witness's proof of evidence was intrinsically credible, and whether it fitted in with at least some of the other evidence in the case.

(e) As to whether there is a 'reasonable explanation' for the failure to adduce evidence at the trial, the case of *R v Beresford* (1971) 56 Cr App R 143, on precisely similar words, decided that the test was whether the evidence could have been obtained with 'reasonable diligence'.

(f) Rules on the receipt of fresh evidence have more relevance to factual evidence than to expert evidence, as experts are interchangeable to a certain extent, and if there is only one expert, and that expert is unavailable, the case may be postponed. See *R v Jones* [1997] 1 Cr App R 86. Fresh expert evidence will be received in appropriate circumstances, however. In *R v Latte* (1996), fresh expert evidence was called and the Court of Appeal accepted that there was a reasonable explanation for not adducing the evidence at trial because the field of expertise (lighting and facial recognition) was highly specialised and not well known.

(g) The role of the Court of Appeal is not to make a finding of fact but to assess new evidence that has become available since the trial and to make a decision on the safety of the earlier conviction (*R v Twitchell* [2000] 1 Cr App R 373).

(h) *R v Guppy* (1995) 16 Cr App R (S) 25, a decision on the old law, held that on a true construction of ss 11(3) and 23(1)(c), the Court of Appeal is empowered to receive fresh evidence of any witness, including the appellant, on an appeal against sentence. It would seem that this decision will be followed under the new formulation of s 23(1)(c).

(i) In *R v Ahluwalia* [1992] 4 All ER 889, the fresh evidence which the appellant wished to adduce raised a defence which was not raised at the trial (psychiatric reports as to the appellant's diminished responsibility). The Court of Appeal admitted the reports as fresh evidence, concluding that there may have been an arguable defence which, for some unexplained reason, was not raised at the trial.

See also *R v Moringiello* [1997] Crim LR 902, where the Court of Appeal did not allow fresh evidence to be called by the appellant's solicitor that the trial judge had fallen asleep during part of the evidence. Such an allegation had to be made at the time so that it could be known which parts of the evidence the judge was supposed to have missed.

12.5 Appeal against sentence

The right of appeal against sentence after conviction on indictment is found in CAA 1968, s 9. However, the Court of Appeal has always recognised that judges approach the question of sentencing in different ways, and must be allowed a measure of discretion in their approach. Thus, the court will not interfere merely because it would have passed a somewhat different sentence in a particular case.

The following are the most widely accepted grounds of appeal:

(a) *The sentence is wrong in law*. Where the judge passes a sentence which he has no jurisdiction to pass, such as a sentence of imprisonment on someone under the age of 21 years, the Court of Appeal will interfere. However, appeals on such grounds are rare.

(b) *The sentence is wrong in principle*. This contention covers two situations:

(i) Where the appellant argues that entirely the wrong type of sentence was imposed, such as a sentence of custody when non-custodial measures were appropriate.

(ii) Where the judge combines two sentences which are inconsistent with each other, such as a sentence of imprisonment and a probation order.

(c) *The sentence is manifestly excessive*. Here the appellant is arguing that the right type of sentence has been imposed, but that in the circumstances it is too severe.

(d) *The judge took the wrong approach to sentencing*. If the trial judge, in passing sentence, has taken into account an irrelevant consideration, such as the fact that the appellant has alleged that the police officers had fabricated their evidence, the sentence is likely to be reduced.

(e) *The judge followed the wrong procedure prior to sentence*. If, following a plea of guilty, there has been a dispute as to the facts of the case, and the judge accepts the prosecution version without any inquiry or investigation, then the Court of Appeal may feel obliged to reduce the sentence. See *R v Newton* (1982) 77 Cr App R 13 and, generally, **11.2.2** above and **13.4.2** below.

(f) *Disparity*. Any disparity between the sentence imposed on co-defendants is probably best seen as merely a factor that the Court of Appeal will take into account when considering an appeal against sentence. It is unlikely, on its own, to support a successful appeal against sentence, but the view of the court has been inconsistent. On the one hand the court says that if the disparity is so marked that one of the former co-defendants is left with a burning sense of grievance, then it would be right to interfere (see *R v Dickinson* [1977] Crim LR 303). On the other hand, the court has also expressed the view that the mere fact that one sentence is wrong (the lighter sentence) is no reason for altering the right sentence and making two wrong sentences (see *R v Stroud* (1977) 65 Cr App R 150).

(g) *Sense of grievance*. If the sentencing procedure and the actual sentence, taken together, leave the offender with a justifiable sense of grievance, then the Court of Appeal may interfere, notwithstanding that the sentence is not in itself too severe, for example where the offender is sentenced to custody after reports have been ordered, leading him actually and legitimately to expect a non-custodial sentence if the reports are good, and the reports are good (see *R v Gillam* (1980) 2 Cr App R (S) 267, *R v Ward* (1982) 4 Cr App R (S) 103, *R v Jackson* [1996] Crim LR 355 and *R v Horton* (1985) 7 Cr App R (S) 299).

12.6 Procedure for appeal

Preliminary notes: The procedure is the same whether the appeal is against conviction or sentence. The procedure is governed by the CAA 1968, the Criminal Appeal Rules 1968 (SI 1968/1262) and 'the Guide', namely 'A Guide to Proceedings in the Court of Appeal Criminal Division', produced by the Registrar of Criminal Appeals. The latest version of the Guide was produced in 1997. Students should also be familiar with *Practice Direction (criminal: consolidated)* [2002] 3 All ER 904.

Within 28 days of conviction (or sentence if the appeal is against sentence) notice of application for leave to appeal should be served on the Crown Court at which the proceedings took place. If appealing against conviction, counsel should observe the 28-day limit, even if there are practical difficulties, if there has been a delay between conviction and sentence.

The notice of application for leave to appeal is in a standard form (form 2), which includes:

- the name and address of the appellant;
- the name of the court where he or she was tried, the name of the judge and the dates of his or her appearances;
- the offences of which he or she was convicted and the sentence imposed; and
- the application being made.

This will include not only the application for leave but also, where appropriate:

- leave to appeal out of time;
- legal aid;
- bail pending determination of the appeal;
- leave to be present at the hearing; or
- leave to call witnesses.

Another standard form (form 3) sets out the grounds of appeal (see **12.6.2** below). The forms are served on the Crown Court where the proceedings took place, and are then forwarded to the Criminal Appeal Office by the Crown Court.

The notice and grounds must be signed either by the appellant or by someone on his or her behalf.

12.6.1 Transcripts

Once the Registrar at the Criminal Appeal Office has the notice and grounds, he or she may then order a transcript of any necessary part of the trial or summing-up as specified by counsel in the grounds of appeal. It is rare to request a transcript of the entire case and counsel should not do so unless it is essential.

12.6.2 Grounds of appeal

Once counsel has received a copy of the transcript, the grounds of appeal can be set out in full, or 'perfected', as counsel will now have, for example, the exact words with which the judge directed the jury. Counsel has 14 days to perfect the grounds of appeal.

No particular form of words is required when settling the grounds of appeal, but each point on which appeal is being made should be clearly identified, and set out in sufficient detail for the court to identify clearly the matters relied on. It is often convenient to make these points in chronological order. The grounds should refer to the transcript by page and paragraph number, and should cite any authorities upon which counsel proposes to rely. If counsel wishes to call a witness at the appeal, the reason why such a course is necessary should be explained fully. Further, any document referred to should be clearly identified.

Paragraphs 15.1 and 15.2 of *Practice Direction (criminal: consolidated)* [2002] 3 All ER 904 provide as follows:

15.1   Advocates should not settle grounds or support them with written advice unless they consider that they are properly arguable. Grounds should be carefully drafted and properly particularised. Advocates should not assume that the court will entertain any ground of appeal not set out and properly particularised. Should leave to amend the grounds be granted it is most unlikely that further grounds will be entertained.

15.2   A copy of the advocate's positive advice about the merits should be attached as part of the grounds.

In appeals against conviction, counsel should send the court a document expanding the grounds of appeal and outlining the arguments he or she intends to place before the court (known as a 'skeleton argument'). This saves time and therefore expense at the hearing of the appeal itself. *Practice Direction (criminal: consolidated)* [2002] 3 All ER 904, paras 17.1 and 17.5 provide as follows:

17.1   In all appeals against conviction a skeleton argument from the advocate for the appellant is to be lodged with the Registrar of Criminal Appeals and served on the prosecuting authority within 14 days of receipt by the advocate of the notification of the grant of leave to appeal against conviction or such longer period as the registrar or the court may direct. The skeleton may refer to an advice, which should be annexed with an indication of which parts of it are relied upon, and should include any additional arguments to be advanced.

17.5   A skeleton argument should contain a numbered list of the points the advocate intends to argue, grouped under each ground of appeal, and stated in no more than one or two sentences. It should be as succinct as possible, the object being to identify each point, not to argue it or elaborate on it. Each listed point should be followed by full references to the material to which the advocate will refer in support of it, ie, the relevant passages in the transcript, authorities etc. It should also contain anything which the advocate would expect to be taken down by the court during the hearing, such as propositions of law, chronologies etc. If more convenient, these can be annexed to the skeletons rather than included in it. For points of law, the skeleton should state the point and cite the principal authority or authorities in support with reference to the passages where the principle is enunciated. Chronologies should, if possible, be agreed with the opposing advocate before the hearing. Respondents' skeletons should follow the same principles.

In order to assist the court, the Criminal Appeal Office prepares a summary of the cases coming before it, once the single judge gives leave to appeal. The summary is entirely objective and does not contain any advice about how the court should deal with the case or any view about its merits. *Practice Direction (criminal: consolidated)* [2002] 3 All ER 904, para 18.1.

The summary consists of two parts. Part I is provided to all advocates in the case (para 18.2), and to unrepresented appellants, unless a judge of the High Court or the Registrar directs to the contrary in a case involving material of an explicitly salacious or sadistic nature (para 18.5). Part I generally contains, according to para 18.2:

- particulars of the proceedings before the Crown Court;
- particulars of the proceedings before the Court of Appeal;

- the facts of the case as drawn from the transcripts, advice of the advocates, witnesses statements and/or exhibits (if an advocate does not want any factual material in his or her advice to be taken into account, this should be stated in his or her advice);

- the submissions and rulings, summing-up and sentencing remarks.

The contents of the summary are a matter for the writer, but if an advocate wishes to suggest any significant alteration, he or she should write to the Registrar. If the writer does not agree, the summary and the letter are put before the court.

Part II is for the court alone, and contains:

- a summary of the grounds of appeal;

- in appeals against sentence (and applications for leave) summaries of the antecedent histories of the parties and any relevant pre-sentence medical or other reports.

12.6.3   The single judge

The application for leave to appeal, and any other applications (see **12.6**), is placed before the single judge. No oral submission or arguments are heard by the single judge, who decides the matter on the basis of the papers before him or her.

If the single judge refuses to grant leave, the appellant has 14 days to renew the application before the full court, whose decision is final. When applying for leave to the single judge, or to the full court, the appellant should bear in mind the court's power to order 'loss of time' (see **12.6.1**).

The court has power to extend the 14-day time limit, but very rarely does so (see *R v Dixon* [2000] 1 WLR 782).

Where the single judge grants leave in respect of certain grounds of appeal, but expressly refuses leave in respect of others, the latter grounds may only be argued on appeal with leave of the full court (*R v Jackson* [1999] 1 All ER 572). Further guidance on this issue was given in *R v Cox and Thomas* [1999] 2 Cr App R 6.

12.7   Powers of the single judge

Most of the powers of the Court of Appeal, short of deciding the appeal itself, are exercised by the single judge of the court under the CAA 1968, s 31. The single judge has power to:

(a) Grant leave to appeal.

(b) Allow the appellant to be present at the hearing of the appeal. Under the CAA 1968, s 22(1), the appellant is entitled to be present at the hearing of an appeal even if he or she is in custody. However, if the appellant is in custody, he or she is not entitled to be present if the appeal is on the ground of law alone, nor on any preliminary application, without leave.

(c) Order a witness to attend for examination. The court may order a witness to appear before it, in pursuance of an appeal under the CAA 1968, s 23. This has the advantage of allowing both parties to the appeal to cross-examine.

(d) Allow bail pending the appeal hearing. Under the CAA 1968, s 19, the court has the power to grant bail to an appellant pending the hearing of the appeal. However, bail is granted only rarely, and only where it appears that the appeal is likely to be successful; or where the sentence is so short that it is likely to have been served before the appeal can be heard. In deciding whether to grant bail, the true test is, 'are there exceptional circumstances which would drive the court to the conclusion that justice can only be done by the granting of bail?' (*per* Geoffrey Lane LJ in *R v Watton* (1978) 68 Cr App R 293).

(e) Make, vary or discharge orders, for example, as to whether the appellant is in custody or on bail pending retrial.

(f) Make orders as to the costs of the appeal, including legal aid.

(g) Give directions for loss of time (see **12.8.1**).

12.7.1 Powers of the Registrar

By virtue of the CAA 1968, s 31A, inserted by the CAA 1995, s 6, certain of these powers may be exercised by the Registrar. These are:

- to extend the time within which notice of application for leave to appeal may be given;

- to order a witness to attend for examination;

- to vary the conditions of bail granted by either the Court of Appeal or the Crown Court. However, he or she may not do so unless satisfied that the prosecution does not object to the variation (s 31A(3)).

If the Registrar refuses any of these applications, the appellant may apply to the single judge.

12.8 Powers of the Court of Appeal

12.8.1 Following appeal against conviction

Having heard the appeal against conviction the Court of Appeal may do any of the following:

(a) Dismiss the appeal.

(b) Allow the appeal and quash the conviction.

(c) Allow part of the appeal and dismiss the other part. If it does this, the court may pass a new sentence on the remaining conviction, but this must not be greater than the sentence as a whole passed by the convicting court (CAA 1968, s 4(3)). For example, the defendant is convicted of two offences and sentenced to one year's imprisonment on each to run consecutively. On appeal, one conviction is quashed. The Court of Appeal may increase the sentence on the remaining conviction to up to two years, this being the total imposed by the convicting court.

(d) Find the appellant guilty of an alternative offence. Under the CAA 1968, s 3, if the appellant has been convicted of one offence, but the jury, under the Criminal Law Act 1967, s 6, could have found him or her guilty of another offence, then the court may substitute a conviction for that other offence. Thus, if the jury has convicted of murder, the court may substitute a verdict of guilty of manslaughter. Further, if the defendant is charged with two counts in the alternative, and is convicted on one but the jury is discharged from giving a verdict on the other, the court may reverse the verdicts. The court must consider that the jury was satisfied of facts which proved him or her guilty of the other offence. See *R v Spratt* [1980] 1 WLR 554 and *R v Peterson* [1997] Crim LR 339. Section 4(3) of the CAA 1968 applies. The power to find the appellant guilty of an alternative offence only applies where the appellant pleaded not guilty at the trial (*R v Horsman* [1998] QB 531).

(e) Determine the appeal summarily under the CAA 1968, s 20. If the Registrar considers that an appeal has no real merit, he or she may put it before the Court for 'summary determination'. The Court may, if it is of the same opinion, simply dismiss it without a full hearing and without hearing argument from either side. This process is to discourage vexatious or frivolous appeals, and applies to all appeals, whether on points of pure law, fact, or mixed fact and law.

(f) Order a retrial. Under the CAA 1968, s 7, the court may order a retrial if it considers that a retrial is required in the interests of justice. The power to order a retrial is generally available, whether the appeal is on the basis of fresh evidence, or because of some irregularity or misdirection in the trial.

(g) Make an order for loss of time. Under the CAA 1968, s 29(1), any time spent in custody pending the determination of the appeal is to be reckoned as part of the term of any custody sentence which has been imposed, subject to any directions to the contrary that the Court may give. Such directions may be given where either the single judge or the full Court refuse leave to appeal.

Practice Direction (crime: consolidated) [2002] 3 All ER 904, para 16.1 provides:

16.1   Both the court and the single judge have power in their discretion to direct that part of the time during which an applicant is in custody after putting in his notice of application for leave to appeal should not count towards sentence. Those who contemplate putting in such a notice and their legal advisers should bear this in mind. It is important that those contemplating an appeal should ask advice and should remember that it was useless to appeal without grounds and that grounds should be substantial and particularised and not a mere formula. Where an application devoid of merit has been refused by the single judge and a direction for loss of time has been made, the full court, on renewal of the application, may direct that additional time shall be lost if it, once again, thinks it right so to exercise its discretion in all the circumstances of the case.

In addition, the Court of Appeal has inherent powers, independent of the CAA 1968, to issue a writ of *venire de novo*. If there has been such an irregularity at the trial that the trial can be said to have been a nullity, and the appellant was never in danger of a valid conviction, then the court may order the writ of *venire de novo* to be issued and the appellant may be retried. The irregularity has to be so fundamental that there could not be said to have been a trial (*R v Rose* [1982] AC 822, followed in *R v Booth, Holland and Wood* [1999] 1 Cr App R 457).

See also Patrick O'Connor, 'The Court of Appeal Retrials and Tribulations' [1990] Crim LR 615.

12.8.2   Following appeal against sentence

Having heard the appeal against sentence the court may:

- Quash any sentence or order which is the subject of the appeal.
- Impose any sentence that was available to the Crown Court, except that it may not deal with the appellant, taking the sentence as a whole, more severely than he or she was originally dealt with.

12.8.3   Following an appeal against sentence after summary conviction

Under the CAA 1968, s 10, the Court of Appeal also has the power to deal with an appeal against a sentence imposed by the Crown Court after the defendant has been convicted summarily. Section 10 covers two separate situations:

(a) *After committal for sentence.*   A defendant who has been summarily convicted and committed to the Crown Court for sentence may appeal against that sentence if:

    (i)   the sentence was to imprisonment or detention in a young offenders institution for a term of six months or more; or

    (ii)   the sentence was one which the magistrates did not have power to pass; or

    (iii)   the sentence included disqualification from driving, a recommendation for deportation, or activation of a suspended sentence.

(b) *Breach of a probation order or conditional discharge.* A defendant who has been summarily convicted of an offence which puts him or her in breach of a probation order or conditional discharge, and who is sentenced by the Crown Court for the original offence, may appeal against that sentence in the same circumstances as set out in (a) above.

12.8.4   The Human Rights Act 1998

The Human Rights Act 1998, s 4, provides the Court of Appeal (together with the other superior courts) with the power to make a declaration of incompatibility, ie that a provision of primary legislation is incompatible with Convention rights. Section 5 further provides that if the Court is considering making such a declaration, the Crown is entitled to notice in accordance with rules of court. The Criminal Appeal (Amendment) Rules 2000 (SI 2000 No. 2036) amend the Criminal Appeal Rules 1968 accordingly.

Section 5(2) of the 1998 Act entitles a Minister of the Crown (or person nominated by him or her), a member of the Scottish Executive, a Northern Ireland Minister or a Northern Ireland department, on giving notice, to be joined as a party to the proceedings.

12.9   The appeal against acquittal and order for retrial

12.9.1   The right to appeal

As from June 2004, the prosecution may appeal against the acquittal of the defendant by the Crown Court, if certain conditions are satisfied, by virtue of CJA 2003 ss 75–97. It also applies to acquittals following a successful appeal against conviction.

The right to appeal under this section is not available for every offence, but only for the offences listed in Sch 5 to the Act. These are the most serious offences and include murder, manslaughter, rape, arson endangering life, and war crimes. There is no appeal under these sections where the defendant was found guilty or found not guilty either by reason of insanity or in respect of which he has been found to be under a disability (CJA 2003, s 75(a), (b) and (c)).

Note that s 75(4) makes provision for the retrial of offences where the offender was acquitted outside the UK.

In order to take advantage of the new right to appeal, under CJA 2003, s 76, a prosecutor applies to the Court of Appeal for an order:

- quashing a person's acquittal; and
- ordering his retrial for the offence.

12.9.2 Procedure

There is a two stage procedure in applying for the above order.

(a) The order may only be applied for with the consent of the Director of Public Prosecutions (s 76). Such consent will only be given if:

   (i)   there is new and compelling evidence (see below);

   (ii) it is in the public interest for the application to proceed; and

   (iii) it does not conflict with the treaty obligations under Article 31 or 34 of the Treaty on European Union (the Articles essentially prevent the bringing of new proceedings as opposed to opening up old proceedings).

(b) The prosecutor must seek the leave of the Court of Appeal. The basic steps are as follows, as set out by CJA 2003, s 80:

   (i)   the prosecution must give notice of application to the Court of Appeal;

   (ii) within two days of such notice, the prosecutor must give notice to the person affected. This time limit may be extended if the person affected is outside the UK;

   (iii) the Court of Appeal must consider the application at a hearing;

   (iv) the person is entitled to be present at the hearing, and whether or not he is present, he is entitled to be represented;

   (v) the Court of Appeal may, if it thinks it necessary in the interests of justice, order the production of any document or exhibit or the appearance of any compellable witness;

   (vi) the Court of Appeal may hear more than one application at one hearing but only if the matters could be tried together on the same indictment.

12.9.3 New and compelling evidence

Section 78 of the CJA 2003 provides that there must be new and compelling evidence against the acquitted person. Under s 78(2), evidence is new if it was not adduced in the proceedings in which the person was acquitted, or from which he appealed. An example of such evidence is new testing techniques.

Under s 78(3), evidence is compelling if:

- it is reliable;
- it is substantial, and
- in the context of the outstanding issues, it appears highly probative of the case against the acquitted person. The outstanding issues are the issues in dispute in the proceedings in which the person was acquitted and, if those were appeal proceedings, any other issues remaining in dispute from earlier proceedings to which the appeal related.

12.9.4   Determination by the Court of Appeal

If the Court of Appeal is dealing with an appeal against acquittal, it must make the order applied for and if not, must dismiss the application, if the requirements under CJA 2003, ss 78 and 79 are met (see above).

In addition, the Court of Appeal must be satisfied, under s 9, that it is in the interests of justice for the court to make the order. In determining this issue, the Court of Appeal will have regard, under s 79, to:

(a) Whether existing circumstances make a fair trial unlikely.

(b) For the purposes of that question and otherwise, the length of time since the offence was committed.

(c) Whether it is likely that the new evidence would have been adduced in the earlier proceedings against the acquitted person but for the failure by an officer or by a prosecutor to act with due diligence.

(d) Whether since those proceedings (or since the commencement of this part of the Act, if later) any officer or prosecutor has failed to act with due diligence.

12.10   Other methods of appeal

12.10.1   The Attorney-General's reference

Under the Criminal Justice Act 1972, s 36(1), where a defendant has been acquitted following a trial on indictment, the Attorney-General may refer any point of law that arose in the case to the Court of Appeal for its opinion. The purpose is to prevent potentially false decisions becoming too widely accepted. Whatever conclusion the Court of Appeal reaches on the point of law, the acquittal is not affected.

In order to bring proceedings under s 36, the Attorney-General serves a notice on the defendant within 28 days, containing the point of law to be argued, a summary of the argument, and the authorities the Attorney-General relies on. The Court of Appeal must hear the argument from the Attorney-General or his representative, and may hear submissions from the defence.

Under s 36(3), the Court of Appeal may refer the point to the House of Lords, either on its own initiative or following an application from either party. The House of Lords then considers the matter and gives its opinion.

12.10.2   Reference by the Attorney-General on a matter of sentence

Under the Criminal Justice Act 1988, ss 35 and 36, the Attorney-General may refer a sentence, which includes any order made by a court when dealing with an offender, to the Court of Appeal for review if:

• he or she considers that the sentence was 'unduly lenient' (this may, but need not, be because the Attorney-General considers that the judge erred in law as to his powers of sentence);

• leave of the Court of Appeal is granted; and

• the offence was triable only on indictment, or was triable either way but specified as reviewable in an order made by the Home Secretary.

By the Criminal Justice Act 1988 (Reviews of Sentencing) Order 1994 (SI 1994/119), indecent assault, threats to kill, cruelty to a person under 16, and attempts or incitement to commit any of these offences are specified as reviewable.

If an offender is sentenced for two separate matters, only one of which is triable only on indictment or specified as reviewable, they are to be treated as having been passed in the same proceeding if they are passed on the same day, or passed on different days but ordered to be treated as one sentence by the sentencing court. Thus, sentences may be reviewed by the Court of Appeal even though they do not fall within (c) above.

The procedure for bringing a sentencing reference is the same as for bringing an appeal against sentence (see **12.6**). The Court of Appeal may quash any sentence, and impose such a sentence as it thinks appropriate, provided it is a sentence which the Crown Court had power to pass.

The correct approach to sentencing references was set out by the Court of Appeal in *Attorney-General's Reference (No 4 of 1989)* [1990] 1 WLR 41:

- the sentence must be *unduly* lenient, that is it must fall out of the range of sentences which the judge could reasonably consider appropriate;

- assuming that it is unduly lenient, the court still has a discretion as to whether to exercise its powers;

- the court's powers are not confined to increasing the sentence.

For recent examples, see *R v Shaw, Attorney-General's Reference (No 28 of 1996)* and *R v Harnett, Attorney-General's Reference (No 60 of 1996)*, both reported in The Times, 27 January 1997 and *Attorney-General's Reference (No 110 of 2002)* [2003] EWCA Crim 540.

Further reading: Ralph Henham, '*Attorney-General's Reference* Revisited' (1998) 62(5) JCL 468.

12.11   Appeal to the House of Lords

Under the CAA 1968, s 33, either the prosecution or defendant may appeal from any decision of the Court of Appeal to the House of Lords if:

- leave is granted by either the Court of Appeal or the House of Lords; and

- the Court of Appeal certifies that the case raises a point of law of general public importance which ought to be considered by the House of Lords. There is no appeal against the court's refusal to grant a certificate. See *R v Tang* The Times, 23 May 1995.

One of the effects of s 33 is that the prosecutor may appeal to the House of Lords against the order of the Court of Appeal quashing the appellant's conviction. If the prosecutor is successful in the House of Lords, the conviction will be restored.

12.12   Reference to the European Court of Justice

Under the Criminal Procedure Rules 2005, Part 75, the Court of Appeal has power to refer a case to the European Court of Justice at any time before the determination of the appeal (see *Archbold*, 2005 edn, paras 7–315 to 7–318 and *Blackstone's Criminal Practice*, 2005 edn, para D27.3 for details).

12.13   The Criminal Cases Review Commission

Prior to 1997, the Home Secretary had the power to refer a case, or any point arising in it, to the Court of Appeal (CAA 1968, s 17). The reference was made in the exercise of the Home Secretary's discretion and could be made whether or not the defendant had made an application to the Home Secretary for the reference to be made. In any event the defendant could not be prejudiced by the reference as the Court of Appeal had no power to order loss of time in these circumstances.

If the whole case was referred, it was treated as if it were an appeal to the Court of Appeal by the defendant, who was then able to raise any questions of law, fact or mixed law and fact.

However, it became clear that the power was not satisfactory. In practice, the Home Secretary only referred cases to the Court of Appeal where there was fresh evidence, or some other significant matter arose which had not been investigated at the trial. In 1991, the then Home Secretary announced the creation of a Royal Commission on Criminal Justice to examine the ways in which alleged miscarriages of justice were dealt with. As a result of the recommendations of the Royal Commission, the Criminal Cases Review Commission (the Commission) was established by the CAA 1995, replacing the Home Secretary's power to refer matters to the Court of Appeal. The Commission started work on 1 April 1997. See the website at www.ccrc.gov.uk.

What follows is a general outline of the work of the Commission. A full discussion is beyond the scope of this Manual.

12.13.1   Membership of the Commission

The Commission is a body corporate and is intended to be independent of government and the courts. It must consist of at least 11 members, appointed by Her Majesty on the recommendation of the Prime Minister. At least one-third must be legally qualified. At least two-thirds must be persons who have knowledge or experience of any aspect of the criminal justice system, and at least one of them should have such knowledge in relation to Northern Ireland. It may be noted that no specific requirement is made as to any representation from ethnic minorities, or of any technical or forensic expertise. Fourteen members have initially been appointed, under the chairmanship of Sir Frederick Crawford.

12.13.2   Making the reference

The Commission may refer to the Court of Appeal any conviction or sentence following a trial on indictment, such a reference being treated as an appeal by the person concerned, under the CAA 1968, s 1 (CAA 1995, s 9). Section 11 makes similar provisions in relation to a person convicted in a magistrates' court, referring the matter to the Crown Court.

Under the CAA 1995, s 13, three conditions must be fulfilled before any matter will be referred to the Court of Appeal:

(a) The Commission must consider that there is a 'real possibility that the conviction, verdict, finding or sentence would not be upheld were the reference to be made'.

(b) The Commission must consider this:

    (i)   in the case of a conviction, on the basis of an argument or evidence not raised in the trial *or* there must be exceptional circumstances which justify the reference;

> (ii) in the case of a sentence, on the basis of an argument on a point of law, or information not raised in the proceedings.

(c) The appeal procedure has been followed without success or leave to appeal has been refused *or* there are exceptional circumstances which justify a reference.

The result of these conditions is that in general a reference will only be made if there is fresh evidence leading to a real possibility that the conviction will be quashed. It remains to be seen whether the Commission will exercise its power to refer a matter in exceptional circumstances in situations where there is no fresh evidence, but the existing evidence is weak and unsatisfactory.

In deciding whether to make a reference, the Commission should also have regard, under s 14(2) and (3), to the following:

(a) Any application or representations made to the Commission by or on behalf of the person to whom it relates. Note that the reference may be made without any application being made to it by the person to whom it relates (s 14(1)).

(b) Any other representations made to the Commission in relation to it.

(c) Any point on which it desires the assistance of the Court of Appeal.

(d) Any other matters which appear to the Commission to be relevant.

Since there is no mention of a time limit in the CAA 1995 and given the retrospectivity of the HRA 1998, s 22(4), the Commission is entitled to refer a case to the Court of Appeal no matter how old the conviction. The only question for the Court of Appeal when hearing an appeal against conviction in these circumstances is whether the conviction was unsafe. See *R v Kansal* [2001] 3 WLR 751.

For an example of a reference by the Commission to the Court of Appeal, see *R v Bentley* [2001] 1 Cr App R 21.

12.13.3   Information to the parties

Where the Commission decides to refer the matter to the court, it shall inform the court, and any likely party to the proceedings, of its reasons for making the reference (s 14(4)). Further, where the Commission decides not to make a reference after an application has been made to it, the Commission must give the applicant the reasons for not so doing.

12.13.4   Investigations

The Commission has no power to carry out investigations into alleged miscarriages of justice. Instead, the police will be asked to carry out investigations for them, acting in a manner which is similar to the Police Complaints Authority. The Commission may require an appropriate person from the body which carried out the original investigation to appoint someone to make enquiries and report back to the Commission (CAA 1995, s 19(1)). In the majority of cases this will be a police force, and the appropriate person will be the Chief Constable. The Chief Constable may be required to appoint someone from his own force or another force.

12.13.5   Relationship with the Court of Appeal

For a discussion of the relationship between the Commission and the Court of Appeal, see *R v Criminal Cases Review Commission, ex p Pearson* [1999] 3 All ER 498, where the appellant was convicted of murder and wished the Commission to refer her case to the Court of Appeal. The Commission refused to do so, on the basis that there was no likelihood that the Court of Appeal would receive the fresh evidence that the appellant wished to adduce, and there was therefore no real possibility that the conviction would be quashed. The appellant sought judicial review, in which the following principles were set out:

(a) The role of the Commission was to try to predict the response of the Court of Appeal, and it could only do this by making its own assessment based on the same process of reasoning that the Court of Appeal might follow. To do so was not to usurp the function of the Court of Appeal.

(b) The Commission's reasoning did not include any defects which would allow the court to interfere, and the conclusion of the Commission was not irrational and not legally misdirected. The issue was within the Commission's discretion and the only role for the court in such cases was to ensure that the Commission had acted lawfully.

Three final points may be made about the Commission:

(a) The Court of Appeal is not restricted to dealing with the matter on the point referred to, but may examine the case as a whole (s 14(5)).

(b) The Court of Appeal has the discretionary power, if practical considerations so demand, to adjourn an appeal referred to it by the Commission (see *R v Smith* [1999] 2 Cr App R 444).

(c) Once a reference has been made to the Court of Appeal on whatever grounds, an appellant may put forward additional grounds of appeal that he or she has been advised could be pursued, arising from the original trial, despite the fact that the Commission has previously rejected them. The Commission does not act in the same way as the 'single judge'. See *R v Smith* [2002] EWCA Crim 2907.

13

Procedure between conviction and sentence

13.1 Advance indications of the sentence

If he or she wishes, a Crown Court judge may — prior to the indictment being put to the accused — indicate that the sentence either will or will not take a particular form, regardless of how the accused pleads (see *R v Turner* [1970] 2 QB 321 at 327). Usually such indications are given to counsel privately in the judge's room, and are then transmitted to the accused.

It is vital that, if an indication of sentence is given, it is not made conditional on how the accused pleads. If the judge were to promise a non-custodial sentence in the event of a guilty plea, and either expressly say that the promise would not apply were the accused to be convicted by a jury, or simply not state what would happen in that event, then the accused would be placed under intolerable pressure to plead guilty. In fact, his or her plea of guilty would, on appeal, be treated as a nullity. The Court of Appeal would quash the conviction and order a retrial at which, presumably, the accused would plead not guilty (see **11.2.7** above).

Anything the judge says privately to counsel about sentence should be passed on to the accused. The court will then be bound by what the judge has indicated, even if there is an adjournment prior to sentence and a different judge actually deals with the accused (see *R v Moss* (1984) 5 Cr App R (S) 209).

Making pre-trial promises about sentence, made only in the minority of cases, restricts the court's freedom of action when the time to sentence arrives. It can do little to influence the plea because of the rule that the promises must not be conditional on how the accused pleads. Perhaps their greatest value is in a case where defence counsel suspects that the client really wants to plead guilty but is terrified that the result will be a custodial sentence. This saves a lot of court time, and is good for the accused as well, because the eventual sentence will reflect the credit he or she has earned by this plea.

Advance indications of sentence may be given in the magistrates' court but only as part of a mode of trial determination (see **4.2.2**). A Crown Court judge, however, can familiarise himself or herself with the case by reading through the commit- tal statements. He or she is also entitled to see the accused's written antecedents and list of previous convictions. Thus the papers in the case give the judge an adequate basis for such indications as to the sentence he or she considers proper to pass.

13.2 Advising on sentence

Counsel has to rely upon knowledge of the tariff for the offence in question and on prior experience (if any) of the judge. There are suggestions (see *R v Cain* [1976] Crim LR 464) that, when completely unsure as to what the penalty is likely to be, counsel can ask the judge for a private *and confidential* indication of what the latter has in mind. In basing advice on such an indication, counsel would not reveal to the accused that he or she had seen the judge. In the light of *R v Turner*, however, it is highly unlikely that this procedure would now be approved by the Court of Appeal, and it is rarely, if at all, resorted to in practice. Either the judge gives a '*Turner*-type' indication which can be passed on openly to the accused, or he or she tells counsel nothing at all about the probable sentence.

An accused should always be told, assuming he or she does not know it already, that credit is given to an offender who pleads guilty. He or she receives a lighter sentence than he or she would have done had he or she pleaded not guilty and been found guilty by a jury. Strong advice, stressing the advantage of a guilty plea from the point of view of the eventual sentence, is permissible (*R v Peace* [1976] Crim LR 119), but it must not be so strong as effectively to deprive the accused of his or her free choice as to how he or she pleads (*R v Inns* (1975) 60 Cr App R 231). See also *R v Keily* [1990] Crim LR 204, *R v Smith* [1990] 1 WLR 1311, *R v Pitman* [1991] 1 All ER 468, CA and *R v Thompson* (1995) 159 JP 568.

13.3 Adjournments

The court does not necessarily sentence the offender on the day on which he or she pleads guilty or is found guilty. It has power to adjourn prior to passing sentence. The Crown Court's power to adjourn is one which it possesses at common law; a magistrates' court's power to do so is governed by the Magistrates' Courts Act 1980 (MCA). During the period of an adjournment before sentence, the offender is remanded in custody or on bail. He or she has a prima facie right to bail by reason of the Bail Act 1976 (BA), s 4, but bail may be refused, not only on the grounds which apply before conviction, but also on the ground that the adjournment is for the purpose of preparing a report and it would be impracticable to do that if the offender were at liberty (see BA 1976, Sch 1, Pt I, para 7). Where an offender remanded for reports is granted bail the court may, at its discretion, include a condition that he or she must be available for interview, etc, so that the report can be compiled (BA 1976, s 3(6)(d)).

13.3.1 Adjournments for reports

Independent reports on offenders are often a vital factor in the sentencing decision, coming from sources such as probation officers and social workers producing presentence reports, or from doctors and psychiatrists producing medical reports. Where an accused intimates an intention to plead guilty and it seems likely that the court will need reports before sentencing, the reports are prepared before the hearing if that is at all possible. If, however, the accused is pleading not guilty, it is unlikely that reports will be prepared. Even if pleading guilty, reports are not prepared automatically. Sometimes the court can properly proceed without reports, but in many cases the sentencer's provisional view of the proper sentence will be such that to pass it without consulting a report would either be positively unlawful or at least bad sentencing practice. The court must then adjourn for reports. Two or three weeks will probably be sufficient, although the Crown Court could in theory adjourn for any period. Section 10(3) of the MCA 1980 provides that when magistrates adjourn for reports it must be for not more than four weeks if the offender is remanded on bail, and for not more than three weeks if he or she is in custody.

Section 10(3) of the MCA 1980, which applies to adjournments for any type of report, is supplemented by the Powers of Criminal Courts (Sentencing) Act 2000 (PCC(S)A), s 11, which applies only to medical reports. The main difference between the two sections is that under s 11 the magistrates can adjourn for a medical report even before convicting the accused, provided they are satisfied that the accused committed the *actus reus* of the offence charged. This may enable them to make a *hospital* order without finding the accused guilty. Adjournments under the MCA 1980, s 10(3), on the other hand, presuppose that the magistrates have convicted the accused. In addition, provisions under ss 35 and 36 of the Mental Health Act (MHA) 1983, allow both the Crown Court and magistrates' courts to remand offenders to a hospital for the preparation of reports.

13.3.2 Adjournments where there are several accused

Sentencing joint offenders together should ensure consistent treatment for them all, with any disparity in sentence being justified by the differing degrees to which they were involved in the criminal conduct or by differences in their records.

If there are consistent pleas by the accused, there should be no problem. But, if one accused (A1) pleads guilty and another accused (A2) pleads not guilty, then difficulties arise. A2 obviously cannot be sentenced unless and until he or she is convicted by a jury. The desirability of dealing with A1 and (if convicted) A2 together has led to a general rule that sentence on A1 should be postponed until after the trial of A2. This has the additional advantage of allowing the judge to hear the evidence called at A2's trial, and proportion his or her sentence according to which, if either, of the accused apparently played the leading role in the offence(s) (see *R v Payne* [1950] 1 All ER 102).

However, a special problem arises if A1 is going to be called by the prosecution at the trial of A2, since he or she might be tempted to give false evidence minimising his or her own part in the crime. For this reason, it used to be the practice in such cases to depart from the general rule and sentence A1 before A2's trial (*Payne*). More recently, the Court of Appeal has indicated strongly that the general rule should always be followed, notwithstanding that A1 will be a prosecution witness (see *R v Weekes* (1982) 74 Cr App R 161). Perhaps, though, the matter should be left to the discretion of the trial judge, who is in the best position to balance the interests of the co-accused (that the accomplice, when he or she testifies, should have no motive for giving false evidence) against the wider interests of justice (that confederates in crime should be sentenced together so as to avoid unjustified differences in sentence).

If the accomplice is sentenced before testifying for the prosecution, defence counsel in mitigation may outline the evidence his or her client proposes to give. This will no doubt secure a significant reduction in sentence. Should the accomplice fail to give the evidence thus foreshadowed, his or her sentence may *not* be increased (*R v Stone* [1970] 1 WLR 1112).

The desirability of sentencing confederates in crime together applies when they are to be dealt with in the magistrates' court just as much as when they are to be dealt with in the Crown Court.

13.3.3 Adjournments where there are outstanding charges

It is desirable that an accused with several charges outstanding against him or her should be sentenced on one occasion for all matters in respect of which he or she is ultimately convicted. If he or she is sentenced piecemeal by different judges (or even by the same judge on different occasions) there is a danger that the aggregate sentence will be out of proportion to the overall gravity of his or her conduct. There is also a danger that the first judge, dealing perhaps with the less serious offences, will pass a non-custodial sentence and thus create a dilemma for the second judge. The latter may feel that a custodial sentence is necessary for the offences with which he or she is dealing, but to pass such a sentence might prevent the earlier non-custodial sentence running its natural course. To avoid such difficulties, it is better that one sentencer should deal with everything on one occasion, even if this means adjournments and some extra administrative work behind the scenes.

Much will depend on whether or not the offences have been joined in the indictment, under r 9 of the Indictment Rules 1971. A court and jury can try only one indictment at a time, so sentence on one indictment where the accused is found guilty may have to be postponed until trial on a second indictment. Furthermore, where an accused has indictments outstanding against him or her at different locations of the Crown Court, it will be necessary for the Crown Court at one location to transfer its indictment to the Crown Court at the second location (see *R v Bennett* (1980) 2 Cr App R (S) 96).

13.4   The facts of the offence

If the accused pleads guilty, the first stage in the procedure (before sentence is passed) is for the prosecution to present the brief facts of the offence. In the Crown Court this is always the task of counsel, or solicitor with rights of audience in the Crown Court, for the prosecution must be legally represented for proceedings on indictment (*R v George Maxwell Developments Ltd* [1980] 2 All ER 99).

In the magistrates' court, the prosecution case will be presented by a Crown Prosecutor (or by an agent instructed by the CPS). The procedure before sentence is passed is essentially the same in both the Crown Court and magistrates' courts, but it is less formal in the latter.

13.4.1   Presenting the facts

The prosecuting advocate in the Crown Court has the benefit of the statements from the committal proceedings. Counsel summarises the prosecution case based on these statements. He or she will probably describe in sequence: (i) the circumstances, method and gravity of the offence; (ii) the manner in which the offender was arrested; and (iii) his or her questioning at the police station.

Concerning the advocate's account of the offence itself, details which should be included will obviously vary according to the nature of the offence. The degree of planning which apparently preceded the commission of the offence is always a relevant factor, as is any other aggravating factor, eg breach of trust in an offence involving dishonesty committed by an employee against his or her employer.

As to the arrest and questioning of the offender, the judge will want to know whether the offender was frank and cooperative with the police. If he or she was, that is useful mitigation. Also, what the offender said to the police may foreshadow what defence counsel will say in his or her speech in mitigation about the way the offence was committed, the motive for it, and the offender's degree of involvement if it was a joint offence. Where the offender followed up verbal admissions by making a written statement under caution, the advocate can either read it out in full or give the gist of it, whichever seems more convenient.

When presenting the facts, the prosecuting advocate should not try to make the offence seem as serious as possible so as to obtain a heavy sentence. Traditionally, the prosecution has taken a neutral attitude to the sentence which ought to be passed, not asking for any particular sentence. So, the advocate must present the facts fairly in the light of the prosecution evidence contained in the committal statements, conceding to the defence those points in mitigation which are apparent from the statements, but equally giving full weight to any aggravating factors which make the offence a serious one of its type. In particular, if the offender (in his or her statements to the police) or defence advocate (in mitigation) puts forward a version of the facts of the offence which does not accord with the evidence the prosecution has available, the advocate should indicate that he or she cannot accept what the defence is saying about the offence.

Two further points should be made:

(a) The prosecuting advocate should apply for compensation, confiscation or forfeiture if appropriate.

(b) Both prosecuting and defence advocates should draw the court's attention to any limits on its sentencing powers (*R v Komsta* [1990] 12 Cr App R (S) 63). In addition, prosecuting advocate should also mention guideline cases (*R v Panayioutou* [1989] 11 Cr App R (S) 535). See also *R v Hartrey* (1993) 14 Cr App R (S) 507.

It is often appropriate for the judge to receive factual information as to the effect of the offence on the victim, a 'victim personal statement'. *Practice Direction (criminal: consolidated)* [2002] 3 All ER 904, para 28, sets out the approach the court should take when dealing with a victim personal statement:

28.1 This section draws attention to a scheme which started on 1 October 2001, to give victims a more formal opportunity to say how a crime has affected them. It may help to identify whether they have a particular need for information, support and protection. It will also enable the court to take the statement into account when determining sentence.

28.2 When a police officer takes a statement from a victim the victim will be told about the scheme and given the chance to make a victim personal statement. A victim personal statement may be made or updated at any time prior to the disposal of the case. The decision about whether or not to make a victim personal statement is entirely for the victim. If the court is presented with a victim personal statement the following approach should be adopted.

(a) The victim personal statement and any evidence in support should be considered and taken into account by the court prior to passing sentence.

(b) Evidence of the effects of an offence on the victim contained in the victim personal statement or other statement, must be in proper form, that is a witness' statement under [s 9 of the Criminal Justice Act 1967] or an expert's report, and served upon the defendant's solicitor or the defendant, if he is not represented, prior to sentence. Except where inferences can properly be drawn from the nature of or circumstances surrounding the offence, a sentencer must not make assumptions unsupported by evidence about the effects of an offence on the victim.

(c) The court must pass what it judges to be the appropriate sentence having regard to the circumstances of the offence and of the offender, taking into account, so far as the court considers it appropriate, the consequences to the victim. The opinions of the victim or the victim's close relatives as to what the sentence should be are therefore not relevant, unlike the consequence of the offence on them. Victims should be advised of this. If, despite this advice, opinions as to sentence are included in the statement, the court should pay no attention to them.

(d) The court should consider whether it is desirable in its sentencing remarks to refer to the evidence provided on behalf of the victim.

13.4.2 Disputes about the facts after a guilty plea

By pleading guilty an offender does not necessarily concede that the prosecution case against him or her is correct in its entirety. He or she admits, of course, that he or she committed the offence described in each of the counts of the indictment to which he or she enters a guilty plea, and if the defence advocate says anything in mitigation which is inconsistent with the pleas the judge will ignore that part of the mitigation or invite the defence to consider a change of plea. But the particulars about an offence given in a count of an indictment are so basic that they only partially reveal whether the offence is a serious or trivial one of its type. Thus, it occasionally happens that an offender quite properly pleads guilty and then, after the facts have been presented by the prosecuting advocate, denies that his or her crime is as grave as has been alleged. However, the sentence can be significantly affected by whether the judge accepts the prosecution statement of facts or the defence mitigation.

Guidance in these circumstances is given by *R v Newton* (1982) 77 Cr App R 13, followed in *R v Costley* (1989) 11 Cr App R (S) 357. After the guilty plea, the judge may either:

- hear whatever evidence the parties wish to call on the disputed issue, and come down on one side or the other (this is usually referred to as a '*Newton* hearing'); or

- act merely on the basis of counsels' respective submissions, in which case he or she must accept the defence version as far as possible; or

- empanel a jury to decide the issue (in such a case a count will be added to the indictment by way of amendment and a trial on that count will ensue, see *R v Eubank* [2001] Crim LR 495).

There have been a considerable number of cases on this area since *Newton*, and the cases considered below are merely examples of the issues which have arisen. Students are referred to *Blackstone's Criminal Practice*, para D18.2 et seq for a full discussion.

Defence solicitor and counsel have a duty to notify the Crown that a guilty plea will be put forward, but that the prosecution version of the facts will be contested, so that the prosecution can ensure the presence of any necessary witnesses to enable a *Newton* hearing to proceed (*R v Mohun* [1992] Crim LR 598, CA; *R v Gardener* [1994] Crim LR 301).

When the judge conducts a *Newton* hearing, the rules of evidence should be strictly followed, and the judge should give himself or herself the same directions which he or she would give to a jury, for example, in accordance with the guidelines in *R v Turnbull* [1977] QB 224 (*R v Gandy* (1989) 11 Cr App R (S) 564). Further the judge should openly direct himself or herself that the facts have to be proved to the criminal standard, though failure to do so will not necessarily be fatal (*R v Kerrigan* (1992) 156 JP 889, CA).

The fact that the judge knows of the defendant's antecedents does not preclude him from conducting a *Newton* hearing, but, where the offence is a serious one, it is preferable to have the benefit of a jury verdict (*R v Eubank* [2002] 1 Cr App R (S) 4).

It is not right, on a *Newton* hearing, to sentence the defendant on the basis of a more serious offence than charged. In *R v Druce* (1993) 14 Cr App R (S) 691, CA, the prosecution alleged rape although the charges were unlawful sexual intercourse and indecent assault. The Court of Appeal held that if that was the prosecution case, the defendant should have been so charged. The judge had no alternative but to deal with the case by giving the defendant the benefit of the doubt, and proceed on the basis that the complainant had consented (cf *R v Nottingham Crown Court, ex p DPP* [1995] Crim LR 902).

It should be noted that the defence cannot frustrate the *Newton* inquiry procedure by declining to give evidence. In these circumstances, where the basic facts are not in dispute, the judge is entitled to draw inferences from these undisputed facts (*R v Mirza* (1992) 14 Cr App R (S) 64, CA).

Where the alleged facts relied upon by the offender to reduce the gravity of the offence are exclusively within his or her knowledge, so that the prosecution cannot reasonably be expected to call evidence in rebuttal, the judge is entitled to reject the offender's evidence of what happened as unbelievable, notwithstanding that it is the only evidence there is (*R v Kerr* (1980) 2 Cr App R (S) 54); and see *R v Hawkins* (1985) 7 Cr App R (S) 351 where it was said that the judge is entitled to reject the defence version without hearing evidence if the story is 'incredible'.

Occasionally, a defendant will decide to change his or her plea halfway through the trial, after at least some evidence has been given for the prosecution. In these circumstances, the judge should hear evidence from the defendant and then decide upon the version of facts upon which he or she is going to sentence, forming his or her view on the whole of the evidence that was given. See *R v Mottram* [1981] 3 Cr App R (S) 123 and *R v Archer* [1994] Crim LR 80.

Section 80(2)(b) of the PCC(S)A 2000 provides for the imposition of longer than normal sentences where the offence is of a violent or sexual nature and the court is of the opinion that it is necessary in order to protect the public from harm from the offender. In such a situation, the court must hold a *Newton* hearing to resolve any important issue relevant to sentence. See *R v Oudkerk* [1994] Crim LR 700.

Credit should be given for a plea of guilty, since court time has been saved, even if the judge rejects the version of the facts put forward by the defendant, taking the view that the plea was put forward on a false basis (*R v Williams* (1990) 12 Cr App R (S) 415).

If the judge wrongly fails to hold a *Newton* hearing, the Court of Appeal may vary the sentence to one which is appropriate on the basis that the defendant's version of events is correct (*R v Mohun* (1993) 14 Cr App R (S) 5).

See *R v Cranston* (1993) 14 Cr App R (S) 103, CA, for a recent example and note that further guidance has been provided by the Court of Appeal in *R v Beswick* (1996) 160 JP 33. See **15.2.2** and *R v Tolera* [1999] 1 Cr App R (S) 25 where the Court of Appeal clarified the practice to be followed where the defendant pleaded guilty but sought to be sentenced on a factual basis other than that which was advanced by the prosecution.

The Court of Appeal may interfere with the decision of the sentencing judge after a *Newton* hearing (*Attorney-General's References (Nos 3 and 4 of 1996)* [1997] 1 Cr App R (S) 29). Any interference, however, is likely to be only in exceptional cases, where the judge has reached a decision which no reasonable jury, properly directed, could have reached.

13.4.3 Disputes about the facts after a not guilty plea

Post-conviction disputes about the circumstances of the offence are not limited to cases where the offender pleaded guilty, for a jury's verdict of guilty after a not guilty plea is not necessarily a total vindication of the prosecution's case. In such cases, it is for the judge to form a personal view of the evidence adduced before the jury, and decide what the facts of the offence were. He or she should not ask the jury the reasons for its verdict or what facts it found proved (*per* Humphreys J in *R v Larkin* [1943] KB 174, although that case recognised an exception to the rule where the jury finds the accused not guilty of murder but guilty of manslaughter, and may be asked whether the verdict was on the basis of provocation, diminished responsibility or something else). The judge is not obliged to adopt as a basis for sentencing the least serious version of events consistent with the jury's verdict (*R v Solomon* (1984) 6 Cr App R (S) 120), but should be 'extremely astute' in giving the benefit of any doubt to the offender (*per* Watkins LJ in *R v Stosiek* (1982) 4 Cr App R (S) 205). In *R v Wood* (1991) 13 Cr App R (S) 207, the Court of Appeal said that it would only interfere with the finding of fact by a judge after hearing evidence in exceptional circumstances.

The view the judge takes of the facts must naturally be consistent with the jury's verdict. Thus, if the jury refuses to find the accused guilty as charged but only convicts him or her of a lesser offence, the sentence must be appropriate to the lesser offence, notwithstanding that the judge is convinced there should have been a conviction for the more serious offence (*R v Hazelwood* (1984) 6 Cr App R (S) 52 and *R v Dowdall* (1992) 13 Cr App R (S) 441, CA).

13.5 Character and antecedents evidence

After the prosecution summary of the facts or, in the case of a not guilty plea, immediately after the guilty verdict, the Crown Prosecutor in the magistrates' court or prosecuting counsel in the Crown Court provides the court with information about the character and antecedents of the offender. Information about the character of the offender will be wholly or principally concerned with the matter of his or her previous convictions, if any. Information about antecedents deals with the offender's general background and circumstances.

13.5.1 The antecedents

Practice Direction (Criminal: Consolidated) 2002 3 All ER 904, Part III. 27 1 WLR 1482 sets out the procedure for the provision of antecedents in magistrates' courts and in the Crown Court.

Antecedents evidence is usually provided by prosecution counsel, provided that defence counsel has agreed that they are not in dispute.

Should the defence challenge anything in the antecedents, the antecedents officer and any other witnesses may have to be called, as the prosecution is expected to provide proper proof of what it has alleged, ie evidence of a type which would be admissible in a trial of a not guilty plea. If it fails to provide such proof, the judge should ignore the challenged allegation, and state that he or she is ignoring it (*R v Campbell* (1911) 6 Cr App R 131). It follows that where the prosecution does not have proper proof of an allegation prejudicial to the offender, it should not make the allegation in the first place (see *R v Van Pelz* [1943] KB 157 and *R v Wilkins* (1977) 66 Cr App R 49). Where the prosecution does propose to adduce first-hand antecedents evidence of a factual nature, but it realises that the facts may well be challenged by the defence, it should give notice of the proposed evidence (*R v Robinson* (1969) 53 Cr App R 314). It is not entirely clear whether the prosecution is ever entitled to refer to the offender as having criminal associates. In *R v Bibby* [1972] Crim LR 513 it was held that it was unfair of the antecedents officer to say that B mixed with criminals, but in *R v Crabtree* [1952] 2 All ER 974 Lord Goddard CJ held such evidence to be acceptable provided the officer could speak from his personal knowledge. In the light of these cases, the safest rule for a police officer giving antecedents evidence must be to restrict himself or herself to what is on the antecedents form, and not make additional allegations likely to be disputed by the defence.

13.5.2 Previous convictions

Section 151(1) of the PCC(S)A 2000 provides that when considering the seriousness of any offence, the court may take into account any previous convictions or any failure of the offender to respond to previous sentences. Prosecutors therefore make available to the court a list of any previous convictions of the offender in accordance with the *Practice Direction*.

Practice Direction (criminal: consolidated) [2002] 3 All ER 904, Part III. 27 provides guidance for the provision of information of antecedents in the Crown Court and magistrates' courts:

27.1   In the Crown Court the police will provide brief details of the circumstances of the last three similar convictions and/or of convictions likely to be of interest to the court, the latter being judged on a case by case basis. This information should be provided separately and attached to the antecedents as set out below.

27.2   Where the current alleged offence could constitute a breach of an existing community order, eg community rehabilitation order, and it is known that that order is still in force then, to enable the court to consider the possibility of revoking that order, details of the circumstances of the offence leading to the community order should be included in the antecedents as set out below.

27.3   [standard formats]

Provision of antecedents to the court and parties

Crown Court

27.4   The Crown Court antecedents will be prepared by the police immediately following committal proceedings, including committals for sentence, transfers under section 4 of the Criminal Justice Act 1987 or section 53 of the Criminal Justice Act 1991, or upon receipt of a notice of appeal, excluding non-imprisonable motoring offences.

. . .

Magistrates' courts

27.8   The magistrates' court antecedents will be prepared by the police and submitted to the CPS with the case file.

. . .

27.10   In instances where antecedents have been provided to the court some time before the hearing the police will, if requested to do so by the CPS, check the record of convictions. Details of any additional convictions will be provided using the standard format above. These will be provided as above and attached to the documents already supplied. Details of any additional outstanding cases will also be provided at this stage.

. . .

13.5.3   Spent convictions

The Rehabilitation of Offenders Act 1974 (ROA) was passed with the aim of helping criminals who had decided to 'go straight' to live down their past. Its main effect is that, once a certain time (the 'rehabilitation period') has elapsed from the date of an offender's conviction, the conviction becomes spent and the offender, in respect of that conviction, is a rehabilitated person. As a rehabilitated person he or she is, for most purposes, treated as if he or she had never committed or been convicted of the offence.

Whether a conviction is capable of becoming spent depends upon the length of the sentence imposed for the offence. The length of the sentence, assuming that it is within the limit, also governs the length of the rehabilitation period.

Section 7 of the ROA 1974 provides that the ban on revealing or asking questions about spent convictions does *not* apply in criminal proceedings. However, *Practice Direction (criminal: consolidated)* [2002] 3 All ER 904, para 6, provides that neither judge nor counsel should refer to a spent conviction where 'such reference can be reasonably avoided'. Mention of a spent conviction always requires the judge's authority, that authority being given only where the interests of justice so require. At the sentencing stage, the list of previous convictions given to the court should mark those which are spent. When passing sentence the judge should say nothing about spent convictions unless it is vital to do so to explain the penalty he or she has decided upon.

13.5.4   Defence questions

If a police officer has testified about the offender's antecedents and previous convictions, defence counsel can ask him or her questions. The questioning is unlikely to be hostile in nature, but counsel might wish to confirm that his or her client was cooperative when questioned about the offence or showed signs of genuine remorse. If there has been a change in the offender's circumstances since the antecedents were prepared the officer can be asked if he or she knows anything about that. Upon the officer leaving the witness box the prosecution case is closed.

13.6   Reports

After information as to character and antecedents has been presented to the court, the judge — if he or she has not already done so before court — reads any reports which have been prepared about the offender. Sometimes sentence may properly be passed without the benefit of reports, but there are many occasions when the court must have them either because there is a statutory provision to that effect or because good sentencing practice demands it.

13.6.1   The necessity for pre-sentence reports

A pre-sentence report is defined by s 162 of the PCC(S)A 2000 as a report in writing which is made or submitted by a probation officer or social worker or member of a youth offending team with a view to assisting the court to reach the most suitable method of dealing with the offender, and contains such information as may be specified by the Secretary of State.

Under s 81(1) of the PCC(S)A 2000, when a court is forming any necessary opinion under s 79(2) or s 80(2) of that Act (whether a custodial sentence should be imposed and the length of that order), the court is under a duty to obtain and consider a pre-sentence report. Section 81(1) does not apply, however, if the offender is aged 18 or over, and in the circumstances of the case, the court is of the opinion that it is unnecessary to obtain a pre-sentence report (s 81(2)). This would apply where the sentence was clear, and the report would, in practice, make no difference.

Failure to obtain a report does not invalidate a sentence, but any court sitting on appeal against sentence must obtain one and consider it, unless it is of the opinion that it is unnecessary (s 81(5) and (6)).

Where the offender is aged under 18, by virtue of s 81(3), the court must obtain and consider a report unless either:

- the offence is triable only on indictment, and the court is of the opinion that it is unnecessary to obtain one; or
- there already exists a report, and the court has considered the information. If more than one report exists, the court should consider the most recent.

When making any of the following orders, the court, under s 36, is under a duty to obtain and consider a pre-sentence report, unless it considers it unnecessary (s 36(5)):

- a community rehabilitation order which includes additional requirements authorised by the PCC(S)A 2000, Sch 2;
- a community punishment order;

- a community punishment and rehabilitation order;
- a drug treatment and testing order; and
- a supervision order which includes requirements authorised by Sch 6.

Section 36 contains provisions relating to failure to obtain a report, and offenders under 18 which are parallel to those in s 81 above.

A probation officer writing a report will draw upon many sources. Of prime importance is the interview with the accused. He or she may also visit the accused's home and speak with members of the family. With permission, he or she might talk to the accused's employer, although great care would obviously have to be taken not to jeopardise continued employment. He or she will also have access to background sources of information such as police antecedents and any records the probation service has of previous contact with the accused. If the accused has recently been released from a custodial sentence, the probation officer could consult the authorities at the relevant establishment to see what effect the sentence apparently had on him or her. Where medical or psychiatric reasons seem to have contributed to the offence, assistance might be sought from the accused's doctor, and the report might suggest the preparation of full medical reports.

13.6.2 Contents of a pre-sentence report

By s 162(1) and (2) a pre-sentence report is defined as a report in writing which:

- with a view to assisting the court in determining the most suitable method of dealing with an offender, is made or submitted by a probation officer or by a social worker of a local authority social services department or a member of a youth offending team; and
- contains information as to such matters, presented in such manner, as may be prescribed by rules made by the Secretary of State.

In the White Paper, 'Punishment and Supervision in the Community' (paras 3.10 and 3.11) the government outlined the purpose of the pre-sentence report:

The purpose of requiring the courts to consider a report by the probation service when a custodial sentence is contemplated will be to provide the court with detailed information about how the offender could be punished in the community, so that option can be fully considered. Its purpose will not be to make recommendations about sentencing or to be a plea in mitigation.

In addition, the Green Paper entitled 'Punishment and Supervision in the Community' described (at para 9.6) what such a report should contain:

The reports should include: information about the offence and the offender's attitude towards it, background information about the offender, an assessment of the offender's ability and willingness to stop committing crimes, and a detailed programme of supervision to achieve this. Preparing a report of this sort needs skill in assessing the likely outcome of various sentencing options; these assessments can be made only against a background of detailed knowledge about court practice, about the resources available for supervising offenders together with knowledge and understanding of offending; judgements involving issues of public safety have to be made; and those preparing the reports exercise their discretion in ways which can have serious and lasting consequences for offenders under sentence.

Report do not contain recommendations, made by the probation officer or social worker involved, as to the appropriate sentence. On the other hand, the contents of reports will need to reflect a clear understanding of sentencing principles and practice. Reports have to deal with the various factors in the commission of the crime that may or may not make it 'serious' for the purposes of s 79(2)(a).

13.6.3   The presentation of pre-sentence reports

A representative of the probation service should always be available at court to hand in reports and assist the court in any other way he or she can (eg by interviewing an offender so as to bring an old report up to date). Unless required to do so by the defence, the probation officer who prepared a report need not attend when its subject appears to be sentenced, although may choose to do so if, for instance, the offence was committed while on probation. Such a practice is confirmed by s 162(1) which indicates that the report is 'made or submitted' by a probation officer, social worker or member of a youth offending team. The report would then be presented by a liaison officer. It is clear from s 162(1) that the pre-sentence reports must be in writing. This ends the occasional practice of probation officers or social workers giving their report orally in court.

A copy of the report must be given to the offender or his or her legal representative, except that in cases of unrepresented juveniles it should be given to their parents (s 156(3)). It is considered bad practice to read out the whole of a pre-sentence report in open court since it may well contain matters which, in the offender's best interests, should not be publicly emphasised. The defence, in mitigation, may, however, refer the sentencer to passages in the report or perhaps read isolated sentences which are especially favourable. The defence can challenge allegations made in the report by requiring the probation officer concerned to attend for questioning in open court.

Particular care must be taken where the allegations in the report contain an admission of the full facts of the offence, not formally accepted in court. In *R v Cunnah* [1996] 1 Cr App R (S) 393, the report contained details of the defendant's admission to the full seriousness of the offences as alleged by the victims, but pleas of guilty had been accepted by the prosecution on a more limited basis. There was no discussion of the implications of this with counsel and, on appeal, the sentence was reduced to the level which was appropriate to the pleas given and accepted.

13.6.4   Other reports

In addition to pre-sentence reports, the court may be assisted by the following types of report:

(a) *Medical reports.*   These may concern the offender's physical condition or his or her mental condition or both. If an offender is remanded on bail, it may be made a condition of bail that he or she attend a hospital, etc, for the preparation of medical reports (BA 1976, s 3(6)(d) and PCC(S)A 2000, s 11(3)). If remanded in custody, he or she may be examined by the prison medical officers. Also, there is now the possibility under the Mental Health Act (MHA) 1983 of a remand to a mental hospital for reports in cases where the court is considering a hospital order under s 37 of the MHA 1983. A hospital order can only be made on the basis of reports from two doctors, one of whom must be a psychiatrist.

A copy of a report on an offender's mental condition must be given to his or her counsel or solicitor, but the offender personally is not entitled to a copy. If unrepresented, he or she should be told the gist of what is in the report (MHA 1983, s 54(3)). The psychiatrist who prepared the report may be required to attend court to give oral evidence.

(b) *Reports on juveniles.*   Having found a juvenile guilty, the youth court sometimes remands him or her to local authority accommodation for two or three weeks so that a detailed report can be prepared. Such a report will deal with intelligence, aptitudes, attitudes to those in authority, relationships with peers and many other matters. The school he or she attends (or fails to attend) may also submit a report, together with a record of attendance.

(c) *Remand centre reports.*   There is nothing to stop the court adjourning for a remand centre report on a young offender (under the age of 21), if it considers that that would be helpful. Generally, reports on the behaviour of offenders held at custodial institutions are more likely to be prepared for the assistance of the Court of Appeal than for sentencers at first instance. In determining an appeal against a custodial sentence, the Court of Appeal is quite often given information about the appellant's progress in prison, young offenders institution, etc, during the period between the passing of the sentence and the hearing of the appeal.

13.7   Defence mitigation

After the judge has read the reports the defence has the opportunity to present mitigation on behalf of the offender. If he or she wishes, defence counsel may call character witnesses. The offender will not be called personally unless either there is a dispute about the facts of the offence, or it is a road traffic case and he or she would be liable to mandatory disqualification unless he or she can show special reasons for not disqualifying. In most cases there will not be any character witnesses, and defence counsel will proceed immediately to make a plea in mitigation. (See the ***Advocacy Manual***.)

There is no set pattern for mitigation, and what ought to be said will obviously vary from case to case. However, a plea in mitigation will usually include a discussion of the facts of the offence, the circumstances which led up to it, and the offender's personal circumstances. As regards the potential sentence, one possible approach is to discuss all the available sentences, explaining why they would not be appropriate in this case, concluding with the sentence that is thought appropriate. However, counsel should bear in mind the seriousness of the offence in deciding what is appropriate. If the offence is so serious that only a custodial sentence would be justified, the judge's patience should not be tried by discussing non-custodial sentences at length. Conversely, counsel will look foolish if he or she virtually concedes that the offender must go to prison, and then the judge imposes a community sentence.

The fact that the defendant has pleaded guilty has always been seen as an important point in mitigation, and has been said to reduce the sentence by as much as a third. Section 152 of the PCC(S)A 2000 provides as follows:

(1)   *In determining what sentence to pass on an offender who has pleaded guilty to an offence in proceedings before that or another court, a court shall take into account —*
   (a)   *the stage in the proceedings for the offence at which the offender indicated his intention to plead guilty, and*
   (b)   *the circumstances in which this indication was given.*
(2)   *If, as a result of taking into account any matter referred to in subsection (1) above, the court imposes a punishment on the offender which is less severe than the punishment it would otherwise have imposed, it shall state in open court that it has done so.*

It should be noted, however, that the section does not go on to provide that failure to comply invalidates the sentence.

Other matters which are generally accepted as being good mitigation include the youth of the offender or his or her age; previous good character; that the offender had assisted the police; that the offender has expressed genuine remorse or made attempts to compensate the victim; that the offender was under some sort of particular stress at the time of the offence; and the potential effect on the offender's family in the event, for example, of a custodial sentence. For a more detailed discussion on mitigation, see the later chapters of this Manual, and the *Advocacy Manual*.

One important point to bear in mind is that counsel almost always has the most up-to-date information on the offender. The antecedents are taken at the time of the arrest, which may have been some considerable time before the trial, and in any event are only an outline of the offender's circumstances. There is not always a pre-sentence report, and even if there is, it may also be out of date, or may not contain the information that is required. Consequently, courts increasingly look to counsel to provide accurate, detailed, up-to-date information concerning the offender.

The Code of Conduct of the Bar, para 610(e), provides that defence counsel must not make statements or ask questions which are merely scandalous or intended or calculated only to vilify, insult or annoy. If the defence asserts facts which the prosecution disputes, this should be drawn to the attention of the defence, and if necessary a *Newton* hearing will be held.

The Criminal Procedure and Investigations Act 1996 (CPIA), ss 58–61, allows the judge to impose reporting restrictions where, under s 58(4), there are substantial grounds for believing that:

- the assertion is derogatory to a person's character, and
- the assertion is false or irrelevant to sentence.

Any order made will not apply to an assertion previously made at trial or during any other proceedings relating to the offence (s 58(5)).

The order may be revoked by the court and if not so revoked will cease to have effect after a period of one year (s 58(8)).

It is an offence to publish material in breach of an order under s 58, the sentence being a fine on summary conviction not exceeding level 5 on the standard scale.

Sometimes, when counsel has concluded his or her mitigation, the judge asks the offender whether he or she personally has anything to say. After that it is for the judge to pronounce sentence.

13.8 Pronouncing sentence

A Crown Court judge sitting alone will normally pronounce sentence immediately after defence mitigation (or after giving the offender the opportunity to make a personal statement). If he or she is sitting with lay magistrates and the decision is a difficult one, they sometimes retire to consider it. Similarly, a lay bench of magistrates may wish to retire to consider sentence, and they may also ask their clerk to retire with them to advise on their sentencing powers. In the magistrates' court, the decision on sentence may be taken by a majority but it is pronounced by the chairman of the bench.

Crown Court judges are encouraged to give their reasons for deciding upon a particular sentence. They should certainly give reasons when the sentence prima facie seems a severe one in the circumstances of the case (see *R v Newman* (1979) 1 Cr App R (S) 252 and ss 79(4) and 80(3) of the PCC(S)A 2000). The reasons will be brief and couched in language which the offender may be expected to understand. The judge might say why he or she could not follow a proposal in the pre-sentence report that the offender be given a non-custodial sentence; or, if he or she does pass a non-custodial sentence, the offender might be warned that this really is a last chance and if he or she offends again the penalty will be severe; or, where the offender is going to prison for the first time after a series of convictions which were dealt with by other means, he or she could be told that he or she still has time to reform but if he or she does not learn his or her lesson now he or she is in danger of becoming an habitual criminal who will spend half his or her life in prison. Occasionally the judge's comments on passing sentence get him or her into trouble. It may be evident that he or she has taken irrelevant matters into account, and for that reason passed a sentence which is more severe than would otherwise have been passed. The Court of Appeal is then likely to reduce the sentence, even if it was a proper sentence in itself.

In a few cases, statute obliges the court to give reasons for its decisions. For instance, both the magistrates' court and the Crown Court must explain a decision not to activate a suspended sentence if they are dealing with an offender who is in breach of such a sentence. In other cases (notably the making of a probation order with a requirement for treatment for mental disorder or for treatment for drug or alcohol dependency) the offender's willingness to comply with such requirement must be sought by the court. In yet other cases (eg suspended sentences) the effect of the sentence must be explained to him or her by the court. See the later chapters of this Manual for details.

The Crown Court may vary or rescind a sentence within 28 days of its being passed (if the offender was jointly indicted with other accused, the period is 56 days from the passing of the sentence or 28 days from the conclusion of the joint trial, whichever expires sooner). The variation must be made by the Crown Court judge who originally passed the sentence, but if he or she was then sitting with lay justices they need not be present for the variation. It is clear that the power to vary may be used to correct technical errors in the original sentence or to alter it in the offender's favour. The extent to which a sentence may be fundamentally varied to the offender's detriment is unclear. The Crown Court's power to vary sentence is now contained in s 155 of the PCC(S)A 2000.

Once the statutory period for variation has expired a court may *not* vary its sentence even if, through inadvertence, it failed to consider including in the sentence an order which really ought to have been included.

Magistrates' courts may also vary or rescind a sentence at any time if it is considered to be in the interest of justice to do so (MCA 1980, s 142) (see **5.1.12**).

13.9   Taking other offences into consideration

An offender is sentenced for the offences to which he or she pleads guilty or of which he or she is found guilty. In deciding on sentence, the judge or magistrates must not be influenced by any circumstances which lead them to think that the offender may also have committed other offences with which he or she has not been charged (eg *R v Courtie* [1984] AC 463). There is one major exception to this rule, namely the practice of taking other offences into consideration.

Other offences taken into consideration when sentence is passed (or 't.i.c.'s as they are colloquially known) are offences of which the offender is never convicted, but which are admitted by him or her in court and, at his or her request, are borne in mind by the judge when passing sentence for the offences in respect of which there is a conviction ('conviction offences'). The sequence of events leading up to offences being 't.i.c.'ed will vary from case to case. Typically it will involve a suspect who has been arrested on suspicion of one or more crimes admitting at the police station that he or she committed those crimes, and making it obvious that he or she is going to plead guilty. The police may then ask him or her about other similar offences which they believe he or she may have committed, but which, in the absence of an admission from him or her, they will find it difficult to prove. Since he or she is resigned to having to plead guilty to the offences for which he or she was arrested, the suspect often decides to make a clean breast of everything on the understanding that some or all the offences he or she is now being asked about will not be the subject of separate charges but will merely be taken into consideration. A list is then drawn up of the offences to be 't.i.c.'ed and the suspect signs the list. The offences for which he or she was arrested and with which he or she was charged are then prosecuted in the normal way, and, if the matter is to be dealt with in the Crown Court, appear as counts on the indictment. He or she duly pleads guilty. Then at some convenient stage during the procedure before sentence is passed, prosecuting counsel mentions to the judge that the offender wants other matters considered. The judge is handed the list of offences signed by the offender at the police station, and he or she (or the court clerk) asks whether he or she admits committing them and whether he or she wants them taken into consideration. Assuming the offender answers 'yes' to both questions, the judge may, at his or her discretion, comply with the request. Prosecuting counsel should be in a position to give the judge brief details of the nature of the offences. The sentence the judge eventually passes for the conviction offences will no doubt be somewhat more severe than it would have been in the absence of 't.i.c.'s, but the addition to the sentence will almost certainly not be as great as the penalty for the offences had they been prosecuted separately. Thus, the system of taking offences into consideration has advantages for offenders. It also has advantages for the police, because they clear up offences which might otherwise have remained unsolved. This is why the system flourishes even though it has no solid basis in law.

The following points about taking offences into consideration should be noted:

(a) The sentence the court may pass is restricted to the maximum permissible for the offence(s) of which the offender has been convicted. This does not in practice deter the courts from 't.i.c.'ing offences because maximum penalties are usually far higher than a sentencer would wish to impose even for a grave instance of the of- fence in question. It is thus possible to add something to the sentence to reflect the 't.i.c.'s without exceeding the maximum penalty.

(b) Which offences to charge and which to refrain from charging in anticipation of their eventually being taken into consideration is essentially a matter for the police and the prosecution. Sometimes the most serious offences are charged and later appear on the indictment, while other less grave but broadly similar crimes are taken into consideration. Or perhaps the most recent offences will be charged and the remainder 't.i.c.'ed. On occasions, the 't.i.c.'s vastly outnumber the conviction offences (see, eg, *R v Sequeira* (1982) 4 Cr App R (S) 65).

(c) Offences should not be taken into consideration unless the offender clearly requests the sentencer to do so. The offender should also admit in open court that he or she committed the offences (*R v Griffiths* (1932) 23 Cr App R 153). It is not, however, necessary to put the particulars of each offence to the offender one by one. Usually the offender is asked whether he or she signed at the police station the list of other offences, whether he or she admits committing those offences, and whether he or she wants them considered.

(d) Since the taking of an offence into consideration does not, as a matter of strict law, amount to a conviction, the offender is unable to bar a subsequent prosecution for the offence by reliance on a plea of autrefois convict (*R v Nicholson* [1947] 2 All ER 535). However, the police do not in practice prosecute for matters which have already been 't.i.c.'ed because to do so would undermine a system which they themselves find very convenient. If a prosecution were to be brought, the court would almost certainly pass a nominal sentence such as an absolute discharge.

(e) Although the 't.i.c.' system is geared to offenders pleading guilty, there is nothing to stop the prosecution using a short adjournment after the accused has been found guilty on a not guilty plea to ask him or her whether, given the outcome of the trial, he or she would now like other offences considered.

(f) The court is not obliged to comply with a request to take offences into consideration. It is generally bad practice to 't.i.c.' offences of a different type from the conviction offences, and the court should never consider offences which carry endorsement of the driving licence and disqualification if the conviction offences are not so punishable (*R v Collins* [1947] KB 560). The reason for this is that taking endorsable offences into consideration will not entitle the court to endorse the licence or disqualify if the conviction offences are non-endorsable, whereas if the offences are prosecuted in the normal way endorsement would be virtually certain and disqualification a possibility.

(g) The practice of taking offences into consideration is as common in the magistrates' courts as it is in the Crown Court. However, magistrates should not 't.i.c.' offences which are triable only on indictment (see *R v Simons* [1953] 1 WLR 1014).

(h) The court should state when passing sentence how many other offences it has taken into consideration.

(i) T.i.c.s can establish or assist in the establishment of a criminal lifestyle as defined by the Proceeds of Crime Act 2002, s 75.

13.10 Sample offences

From time to time, the prosecution may invite the judge to treat the offences on which he or she is now passing sentence as samples of a continuing course of conduct over a period of time. This is a convenient way of proceeding if the offences are numerous and were committed over a long period. It would be possible to include all the offences as 't.i.c.'s but this may result in an over-long list, as in *R v Sequeira* (1982) 4 Cr App R (S) 65, where the defendant admitted 150 offences.

The problem for the court is how such sample offences should be sentenced. Recent authorities take the view that the defendant should not be sentenced for offences for which he or she has not pleaded guilty or been found guilty. Thus the fact that the offences are described as 'specimens' does not entitle the court to sentence him or her as if he or she had been found guilty of offences not included in the indictment (*R v Burfoot* (1990) 12 Cr App R (S) 252), unless the offender admitted them (*R v Clark* [1996] 2 Cr App R (S) 351 and *R v Canavan* [1998] 1 Cr App R 79). Previous authority to the contrary (*R v Mills* (1979) 68 Cr App R 154; *R v Singh* (1981) 3 Cr App R (S) 90; and *R v Bradshaw* [1997] 2 Cr App R (S) 128) was rejected.

Two further points should be made:

(a) Prosecutors should ensure that offenders are charged with sufficient offences to reflect the overall criminality involved.

(b) The PCC(S)A 2000, s 80(2)(a), provides that the sentence shall be 'commensurate with the seriousness of the offence, or the combination of the offence and one or more offences associated with it'. Included in the definition of an associated offence is where the offender has admitted the offence and 'requests the court to take it into consideration in sentencing him for that offence' (s 161). It would seem that the court is therefore precluded from sentencing on any other offences.

13.11   Legal representation

The offender can, of course, represent himself or herself if he or she so wishes, and present his or her own mitigation. If the offence is a trivial one, for which the offender is obviously only going to be fined, he or she would be well advised not to employ a lawyer because his or her solicitor's bill would exceed any slight reduction in the fine which might be achieved by eloquent mitigation. In more serious cases, especially where the offender's liberty is at stake, legal representation is desirable.

Legal representation not only assists the offender but it should assist the court, in that the lawyer can clarify the issues, highlight those matters which are in the offender's favour and remind the judge that although the offender might qualify for a custodial sentence, the court is still under a duty to consider whether such sentence is appropriate having regard to the mitigating factors available and relevant to the offender (see *R v Cox* [1993] 1 WLR 188). The court will not want to resort to the drastic expedient of prison unless there is really no alternative. The same applies whenever a custodial sentence of any description is contemplated for a young offender. So, in these types of cases the offender is not merely allowed to have legal representation, but is positively encouraged to have it by the grant of the right to funded representation as part of the Criminal Defence Service.

The general effect of the relevant legislation is that, when dealing with an offender who is not legally represented in court, the court *must* give him or her an opportunity to apply for funded representation before doing any of the following:

- passing a sentence of imprisonment if the offender has never previously been sentenced to imprisonment (PCC(S)A 2000, s 83(1));
- passing a sentence of detention in a young offenders institution, custody for life, detention during Her Majesty's pleasure or making a detention and training order (PCC(S)A 2000, s 83(2));
- making an order for detention under PCC(S)A 2000, s 91.

The first situation applies both to the passing of an immediate sentence of imprisonment and to the passing of a suspended sentence, but in deciding whether an offender has previously been sentenced to imprisonment, a suspended sentence which has not been brought into effect must be ignored. Points two and three apply irrespective of whether the offender has previously received the sentence in question.

The court must not pass the relevant sentence on an unrepresented offender unless either:

- he or she was granted a right to funded representation as part of the Criminal Defence Service but the right was withdrawn because of his or her conduct; or
- having been informed of his or her right to apply for funded representation and having had the opportunity to do so, he or she refused or failed to apply (PCC(S)A 2000, s 83(3)).

The effect of the legislation is that, if the court is considering a first sentence of imprisonment, etc, for an unrepresented offender, it must (if it has not been done already) tell him or her that he or she can apply for funded representation as part of the Criminal Defence Service and grant him or her an adjournment of sufficient length to make the application and instruct solicitors. If the offender fails to use the adjournment for the purpose for which it was granted, that is his or her fault, and the court at the resumed hearing can pass whatever sentence it considers appropriate even if the offender is still unrepresented.

If s 83 of PCC(S)A 2000 is not complied with, but a sentence of imprisonment is nonetheless passed on an offender who has not previously been so sentenced, it would seem that the consequences of the error depend on which court makes it. If it was a magistrates' court which failed to comply with s 83, the Crown Court (which hears appeals against sentences passed in the magistrates' courts) must replace the sentence of imprisonment with a sentence the magistrates could lawfully have passed on the occasion on which they dealt with the offender. So the replacement sentence cannot be a sentence of imprisonment (*R v Birmingham Justices, ex p Wyatt* [1976] 1 WLR 260). If it was the Crown Court which failed to comply with s 83, the Court of Appeal can uphold the lower court's sentence if, notwithstanding the procedural irregularity, it considers that the sentence was the appropriate one for the offender (*R v McGinlay* (1976) 52 Cr App R 156). Presumably the same consequences will flow from breach of any of the other sections requiring the court to allow time for an application for funded representation to be made.

13.12 Differences between sentencing procedure in the Crown Court and in the magistrates' courts

The procedure before sentence is passed is essentially the same whatever the court. The practice of taking other offences into consideration and the power to defer sentence are equally applicable to both the Crown Court and the magistrates' courts. For minor driving matters, the court relies merely on the endorsements, if any, on the offender's licence.

The principles of sentencing

14.1 Introduction

Chapter 13 sets out the procedure to be followed prior to passing sentence. In brief, the prosecutor provides a summary of the facts of the case (unless sentence is being passed immediately after the trial has taken place) and the defence advocate makes a plea in mitigation.

In many cases, there will be an adjournment prior to the passing of sentence. The most common reason for such an adjournment is where the court requires a pre-sentence report before passing sentence. In the magistrates' court, adjournments after conviction must not exceed four weeks where the offender is granted bail or three weeks if he is remanded in custody (see s 10(3) of the MCA 1980). The Crown Court normally adopts the same periods.

Where the court adjourns between conviction and sentence, it has to be made clear to the offender that all sentencing options remain open to the court when sentence is passed if that is the intention of the court. If the offender is led to believe that a particular type of disposal — for example, custody or, where the offender has pleaded guilty in the magistrates' court, committal for sentence — will not be used, the sentencer has to abide by this indication. See, for example, *Gillam* (1980) 2 Cr App R(S) 267 and *Moss* (1984) 5 Cr App R 209.

14.2 Sentencing Guidelines Council

Section 167 of the CJA 2003 establishes the Sentencing Guidelines Council ('SGC'), chaired by the Lord Chief Justice. One of the main objectives of the SGC (which is assisted by the Sentencing Advisory Panel under s 169 of the Act) is to promote consistency in sentencing (see s 170(5)(a)). Under s 170(7) the sentencing guidelines issued in respect of any offence (or category of offences) 'must include criteria for determining the seriousness of the offence or offences, including (where appropriate) criteria for determining the weight to be given to any previous convictions of offenders'.

At the time of writing the SGC has issued the following guidance (all of which is available from the SGC web site: www.sentencing-guidelines.gov.uk/guidelines/council/final.html):

- 'Overarching Principles: Seriousness'
- 'Reduction in Sentence for a Guilty Plea'
- 'New Sentences: Criminal Justice Act 2003'

Under CJA 2003, s 172(1),

every court must—

(a) *in sentencing an offender, have regard to any guidelines which are relevant to the offender's case, and*

(b) *in exercising any other function relating to the sentencing of offenders, have regard to any guidelines which are relevant to the exercise of the function.*

14.3 Purposes of sentencing

CJA 2003, s 142(1), sets out the objectives of sentencing, to which the courts are required to have regard when dealing with offenders. Those objectives are:

- Punishment of offenders.
- Reduction of crime (including reduction by deterrence).
- Reform and rehabilitation of offenders.
- Protection of the public.
- Making of reparation by offenders to persons affected by their offences.

14.4 The sentencing process

In essence, the sentencing process requires consideration of both aggravating and mitigating factors. It involves a two-stage process:

- What sentence does the seriousness of the offence itself merit?
- Can that sentence be reduced in light of mitigation relating to the offender?

14.5 The concept of seriousness

Seriousness is an important concept. The SGC guidance on seriousness points out that seriousness is significant because it:

- determines which of the sentencing thresholds has been crossed (see below);
- indicates whether a custodial, community or other sentence is the most appropriate; and
- is the key factor in deciding the length of a custodial sentence, the onerousness of requirements to be incorporated in a community sentence and the amount of any fine imposed.

The concept of 'thresholds' is exemplified by two provisions in the CJA 2003. As regards custodial sentences, s 152(2) provides that:

The court must not pass a custodial sentence unless it is of the opinion that the offence, or the combination of the offence and one or more offences associated with it, was so serious that neither a fine alone nor a community sentence can be justified for the offence.

As regards community orders, s 148(1) provides that:

A court must not pass a community sentence on an offender unless it is of the opinion that the offence, or the combination of the offence and one or more offences associated with it, was serious enough to warrant such a sentence.

14.5.1 Seriousness according to type of offence

As well as the general guidance issued by the SGC, there are guidelines on particular factors which may make specific offences more, or less, serious. These guidelines can currently be found in Court of Appeal guidelines cases (which may be found in the commentary on the offences themselves in *Blackstone's Criminal Practice* and *Archbold*) and the Magistrates' Association Sentencing Guidelines. However, both these sources will be superseded by guidelines on specific offences to be issued by the SGC.

14.5.2 General factors affecting seriousness — statutory factors

CJA 2003, s 143(1) provides that:

the offender's culpability in committing the offence and any harm which the offence caused, was intended to cause or might foreseeably have caused.

Thus, culpability is the initial factor in determining the seriousness of an offence. The SGC guidance on Seriousness identifies four levels of culpability:

(a) *Intention* to cause harm: highest culpability when an offence is planned; the worse the harm intended, the greater the seriousness.

(b) *Recklessness* as to whether harm is caused (appreciates some harm would be caused but proceeds, giving no thought to consequences even though extent of risk would be obvious to most people).

(c) *Knowledge* of specific risks entailed by actions but does not intend to cause the harm that results.

(d) *Negligence.*

The SGC guidance also notes that culpability is greater if:

- the offender deliberately causes more harm than is necessary for the commission of the offence, or
- the offender targets a victim who is vulnerable (because of old age or youth, disability or by virtue of the job they do).

As well as giving this general guidance, the SGC suggests a number of general factors which are relevant to assessing the seriousness of an offence. This guidance lists a number of factors that indicate **higher culpability**:

- Offence committed whilst on bail for other offences. This is a statutory aggravating factor — see s 143(3) of the CJA 2003, which provides that if the offence was committed while the offender was on bail, the court must treat that as an aggravating factor.
- Failure to respond to previous sentences.
- Offence was racially or religiously aggravated. Racial or religious aggravation is a statutory aggravating factor under s 145 of the CJA 2003, which provides that if the offence was racially or religiously aggravated, the court must treat this as an aggravating factor.

- Offence motivated by, or demonstrating, hostility to the victim based on his or her sexual orientation (or presumed sexual orientation) or disability (or presumed disability). Again, these are statutory aggravating features. Section 146(2) of the CJA 2003 provides that the court must treat circumstances as aggravating where (a) at the time of committing the offence, or immediately before or after doing so, the offender demonstrated towards the victim of the offence hostility based on (i) the sexual orientation (or presumed sexual orientation) of the victim, or (ii) a disability (or presumed disability) of the victim, or (b) the offence is motivated (wholly or partly) (i) by hostility towards persons who are of a particular sexual orientation, or (ii) by hostility towards persons who have a disability or a particular disability. Under s 146(4), it is immaterial whether or not the offender's hostility is also based, to any extent, on any other factors. For these purposes 'disability' means any physical or mental impairment: s 146(5).
- Previous conviction(s), particularly where a pattern of repeat offending is disclosed. The effect of previous convictions is dealt with by s 143(2) of the CJA 2003 (see below).
- Planning of an offence.
- An intention to commit more serious harm than actually resulted from the offence.
- Offenders operating in groups or gangs.
- 'Professional' offending.
- Commission of the offence for financial gain (where this is not inherent in the offence itself).
- High level of profit from the offence.
- An attempt to conceal or dispose of evidence.
- Failure to respond to warnings or concerns expressed by others about the offender's behaviour.
- Offence committed whilst on licence (ie following release from a custodial sentence).
- Offence motivated by hostility towards a minority group, or a member or members of it.
- Deliberate targeting of vulnerable victim(s).
- Commission of an offence while under the influence of alcohol or drugs.
- Use of a weapon to frighten or injure victim.
- Deliberate and gratuitous violence or damage to property, over and above what is needed to carry out the offence.
- Abuse of power.
- Abuse of a position of trust.

The SGC guidance goes on to identify factors that indicate a **more than usually serious degree of harm**:

- Multiple victims.
- An especially serious physical or psychological effect on the victim, even if unintended (on the use of 'victim person statements' see para III.28 of the *Consolidated Practice Direction*).
- A sustained assault or repeated assaults on the same victim.
- Victim is particularly vulnerable.
- Location of the offence (for example, in an isolated place).

- Offence is committed against those working in the public sector or providing a service to the public.
- Presence of others eg relatives, especially children or partner of the victim.
- Additional degradation of the victim (eg taking photographs of a victim as part of a sexual offence).
- In property offences, high value (including sentimental value) of property to the victim, or substantial consequential loss (eg where the theft of equipment causes serious disruption to a victim's life or business).

The list of factors identified by the SGC as indicating **significantly lower culpability** is somewhat shorter:

- A greater degree of provocation than normally expected.
- Mental illness or disability.
- Youth or age, where it affects the responsibility of the individual defendant.
- The fact that the offender played only a minor role in the offence.

14.6 Credit for guilty plea

Pleading guilty is, in itself, good mitigation. Section 144(1) of the CJA 2003 requires the sentencer to have regard to the fact that the offender pleaded guilty and to take into account (a) the stage of the proceedings at which the offender indicated an intention to plead guilty and (b) the circumstances in which that indication was given.

Cases such as *Buffery* (1993) 14 Cr App R(S) 511 and *Costen* (1989) 11 Cr App R(S) 511 established that an offender should receive a one-third discount if the guilty plea is entered at the earliest opportunity. In *R v Rafferty* (1999) 1 Cr App R 235 and *R v Barber* [2002] 1 Cr App R(S) 130, the Court of Appeal emphasised that the earliest opportunity in 'either way' cases is at the 'plea before venue' hearing, where the defendant is asked to indicate his intention as regards plea (and is regarded as having pleaded guilty if he or she indicates an intention to plead guilty).

The SGC guidance on guilty pleas points out that a reduction in sentence as a result of a guilty plea is appropriate because that plea avoids the need for a trial (enabling other cases to be disposed of more expeditiously); shortens the gap between charge and sentence; saves considerable cost; and saves victims and witnesses from having to give evidence.

A guilty plea is often regarded as evidence of remorse on the part of the offender. However, the SGC guidance says that the sentencer should address remorse separately, when deciding most appropriate length of sentence before calculating reduction for guilty plea.

The SGC guidance also points out that the giving of a discount for pleading guilty is not relevant only to the length of any custodial sentence to be passed. Where the offence crosses the threshold for the imposition of a community or a custodial sentence, application of the reduction principle may properly form the basis for imposing a fine or discharge rather than a community sentence, or an alternative to an immediate custodial sentence. Where the reduction is applied in this way, the actual sentence imposed incorporates the reduction and so no further discount is appropriate.

The SGC guidelines provide that discount for pleading guilty should be based on a sliding scale, so that the offender gets more credit for pleading guilty at the earliest opportunity (and less credit for pleading guilty at a later stage). Under that sliding scale, the offender receives:

- the [normal] maximum of one third where the guilty plea was entered at the first reasonable opportunity;
- a maximum of one quarter where a trial date has been set;
- a maximum of one tenth for a guilty plea entered at the 'door of the court' or after the trial has begun.

The guidelines summarise the effect of this sliding scale:

- The maximum reduction (of one third) is to be given only where the offender indicated willingness to admit guilt at the first reasonable opportunity.
- Where the admission of guilt comes later than the first reasonable opportunity, the reduction will be less than one third.
- Where the plea of guilty comes very late, it is still appropriate to give some reduction (albeit much reduced).
- If the 'not guilty' plea was entered and maintained for tactical reasons, a late guilty plea should attract very little, if any, discount.

The SGC guidance also makes it clear that where there is a *Newton* hearing (because the defendant puts forward a version of events that differs significantly from the prosecution version, and the court is not willing simply to accept the defendant's version), and the defendant's version of events is rejected, this should be taken into account in determining the level of reduction in sentence. In other words, the defendant will lose some of the discount for pleading guilty in such a case.

It is also worthy of note that in *Landy* (1995) 16 Cr App R(S) 908, it had been held that the discount for pleading guilty should be withheld if the offender had been caught 'red-handed'. However, the SGC guidelines state that, 'Since the purpose of giving credit is to encourage those who are guilty to plead at the earliest opportunity, there is no reason why credit should be withheld or reduced on these grounds alone. The normal sliding scale should apply' (para 5.2).

The SGC guidance sets out the recommended approach to giving the offender credit for pleading guilty by setting out four steps:

1. The court decides the sentence for the offence(s), taking into account any offences to be taken into consideration (TICs).
2. The court selects the amount of the reduction by reference to the sliding scale.
3. The court applies that reduction to the sentence initially decided on.
4. When pronouncing sentence, the court should usually state what sentence would have been imposed if there had been no reduction as a result of guilty plea.

14.7   Effect of previous convictions

CJA 2003, s 143(2), provides that:

. . . the court must treat each previous conviction as an aggravating factor if (in the case of that conviction) the court considers that it can reasonably be so treated having regard, in particular, to

(a) the nature of the offence to which the conviction relates and its relevance to the current offence, and

(b) the time that has elapsed since the conviction.

In other words, an offence is to be regarded as more serious if committed by someone with relevant previous convictions (relevance depending on how old the previous convictions are and how similar in type they are to the present offence).

The approach prior to the implementation of the CJA 2003 was to regard the existence of relevant previous convictions as resulting in a 'progressive loss' of 'good character mitigation' (see, for example, *Carlton* [1993] Crim LR 981). This meant that an offender without relevant previous convictions would receive a discount in the sense to reflect previous good character. The more relevant previous convictions recorded against the offender, the more discount was lost. Under the CJA 2003, it seems likely that courts will increase the sentence imposed on the offender in order to reflect previous convictions.

It will remain the case that a custodial sentence may be imposed because of previous failures to respond to non-custodial sentences. For example, where the offence crosses the custody threshold but the defence argue that mitigating circumstances justify the imposition of a community sentence instead, the court may reject the suggestion of a community sentence on the basis that such sentences have been tried previously but the offender has nonetheless committed further offences (see, for example, *Oliver & Little* [1993] 2 All ER 9). It should be borne in mind, however, that even if the offender has a very bad record, the defence may argue for a non-custodial sentence to give the offender 'one last chance' to break the cycle of offending (see, for example, *Bowles* [1996] 2 Cr App R(S) 248).

14.8   Specimen/sample counts

It used to be the practice, where the defendant was alleged to have committed a large number of offences, to charge 'sample' or 'specimen' charges/counts. This practice was outlawed by the Court of Appeal in a series of cases: *Clark* [1996] 2 Cr App R(s) 351; *Kidd* [1998] 1 All ER 42; and *Rosenburg* [1999] 1 Cr App R(S) 365. These cases emphasise that an offender can only be sentenced for offences to which he or she has pleaded guilty or been found guilty or has admitted by asking the court to take them into consideration (see below).

14.9   'TICs' (Offences 'taken into consideration')

Where an offender pleads guilty to one or more charges/counts, he can also ask for other offences to be 'taken into consideration'. These offences are not the subject of separate charges/counts but the court will take account of them when passing sentence for the offences to which the offender has pleaded guilty. This is advantageous to the offender because (despite a small increase in sentence to reflect the admission of guilt of other crimes) the agreement to 'wipe the slate clean' is good evidence of remorse (a mitigating factor which serves to reduce the sentence); also, as a matter of practice, where offences have been taken into consideration, they will not be the subject of separate prosecution (and the small increase in sentence that results from such offences being taken into consideration is considerably less than the sentence that would be imposed if the offender were to be convicted — and sentenced separately — for those offences).

Non-custodial sentences in the magistrates' court

In this chapter we look at the various non-custodial sentences that may be imposed by a magistrates' court.

Most of the law relating to non-custodial sentences can be found in the Powers of Criminal Courts (Sentencing) Act 2000 (PCC(S)A).

15.1 Absolute discharge

An absolute discharge (PCC(S)A 2000, s 12(1)(a)) is ordered where the court decides that it is inappropriate to inflict any punishment. Such an order may be appropriate where the circumstances of the offence disclose little or no blame on the part of the offender (for example, *R v O'Toole* (1971) 55 Cr App R 206, where an ambulance driver collided with another vehicle while responding to an emergency call).

15.2 Conditional discharge

Where a conditional discharge is imposed (PCC(S)A, s 12(1)(b)), the offender is discharged on condition that he or she does not commit a further offence during the period specified by the court (which can be up to three years). If the offender does commit a further offence during the period of the conditional discharge, he or she can be re-sentenced for the offence in respect of which the conditional discharge was imposed, as well as sentenced for the later offence.

One magistrates' court can deal with the breach of a conditional discharge imposed by another magistrates' court, but only with the consent of that court (s 13(8)). If the Crown Court is dealing with the breach of a conditional discharge imposed by a magistrates' court, the powers of the Crown Court when re-sentencing are limited to those of a magistrates' court (s 13(7)). If the conditional discharge was imposed by the Crown Court, only the Crown Court can re-sentence; so if a magistrates' court convicts someone of an offence committed in breach of a conditional discharge imposed by the Crown Court, the magistrates are empowered to commit the offender to the Crown Court to be dealt with for the breach of the conditional discharge (s 13(5)).

The court which re-sentences the offender for the original offence can impose any sentence which could have been passed when the conditional discharge was ordered (PCC(S)A 2000, s 13(6)).

See *Blackstone's Criminal Practice*, 2005 edn, section E14.

15.3 Fines

More offenders are dealt with by means of a fine than by means of any other sentence.

15.3.1 The maximum fine

For summary offences, fines are expressed in terms of a standard scale containing five 'levels' (Criminal Justice Act 1982, s 37(2), as amended):

Level	Maximum fine
1	£200
2	£500
3	£1,000
4	£2,500
5	£5,000

For offences that are triable either way, the maximum fine is £5,000 (a figure sometimes referred to as the 'statutory maximum'), unless the statute creating the offence prescribes a larger maximum fine (Magistrates' Courts Act 1980 (MCA), s 32).

These limits apply to the fine for each individual offence. So if, for example, the offender is being dealt with for five either way offences, he could be fined a total of £25,000.

The Management of Offenders and Sentencing Bill 2005 proposed increases in these fines. The maximum fine for an either way offence would be increased to £15,000. For summary offences, the fines would become:

Level	Maximum fine (£)
1	£750
2	£1,500
3	£3,000
4	£7,500
5	£15,000

15.3.2 Fixing the amount of the fine

The procedure for fixing the amount of a fine is set out in CJA 2003, s 162. There are three stages:

(a) The court begins by deciding what fine is appropriate in light of the seriousness of the offence.

(b) Next, the court considers whether the fine should be reduced on the basis of any mitigating circumstances relating to the offender. The fine should also be reduced to reflect an early plea of guilty.

(c) Finally, the court takes account of the financial circumstances of the offender. The means of the offender can operate to increase or decrease the amount of the fine.

Under CJA 2003, s 162, the court can make a 'financial circumstances order' against the offender, requiring the offender to provide a statement of means within the period specified in the order.

If the offender spent time remanded in custody but subsequently receives a fine rather than a custodial sentence for the offence, the fine should be reduced to reflect the time spent in custody (*R v Warden* [1996] 2 Cr App R 269).

The Magistrates' Courts Sentencing Guidelines provide guidance on fines to be imposed based on the seriousness of the offence and the means of the offender.

15.3.3 Enforcement of fines

Where a fine is imposed, payment is due immediately. However, where the offender does not have the means to pay the fine forthwith, the magistrates are empowered to allow time for payment or to order payment by instalments (MCA 1980, s 75(1)). Where payment by instalments is ordered, the total fine should usually be one that the offender will be able to pay off within 12 months.

A magistrates' court, when it imposes a fine, may only fix a term of imprisonment in default if either the offence is punishable with imprisonment and it appears to the court that the offender has sufficient means to pay the fine immediately, or if it appears to the court that the offender is unlikely to remain long enough at an address where he can be found (so that enforcement of the fine by other methods is likely to be impossible) (MCA 1980, s 82(1)).

Enforcement of fines is carried out by the offender's local magistrates' court. If the offender fails to pay the fine (or fails to pay the instalments as ordered), the magistrates' court can issue a summons requiring the offender to attend court (or the court can issue a warrant for the offender's arrest) (MCA 1980, s 83). At the hearing, the court will investigate the offender's means (and the offender can be required to produce evidence of income and outgoings).

If the offender fails to pay some or all of the fine and the court is satisfied that this is because of inability (rather than refusal) to pay, the court may remit the whole or part of the fine (PCC(S)A 2000, s 129).

Otherwise, the sanctions for non-payment of a fine are as follows:

(a) A 'distress warrant' authorising seizure and sale of goods owned by the offender.

(b) An 'attachment of earnings order', so that money is deducted from the offender's wages (Attachment of Earnings Act 1972).

(c) An order for deduction of money from the offender's income support or income-based job-seeker's allowance (Fines (Deductions from Income Support) Regulations 1992 (SI 1992/2182)).

(d) An attendance centre order (if the offender is under 25).

(e) A community punishment order or curfew order (Crime Sentences Act 1997, s 35). Crime Sentences Act 1997, s 35, is amended by CJA 2003, s 300, empowering the court to order the offender to comply with an unpaid work requirement or a curfew requirement (with electronic monitoring) instead.

(f) Disqualification from driving for up to 12 months (Crime Sentences Act 1997, s 40 which is re-enacted in CJA 2003, s 301).

(g) Imprisonment, but only if either (a) the offence for which the fine was imposed is imprisonable and the offender has sufficient means to pay forthwith, or (b) the court is satisfied that the offender's failure to pay the fine is due to 'wilful refusal' or 'culpable neglect' and the court has considered or tried all other methods of enforcement but it appears to the court that they are inappropriate or have been unsuccessful (MCA 1980, s 82(4)).

Schedule 5 to the Courts Act 2003 puts in place an additional set of powers to aid the enforcement of fines. It complements (rather than replaces) the existing mechanisms for enforcement. It offers an incentive by fixing a discount for prompt payment of fines; there is also provision for fines to be increased in the event of non-payment. The Act also enables the offender's vehicle to be clamped, and then sold, if a fine remains unpaid. Schedule 6 enables the court to allow an offender over the age of 18 to discharge a fine by means of unpaid work (under a 'work order').

See *Blackstone's Criminal Practice*, 2005 edn, section E17.

15.4 Community sentences under the Criminal Justice Act 2003

The Criminal Justice Act 2003 aims to simplify the regime of community sentences. Essentially it gives the court a 'pick-and-mix' menu to enable it to construct a community order that is appropriate to the particular offender.

The starting point is the definition of 'community order' in s 177(1) of the Act. This provides that where a person aged 16 or over is convicted of an offence, the court may make an order (a 'community order') imposing on him any one or more of the following requirements:

- an unpaid work requirement (as defined by s 199);
- an activity requirement (as defined by s 201);
- a programme requirement (as defined by s 202);
- a prohibited activity requirement (as defined by s 203);
- a curfew requirement (as defined by s 204);
- an exclusion requirement (as defined by s 205);
- a residence requirement (as defined by s 206);
- a mental health treatment requirement (as defined by s 207);
- a drug rehabilitation requirement (as defined by s 209);
- an alcohol treatment requirement (as defined by s 212);
- a supervision requirement (as defined by s 213); and
- in a case where the offender is aged under 25, an attendance centre requirement (as defined by s 214).

Under s 177(3), where the court makes a community order imposing a curfew requirement or an exclusion requirement, it must normally impose an electronic monitoring requirement as well; under s 177(4), the court may impose an electronic monitoring requirement when it makes a community order containing any of the other requirements.

Under s 177(5), a community order must specify a date by which all the requirements in it must have been complied with; this date must be no more than three years after the date of the order. Section 177(6) provides that, before making a community order imposing two or more different requirements, the court must consider whether, in the circumstances of the case, the requirements are compatible with each other. Thus, a community order can last for up to three years, and the components of the order must be compatible with each other.

Section 178 of the Act empowers the Secretary of State to introduce delegated legislation which enables or requires a court making a community order to provide for that order 'to be reviewed periodically by that or another court'. In other words, the court should continue to have involvement with the case after it has passed sentence.

15.4.1 Community sentence threshold

A community sentence under the Criminal Justice Act 2003 can only be imposed if the seriousness of the case merits such a sentence; in other words, the community sentence 'threshold' has to be met. Section 148 of the 2003 Act provides as follows:

Restrictions on imposing community sentences

(1) A court must not pass a community sentence on an offender unless it is of the opinion that the offence, or the combination of the offence and one or more offences associated with it, was serious enough to warrant such a sentence.

(2) Where a court passes a community sentence which consists of or includes a community order—

(a) the particular requirement or requirements forming part of the community order must be such as, in the opinion of the court, is, or taken together are, the most suitable for the offender, and

(b) the restrictions on liberty imposed by the order must be such as in the opinion of the court are commensurate with the seriousness of the offence, or the combination of the offence and one or more offences associated with it.

. . .

Section 166(2) of the CJA 2003 makes it clear that a court is not prevented, after taking into account any matters that are, in the opinion of the court, relevant in mitigation of sentence, from passing a community sentence even though it is of the opinion that the offence(s) is/are so serious that a community sentence could not normally be justified for the offence(s). In other words, the fact the case crosses the custody threshold does not mean that custody is inevitable. If there is sufficient mitigation, it is open to the court to impose a community sentence instead.

15.4.2 Requirements that may be imposed under a community order

The requirements that may be imposed as part of a community order are listed in CJA 2003, s 177(1).

15.4.2.1 Unpaid work requirement (s 199, 200)

This is a requirement that the offender must perform unpaid work in accordance with CJA 2003, s 200. The number of hours' work that may be required under an unpaid work requirement must be specified in the order and must be between 40 and 300. The Court may only impose an unpaid work requirement if satisfied that the offender is a suitable person to perform work under such a requirement. Thus, the unpaid work requirement is the same as a 'community punishment order' under the PCC(S)A 2000, save that the maximum order is increased from 240 to 300 hours. Under s 200(1), the offender 'must perform for the number of hours specified in the order such work at such times as he may be instructed by the responsible officer'. Subsection (2) states that the work should normally be performed during a period of 12 months. However, under subsection (3), unless it is revoked, a community order imposing an unpaid work requirement remains in force until the offender has worked under it for the number of hours specified in it.

15.4.2.2 Activity requirement (s 201)

This is a requirement that the offender must:

- present himself to a person or persons specified in the relevant order at a place or places so specified on such number of days as may be so specified; and/or

- participate in activities specified in the order on such number of days as may be so specified.

The specified activities may consist of, or include, activities whose purpose is reparation (including activities involving contact between the offender and people affected by the offences). Such a requirement may only be added if the court is satisfied that it is feasible to secure compliance with the requirement. The aggregate of the number of days specified for the requirement must not exceed 60.

The place specified under subsection (1)(a) will usually be a 'community rehabilitation centre' (that is, premises at which non-residential facilities are provided for use in connection with the rehabilitation of offenders).

15.4.2.3   Programme requirement (s 202)

This is a requirement that the offender must participate in an accredited programme (comprising a systematic set of activities) specified in the order at a place so specified on such number of days as may be so specified. The court can only include such a requirement if the programme has been recommended to the court as being suitable for the offender by the probation service or (for offenders under 18) youth offending team.

15.4.2.4   Prohibited activity requirement (s 203)

This is a requirement that the offender must refrain from participating in activities specified in the order on a day or days so specified, or during a period so specified. Before including such a requirement, the court must consult a probation officer or (for offenders under 18) a member of a youth offending team.

15.4.2.5   Curfew requirement (s 204)

This is a requirement that the offender must remain, for periods specified in the order, at a place specified in the order. The order may specify different places or different periods for different days, but may not specify periods which amount to less than two hours or more than 12 hours in any day. The order may only specify periods that fall within six months from the date when the order was made.

15.4.2.6   Exclusion requirement (s 205)

This has the effect of prohibiting the offender from entering a place specified in the order for a period specified in the order. This period cannot be for more than two years. An exclusion requirement may provide for the prohibition to operate only during the periods specified in the order, and may specify different places for different periods or days.

15.4.2.7   Residence requirement (s 206)

This is a requirement that, during a period specified in the order, the offender must reside at a place specified in the order. Before imposing such a requirement, the court must consider the home surroundings of the offender. The court cannot specify a hostel or other institution as the place where the offender must reside, except on the recommendation of a probation officer.

15.4.2.8   Mental health treatment requirement (s 207)

This is a requirement that the offender must submit, during the period(s) specified in the order, to treatment by a registered medical practitioner or a chartered psychologist with a view to the improvement of the offender's mental condition. The treatment may be on an in-patient or out-patient basis. The court may only impose such a requirement if satisfied, on the evidence of a registered medical practitioner, that the mental condition of the offender is such as requires (and may be susceptible to) treatment, but is not such as to warrant the making of a hospital order or guardianship order under the Mental Health Act 1983 and the offender has expressed his willingness to comply with such a requirement.

15.4.2.9   Drug rehabilitation requirement (s 209)

This is a requirement that, during the period specified in the order ('the treatment and testing period'), the offender must submit to treatment by an appropriately qualified person with a view to the reduction or elimination of the offender's dependency on or propensity to misuse drugs; the order also requires that, for the purpose of ascertaining whether he has any drug in his body during that period, the offender must provide samples for testing. Such a requirement can only be imposed if the court is satisfied that the offender is dependent on, or has a propensity to misuse, drugs, and that his dependency or propensity is such as requires and may be susceptible to treatment. Also, the requirement must have been recommended to the court as being suitable for the offender by a probation officer or (for an offender under 18) a member of a youth offending team; and the offender must have expressed willingness to comply with the requirement. The treatment and testing period must be at least six months. The treatment required under the order can be on an in-patient or out-patient basis.

Sections 210 and 211 provide for review by the court where a drug rehabilitation requirement has been imposed. Under s 210, a community order imposing a drug rehabilitation requirement may (or must if the treatment and testing period is more than 12 months) provide for the requirement to be reviewed periodically at intervals of not less than one month, at a 'review hearing' convened by the court. Under s 211, at a review hearing, the court may, after considering the responsible officer's report, amend the drug rehabilitation requirement. Such an amendment can only be made if the offender expresses willingness to comply with the requirement as amended. If the offender withholds consent to the amendment, the court may revoke the community order and deal with him (for the offence in respect of which the order was made) in any way in which he could have been dealt with for that offence by the court which made the order. If the offender is re-sentenced, the court must take into account the extent to which the offender has complied with the requirements of the order; the court can impose a custodial sentence even if the offence did not cross the custody threshold. If, at a review hearing, the court is of the opinion that the offender's progress under the requirement is satisfactory, the court may amend the order to provide for subsequent reviews to be without a hearing. If at a review without a hearing, the court is of the opinion that the offender's progress under the requirement is no longer satisfactory, it may require the offender to attend a hearing at the court, and the court may order that subsequent reviews are carried out at review hearings.

15.4.2.10   Alcohol treatment requirement (s 212)

This is a requirement that the offender must submit, during the period specified in the order, to treatment by a suitably qualified person with a view to the reduction or elimination of the offender's dependency on alcohol. Such a requirement may only be imposed if the court is satisfied that the offender is dependent on alcohol, and that this dependency is such as requires (and may be susceptible to) treatment. The court may not impose an alcohol treatment requirement unless the offender expresses willingness to comply with its requirements. The period for which the alcohol treatment requirement has effect must be not less than six months. The treatment can be on an in-patient or out-patient basis.

15.4.2.11   Supervision requirement (s 213)

This is a requirement that, during the time that the community order remains in force, the offender must attend appointments with the responsible officer at times and places determined by the officer. The purpose for which a supervision requirement may be imposed is that of promoting the offender's rehabilitation.

15.4.2.12   Attendance centre requirement (s 214)

Section 221(2) defines an 'attendance centre' as 'a place at which offenders aged under 25 may be required to attend and be given under supervision appropriate occupation or instruction'. Thus the definition of the attendance centre is unchanged. Attendance centre requirements are governed by s 214, which provides that an attendance centre requirement is a requirement that the offender must attend an attendance centre for the number of hours specified in the order. The maximum total number of hours must be between 12 and 36.

The offender cannot be required to attend an attendance centre on more than one occasion on any day, or for more than three hours on any occasion.

15.4.2.13   Electronic monitoring requirement (s 215)

Under s 215, an electronic monitoring requirement is a requirement for securing the electronic monitoring of the offender's compliance with other requirements under a community order.

15.4.2.14   Restrictions on community orders

Section 217 requires that:

> (1)   The court must ensure, as far as practicable, that any requirement imposed by a relevant order is such as to avoid —
>> (a)   any conflict with the offender's religious beliefs or with the requirements of any other relevant order to which he may be subject; and
>> (b)   any interference with the times, if any, at which he normally works or attends school or any other educational establishment.
>
> (2)   The responsible officer in relation to an offender to whom a relevant order relates must ensure, as far as practicable, that any instruction given or requirement imposed by him in pursuance of the order is such as to avoid the conflict or interference mentioned in subsection (1).
>
> . . . .

15.4.2.15   Other duties of offenders subject to community orders

Section 220 imposes a duty on the offender to keep in touch with the responsible officer in accordance with such instructions as he may from time to time be given by that officer, and to notify him of any change of address.

15.4.2.16   Persistent offenders

CJA 2003, s 151, replaces PCC(S)A 2000, s 59. It deals with the imposition of community orders on certain persistent offenders by providing the court with an additional (discretionary) power for dealing with persistent petty offenders. Where an offender aged 16 or over has been sentenced to a fine on at least three previous occasions, the court may impose a community sentence, instead of a fine, even if the current offence does not cross the community sentence threshold. It does not matter whether the offender has on previous sentencing occasions received community or custodial sentences.

15.5 Procedural requirements

Before deciding that the offence is sufficiently serious to merit a community sentence and before deciding what restrictions on the offender's liberty would be commensurate with the seriousness of the offence and whether the offender is suitable for the imposition of particular requirements, the court must obtain and consider a pre-sentence report (unless, in the case of an offender who has attained the age of 18, the court takes the view that such a report is unnecessary): see s 156 of the CJA 2003.

15.6 Restrictions on community orders

Under s 148(1) of the CJA 2003, the community sentence threshold has to be crossed before a community sentence can be imposed.

A court must not pass a community sentence on an offender unless it is of the opinion that the offence, or the combination of the offence and one or more offences associated with it, was serious enough to warrant such a sentence.

Under s 148(2) of the Act, the court has to ensure that the order is both suitable for the offender and commensurate with the seriousness of the offence:

Where a court passes a community sentence which consists of or includes a community order—

   (a) the particular requirement or requirements forming part of the community order must be such as, in the opinion of the court, is, or taken together are, the most suitable for the offender, and

   (b) the restrictions on liberty imposed by the order must be such as in the opinion of the court are commensurate with the seriousness of the offence, or the combination of the offence and one or more offences associated with it.

Under s 177(7) of the Act, the court has to ensure that, where two or more requirements are imposed under a community order, the requirements are compatible:

Before making a community order imposing two or more different requirements . . . the court must consider whether, in the circumstances of the case, the requirements are compatible with each other.

Finally, the maximum duration of a community order is three years: s 177(5).

15.7 Guidance from the Sentencing Guidelines Council

The SGC suggests that the following approach be taken to community sentences:

In community sentences, the guiding principles are proportionality and suitability. Once a court has decided that the offence has crossed the community sentence threshold and that a community sentence is justified, the initial factor in defining which requirements to include in a community sentence should be the seriousness of the offence committed.

The SGC guidance also makes the point that:

Where an offender is being sentenced for a non-imprisonable offence or offences, great care will be needed in assessing whether a community sentence is appropriate since failure to comply could result in a custodial sentence.

The SGC guidance suggests appropriate community sentences according to the seriousness of the offence (based on a three-fold classification of 'low', 'medium' and 'high'). The suggestions are:

'Low' range

This category comprises offences 'only just crossing the community sentence threshold':

- 40–80 hours of unpaid work,
- a curfew requirement within the lowest range (eg up to 12 hours per day for a few weeks),
- an exclusion requirement lasting a few months,
- a prohibited activity requirement, or
- an attendance centre requirement.

'Medium range'

- a greater number (eg 80–150) of hours of unpaid work,
- an activity requirement in the middle range (20–30 days),
- a curfew requirement within the middle range (eg up to 12 hours for 2–3 months),
- an exclusion requirement lasting in the region of six months, or
- a prohibited activity requirement.

'High' range

This category comprises offences that 'only just fall below the custody threshold' or where the custody threshold has been crossed but a community sentence is more appropriate. A more intensive sentence, which combines two or more requirements, may be appropriate at this level.

- an unpaid work order of 150–300 hours,
- an activity requirement up to maximum 60 days,
- an exclusion order lasting in region of 12 months,
- a curfew requirement of up to 12 hours a day for four to six months.

15.8 Persistent offenders

Section 151 of the Criminal Justice Act 2003 deals with the imposition of community orders on certain persistent offenders by providing the court with an additional (discretionary) power for dealing with persistent petty offenders. Where an offender aged 16 or over has been sentenced to a fine on at least three previous occasions, the court may impose a community sentence, instead of a fine, even if the current offence does not cross the community sentence threshold. It does not matter whether the offender has on previous sentencing occasions received community or custodial sentences.

The SGC guidance on community sentences under the CJA 2003 make the point that the:

. . . justification for imposing a community sentence in response to persistent petty offending is the persistence of the offending behaviour rather than the seriousness of the offences being committed.

The requirements imposed should ensure that the restriction on liberty is proportionate to the seriousness of the offending, to reflect the fact that the offences, of themselves, are not sufficiently serious to merit a community sentence.

The guidance suggests that such offenders would merit a 'light touch' approach, for example, a single requirement such as a short period of unpaid work, or a curfew, or a prohibited activity requirement or an exclusion requirement (where the circumstances of the case mean that this would be an appropriate disposal without electronic monitoring).

15.9 Credit for time spent on remand

Section 149(1) of the CJA 2003 provides that:

In determining the restrictions on liberty to be imposed by a community order . . . in respect of an offence, the court may have regard to any period for which the offender has been remanded in custody in connection with the offence . . .

The SGC guidance says that the court should seek to give credit for time spent on remand in all cases where the offender was remanded in custody prior to conviction/sentence. Thus, the offender may receive a more lenient community sentence to reflect the fact that he or she has already spent some time in custody in connection with the offence for which sentence is now being passed.

The guidance adds that the court should make clear, when announcing sentence, whether or not credit for time on remand has been given and should explain its reasons for not giving credit when it considers that this is not justified, would not be practical, or would not be in the best interests of the offender.

15.10 Breach of community orders under the Criminal Justice Act 2003

CJA 2003, s 179 gives effect to Sch 8, which deals with breach, revocation and amendment of community orders. This Schedule largely reproduces (with some amendments) the provisions of PCC(S)A 2000, Sch 3.

Under para 5(1), if the responsible officer is of the opinion that the offender has failed without reasonable excuse to comply with any of the requirements of a community order, the officer must give him a warning unless the offender has received such a warning during the last 12 months or the responsible officer decides to refer the matter back to the court. If a warning is given, it must inform the offender that if, within the next 12 months, he again fails to comply with any requirement of the order, he will be liable to be brought before the court (para 5 (2)).

Paragraph 6(1), which deals with further non-compliance after a warning, is cast in mandatory terms. It provides that if the responsible officer has given the offender a warning under para 5 and, during the next 12 months, the offender again fails (without reasonable excuse) to comply with any of the requirements of the order, the officer *must* refer the case back to the court. Under para 7, the court can issue a summons, or an arrest warrant, to secure the offender's attendance. If a summons is issued but the offender fails to appear in answer to the summons, the court may issue a warrant for his arrest.

Under para 9(1), if it is proved to the satisfaction of the court that the offender has failed without reasonable excuse to comply with any of the requirements of the community order, the court must deal with him in respect of the failure in any one of the following ways:

> *(a) by amending the terms of the community order so as to impose more onerous requirements which the court could include if it were then making the order;*
>
> *(b) where the community order was made by a magistrates' court, by dealing with him, for the offence in respect of which the order was made, in any way in which the court could deal with him if he had just been convicted by it of the offence;*
>
> *(c) where —*
>
> > *(i)   the community order was made by a magistrates' court,*
> >
> > *(ii)   the offence in respect of which the order was made was not an offence punishable by imprisonment,*
> >
> > *(iii) the offender is aged 18 or over, and*
> >
> > *(iv)   the offender has wilfully and persistently failed to comply with the requirements of the order,*
>
> *by dealing with him, in respect of that offence, by imposing a sentence of imprisonment for a term not exceeding 51 weeks.*

Option (a) would, for example, empower the court to extend the duration of a particular requirement, but not beyond the maximum duration applicable to that requirement and not beyond the three-year limit applicable to the duration of a community order (para 9(3)).

Option (b) involves revocation of the order (if it is still in force at the date of the hearing) and then re-sentencing (subject to the limitation on the court's sentencing powers when it was first dealing with the offender). Paragraph 9(4) empowers the court to impose a custodial sentence even if the offence did not cross the custody threshold.

Option (c) enables the court to punish wilful and persistent non-compliance with a custodial sentence even though the offence for which the order was made was non-imprisonable. As with (b), the community order is revoked if this option is chosen.

When dealing with the non-compliance, the court must take into account the extent to which the offender has complied with the order (para 9(2)). If the offender is re-sentenced, he can appeal to the Crown Court against the new sentence (para 9(8)).

Where the order was made by the Crown Court (and that court directed that failures to comply should be dealt with by the magistrates' court) the magistrates' court dealing with the breach can commit him, in custody or on bail, to be dealt with by the Crown Court (para 9(6)). The powers of the Crown Court in such a case are discussed in **19.3** below.

Paragraph 11(1) provides that:

- if an offender has refused to comply with a mental health treatment requirement, a drug rehabilitation requirement, or an alcohol treatment requirement, and

- the refusal was a refusal to undergo 'any surgical, electrical or other treatment', and

- the court decides that the refusal was reasonable in all the circumstances, then the refusal is not to be treated as a breach of the order.

Paragraph 12 deals with cases where a community order was made by a youth court in respect of an offender who was being dealt with for an indictable-only offence and who was under 18 years of age when the order was made but has attained the age of 18 by the time of the enforcement proceedings. Where the court revokes the community order and re-sentences the offender, its powers are limited to:

- imposing a fine not exceeding £5,000 for the offence in respect of which the order was made, or

- dealing with the offender for that offence in any way in which a magistrates' court could deal with him if it had just convicted him of an offence punishable with imprisonment for a term not exceeding 51 weeks.

The SGC guidance on community sentences give the following guidance on sentencing for breach of a community order:

- The primary objective is to ensure that the requirements of the community sentence are completed.
- A court sentencing for breach must take account of the extent to which the offender has complied with the requirements of the community order, the reasons for breach and the point at which the breach has occurred.
- Custody should be the last resort, reserved for those cases of deliberate and repeated breach where all reasonable efforts to ensure that the offender complies have failed.
- Before increasing the onerousness of the requirements of a community sentence, the sentencer should take account of the offender's ability to comply and should avoid precipitating further breach by overloading the offender with too many or conflicting requirements.
- It may be necessary to consider re-sentencing to a differently constructed community sentence in order to secure compliance with the purposes of the original sentence.

The guidance also suggests that:

When increasing the onerousness of requirements, the court must consider the impact on the offender's ability to comply and the possibility of precipitating a custodial sentence for further breach. For that reason, and particularly where the breach occurs towards the end of the sentence, the court should take account of compliance to date and may consider that extending the supervision or operational periods will be more sensible; in other cases it might choose to add punitive or rehabilitative requirements instead.

From this it is clear that the emphasis is on achieving the objectives of the original sentence rather than punishing the offender for failure to comply with the terms of that original sentence.

15.10.1 Revocation of community orders other than for breach

Part 3 of Sch 8 deals with the revocation of community orders other than in the case of a breach of the requirement of the order. Paragraph 13 states that (provided the order is still in force) either the offender or the responsible officer may apply to the magistrates' court for the revocation of the order, or for the offender to be dealt with in some other way for the offence in respect of which the order was made, if — having regard to circumstances which have arisen since the order was made — it would be in the interests of justice to do so.

Under para 13(3), the circumstances in which a community order may be revoked include the fact that the offender is making good progress or is responding satisfactorily to supervision or treatment under the order. The revocation of the order may also be appropriate if, for example, the offender is taken ill or becomes disabled, and so becomes unable to complete the requirements of the order.

If the court re-sentences the offender, it must take into account the extent to which the offender complied with the original order (para 13(4)). If a new sentence is passed, the offender can appeal against that sentence (para 13(5)).

Paragraph 13 applies to a community order made by the Crown Court unless the order does not include a direction enabling a magistrates' court to deal with any failure to comply with the order.

15.11 Amendment of community orders

Part 4 of Sch 8 to the Criminal Justice Act 2003 deals with the amendment of community orders.

Paragraph 16 deals with amendments made necessary because the offender has changed residence and is living in a different area (and so should be supervised by a different magistrates' court).

Under para 17(1), the court may, on the application of the offender or the responsible officer, amend a community order by cancelling any of the requirements of the order, or by replacing any of those requirements with a requirement of the same kind, which the court could include if it were then making the order.

The court cannot add a wholly new requirement or substitute a different requirement for one that was originally specified in the order. However, the court can cancel a requirement or adjust it (for example, changing the hours of a curfew or substituting one specified activity for another). The court is also empowered to add electronic monitoring to any of the original requirements under the order.

The court cannot amend a drug rehabilitation, alcohol treatment or mental health treatment requirement without the offender's consent. If the offender withholds consent, the court can revoke the order and re-sentence him; if it re-sentences him it must take into account the extent to which he has complied with the requirements of the community order. The court can impose a custodial sentence if the original offence was punishable with imprisonment.

Paragraph 18 provides that, where a community order includes a drug rehabilitation, alcohol treatment or mental health treatment requirement, and the medical practitioner (or other person responsible for the treatment) is of the opinion that the treatment of the offender should be continued beyond the period specified in that behalf in the order, or the offender needs different treatment, or the offender is not susceptible to treatment, or the offender does not require further treatment, or the doctor is for any reason unwilling to continue to treat or direct the treatment of the offender, then he must make a written report to that effect to the responsible officer; the responsible officer must then apply (under para 17) to the court for the variation or cancellation of the requirement.

Paragraph 19 provides that where a community order includes a drug rehabilitation requirement with provision for review, the responsible officer may apply to the court (under para 17) to amend the order to provide for each subsequent periodic review (see s 211) to be made without a hearing instead of at a review hearing, or vice versa.

Paragraph 20 provides that, on the application of the offender or the responsible officer, the court may extend an unpaid work requirement beyond the 12-month limit (specified in s 200(2)) if it believes it to be in the interests of justice to do so having regard to circumstances which have arisen since the order was made.

15.12 Commission of subsequent offences

Part 5 of Sch 8 deals with the powers of the court in relation to a community order where the offender is subsequently convicted for another offence.

Paragraph 21 provides that where an offender in respect of whom a community order made by a magistrates' court is in force is convicted of an offence by a magistrates' court, and it appears to the court that it would be in the interests of justice to do so so, having regard to circumstances which have arisen since the community order was made, the magistrates' court may either (a) revoke the order, or (b) revoke the order and deal with the offender, for the offence in respect of which the order was made, in any way in which he could have been dealt with for that offence by the court which made the order. If it resentences him, the court must take into account the extent to which he complied with the order (para 21(3)), and the offender has a right of appeal to the Crown Court (para 21(4)).

If the magistrates' court is dealing with the later offence but the community order was made in the Crown Court, the magistrates may commit the offender, in custody or on bail, to appear at the Crown Court (para 22(1)). The powers of the Crown Court in such a case are discussed in **19.4** below.

15.13 Disqualification under PCC(S)A 2000, s 146

Section 146 of the PCC(S)A 2000 provides that, in addition to or instead of dealing with an offender in any other way, a court may disqualify him from driving for such period as it thinks fit. In *R v Cliff* [2004] EWCA Crim 3139; The Times, December 1 2004, it was held that the ambit of s 146 is not limited to any particular offence, and so it is not necessary that the offence should be connected in any way with the use of a motor vehicle. The Court said that the Act provides an additional form of punishment where a person might be disqualified from driving notwithstanding that the offence of which he has been convicted was not connected with the use of a vehicle.

15.14 Surcharges

Section 14 of the Domestic Violence, Crime and Victims Act 2004 makes provision for 'surcharges' to be payable on conviction. It inserts ss 161A and 161B into the Criminal Justice Act 2003. Section 161A provides that where the court is dealing with an offender for one or more offences, it must also order him to pay a surcharge unless either the case falls within a category exempted by the Secretary of State or else the court consider that it would be appropriate to make a compensation order but the offender does not have sufficient means to pay both the surcharge and appropriate compensation (in which case the court must reduce the amount of the surcharge, if necessary to nil). Under s 161B, the amount of the surcharge will be specified by statutory instrument.

Section 14(2) of the 2004 Act inserts subsection 164(4A) into the 2003 Act to make it clear that a court must not reduce the amount of a fine on account of any surcharge it orders the offender to pay under section 161A, except to the extent that the offender has insufficient means to pay both.

15.15 Recovery orders

Section 57 of the Domestic Violence, Crime and Victims Act 2004 makes amendments to the Criminal Injuries Compensation Act 1995. It inserts ss 7A–7D into the 1995 Act. Section 7A enables the making of regulations to provide for the recovery from an 'appropriate person' of an amount 'equal to all or part of the compensation paid in respect of a criminal injury' (s 7A(1)). An 'appropriate person' means 'a person who has been convicted of an offence in respect of the criminal injury' (s 7A(2)). Under s 7A(3), the amount recoverable under the regulations 'must be determined by reference only to the extent to which the criminal injury is directly attributable to an offence of which he has been convicted'. Section 7B provides for 'recovery notices' which require the offender to pay the amount specified in the notice.

Section 7C provides for review of a determination that an amount is recoverable from a person and of the amount determined as recoverable from a person. Subsection (2) sets out the only grounds for such review, namely:

(a) *that he has not been convicted of an offence to which the injury is directly attributable;*

(b) *that the compensation paid was not determined in accordance with the Scheme;*

(c) *that the amount determined as recoverable from him was not determined in accordance with the regulations.*

Under subsection (4), the person conducting any such review may:

(a) *set aside the determination that the amount is recoverable;*

(b) *reduce the amount determined as recoverable;*

(c) *increase the amount determined as recoverable;*

(d) *determine to take no action under paragraphs (a) to (c).*

Subsection (5) provides that the person conducting the review may increase the amount determined as recoverable if (but only if) it appears to that person that the interests of justice require the amount to be increased.

Section 7D makes provision for recovery proceedings where a person has been given a recovery notice (see above) but has failed to pay the amount in accordance with the notice. Under subsection (2), it is a defence in such proceedings for the person to show:

(a) *that he has not been convicted of an offence to which the injury is directly attributable;*

(b) *that the compensation paid was not determined in accordance with the Scheme; or*

(c) *that the amount determined as recoverable from him was not determined in accordance with regulations under section 7A.*

Custodial sentences in the magistrates' court

16.1 Introduction

In this Chapter, we examine the custodial powers of the magistrates' court. These powers differ according to whether the offender is aged 18–20 or has attained the age of 21.

16.2 Magistrates' powers of custodial sentencing

For imprisonable summary offences, the maximum sentence can be up to 51 weeks. CJA 2003, Sch 26, lists a large number of summary offences for which this is the maximum penalty. For summary offences not listed in this schedule, the maximum (assuming the offence carries a custodial sentence — many summary offences do not) is specified by the statute which creates the offence.

For either way offences, the magistrates' court can impose up to 12 months for a single offence (s 282 of the CJA 2003).

Where the magistrates are dealing with offender for two or more offences (whether triable either way or summarily only), the maximum aggregate sentence is 65 weeks (see s 155 of the CJA 2003).

16.3 Imprisonment

Sentences of imprisonment imposed by a magistrates' court can take three forms: 'custody plus'; a suspended sentence; intermittent custody. However, before a custodial sentence can be imposed, the case has to be regarded as sufficiently serious to cross the custody threshold.

16.3.1 The custody threshold

Section 152(2) of the CJA 2003 provides that:

The court must not pass a custodial sentence unless it is of the opinion that the offence, or the combination of the offence and one or more offences associated with it, was so serious that neither a fine alone nor a community sentence can be justified for the offence.

The SGC guidance on seriousness emphasises two key points about the custody threshold:

- Parliament's clear intention is to reserve imprisonment as a punishment for the most serious offences;
- Passing the custody threshold does **not** mean that a custodial sentence should be regarded as inevitable: custody can still be avoided in light of personal mitigation or where there is a suitable intervention in the community which provides sufficient restriction (by way of punishment) while addressing the rehabilitation of the offender to prevent future crime.

The custody threshold under the legislation that preceded the CJA 2003 had been considered in *R v Cox* [1993] 1 WLR 188. It was held that an offence is 'so serious that only a custodial sentence can be justified' (the test then applicable) if it is such as to make all right-thinking members of the public, knowing all the facts, feel that justice would not be done by the passing of anything other than custodial sentence.

In *R v Howells* [1999] 1 WLR 307, the Court of Appeal expressed the view that this test was not particularly helpful. The Court chose not to replace the test with a different form of words, but did helpfully set out some factors that could make the difference between a custodial or non-custodial sentence. Lord Bingham CJ said that:

. . . in approaching cases which are on or near the custody threshold courts will usually find it helpful to begin by considering the nature and extent of the defendant's criminal intention and the nature and extent of any injury or damage caused to the victim. Other things being equal, an offence which is deliberate and premeditated will usually be more serious than one which is spontaneous and unpremeditated or which involves an excessive response to provocation; an offence which inflicts personal injury or mental trauma, particularly if permanent, will usually be more serious than one which inflicts financial loss only. In considering the seriousness of any offence the court may take into account any previous convictions of the offender or any failure to respond to previous sentences . . . and must treat it as an aggravating factor if the offence was committed while the offender was on bail . . . .

In deciding whether to impose a custodial sentence in borderline cases the sentencing court will ordinarily take account of matters relating to the offender.

(a) The court will have regard to an offender's admission of responsibility for the offence, particularly if reflected in a plea of guilty tendered at the earliest opportunity and accompanied by hard evidence of genuine remorse, as shown (for example) by an expression of regret to the victim and an offer of compensation . . .
(b) Where offending has been fuelled by addiction to drink or drugs, the court will be inclined to look more favourably on an offender who has already demonstrated (by taking practical steps to that end) a genuine, self-motivated determination to address his addiction.
(c) Youth and immaturity, while affording no defence, will often justify a less rigorous penalty than would be appropriate for an adult.
(d) Some measure of leniency will ordinarily be extended to offenders of previous good character, the more so if there is evidence of positive good character (such as a solid employment record or faithful discharge of family duties) as opposed to a mere absence of previous convictions. It will sometimes be appropriate to take account of family responsibilities, or physical or mental disability.
(e) While the court will never impose a custodial sentence unless satisfied that it is necessary to do so, there will be even greater reluctance to impose a custodial sentence on an offender who has never before served such a sentence.

One issue is the extent to which the prevalence of an offence can affect its seriousness. The SGC notes that the key factor in determining whether sentencing levels should be enhanced in response to the prevalence of the particular offence is the level of harm that is being caused in the locality. The guidance emphasises that 'enhanced' sentences should be exceptional and in response only to exceptional circumstances, and that sentencers must sentence within the sentencing guidelines once prevalence has been addressed.

The Court of Appeal has encouraged sentencers to consider sentences other than custody — for example, imposing a fine instead. See, for example, *R v Kefford* [2002] EWCA Crim 519; [2002] 2 Cr App R (S) 106, and *R v Baldwin* [2002] EWCA Crim 2647; The Times, November 22 2002.

16.3.2 Proviso to the custody threshold

Section 152(3) of the CJA 2003 contains a proviso to s 152(2), that:

Nothing in subsection (2) prevents the court from passing a custodial sentence on the offender if—

> (a) *he fails to express his willingness to comply with a requirement which is proposed by the court to be included in a community order and which requires an expression of such willingness . . .*

16.3.3 Length of sentence

Section 153(2) of the CJA 2003 provides that (apart from mandatory minimum sentence cases (see **Chapter 19**)):

the custodial sentence must be for the shortest term (not exceeding the permitted maximum) that in the opinion of the court is commensurate with the seriousness of the offence, or the combination of the offence and one or more offences associated with it.

In *R v Howells* [1999] 1 WLR 307 (following such cases as *R v Ollerenshaw* [1999] 1 Cr App R(S) 65), Lord Bingham said that:

> Where the court is of the opinion that an offence, or the combination of an offence and one or more offences associated with it, is so serious that only a custodial sentence can be justified and that such a sentence should be passed, the sentence imposed should be no longer than is necessary to meet the penal purpose which the court has in mind.

This is particularly so in the case of the offender who has not previously served a custodial sentence. For that offender, the effect of the 'clang of the prison gates' is spent after a comparatively short time in custody.

Where the offender is being sentenced for two or more offences, the court can make the terms run concurrently or consecutively. Essentially, this will depend on whether the offences constitute a single series of incidents (in which case, concurrent terms would be appropriate) or unrelated offences (in which case, consecutive terms would be appropriate). CJA 2003, s 166(3)(b), preserved the 'totality' principle, which requires that where consecutive sentences are imposed, the court must ensure that the total time to be served is commensurate with the seriousness of the overall course of offending that is being dealt with.

In calculating the time to be served, account has to be taken of any time spent on remand prior to conviction/sentence (see s 240 of the CJA 2003).

Section I.7.2 of the *Consolidated Practice Direction* stipulates that whenever a custodial sentence is imposed on an offender, the court should explain the practical effect of the sentence in addition to complying with existing statutory requirements.

Section I.8.1 goes on to stipulate that where a court passes more than one term of imprisonment, the court should state in the presence of the defendant whether the terms are to be concurrent or consecutive.

16.3.4   Procedure

Section 156 of the CJA 2003 requires the court to obtain and consider a pre-sentence report in order to decide whether the case is sufficiently serious for a custodial sentence and, if so, what length of sentence would be commensurate with the seriousness of the offence. If the offender has attained the age of 18, the court may refrain from seeking a report on the basis that it is unnecessary to obtain one.

In *Gillette* The Times, 3 December 1999, the Court of Appeal said that the court should always seek a pre-sentence report before passing a custodial sentence on someone who has not previously served a custodial sentence. However, in *Armsaramah* (2000) 164 JP 709, the Court of Appeal accepted that there may be cases where it is open to court to pass a custodial sentence without seeking a pre-sentence report even where the offender has not served a custodial sentence before.

16.3.5   Custody options in the magistrates' court

Under the CJA 2003, custodial sentences of under 12 months (or 65 weeks where the offender is being sentenced for more than one offence) may take one of three forms:

- 'custody plus';
- intermittent custody;
- a suspended sentence.

The SGC has given guidance on the order in which those alternatives should be considered (assuming that case is one where the custody threshold has been crossed):

(a) has the custody threshold been passed?

(b) if so, is a custodial sentence unavoidable?

(c) if so, can the sentence be suspended?

(d) if not, can the sentence be served intermittently?

(e) if not, impose a sentence which takes immediate effect for term commensurate with seriousness of offence.

16.4   Prison sentences of less than 12 months: 'custody plus'

The objectives of 'custody plus' are twofold:

- to make short prison sentences more onerous, and
- to make sure that the offender receives supervision after release from prison (rather than simply being released on licence and left to his or her own devices).

A 'custody plus' sentence comprises a custodial period (time spent behind bars) and licence period (time spent in the community).

Under s 181(2) of the CJA 2003, the term of the sentence 'must be expressed in weeks', and must be between 28 and 51 weeks.

The 'custodial period' has to be between two and 13 weeks (s 181(5)). The licence period has to be at least 26 weeks (s 181(6)).

Where the court is dealing with two or more offences and imposes consecutive prison sentences, under s 181(7), the aggregate length of the terms of imprisonment must not be more than 65 weeks, and the aggregate length of the custodial periods must not be more than 26 weeks.

During the licence period, the offender can be made subject to a number of require-ments (effectively combining the custodial sentence with a community sentence). The requirements that can be specified are set out in s 182(1) of the CJA 2003:

- an unpaid work requirement;
- an activity requirement;
- a programme requirement;
- a prohibited activity requirement;
- a curfew requirement;
- an exclusion requirement;
- a supervision requirement;
- an attendance centre requirement (provided that the offender is under 25).

16.5 Suspended sentences

Suspended sentences of imprisonment are governed by ss 189–191 of the CJA 2003.

Where the custodial term is between 28 and 51 weeks (or between 28 and 65 weeks if the court is imposing consecutive sentences for more than one offence), the court may suspend that sentence, ordering that the sentence of imprisonment is not to take effect unless either (i) during the 'supervision period', the offender fails to comply with a requirement imposed under the order, or (ii) during the 'operational period', the offender commits another offence (whether or not punishable with imprisonment): s 189(1)(b).

Thus, where the court passes a suspended sentence it must specify an 'operational period' (the time for which the sentence is suspended) and a 'supervision period' (the time during which the offender has to comply with community sentence requirements).

The 'supervision period' and the 'operational period' both have to be between six months and two years (s 189(3)).

The 'supervision period' must end not later than the operational period (s 189(4)).

During the supervision period, the offender can be required to comply with additional requirements which are the same as those which comprise a community order: s 190 of the CJA 2003, namely:

(a) an unpaid work requirement,

(b) an activity requirement,

(c) a programme requirement,

(d) a prohibited activity requirement,

(e) a curfew requirement,

(f) an exclusion requirement,

(g) a residence requirement,

(h) a mental health treatment requirement,

(i) a drug rehabilitation requirement,

(j) an alcohol treatment requirement,

(k) a supervision requirement, or

(l) in a case where the offender is aged under 25, an attendance centre requirement.

Sections 191 and 192 provide for periodic reviews by the court of the offender's progress in complying with the requirements of the sentence; these reviews will be informed by a report from the 'responsible officer' who is supervising the offender during the 'supervision period'.

It should be emphasised that a suspended sentence counts as a custodial sentence and so is appropriate only for an offence that passes the custody threshold and for which imprisonment is the only option.

The SGC guidance on custodial sentences under the CJA 2003 implies that, in the case of sentences under 12 months (or 65 weeks for two or more offences), there is a presumption in favour of suspending the sentence (in that suspension has to be considered as the court considers intermittent custody or an ordinary custodial sentence). As noted above, the order of questions to be considered by the court is:

- Has the custody threshold been passed?
- If so, is it unavoidable that a custodial sentence be imposed?
- If so, can that sentence be suspended?
- If not, can the sentence be served intermittently?
- If not, impose a sentence which takes immediate effect for the term commensurate with the seriousness of the offence.

The SGC guidance also points out that the operational period should reflect the length of sentence being suspended. For example, an operational period of up to 18 months might be appropriate for a suspended sentence of up to 12 months.

The SGC also gives guidance on the imposition of requirements during the supervision period, saying that:

In order to ensure that the overall terms of the sentence are commensurate with the seriousness of the offence, it is likely that the requirements to be undertaken during the supervision period would be less onerous than if a community sentence had been imposed. These requirements will need to ensure that they properly address those factors that are most likely to reduce the risk of re-offending.

Because of the very clear deterrent threat involved in a suspended sentence, requirements imposed as part of that sentence should generally be less onerous than those imposed as part of a community sentence. A court wishing to impose onerous or intensive requirements on an offender should reconsider its decision to suspend sentence and consider whether a community sentence might be more appropriate.

16.5.1   Breach of suspended sentence or re-offending during the operational period

This is governed by Sch 12 of the CJA 2003.

Where an offender has breached any of the requirements without reasonable excuse for the first time, the responsible officer must either give a warning or initiate breach proceedings. Where there is a further breach within a 12-month period, breach proceedings must be initiated.

If the offender is brought to court because he or she:

- has failed, without reasonable excuse, to comply with any of the community requirements of the suspended sentence order, or
- is convicted of an offence committed during the operational period of a suspended sentence,

then the court has three options:

1. order that the suspended sentence take effect with its original term and custodial period unaltered; or

2. order that the sentence take effect but with a shorter period of custody; or

3. amend the order by:
    - imposing more onerous community requirements
    - extending the supervision period, or
    - extending the operational period.

There is a presumption that the suspended prison sentence will be activated (either with its original custodial term or a lesser term) unless the court takes the view that this would, in all the circumstances, be unjust. In reaching this decision, the court may take into account both the extent to which the offender has complied with the requirements and the facts of the new offence.

The SGC has given guidance on the action to be taken where the offender commits a further offence during the operational period of the suspended sentence:

- If the new offence is committed near the end of the operational period (the offender having complied with the requirements imposed), it may be more appropriate to amend the order rather than activate the custodial term.

- If the new offence is of a less serious nature than the offence for which the suspended sentence was passed, this may justify activating the suspended sentence with a reduced term or amending the terms of the order.

- It is expected that any activated suspended sentence will be consecutive to the sentence imposed for the new offence.

- If the new offence is non-imprisonable, the sentencer should consider whether it is appropriate to activate the suspended sentence at all (the implication being that it would generally not be appropriate).

- Where the court decides to amend a suspended sentence order rather than activate the custodial sentence, it should give serious consideration to extending the supervision or operational periods (within statutory limits) rather than making the requirements more onerous.

16.6 Intermittent custody

Again, this sentence (which is governed by s 183 of the CJA 2003) applies to sentences of under 12 months. The court specifies a number of 'custodial days', but these are not served all in one go. Rather, the offender is released on temporary licence at set intervals throughout the sentence. The court may only impose intermittent custody if the offender consents to serving the custodial part of the sentence intermittently.

Under s 183(4), the term of the sentence must be expressed in weeks, must be at least 28 weeks, and must not be more than 51 weeks in respect of any one offence.

Under s 183(5), the 'custodial days' have to number between 14 and 90 (unless the offender is being dealt with for two or more offences, in which case the maximum is 180 custodial days).

Where the court is sentencing for two or more offences and imposes consecutive terms of imprisonment, the aggregate length of the terms of imprisonment must not be more than 65 weeks, and the aggregate of the numbers of custodial days must not be more than 180 (see s 183(7)).

Paragraph 7 of Sch 6 to the Domestic Violence, Crime and Victims Act 2004 amends the Criminal Justice Act 2003 to add a s 264A to deal with intermittent custody in the case of consecutive terms. In such a case, under s 264A(2), the offender is not to be treated as having served all the required custodial days in relation to any of the terms of imprisonment until he has served the aggregate of all the required custodial days in relation to each of them. Under subsection (3), after the number of days served by the offender in prison is equal to the aggregate of the required custodial days in relation to each of the terms of imprisonment, the offender is to be on licence until the 'relevant time' (ie the time when the offender would, but for his release, have served a term equal in length to the aggregate of (a) all the required custodial days in relation to the terms of imprisonment, and (b) the longest of the total licence periods in relation to those terms: s 264A(4)).

Under s 185 of the CJA 2003, licence conditions can be imposed for those periods when the offender is released on licence:

- an unpaid work requirement;
- an activity requirement;
- a programme requirement;
- a prohibited activity requirement.

The SGC guidance on the use of intermittent custody stipulates that:

- the court must be satisfied that a custodial sentence of less than 12 months is justified and that neither a community sentence nor a suspended sentence is appropriate before considering whether to make an intermittent custody order;
- when imposing a custodial sentence of less than 12 months, the court should always consider whether it would be appropriate to sentence the offender to intermittent custody. Primary considerations will be public safety, offender suitability and sentence availability.

The guidance suggests that suitable candidates for weekend custody might include offenders who are: full-time carers; employed; or in education.

As regards sentence length where the court decides to impose intermittent custody, the SGC guidelines say that the disruptive effect on family life, the psychological impact of going in and out of custody, and the responsibility on the offender to travel to and from the custodial establishment on many occasions, all make the sentence more onerous than ordinary custody. On this basis, the guidance stipulates that, once the court has decided that an offender should be sent to prison and has determined the length of the sentence, it should reduce the overall length of the sentence because it is to be served intermittently.

16.7 Offenders aged 18–20: detention in a young offender institution

Under s 96 of the PCC(S)A 2000, the custodial sentence applicable to an offender who is aged 18, 19 or 20 at the date of conviction is 'detention in a young offender institution'.

The maximum term of such detention is the same as the maximum term of imprisonment that the court may impose on an adult for that offence.

This sentence is due to be abolished (so that offenders aged 18–20 would be sentenced to the custodial sentences that are currently available in the case of offenders who have attained the age of 21). However, the provision that repeals s 96 of the 2000 Act (s 61 of the Criminal Justice and Court Services Act 2000) has not yet been brought into force.

17

Non-custodial sentences in the youth court

17.1 Introduction

In this chapter, we look at the non-custodial sentences available where the offender is under the age of 18. Offenders under the age of 18 are subject to a different range of non-custodial sentences to adult offenders (see **Chapter 15**). However, where the offender is aged 16 or 17 at the date of conviction, the court may impose either a community order applicable to adult offenders or a sentence applicable to young offenders.

17.2 Fines and discharges

Young offenders may be dealt with by means of a fine or an absolute or conditional discharge.

17.2.1 Absolute discharge

See **15.1**.

17.2.2 Conditional discharge

See **15.2**. In the case of young offenders, it should be noted that s 66(4) of the Crime and Disorder Act 1998 provides that where a juvenile who has received a warning under s 65 is convicted of an offence committed within two years of the warning, the court is not permitted to order a conditional discharge in respect of the offence unless it is of the opinion that there are exceptional circumstances relating to the offence or the offender which justify its doing so.

17.2.3 Fines

Where the offender is aged 15, 16, or 17, the maximum fine that may be imposed is £1,000. Where the offender is aged between 10 and 14, the maximum fine is £250, the Management of Offenders and Sentencing Bill 2005 proposed increasing these figures to £3,000 and £750 respectively.

Where the offender is under 16, the court *must* order that the fine is paid by the offender's parents (and so the means of the parents have to be taken into account in assessing the amount of the fine). If the offender is aged 16 or 17, the court *may* order the parents to pay the fine. See s 137 of the PCC(S)A 2000; **6.4.3**.

17.2.4 Binding over

Where the offender is under the age of 16, the court must consider binding over the parents to take proper care of, and exercise proper control over, the offender. In fact, such orders are comparatively rare. See s 150 of the PCC(S)A 2000.

17.3 Non-custodial sentences specific to young offenders

Where the offender is under the age of 18 at the date of conviction, the youth court has a wide range of non-custodial orders at its disposal. These include:

- supervision orders;
- attendance centre orders;
- action plan orders;
- reparation orders;
- exclusion orders;
- referral orders.

Section 156 requires the court to obtain a pre-sentence report before deciding that an offence is sufficiently serious to merit a community order and before deciding what restrictions on the offender's liberty are commensurate with the seriousness of the offence. Where the offender has attained the age of 18, the court can take the view that a report is unnecessary. However, under s 156(5), if the offender is under the age of 18, the court cannot dispense with a pre-sentence report unless there exists a previous pre-sentence report obtained in respect of the offender, and the court has had regard to the information contained in that report (or, if there is more than one such report, the most recent report).

17.4 Supervision orders

Under s 63 of the PCC(S)A 2000, a supervision order may be imposed on an offender aged between 10 and 17. The order requires that the offender be placed under the supervision of a social worker for a period of up to three years. The role of the supervisor is to 'advise, assist and befriend' the offender (s 64(4)).

The Court can include additional requirements (set out in Sch 6 of the PCC(S)A 2000) in the supervision order, for example:

- A residence requirement (that the offender must reside with a named individual).
- A requirement that the offender take part in activities specified by the supervisor (for a maximum of 180 days).
- A requirement that the offender engage in activities that have been specified by the court ('court-nominated activities'), for a maximum of 180 days.

- A requirement that the offender make reparation (either to the victim of the offence or to the community at large).
- Night restrictions (essentially, a curfew), for a maximum of 30 days.
- 'Negative requirements', that the offender refrain from doing the things specified in the order.

17.4.1 Breach of supervision order

This is governed by Sch 7 of the PCC(S)A 2000.

If the offender fails to comply with the provisions of the supervision order, the court may:

- impose a fine up to £1,000, or
- impose a curfew order or an attendance centre order, or
- discharge the supervision order and re-sentence the offender for the original offence.

17.5 Attendance centre order

Section 60 of the PCC(S)A 2000 (as amended by the CJA 2003) enables the court to make an attendance centre order where the offender is under the age of 16.

The order requires the offender to attend a specified place in order to be 'given, under supervision, appropriate occupation or instruction' (see s 221(2) of the CJA 2003).

The aggregate number of hours for which an attendance centre order may require the offender to attend the attendance centre must be at least 12, unless the offender is under the age of 14 and the court takes the view that 12 hours would be excessive, having regard to his age or any other circumstances (s 60(3) of the 2000 Act). The aggregate number of hours cannot exceed 12 unless the court is of the opinion, having regard to all the circumstances, that 12 hours would be inadequate; in that case, the maximum number of hours is 24 (s 60(4)).

Under s 60(10), an offender cannot be required to attend at an attendance centre on more than one occasion on any day, or for more than three hours on any occasion. Thus, these orders are served in blocks of, say, two or three hours (often on Saturday afternoons).

At the attendance centre, the offender has to participate in whatever activities are taking place there. The purposes of the order are keeping the offender out of trouble and (to quote from Home Office guidance) to teach him 'something of constructive use of leisure'.

17.5.1 Breach of attendance centre order

If the offender fails to comply with the attendance centre order, the magistrates may:

- impose a fine to £1,000, or
- (if the order was made by a magistrates' court) re-sentence the offender for the original offence, or
- (if the order was made by the Crown Court) commit the offender to the Crown Court to be dealt with (that court may impose a fine up to £1,000 or re-sentence).

17.6 Reparation order

Section 73 of the PCC(S)A 2000 empowers the court to impose a reparation order where the offender is aged between 10 and 17.

Under the order, the offender is required to make reparation to the victim(s) of the offence (provided that the victim consents to this) or to the community at large.

This reparation must be carried out, over a maximum period of 24 hours, under the supervision of a probation officer, social worker or member of the youth offending team.

The reparation required by the order has to be completed within three months of the making of the order.

17.7 Action plan order

Section 69 of the PCC(S)A 2000 enables the court to make an action plan order where the offender is aged between 10 and 17.

The order can last for up to three months. During that time, the offender is under the supervision of a probation officer, social worker or member of the youth offending team.

The action plan can include a number of requirements (see s 70 of the 2000 Act), for example:

- to participate in specified activities,
- to attend an attendance centre,
- to stay away from specified places,
- to make reparation to the victim (with the consent of the victim) or to the community.

This is intended as a 'short, sharp' period in which the offender is encouraged to address their offending behaviour.

17.8 Exclusion order

Section 40A of the PCC(S)A 2000 empowers the court to impose an 'exclusion order'. This is an order prohibiting the offender from entering any place specified in the order for a specified period of up to one year (or three months if the offender is aged under 16). The order may provide for the prohibition to operate only during the periods specified in the order or may specify different places for different periods or days (s 40A(3)).

17.9 Curfew order

Section 37 of the PCC(S)A 2000 (as amended by the CJA 2003) empowers the court to make a 'curfew order' where the offender is under the age of 16. Under s 37(3), a curfew order may specify different places or different periods for different days, but cannot last for longer than six months from the date when the order is made and has to operate for between two and 12 hours on the days when it is effective.

17.10   Referral order

Provision for referral orders is made by ss 16–18 of the PCC(S)A 2000.

The making of a referral order is *mandatory* (unless the court is considering either an absolute discharge or the imposition of a custodial sentence) if the offender pleads guilty to an imprisonable offence and has not previously been convicted of any offence.

The making of a referral order is *discretionary* if the offender being dealt with for two or more connected offences, pleads guilty to at least one of them and has not previously been convicted of any offence.

Under s 19(4), where the court makes a referral order, it cannot also impose a community sentence, a fine, a reparation order, or a conditional discharge, nor can it bind the offender's parents over.

As part of complying with the referral order, the offender has to attend meetings with a 'youth offender panel', over a period of between three and 12 months.

In addition, the offender can be required to comply with additional requirements (see s 23), such as:

- making reparation;
- undergoing mediation;
- carrying out unpaid work;
- taking part in specified activities; or
- refraining from taking part in specified activities.

17.11   Offenders aged 16 and 17 — adult community orders

The 'adult' community orders listed in s 177 of the CJA 2003 (see **Chapter 15**) are available where the offender has attained the age of 16.

This means, for example, that if the court wishes to impose a sentence which requires the offender to be placed under supervision, it can either make a supervision order or impose an adult community order with a supervision requirement.

Custodial sentences in the youth court

18.1 Introduction

In this chapter, we look at the detention and training order, which is the custodial sentence applicable to offenders who fall within the jurisdiction of the youth court (ie offenders under the age of 18).

18.2 Detention and training orders

Under PCC(S)A 2000, s 100, an offender aged under 18 at the date of conviction may be sentenced to a detention and training order ('DTO').

The minimum age for such a sentence is 12 (although the Secretary of State has power to include 10 and 11 year olds).

If the offender was under 15 at the date of conviction, a DTO can be imposed only if the juvenile is a 'persistent offender'. Surprisingly, this term is not defined in the legislation. Normally, a juvenile will be regarded as a persistent offender because of the number of previous findings of guilt. However, a juvenile can be regarded as a persistent offender on the basis that he or she is being dealt with for several offences (see *R v Charlton* (2000) 164 JP 685).

A sentence of DTO is a custodial sentence (and so the custody threshold criteria have to be met).

The total length of the DTO has to be 4, 6, 8, 10, 12, 18 or 24 months.

The offender is placed in detention for half of the term of the order. On release, the juvenile is placed under supervision for the rest of the order (supervision being provided by a probation officer, social worker or member of youth offending team).

It should be noted that, as regards the DTO, the powers of the youth court and the Crown Court are identical, as neither court can exceed the maximum duration of 24 months.

If the juvenile fails to comply with the supervision requirement under the DTO, the court can either:

- order his or her return to custody (for three months or for the remainder of the order, whichever is less); or
- impose a fine of up to £1,000.

If the juvenile re-offends during the second half of the DTO, the court may (as well as dealing with the juvenile for the later offence) order that he or she return to custody for the length of time between the date of the offence and the expiry of the original order.

18.3   More serious offences

If the juvenile is charged with an offence which falls within the scope of s 91 of the PCC(S)A 2000 (see **Chapter 20**) and he or she indicates an intention to plead not guilty, the youth court has to decide whether to try the case or to send the juvenile to the Crown Court for trial. Where the juvenile indicates a guilty plea to an offence to which s 91 applies, the youth court has to decide whether to pass sentence itself (bearing in mind the limitations on both the length of the DTO and the offenders who can be made subject to a DTO) or to commit the juvenile to the Crown Court (which may then pass a sentence under s 91).

18.4   Summary: custodial sentences available according to age

- 10–11: the only custodial sentence available is detention under s 91 of the PCC(S)A 2000 (and only the Crown Court can impose such a sentence);

- 12, 13 or 14: a 'DTO' is available, provided that the juvenile is a 'persistent offender'; detention under s 91 is also available in appropriate cases;

- 15, 16, or 17: a 'DTO' is available; detention under s 91 is also available in appropriate cases.

Non-custodial sentences in the Crown Court

Besides the amount of any fine, the powers of the Crown Court to impose non-custodial sentences are identical to those of the magistrates' court, set out in **Chapter 15** of this Manual. This chapter will therefore simply summarise some of the key points

19.1 Fines

The Crown Court is empowered to impose a fine instead of, or in addition to, dealing with the offender in any other way (the CJA 2003, s 163). This is so whether the offender was convicted in the Crown Court or committed to the Crown Court for sentence under the PCC(S)A 2000, s 3.

There is no statutory limit on the amount of a fine imposed by the Crown Court.

Where the Crown Court imposes a fine it must fix a term of imprisonment (if the offender is aged 21 or over) or detention in a young offenders institution (if the offender is aged between 18 and 20) in default. The maximum term set in default depends on the amount of the fine (see PCC(S)A 2000, s 139(4)):

Fine (£)	Term (maximum)
1–200	7 days
201–500	14 days
501–1,000	28 days
1,001–2,500	45 days
2,501–5,000	3 months
5,001–10,000	6 months
10,001–20,000	12 months
20,001–50,000	18 months
50,001–100,000	2 years
100,001–250,000	3 years
250,001–1,000,000	5 years
over 1,000,000	10 years

The Management of Offenders and Sentencing Bill 2005 proposed revision of these provisions:

Fine (£)	Term (maximum)
0–750	21 days
751–1,500	35 days
1,501–3,000	49 days
3,001–7,500	70 days
7,501–15,000	3 months
15,001–30,000	6 months
30,001–50,000	12 months
50,001–75,000	18 months
75,001–100,000	2 years
100,001–250,000	3 years
250,001–1,000,000	5 years
over 1,000,000	10 years

19.2 Other non-custodial sentences

Like the magistrates' court, the Crown Court is empowered to impose any of the following:

- absolute discharge;
- conditional discharge (1–3 years);
- community order.

Where the Crown Court is dealing with a juvenile (for example, where the juvenile was charged alongside an adult and the magistrates decided that it was in the interests of justice for the juvenile to be sent to the Crown Court to be tried with the adult), there is a statutory presumption that the Crown Court should remit the juvenile to the youth court for sentence. Section 8(2) of the PCC(S)A 2000 provides that in such a case the court shall, unless satisfied that it would be undesirable to do so, remit the case to the youth court. However, in *R v Lewis* (1984) 79 Cr App R 94, Lord Lane CJ pointed out that declining to remit to the youth court could be justified for a number of reasons (for example, the Crown Court judge will, after the trial, be better informed about the facts of the offence and general nature of the case than the youth court could hope to be; sentencing the juvenile in the Crown Court will avoid the risk of unjustifiable disparity in sentencing that could otherwise arise if the juvenile and adult are sentenced by separate courts; and remitting the case would cause delay, unnecessary duplication of proceedings and extra expense). Where the Crown Court does pass sentence on the juvenile, all the non-custodial options available to youth court are available to the Crown Court (see **Chapter 17**).

19.3 Breach of community order imposed by the Crown Court

Where the Crown Court imposes a community order, it can include in the order a direction that any failure to comply with the requirements of the order is to be dealt with by a magistrates' court. Where the order does not contain such a stipulation and the offender breaches the order, he or she will be brought before the Crown Court pursuant to para 8(2) of Sch 8 to the CJA 2003, which provides that, if it appears to the Crown Court that the offender has failed to comply with any of the requirements of the order, it may issue a summons requiring the attendance of the offender or, if the information is in writing and on oath, issue a warrant for the offender's arrest. Under para 8(4), if a summons is issued but the offender fails to appear before the Crown Court, a warrant may be issued for the arrest of the offender.

Under para 9(6), where a community order was made by the Crown Court and the order provided that any failure to comply could be dealt with by a magistrates' court, and the offender is brought before the magistrates for non-compliance with the order, the magistrates have a discretion to commit the offender (in custody or on bail) to the Crown Court to be dealt with for the breach.

Paragraph 10(1) sets out the powers of the Crown Court where it is dealing with an offender for breach of a community order. If it is proved to the satisfaction of the court that the offender has failed, without reasonable excuse, to comply with any of the requirements of the community order, the Crown Court *must* deal with the offender in one of the following ways:

(a) *by amending the terms of the community order so as to impose more onerous requirements which the Crown Court could impose if it were then making the order;*

(b) *by dealing with him, for the offence in respect of which the order was made, in any way in which he could have been dealt with for that offence by the court which made the order if the order had not been made;*

(c) *where—*

(i) *the offence in respect of which the order was made was not an offence punishable by imprisonment,*

(ii) *the offender is aged 18 or over,*

(iii) *the offender has wilfully and persistently failed to comply with the requirements of the order,*

by dealing with him, in respect of that offence, by imposing a sentence of imprisonment for a term not exceeding 51 weeks.

Paragraph 10(2) requires the Crown Court to take account of the extent to which the offender has complied with the requirements of the community order.

Paragraph 10(3) makes it clear that, if the Crown Court adopts the option set out in para 10(1)(a), it may extend the duration of particular requirements under the community order, but not beyond the three-year maximum duration of community order fixed by s 177(5) of the Act.

Paragraph 10(4) goes on to provide that where the Crown Court adopts the option set out in para 10(1)(b) in the case of an offender who has wilfully and persistently failed to comply with the requirements of the community order, it may impose a custodial sentence (provided the offence for which the community order was imposed was an imprisonable offence) whether or not the original offence crossed the custody threshold contained in s 152(2) of the Act.

Under para 10(5), if the Crown Court chooses either of the options set out in para 10(1)(b) or (c), it must also revoke the community order if it is still in force.

Finally, para 10(6) makes it clear that the question whether the offender has complied with the requirements of the community order is to be determined by a Crown Court judge sitting alone (without a jury).

19.4 Revocation of Crown Court community orders other than for breach

Under para 14(1) of Schedule 8 to the CJA 2003, where the community order was made by the Crown Court and does not include a direction that any failure to comply with the requirements of the order is to be dealt with by a magistrates' court, any application by the offender or by the 'responsible officer' for the order to be revoked, or for the offender to be dealt with in some other way for the original offence, has to be made to the Crown Court.

Where such an application is made, para 14(2) empowers the Crown Court, if it takes the view that it is in the interests of justice to do so (having regard to circumstances which have arisen since the order was made), either to revoke the order or else both to revoke the order and re-sentence the offender for the original offence.

Para 14(3) provides that the circumstances in which a community order may be revoked include the fact that the offender is making good progress or is responding satisfactorily to supervision or treatment.

If the court re-sentences the offender for the original offence, it must take into account the extent to which the offender has complied with the requirements of the community order.

19.5 Commission of subsequent offences

Paragraph 22(1) of Sch 8 to the CJA 2003 provides that where an offender is subject to a community order made by the Crown Court and is convicted of an offence by a magistrates' court, the magistrates' court may commit the offender (in custody or on bail) to the Crown Court.

Under para 23(1) and (2), where an offender in respect of whom a community order is in force is either convicted of an offence by the Crown Court, or sent to the Crown Court under para 22, the Crown Court may either revoke the order or else both revoke the order and re-sentence the offender for the original offence.

Paragraph 23(1)(b) stipulates that the Crown Court may only exercise the power conferred by para 23 if it would be in the interests of justice to do so, having regard to circumstances which have arisen since the community order was made.

If the court re-sentences the offender for the original offence, it must take into account the extent to which the offender has complied with the requirements of the community order.

Custodial sentences in the Crown Court

20.1 Introduction

In this chapter we consider the custodial sentences that can be imposed by the Crown Court on offenders who have attained the age of 18.

Where the offender is aged 18–20 (inclusive) the appropriate custodial sentence is 'detention in a young offender institution' (see **Chapter 16**). The maximum sentence is the same as that applicable to offenders who have attained the age of 21.

Where the offender has attained the age of 21, the custodial sentences available to the Crown Court are:

(a) Sentences of less than 12 months:
    (i)   custody plus;
    (ii) suspended sentence;
    (iii) intermittent custody.
(b) Sentences of over 12 months.

Sentences of less than 12 months are considered in **Chapter 16**.

20.2 Sentences over 12 months — release on licence

Prisoners serving sentences of 12 months or more (apart from dangerous offenders and life sentence prisoners, for whom there is separate provision) must be released on licence after serving half of their sentence. This release is subject to 'standard' and 'prescribed' conditions (and so, in effect, the second half of the sentence is 'served in the community').

The SGC Guidance on the sentences created by the CJA 2003 Act says that:

- A court may sensibly suggest interventions that could be useful when passing sentence, but should only make specific recommendations about the requirements to be imposed on licence when announcing short sentences and where it is reasonable to anticipate their relevance at the point of release. The Governor and Probation Service should have due regard to any recommendations made by the sentencing court but its decision should be contingent upon any changed circumstances during the custodial period.
- The court should make it clear, at the point of sentence, that the requirements to be imposed on licence will ultimately be the responsibility of the Governor and Probation Service and that they are entitled to review any recommendations made by the court in the light of any changed circumstances.

In *R (Carman) v Secretary of State for the Home Dept* [2004] EWHC 2400; The Times, October 11 2004, it was said that the court should only interfere with the conditions of release of a prisoner on licence in exceptional cases.

20.3 Life sentences — murder

An offender aged 21 or over who is convicted of murder must be sentenced to imprisonment for life. In fact, as is well known, life generally does not mean life. The offender will be eligible for release after serving a specified minimum period of detention. The setting of the 'tariff' for such cases is governed in part by Sch 21 to the CJA 2003. However, in *R v Last* [2005] EWCA Crim 106; The Times, January 31 2005, the Court of Appeal said that Sch 21 to the CJA 2003 (and the Sentencing Guidelines Council *Guidance on Reduction in Sentence for Guilty Pleas*, which includes a section on life sentence cases) does not remove the trial judge's discretion to calculate the actual minimum period to be served by the offender. Those provisions merely indicate the matters to which the judge is to have regard when exercising the discretion; the court is free to depart from them, provided reasons are given explaining what it has done.

20.4 Mandatory life sentences — second 'serious' offence

Section 109 of the PCC(S)A 2000 makes provision for the imposition of a mandatory life sentence where the offender is convicted of a second 'serious' offence (such offences being defined by the Act). The court has to impose a life sentence unless satisfied that there are 'exceptional circumstances'.

These provisions have been considered in a number of cases — see especially *R v Offen (No 2)* [2001] 1 WLR 253, *R v Kelly* [2002] 1 Cr App R(S) 85 and *R v Drew* [2003] UKHL 25; [2003] 1 WLR 1213. The key question is whether or not the offender constitutes a significant risk to the public. If he does not, that fact amounts to an exceptional circumstance, and so the court should not impose a life sentence.

20.5 Mandatory minimum sentences

Under PCC(S)A 2000, s 110, the court must impose a mandatory minimum sentence of seven years' custody where the offender is convicted for the third time of trafficking in class A drugs unless 'particular circumstances' (relating to the offences or the offender) make this unjust.

Under s 111 of the same Act, the court must impose a sentence of at least three years' custody where the offender is convicted for the third time of domestic burglary unless 'particular circumstances' (relating to the offences or the offender) make this unjust.

Finally, s 287 of the CJA 2003 lays down mandatory minimum sentences for certain firearms offences under the Firearms Act 1968: a minimum term of five years in the case of an offender who was aged 18 or over when he committed the offence or three years in the case of an offender who was under 18 at that time. The court has to impose a sentence of not less than this minimum term unless it is of the opinion that there are exceptional circumstances relating to the offence or to the offender which justify its not doing so. In *R v Redfern* [2004] EWCA Crim 3291, the Court of Appeal expressed the view that cases where there are exceptional circumstances will be rare.

20.6 Dangerous offenders

Sections 224–236 of the CJA 2003 deal with dangerous offenders. These provisions apply only to certain offences. Section 224 defines the key terms. A 'specified offence' means a violent offence specified in Part 1 of Sch 15 to the Act or a sexual offence specified in Part 2 of that Schedule. A 'serious offence' means a violent or sexual offence specified in Sch 15 punishable with life imprisonment or a determinate sentence of at least ten years' imprisonment. The phrase 'serious harm' means death or serious personal injury (whether physical or psychological).

Section 225 enables the court to impose imprisonment for public protection where an offender aged 18 or over is convicted of a 'serious offence' and the court is of the opinion that there is a significant risk to members of the public of serious harm occasioned by the commission by him of further specified offences (ie offences specified in Sch 15). Under s 225(2), if the offence is punishable with life imprisonment and the court considers that the seriousness of the offence (or of the offence and one or more offences associated with it) is such as to justify the imposition of a sentence of imprisonment for life, then the court must impose a life sentence. In all other cases which fall within s 225 but not within s 225(2), the court must impose a sentence of imprisonment for public protection (s 225(3)); this sentence is for an indeterminate period (s 225(4)). Section 226 applies the same principles to offenders under the age of 18.

Section 227 requires the court to impose an 'extended sentence' where the offender has attained the age of 18 and is convicted of a specified violent or sexual offence and the court considers that there is a significant risk to members of the public of serious harm, caused by the offender committing further specified offences (ie offences specified in Sch 15). Section 227(2) defines an 'extended sentence of imprisonment' as:

a sentence of imprisonment the term of which is equal to the aggregate of—

(a) *the appropriate custodial term [defined in s 227(3) as the term that is commensurate with the seriousness of the offence], and*

(b) *a further period ('the extension period') for which the offender is to be subject to a licence and which is of such length as the court considers necessary for the purpose of protecting members of the public from serious harm occasioned by the commission by him of further specified offences.*

Section 227(4) provides that the extension period must not exceed five years in the case of a specified violent offence, and eight years in the case of a specified sexual offence. In any event, the term of an extended sentence of imprisonment must not exceed the maximum term permitted for the offence.

Section 228 applies the same provisions to offenders under the age of 18.

Section 229(3) provides that, where the offender was aged 18 or over when the offence was committed, the court must assume that there is a significant risk to members of the public of serious harm from the offender unless, after taking into account all the available information the court considers that it would be unreasonable to conclude that there is such a risk. This creates a strong presumption that the court will find that the offender is dangerous, since the court 'must' do so unless it would be 'unreasonable'.

20.7   Young offenders — long-term detention under PCC(S)A 2000, s 91

Under s 91 of the PCC(S)A 2000, the Crown Court may impose a sentence of long-term detention (the maximum length of the sentence being the same as for an adult offender) where an offender under the age of 18 is convicted of an offence which is punishable (in the case of an adult offender) with 14 years' imprisonment or more (or the offence is one of those specified in s 91 itself, such as sexual assault).

This power is available in two circumstances:

(a) where the offender indicates an intention to plead guilty at the 'plea before venue' hearing in the youth court and the youth court decides that the case is too serious for them to deal with: the offender is committed to the Crown Court to be sentenced; or

(b) where the accused indicates an intention to plead not guilty at the 'plea before venue' hearing in the youth court and the youth court, having heard a summary of the case from the prosecution (and any representations from the defence) decide that, in the event of conviction, a sentence of detention under s 91 of the 2000 Act ought to be available: the accused is sent to the Crown Court for trial.

Section 91 has two important effects:

(a) it enables the Crown Court to impose a sentence of detention that is longer than a detention and training order (which is limited to a total of no more than 24 months, of which half is spent in custody and half is spent, under supervision, in the community: see **Chapter 18**); and

(b) it enables the Crown Court to impose a custodial sentence on young offenders for whom a detention and training order is not available (namely (i) those aged 10 and 11, and (ii) those aged 12–14 and who are not 'persistent offenders')

In *R(C) v Balham Youth Court* [2003] EWHC (Admin) 1332; [2004] 1 Cr App R (S) 22, Scott Baker LJ (at paragraph 33) said that 'the fact than an offender . . . does not qualify for a detention and training order because he is only 14 and not a persistent offender is not an exceptional circumstance to justify passing a sentence of less than two years under s 91 of the 2000 Act'. At para 34 he said that the relevant question in that case was whether it was such a serious case that detention above two years would or might realistically be required. In *R(M and W) v West London Youth Court* [2004] EWHC (Admin) 1144 Leveson J (at para 17) put the same question in slightly different terms:

Whether there is a real prospect that a custodial sentence of, or in excess of, two years might be required, or is there any unusual feature of this case which might justify a sentence of less than two years, pursuant to section 91(3), for which purpose the absence of a power to impose a detention and training order because the offender is under the age of 15 is not an unusual feature?

In *R (H) v Southampton Youth Court* [2004] EWHC 2912 (Admin), it was emphasised that offenders under 18, and in particular those under 15, should be tried in the youth court, with Crown Court jurisdiction being reserved for the most serious crimes. It would, said the Court, only be in exceptional cases that an offender aged 12–14 should be sent for trial to the Crown Court. Leveson J summarised the relevant principles as follows (paras 33–35):

33. The general policy of the legislature is that those who are under 18 years of age, and in particular children of under 15 years of age, should, wherever possible, be tried in the youth court. It is that court which is best designed to meet their specific needs. A trial in the Crown Court with the

inevitably greater formality and greatly increased number of people involved (including a jury and the public) should be reserved for the most serious cases.

34. It is a further policy of the legislature that, generally speaking, first-time offenders aged 12 to 14 and all offenders under 12 should not be detained in custody and decisions as to jurisdiction should have regard to the fact that the exceptional power to detain for grave offences should not be used to water down the general principle. Those under 15 will rarely attract a period of detention and, even more rarely, those who are under 12.

35. In each case the court should ask itself whether there is a real prospect, having regard to his or her age, that this defendant whose case they are considering might require a sentence of, or in excess of, two years or, alternatively, whether although the sentence might be less than two years, there is some unusual feature of the case which justifies declining jurisdiction, bearing in mind that the absence of a power to impose a detention and training order because the defendant is under 15 is not an unusual feature.

APPENDIX 1
SMALL GROUP QUESTIONS

Small Group Session 1

Objectives

By the conclusion of this class you should:

- understand police powers of detention;
- understand the nature of preliminary hearings in a criminal case, and the meaning of terms in common usage;
- understand the principles applicable to the grant of public funding in a criminal case;
- understand the procedure to be followed on a bail application;
- understand the principles which govern the grant/withholding of bail;
- be able to advise a defendant on matters relating to bail, including appealing (defence and prosecution) against a refusal by the magistrates' court;
- be able to put forward effective arguments on the grant/withholding of bail, both on behalf of the defence and prosecution;
- understand the principles applicable to the making of costs orders in a criminal case.

Research

Chapters 1, 2 and **3**.
Blackstone's Criminal Practice, 2005 edn, sections D1, D4, D5 and D28.
PACE, ss 34–46.
Prosecution of Offences Act 1985, ss 16–21.
Access to Justice Act 1999, ss 12–14, Sch 3, para 5.
Bail Act 1976, ss 1–9, Sch 1, Pt I.
Criminal Justice Act 2003, ss 4, 6, 7, 13–31, 154 and 280–282.

Preparation

You will need to prepare questions 1 and 2.

Question 2 deals with the *R v Bruce* brief. The main aim of this question will be to use this case to help students appreciate how to apply the principles which govern the grant or refusal of bail in an application for bail. The accused is in custody, the case is to be remanded today by the magistrates, and the accused wishes to apply for bail.

Before the class, it will help if you look at **Chapter 38** of the *Advocacy Manual*. Consider the order in which people will do things and what those things are. What ought to happen if the question of bail arises? Plan what you should do as counsel, basing your plan upon the brief either for the prosecution or defence (you will be told at class which party you represent; remember the opponent's instructions are confidential). Also, you may be called on to play one of the roles in the hearing — perhaps a barrister, court clerk, or the accused. The more you have thought about how the hearing as a whole should be conducted and what everyone's part will be in it, the easier the class should be.

After the 'hearing' has taken place, there will be a class discussion on how the hearing went — maybe you would have decided the question of bail differently from the 'court', or you had different suggestions that could have been made in the application.

Tutorial questions

1. You are briefed to appear at Casterbridge Magistrates' Court on 26 May to represent Amanda, who has been charged that, on 11 May, she stole from a department store a china figure worth £50. Amanda is aged 22, single, unemployed and in receipt of social security benefits. She has one previous conviction, that also being for shoplifting. She was given a conditional discharge by the Sanditon Magistrates' Court of which she will be in breach if convicted. Amanda has made one previous court appearance in connection with the present charge, that being on 12 May when she was unrepresented and was remanded for a fortnight on unconditional bail. Your solicitors state that Amanda did not instruct them until the morning of the 22nd and that it has not been possible in that time to make an application for representation by the Criminal Defence Service. They therefore ask you to take whatever steps are necessary to obtain publicly funded representation for Amanda.

(a) Describe what you would do to comply with your instructing solicitors' request and summarise the considerations which will be taken into account in deciding whether or not the application should be granted.

(b) Assuming that the application is refused, what further steps could the defence take?

2. *R v Bruce*

IN THE BLACKHEATH MAGISTRATES' COURT

R

— v —

Barry Bruce   Defendant

Instructions to Council for the Defence

Counsel has herewith:

1. Summary of the charges

2. Proof of evidence from the Defendant

3. Letter from the Defendant's father

4. Defendant's antecedents

Counsel is instructed to represent Mr Bruce at the next hearing of the case. He faces two charges — one of theft, the other of handling stolen goods, both contrary to the Theft Act 1968. He will plead Not Guilty to both charges. His Proof of Evidence will fill in the details of the defence case.

He is currently on remand in custody, having consented to summary trial, and Counsel is requested to make an application for bail at the next appearance, next Thursday at 10.00 am.

Counsel is advised that the court refused bail on the only other application, made last week by Instructing Solicitors, on the ground that Mr Bruce might interfere with the main Prosecution witness — Ashley Arthur — who is known to him.

Mr Bruce lives quite near to Mr Arthur in Blackheath. However, Mr Bruce's parents live in Ealing, some considerable distance away, and if he went to live there, there could be little chance of contact with the witness in the ordinary course of events.

Also, Mr Bruce (currently unemployed) now has the offer of a job from his uncle, Charlie Campbell, doing painting and decorating. It is unlikely that Mr Campbell will be able to attend the hearing as this is a busy time of year for him. Mr Bruce's father is in hospital but has given Instructing Solicitors a written assurance that his son may live with him, pending the outcome of these proceedings.

Counsel is asked to use his best endeavours in the circumstances and make a strong application. Mr Bruce is a regular client of Instructing Solicitors — our experience indicates that he 'does not suffer fools (or timidity) gladly'!

Copy of letter from Mr Bruce's father:

> 364B Buttermelt Tower,
> Ealing, West London

1st of September 2005

To whom it may concern,

I know that my son is in trouble with the law again. I am going into hospital on the 1st of October for an operation and will be in for about two weeks. Barry can come and stay but only until his trial comes up. He's always been a handful and as his mother and I get older, we can't control him. If he does not behave this time, he'll have to go back inside as we don't want the aggravation at our age. Still, he is our son and this will always be his home.

> Yours faithfully,
>
> (signed) J. Bruce

Details of charges (taken by Instructing Solicitors from charge sheet)

Charge 1:   On a day unknown between the 3rd August 2005 and 10th August 2005, Barry Bruce dishonestly received stolen goods, namely an IBM laptop computer, knowing or believing it to be stolen.

Charge 2:   On the 9th of August 2005 Barry Bruce stole a DVD entitled 'Twelve Angry Men', the property of AA Newsagents Limited.

Proof of Evidence

Mr Barry Bruce of 255, Hazlitt Gardens, Blackheath, who will say—

I have been falsely accused of two crimes. They are both supposed to have occurred when I was in the local newsagent's shop. The owner, Ashley Arthur, is someone I know from my local pub, The Red Herring. Occasionally, I have sold him some stuff that I had got from other friends — boxes of video tapes, CDs, jewellery and the like. It's all been no questions asked and went smoothly till the last time. I was promised by a friend that he was due to take delivery of some top quality computer equipment. It was going to cost me a monkey but I managed to persuade Arthur to buy it from me (unseen) for a straight £1,000.

Unfortunately, after he took delivery of it Arthur's place got raided by the police. I think he was clean except for the computer, which he persuaded them he come by innocently. The police took the computer away and I think Arthur blamed me for tipping them off (which I did not do). Anyway, the next time I went into Arthur's shop we had a bit of a barney about the raid and his computer. At one point he disappeared out the back of the shop for a couple of minutes. That must be when he rung the police because they turned up about five minutes later. The police came in the shop and spoke to Arthur. He said something like 'That's the man'. One of the police then grabbed hold of me and arrested me for handling.

At the police station, I was searched and they found a DVD. This was from a batch that I had sold on to Arthur a couple of weeks previous but I had kept about 12 for myself. I know Arthur has been knocking them out in his shop but there is no way that mine came from there. They already had price labels on when I got them. I got a bit violent in the shop and started swearing but this was because I had been fitted up. I said to Arthur that I would tear his head off and spit down his throat but it was in the heat of the moment. I have had time to reflect on matters in custody and am quite content to see that justice is done in the court.

I have spoken to my father on the telephone and understand I can live with him until my trial. Also, my mum told me on a visit that my uncle, Charlie Campbell, is holding a job open for me with his firm. Although the job is based in Blackheath, I won't be there much as we will be doing jobs all over London.

I badly want bail as I am very worried about leaving my girlfriend alone in the last few months of her pregnancy.

I can remember my last three convictions. Two were in Ealing Magistrates' Court in 2002 for burglary (I got Community Service, about 150 hours) and one in 2004 at Blackheath Magistrates. That was for a fight in a pub — I was done for simple GBH and got a three-month suspended sentence.

Metropolitan Police

Antecedents of:	Barry BRUCE
Address:	255, Hazlitt Gardens, Blackheath, London
Age:	22
Date of Birth:	31.3.83
Place of Birth:	Paddington, West London
Date of 1st entry into UK:	N/A
Occupation:	Unemployed

Education: He attended Boyson Comprehensive School, leaving aged 16, with 3 GCSEs in English, General Studies and Art.

Main employments during last 5 years
Has had several jobs of short duration since leaving school. These include casual labour for market stallholders and delivering community (free) newspapers.

Home conditions and domestic circumstances
Lives with his girlfriend (who is expecting their child) in a one bedroom flat. Is not claiming Income Support as such, although the rent for the flat is paid by the DSS. No regular commitments. Girlfriend's parents sometimes help with shopping bills.

Outstanding matters

If convicted, will be in breach of a three-month suspended sentence imposed by Blackheath Magistrates' Court on 2.12.04.

List of previous convictions attached:	Yes/No
Date of arrest: 9.8.05	— /In custody

Officer in case: DC Duncan
Station: Blackheath East
Telephone number: Date: 6.9.05
Supervising Officer:

Convictions Recorded Against: Barry Bruce	CRO No. 34567/05
Charged in name of Barry Bruce	Date of Birth 31.3.83

Date	Court	Offences	Sentence

Total number of convictions 6. Has not previously served a custodial sentence.

Date	Court	Offences	Sentence
5.7.99	B'heath M/C	Theft	Fine £30
15.9.99	Greenwich M/C	1. Handling	Con. Dis.
		2. Handling	1 year
1.5.02	Ealing M/C	1. Burglary	Comm. Serv.
		2. Burglary	150 hours
2.12.04	B'heath M/C	Causing GBH	3 months' imprisonment suspended for 1 year

IN THE BLACKHEATH MAGISTRATES' COURT

R

— v —

Barry Bruce   (Defendant)

Instructions to Prosecute

Herewith:

1. The charges against the accused

2. List of objections to bail

3. Antecedents/CRO form

4. Case summary

This case is due in court again next Thursday. The accused has elected summary trial and a date is likely to be fixed by the court at the next hearing. There are two civilian witnesses and two police officers. The time estimate is — half a day.

The accused is currently remanded in custody. On the last occasion that bail was actively considered by the court, it was denied due to possible interference with the chief prosecution witness, Mr Ashley ARTHUR.

Charges: —

1: On a day unknown between 3rd August 2005 and 10th August 2005, Barry Bruce dishonestly received stolen goods, namely an IBM laptop computer, knowing or believing it to be stolen.

2:   On 9th of August 2005 Barry Bruce stole a DVD, the property of AA Newsagents Limited.

Objections to bail on substantial grounds for believing the Defendant may:_

1.   Interfere with prosecution witness — the accused knows him and lives nearby.
2.   Commit further offences — has a record of similar crimes in his record. No apparent income. See antecedents.
3.   Abscond. If convicted of either charge, the accused will be in breach of a suspended sentence. See antecedents.

Case summary: —

In late July 2005, ARTHUR was offered by BRUCE (and agreed to buy) an IBM laptop computer. On 4th August, a Mr Smollett was the victim of a burglary at his flat. Among items taken was an expensive computer. This was later sold by BRUCE to ARTHUR; it was recovered from ARTHUR on the 7th and identified by SMOLLETT as his.

ARTHUR owns a shop in Blackheath. On 9th August, BRUCE went in and ARTHUR called the police.

BRUCE was arrested in the shop and became very aggressive and abusive towards ARTHUR, threatening him with serious injury.

A DVD was later found on BRUCE at the police station. This was identified by ARTHUR as coming from his shop. BRUCE had not bought it.

At the station, BRUCE made a full confession of both offences to DC Duncan and PC Ewart.

[Note: Antecedents and CRO form are not copied — see the Defence brief.]

Small Group Session 2

Objectives

By the conclusion of this class you should:

*   understand the 'plea before venue' procedure and the possible outcomes of that procedure;
*   understand the factors that are relevant to the decision as to mode of trail of either way offences;
*   understand the procedure for determining mode of trial;
*   be able to advise a client (defendant/prosecution) on matters likely to arise in the context of a mode of trial hearing;
*   understand the effect of ss 40 and 41 of the Criminal Justice Act 1988;
*   have a basic understanding of summary trial procedure.

Research

Chapters 4 and **5.**
Blackstone's Criminal Practice, 2005 edn, section D3.
Powers of Criminal Courts (Sentencing) Act 2000, ss 3, 4.
Magistrates' Courts Act 1980, ss 17, 21, 22, 29, 38.
Criminal Justice Act 1988, ss 40 and 41.

Courts Act 2003, s 45 and Sch 3.

Criminal Justice Act 2003, s 41 and Sch 3.

PACE Code C.

Magistrates' Courts (Advance Information) Rules 1985.

National Mode of Trial Guidelines.

Preparation

You will need to prepare questions 1, 2, 3, 4, 5 and 6.

Questions 1 and 2 deal with the procedure for determining which court a defendant may be tried in.

Questions 3 and 6 deal with the issues that determine whether to elect Crown Court trial.

All the questions are problem questions and you should come to class having made notes on each question. Not all the questions have definite answers, some depend upon the circumstances of each case and decisions will be reached using the judgement of counsel.

Tutorial questions

Mode of trial

Questions 1 and 2 deal with the procedure for determining the court in which the defendant will be tried.

1. Edward appears before Muggleton Magistrates' Court charged with:

    (a) dangerous driving;

    (b) taking a motor vehicle without the owner's consent; and

    (c) driving while disqualified.

The prosecution case is that officers in a marked police vehicle saw Edward driving a car on a public road. Knowing him to be disqualified, they signalled to him to stop but he accelerated, driving at speeds of 70 mph in a built-up area, going onto the wrong side of the road, causing oncoming traffic to brake sharply, and eventually crashing the car into a lamppost. He then escaped on foot but was later arrested at his home address. During the course of the arrest, he punched one of the police officers. Enquiries revealed that the car Edward was allegedly driving was taken without the owner's consent earlier that day. It is expected that Edward will plead not guilty to all charges and allege mistaken identification on the part of the police. Dangerous driving is an offence triable either way; driving while disqualified, taking a vehicle without the owner's consent and assaulting a police officer in the execution of his duty are summary offences.

   (a) Describe the procedure by which the mode of trial for the dangerous driving charge will be determined.

   (b) Advise Edward of the extent to which he is entitled to know the nature of the prosecution case in advance of trial (i) if he is charged with a triable either way offence and (ii) if he is charged with a summary only offence?

   (c) Advise the prosecution on whether, if the dangerous driving charge is committed for trial, it will be possible for the other charges to be tried on indictment also.

2. David appears before Kingsport Magistrates' Court charged with two offences of criminal damage. The first charge alleges that, on 1 September, he intentionally damaged a motor vehicle; the second alleges that, on 3 September, he intentionally damaged a window.

The prosecution case as regards the first offence is that, following an argument with a relative, he threw a stone at the windscreen of the relative's car as he was driving away from David's house. As regards the second offence, the case is that, after being told to leave a public house because he was the worse for drink, he threw a brick through a window of the pub. The value of the damage involved in the first charge was £250; the value of the damage in the second was £1,000. David wishes to be tried on indictment.

Advise him as to whether he has a right to be so tried.

Election

Questions 3 to 6 deal with the defendant's decision whether to elect Crown Court trial.

In each of these situations, you are defence counsel in the magistrates' court. Today the court will determine the mode of trial for the defendant. He or she may be asked to choose whether he or she wishes to be tried in the magistrates' court or Crown Court. The defendant is likely to want your advice on this matter. Consider what you could say.

3. Arnold (aged 32) appears at the magistrates' court on two charges. The first (theft) alleges that he stole two loaves of bread and a pint of milk from a local store. The second (making off without payment) alleges that, having ordered and consumed a fried breakfast, Arnold tried to leave a cafe without paying for his meal. According to prosecution witnesses, he was caught 'red-handed' on both occasions.

Arnold has no fixed address, staying in hostels when he can afford to do so. His employment record consists largely of casual jobs which were menial and low-paid. He has seven convictions, covering the last 10 years. Offences involve dishonesty (of a minor nature) or violence/breaches of the peace. If convicted of either of the two latest offences, he will be in breach of a conditional discharge imposed five months ago by another court.

Instructions from the client: Arnold is in custody and would like to stay there for the winter months. He intends to plead Not Guilty, insisting he is innocent, but he has no witnesses. He says the prosecution eye witnesses are lying and have grudges against him.

4. Bertie has been charged with theft from his employer. The allegation is that he took stock (electrical components) from his employer's warehouse over a period of several months, with a total value of £9,500. No property has been recovered.

There are two main prosecution witnesses, the works supervisor and another colleague from Bertie's former place of work. Both say they saw him walk out of the warehouse with items, place them in the boot of his car in the car park and eventually drive home with the items at the end of his shift. Bertie made no admissions to police officers, and refused to be interviewed without his solicitor being present.

Bertie is aged 26 and has no previous convictions. He is married with two young children.

Instructions from the client: Bertie says he can call his ex-employer to testify that he was being considered for promotion at the time of his arrest. He says that he suspected the two prosecution witnesses of stealing the stock that he is charged with stealing.

5. Craig is aged 34. He is charged with stealing a car. The car was recovered from a multi-storey car park attached to a block of flats some 200 metres from Craig's house. Police arrested Craig inside the car. He has four previous convictions for theft (not of cars) and has been in prison on two occasions. He is alleged to have made a full confession on the way to the police station. There are no eye witnesses to the theft.

Instructions from the client: Craig will plead Not Guilty. He says that the car had been in the car park for three days before his arrest and that he thought it had been abandoned. He was thinking about using it for spares for his own car. He denies making the confession, saying that he has always maintained his innocence.

6. Dennis is charged with assault occasioning actual bodily harm. The incident occurred at a nightclub when an argument developed over who was going to drive a young lady

home. The victim (and main prosecution witness) suffered a broken nose and lost two teeth. Dennis (aged 18) is a promising amateur boxer and was not marked.

The victim (aged 24) has several previous convictions for offences of violence. Dennis has no previous convictions. At the police station, Dennis expressed contrition for his part in the incident.

Instructions from the client: Dennis will plead Not Guilty, relying on self-defence. He has no witnesses. He says his 'admission' was an expression of regret for losing his self- control but was not meant to be an acceptance of guilt.

Now go through those situations again and think about how you, as prosecuting counsel, might address the court on the suitable location for the case to be dealt with. (Remember you should liaise with the staff of the Crown Prosecution Service if this is a CPS prosecution.)

Small Group Session 3

Objectives

By the conclusion of this class you should:

- understand the nature of summary trial procedure specifically in relation to juveniles;
- understand in outline how to carry out fact management of a set of papers;
- be aware of the differences and similarities between summary trial of adults and summary trial of juveniles;
- understand the circumstances in which a juvenile may be tried other than in a youth court;
- understand the procedural rules applicable where an adult and a juvenile appear together in an adult magistrates' court;
- appreciate the potential impact of the Human Rights Act 1998 on criminal procedure.

Research

Chapters 5, 6 and **18.**
Blackstone's Criminal Practice, 2005 edn, section D22.
Powers of Criminal Courts (Sentencing) Act 2000, ss 8, 91, 100.
Magistrates' Courts Act 1980, ss 24, 29.
Human Rights Act 1998 and Article 6 of the European Convention on Human Rights.
Criminal Justice Act 2003, Sch 3, paras 9, 18, 22.

Preparation

You will need to prepare questions 1 and 2.

Question 1 deals with the discretionary sentencing powers available regarding juveniles and the committal powers available to the youth court. You should read generally **Chapters 5, 6** and **18,** and make notes of the various custodial sentencing options and the powers of committal available to the youth and magistrates' courts when dealing with juveniles.

Question 2 also considers how to fact manage a set of brief papers (*R v Barley*). This is a simple case of theft. You should set out on a piece of paper what you consider to be the issues in the case and research any legal points that may arise. You should prepare this as you would for any summary trial. You should ask whether you believe the court will make a finding of guilt or not guilty and the reasons for coming to either conclusion. There will be a detailed discussion in class of the brief, how to manage the papers, what the relevant issues may be, and the likely outcome.

You should then consider and makes notes of the procedure and options available to the courts should the juvenile be alleged to have been acting in concert with an adult. The various options and procedure will be discussed in class. Finally, for the class you should make some brief notes of the principal differences between a youth court and a magistrates' court, in procedure, layout and constitution.

Tutorial questions

1.   Fiona (aged 16), Gillian (aged 14) and her twin brother, George, are all found guilty in the youth court of three offences of burglary and one of inflicting grievous bodily harm (contrary to s 20 of the Offences Against the Person Act 1861). On each occasion, they went to a house where an elderly person lived alone, tricked their way in by asking to use the lavatory, after which two of them would search the premises while the third kept the victim occupied in conversation. Pension money, savings and jewellery were stolen to a total value of approximately £1,000. On the third occasion, the victim became suspicious and tried to stop them leaving. They knocked her to the ground, causing bruising and a head wound which required 20 stitches. Reports reveal that Gillian and George have a difficult background. Their mother admits that she cannot keep control of them. Moreover, their father and older siblings all have criminal records. George has previous findings of guilt for shoplifting and stealing a car radio, but Gillian has not been in trouble before. Fiona is also of previous good character. She comes from an excellent home, and the report can give no explanation for her involvement in the offences other than 'a desire for thrills'. She apparently met Gillian and George at a youth club where together they planned the offences.

   (a) What are the youth court magistrates' maximum custodial sentencing powers?

   (b) What are their powers, if any, to commit for sentence?

   (c) Was this an appropriate case to be tried in the youth court?

2.   *R v Barley*

IN THE BLACKHEATH MAGISTRATES' COURT

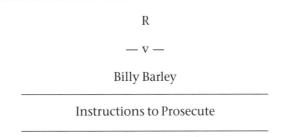

R

— v —

Billy Barley

Instructions to Prosecute

Billy Barley is charged with theft. He is alleged to have stolen a leather jacket, the property of Newtrend Limited, on 3rd August 2005. He was stopped by a store detective, employed by the company, a short distance from their shop after a chase. The jacket was recovered from him. Police were called and Constable Field attended the scene. No admissions were made.

Both witnesses — the store detective, Ellis Farmer, and Constable Field — have been warned to attend court on the next hearing.

Billy Barley is in receipt of publicly funded representation and has instructed Messrs Planter and Reaper of 22 Harvest Street, WC5.

Barley's date of birth is 1st February 1992.

STATEMENT OF WITNESS

Statement of:	Ellis FARMER
Age of witness:	Over 18
Occupation of witness:	Store detective
[Usual declaration omitted]	

Signed: E. Farmer

Signature witnessed by: Drew Field, PC 202Y

I am employed as a store detective by Newtrend Limited. I have held this position for 3 years. For the last 6 months I have been at the Oxford Street Branch.

On the 3rd August 2005, I was on duty on the ground floor of the shop when my attention was caught by a youth who I now know to be Billy BARLEY. He was standing by a mirror and was wearing one of our new leather jackets. He seemed to be more interested in watching what was going on around him than looking in the mirror.

I moved to a different position, keeping him under observation the whole time. After I had been observing him for about thirty seconds, he suddenly ran towards the exit, still wearing the jacket. I was unable to stop him before he left as several customers were between us.

When I got outside, I saw him running through the mall and gave chase. I caught him just around the corner in Orchard Street, some 300 metres from the shop. He had taken the jacket off and appeared to be about to hide it. I took him by the arm and said, 'You're coming with me. The police will have to come. You've stolen this jacket and it's store policy always to prosecute.' He said, 'I don't know what you're talking about. A boy just gave this to me.' I replied, 'We'll let the police sort this out. Come with me'.

We returned to the shop where I called the police and eventually repeated my story to Constable Field in the presence of Billy Barley. The jacket was recovered intact and there is no claim for compensation.

Dated 4.8.05

Signed: E. Farmer

Signature witnessed by: D. Field

STATEMENT OF WITNESS

Statement of:	Drew FIELD
Age of witness:	Over 18
Occupation of witness:	Police Constable 202Y
[Usual declaration omitted]	

Signed: D. Field

Signature witnessed by: G. Fallow P. Sgt 545Z

On the 3rd August 2005 at 4.25 pm I was on duty in Oxford Street when, as a result of information received, I attended the premises of Newtrend Limited at 755 Oxford Street. There I spoke to an employee of the store, Ellis FARMER, and then I asked a youth, who I know to be Billy BARLEY, 'The store detective says you were seen trying the jacket on and then you ran out of the store without paying for it. What have you got to say?' He replied, 'It's a mistake. I was waiting for my bus when a boy came running around the corner, threw the coat down and kept running. I went to pick it up when this person came up and arrested me.'

The store detective said, 'I got a good look at him in the shop. I know it was him.' I said to BARLEY, 'I am not satisfied with your answer. I am arresting you for theft of this leather jacket from Newtrend.' I then cautioned BARLEY and he said 'Can I ring my Mum?' We then went to Paddington Green Police Station where, at 7.45 pm and in the presence of his parents, he was charged with theft of the jacket, cautioned and made no reply.

Dated 10.8.05

Signed: D. Field

Signature witnessed by: G. Fallow

Extract from Record of previous Findings of Guilt:

Billy BARLEY (d.o.b. 1.02.92) has 2 findings of guilt recorded against him, both in the Westminster Youth Court. Both offences were for burglary of dwelling houses. The first finding of guilt, recorded on 13.05.04, resulted in an order that there be a fine of £50. The second, dated 10.02.05, resulted in an order that he be conditionally discharged for 1 year.

WESTMINSTER YOUTH COURT
Sitting at Seymour Place, W1

R

— v —

Billy Barley

Instructions to Counsel for the Defence

Counsel is instructed to represent Billy Barley at Seymour Place Youth Court on his trial. He is charged with shoplifting — taking a leather jacket from a Newtrend shop in Oxford Street. No one else is alleged to be involved. He will plead *Not Guilty*.

Instructing Solicitors understand that there are 2 Prosecution witnesses, a store detective and arresting officer.

The evidence seems quite weak, in the opinion of Instructing Solicitors, with the case turning on identification. Counsel is, of course, familiar with the guidelines for such cases, laid down by the Court of Appeal in *R v Turnbull* [1977] QB 224. Billy Barley was found in possession of the jacket, a fact which he does not deny, but he has an explanation which he told the arresting officer.

There are no defence witnesses, apart from Billy, although his parents have been told by Instructing Solicitors to attend Court with him. Counsel is asked to use his best endeavours to secure an acquittal.

Proof of Evidence

Billy Barley of 65 Plough Lane, London W9, who will say:

On the day in August when I was supposed to have stolen the jacket, I was in Oxford Street, looking around the shops. I had arrived there at about 2 pm and saw all that I wanted to by about 4.30. Then I went to catch the bus home. This is a number 85 which stops in Orchard Street, just off of Oxford Street.

I had just got to the stop when a boy came running around the corner from Oxford Street. He was running hard so I watched to see why. He had something in his hand and threw it to the ground as he went past the bus stop. He kept going, up towards Baker Street.

I was curious about what he had thrown away so I went and picked it up. It was a leather jacket, brand new. I saw it still had the price ticket in and was just looking to see the size when this person came up and told me I was under arrest for shoplifting. I said I did not know anything about it but I was taken to a shop, Newtrend, in Oxford Street.

I did not know what to do but eventually the police came. The store detective said that I had been under observation in the shop and had run out with the jacket. When the police officer asked me if that was true, I denied it and told them what happened. No one believed me and I was taken to the police station.

My Mum and Dad were called down to the station and got me. I have never admitted to stealing the jacket. I would not recognise the boy who had the jacket. I did not know him. There were some other people at the bus stop who must have seen it all but there is no way I could trace them.

I think the jacket is a size 40-inch chest. That is too big for me.

In the case of *R v Billy Barley* (see above), assume that Billy is alleged to have been acting in concert with his cousin Charlotte (aged 18). How would the procedure differ?

Small Group Session 4

Objectives

By the conclusion of this class you should:

- be able to identify the various forms of appeal against the decisions of magistrates;
- explain and apply the procedure for exercising those rights of appeal, and why;
- identify the circumstances in which a defendant may be committed for sentence to the Crown Court.

Research

Chapter 8, 5.1.4 and **5.3**.
Blackstone's Criminal Practice, 2005 edn, section D26.
Powers of Criminal Courts (Sentencing) Act 2000, ss 3, 4, 6, 119, 120.
Magistrates' Courts Act 1980, s 142.
Criminal Justice Act 2003, sch 3, para 22.

Preparation

You will need to prepare questions 1 to 5.

Questions 1–4 all deal with appeals. You need to consider and make notes about which form of appeal is most appropriate in each of the problems and why. In addition you need to be able to state the procedures applicable to each type of appeal.

Questions 5 and 6 deal with committals for sentence. You need to consider the circumstances in which the magistrates' court may commit a defendant to the Crown Court for sentence. You should also be able to state the statutory powers available to the magistrates' court to commit for related/unrelated offences, and summary and either way offences. The different statutory powers and their applicability will be discussed in class.

Tutorial questions

Appeals from the magistrates' court

1.   Christine is charged with stealing an expensive box of chocolates from Harridges, a large department store. She is jointly charged with her husband, Harold. She agrees to summary trial. Christine pleads guilty and Harold not guilty. In view of her plea, the prosecution offers no evidence against Harold. Having learnt that Christine has previous convictions for shoplifting and considered a pre-sentence report, the magistrates pass a sentence of three months' imprisonment. When the defence counsel goes to see Christine in the cells, she tells him for the first time that Harold made her steal the chocolates by threatening her with violence if she did not do so. Also, on the morning of her first appearance before the magistrates, he had said to her, 'You'd better not tell them I made you do it or it will be the worse for you when I get you home'.

Is it possible for Christine to appeal to the Crown Court against conviction? If so, how do you think the Crown Court would deal with the case?

2.   Ben, aged 23, is charged with wounding Claude. The offence is alleged to have taken place in a public house shortly after a football match between 'United' and 'City'. Ben is a 'United' supporter whereas Claude supports 'City'. Ben intends to plead not guilty — he says he was acting in self-defence and that he was attacked by Claude and other 'City' supporters. Ben has two previous convictions for offences of violence. He appears at the Whitehaven Magistrates' Court and elects summary trial. Ben does not give evidence at his trial. After hearing all the evidence the magistrates convict Ben and sentence him to three months' imprisonment.

A week after the hearing Ben's solicitors discover that the police had taken a statement from Desmond, a witness whose evidence supported Ben's account. Neither Ben nor his solicitors knew about Desmond. Ben wishes to appeal against both conviction and sentence. Advise Ben as to his rights of appeal.

3.   Francis appears at Blackacre Magistrates' Court charged with theft. The magistrates find the matter is suitable for summary trial and Francis elects summary trial. At the end of the prosecution evidence, his solicitor makes a submission that there is no case to answer. The magistrates retire to consider and when they return the chairman announces that they find Francis guilty. What steps can be taken to quash the conviction? Describe in brief outline the appropriate procedure.

4.   Alan is charged with having an offensive weapon (contrary to the Prevention of Crime Act 1953, s 1). He was found by the police standing in someone's front garden in possession of a flick knife. Alan makes a submission of no case to answer on the grounds

that the knife was not an offensive weapon per se and that a private garden is not a public place for the purposes of the Act. The justices agree and acquit Alan.

Advice the CPS on:

(a) the most appropriate avenue of appeal; and

(b) the procedure that should be followed.

Committals for sentence

5.   Sid is charged with assault occasioning actual bodily harm, to which he indicated that he wishes to plead guilty. The information is put to Sid and he pleads guilty. The prosecuting solicitor tells the magistrates that Sid is a police officer who committed the offence when off duty, as a result of the victim provoking him deliberately by making offensive remarks about the police. The magistrates were not previously aware that Sid was a police officer. Antecedent evidence shows Sid to have no previous convictions. No other offences are taken into consideration. Can the magistrates properly commit Sid to the Crown Court to be sentenced under s 3 of the Powers of Criminal Courts (Sentencing) Act 2000?

6.   Martin, aged 22, appears in Barchester Magistrates' Court charged with obtaining property by deception, contrary to s 15 of the Theft Act 1968. At the plea before venue hearing, Martin indicates a plea of guilty. Martin is further charged with having (on another occasion) interfered with a motor vehicle, contrary to s 9 of the Criminal Attempts Act 1981. This is a summary offence punishable with a maximum of three months' imprisonment. Martin again pleads guilty. He has previous convictions for dishonesty.

What powers to commit for sentence do the magistrates possess in respect of Martin and what powers of sentence will the Crown Court possess in the event of such committal?

Small Group Session 5

Objectives

By the conclusion of this class you should understand:

- the rules which govern the contents of an indictment;
- how an indictment is drafted;
- what considerations determine what offences appear on an indictment;
- the rules applicable to reporting of cases by the media.

Research

Chapter 10.
Drafting Manual (**Chapter 24**).
Blackstone's Criminal Practice, 2005 edn, section D10.
Indictments Act 1915, ss 3 and 5.
Indictment Rules 1971, rr 3–9.
Code for Crown Prosecutors.
PACE, s 78.
Firearms Act 1968.

Preparation

You will need to prepare the tutorial question *R v Lewis*. You should consider the evidence in the papers and after doing so you should prepare a list of possible defendants and counts against each defendant. You should also consider any evidential questions that may arise. You should be ready in class to justify the charges against your chosen defendants on a legal and evidential basis, and bearing in mind the Code for Crown Prosecutors. There will be a detailed discussion in class of who should be indicted and for what offence(s). You can if you wish attempt to draft your own indictment.

Tutorial question

R v Lewis and others

IN THE CROWN COURT SITTING AT LEWES

R

— v —

Lewis and others

Instructions to Counsel for the Prosecution

Counsel has herewith:

1. Bundle of depositions and witness statements

2. Antecedent history of the accused

Counsel is instructed

(i)   to prosecute in this matter;

(ii) to settle the appropriate indictment; and

(iii) to advise on the procedure to be adopted in relation to any counts added to the indictment.

Case Summary

On 17.4.05 a branch of the South Downs Building Society was held up at gunpoint by two masked men. One kept watch by the door, observing both the people inside the branch and passers-by. The other demanded money from a cashier. On obtaining a holdall containing £15,967, the two men fled on foot. They were pursued by a passer-by and one of the men stopped and shot the pursuer, a Mr Goodbody. They then made good their escape, using a car parked nearby.

The prosecution case was that three of the accused, namely Lewis, Duke and Ella, were involved in the actual robbery with Ella as the driver of the escape vehicle, a stolen Audi TT Coupe. The fourth accused, Peterson, stored the vehicle in his garage for several days prior to the robbery.

Original charge

Against Finlay LEWIS, Arthur DUKE, Gerald ELLA and Leonard PETERSON

You are charged that, on the 17th day of April 2005, you did rob Mary Penny of £15,967, contrary to the Theft Act 1968, s 8(1).

<u>STATEMENT OF WITNESS</u>

Statement of: Mary PENNY
Age: Over 18
Occupation: Building society cashier
[Usual declaration omitted]

Dated 3rd May 2005

I am a cashier for the South Downs Building Society. I work in the Churchill Square Branch. I have been there for about 4 years.

I remember the 17th of April 2005. I was at work that morning. At about 10 am two men entered the branch. Both were wearing dark-coloured donkey jackets which had orange fluorescent material on the top half. They had on dark balaclava helmets with 'Porky Pig' masks. They were both carrying what looked like sawn-off shotguns.

One of the men shouted for everyone to get on the floor. There was some screaming and the same man shouted to shut up.

He came to my window and said 'fill this with money and nobody will get hurt'.

He produced a nylon holdall and passed it through the window. I looked to the manager who indicated that I should do as the man asked.

I emptied the contents of the tills into the bag. This was both cash and cheques. Then I gave it back to the man at the counter.

All this time the other man had just stood by the entrance door, pointing his gun at the staff and customers.

The man with the holdall joined the other one by the door. One of them shouted 'Nobody move and you won't get hurt' and they both ran out. I think it was the man with the holdall who shouted.

I had pressed the silent alarm as the man approached my window and about two minutes after the men left, several police officers arrived.

I would describe the man with the holdall as about 6 feet tall and medium build. His voice was unusual. He had an accent. Irish is how I would describe it.

I saw his hands when he gave me the bag — they were white.

On the 26th of April I attended a video identification parade at Brighton Police Station where I saw a number of men. They all looked about the same height and build as the man with the holdall.

They each said the words 'fill this with money and nobody will get hurt'. I picked out the 5th man. I am sure he was the man with the holdall.

I did not get a good look at the second man. I think he was about 2 inches shorter than the other one, again medium build. I would not recognise him again.

The whole incident lasted for about 5 minutes.

I did not see the face of either man. I did not see their hair, they were both wearing balaclava helmets.

Their jackets were not tight on them. They could have been slimmer than medium build.

I saw no distinctive features on either man. The voice was distinctive.

I would call it Irish. I have no Irish relations or friends. I have not been to Ireland on holiday. I have never been to Scotland.

I can recall the voice of the man with the holdall. I am sure that the man I picked out at the identification parade had the same voice. I am not mistaken. I am not an expert on voices or regional accents.

Signed: Mary Penny
Signature witnessed by: D. Law, DS

STATEMENT OF WITNESS

Statement of:	Reginald GOODBODY
Age:	Over 18
Occupation:	Retired grocer

[Usual declaration omitted]

Dated 3.5.05

(Witness sworn)

On the 17.4.05 I was in Brighton for some shopping. My wife was with me.

We started looking around the shops in Churchill Square. Just after 10 o'clock we were going past a small parade of shops when two men ran out of the South Downs Building Society premises there.

I was about 20 yards away from them. They ran towards me and my wife. They had a bag and guns. They were wearing balaclava helmets. They had workmen's jackets on — black I think, with orange patches.

I realised they had robbed the Building Society and I put up my arms to try and stop them. One got past me but I caught hold of the bag that the other one was carrying.

We got into a bit of a struggle over the bag. I think people were coming out of the Building Society by now.

The other man ran back and shouted at me to let go. When I said No, he shot me in the leg with his gun.

I fell over and let go of the bag. Both of them ran off.

The one I was struggling with was about my height and build. I am 6 feet tall and weigh about 13 stone. The other one was about the same. I can't recall him clearly.

I would not recognise either of them again. Their features were quite obscured by their helmets.

I went to hospital in an ambulance with my wife. The Royal Sussex Hospital in Brighton.

I was there for 8 days. My leg was badly damaged by the gun. It was a shotgun cartridge. I lost some blood and quite a bit of muscle and flesh in my calf.

I now have to walk with a stick. I find my mobility is very restricted. I attend the hospital physiotherapy department every week to build my leg up.

The one with the bag shot me. The gun did not go off in the struggle — I am quite sure.

I do not think it can have been an accident — he deliberately took aim and fired. There was nothing I could do.

The man who shot me shouted at me to let go of the bag. I cannot recall his exact words. He did not have an accent. I did not notice any accent.

The other one never spoke at all.

Signed: R. Goodbody
Signature witnessed by: D. Law, DS

STATEMENT OF WITNESS

Statement of: Brenda BROWSE
Age: Over 18
Occupation: Housekeeper

[Usual declaration omitted]

Signed by: B. Browse
Signature witnessed by: D. Law, DS 494P

Dated 11.5.2005

On the 17th of April 2005 I left my home to meet a friend in Brighton. We had arranged to meet by the Oxfam shop, just along the road from Churchill Square. I got there early, at about 9.30 am. There were several cars parked around the area but I did not take any notice of them. I went to a cafe over the road for a cup of tea.

While I was in the cafe, I could see the road ahead — Mountfort Road. There was a dark blue Audi TT parked there with a man sitting behind the wheel. The car was there the whole time I was in the cafe. At about 10 o'clock, as I was about to leave, two men came running along the road, shouting something. The man in the car started the engine and the two men leaped into the car. It tore off down the road, towards the junction by the cafe and straight over without waiting to see if anyone was crossing the road.

I was astonished by this behaviour and made a note of the car registration number. It was W838 JPO.

I would not recognise the two men who jumped into the car again but both were wearing workmen's jackets with orange fluorescent patches like Council workmen wear. I think they both had dark hair.

The man in the car was quite slim with dark wavy hair, fair-skinned and in his early twenties. I would recognise him again.

I am willing to attend court to give evidence.

Signed: B. Browse
Signature witnessed by: D. Law, DS

STATEMENT OF WITNESS

Statement of: Brenda BROWSE
Age: (Details as above)
Occupation:
Address:

Dated 15.5.05

Further to my statement of 11th May 2005, on the 15th of May 2005 I was asked to attend Brighton Police Station. I was met by Inspector Charger who explained that there was going to be a parade where the man I saw in the Audi TT might be. He explained that the man might not be there and I was to look at all of the men very carefully. He said only if I was sure I saw the same man, I should indicate his position.

I was escorted into a waiting room by a WPC and eventually taken to a room with a glass screen. Several men were lined up against one wall on the other side of the screen. I went to one end of the line and walked along it. The seventh man was the one I had seen driving the Audi TT on the 17th of April. I was quite sure and indicated as such. The Inspector asked me to leave the room as the parade was now over.

I was then brought to a room where I wrote this statement.

Signed: Brenda Browse
Signature witnessed by: D. Law, DS

STATEMENT OF WITNESS

Statement of: David LAW
Age: Over 18
Occupation: Detective Sergeant 494P, Brighton C.I.D.

[Usual declaration omitted]

Signed: D. Law
Signature witnessed by: A. Libby, DC 675P

Dated 18.5.05

On 17th April 2005 at 12.10 pm, as a result of information received, I went to 33 Dials Lane in Brighton where I found a navy blue Audi TT Coupe which appeared to have been abandoned in a hurry. The doors were wide open. Under the driver's seat were some shotgun cartridges. The registration number of the vehicle was W838 JPO.

I had reason to believe that this vehicle had been used in an armed robbery which had occurred earlier that day in Brighton and I requested that a Scenes of Crime Officer attend the location in Dials Lane.

On 11th May, I went to a private house at 72 Power Station Row, Southwick. The door was opened by a woman who identified herself as Sharon Ella. I asked her if I could speak to Gerald Ella — she replied that he was not in. Subsequently, I attended the rear of the house where colleagues had apprehended Gerald ELLA, while he was climbing over a fence in the garden of number 72.

I said to him, 'Are you Gerald Ella?' He replied, 'What if I am?' I said to him, 'I have reason to believe you were involved in an armed robbery on the South Downs Building Society in Brighton on the 17th of April, specifically as the driver of the getaway vehicle.' He replied, 'You've got a very good imagination for a copper'.

I then told him that his fingerprints had been identified on the getaway vehicle, the navy blue Audi TT. He seemed to be about to fall down so I grabbed him and said, 'I am arresting you for your part in the South Downs robbery on the 17th of April 2005. You do not have to say anything. But it may harm your defence if you do not mention when questioned something which you later rely on in court. Anything you do say may be given in evidence'. He made no reply and was taken to Brighton Central Police Station under escort.

He was later seen by myself and DC Libby in an interview room at Brighton Central at 10.25 pm on the 11th. He was reminded of the caution and I then asked him if he was prepared to talk to us about the robbery. He indicated that he did not wish to talk to us and he was returned to his cell at 10.28 pm.

I was present at 7.35 am on the 12th of May when ELLA was charged with robbery, the charge was read over to him, he was cautioned and made no reply.

At 2.40 pm on the 12th of May I interviewed Arthur DUKE at Brighton Central Police Station where he was in custody. The interview was tape-recorded and was concluded at 3.02 pm.

At 6.00 am on the 13th of May 2005 I went to 22 Bramber Street, Brighton. There I saw a man I now know to be Finlay LEWIS. I said to him, 'Are you Finlay Lewis?' He said, 'Yes, why?' I told him that he had been implicated in the robbery of the South Downs Building Society in Brighton and he replied, 'Someone's a grass. I'm saying nothing till I see my solicitor.'

After a brief search of the premises, I told LEWIS that he was under arrest for robbery and cautioned him. He replied 'I'll be wanting a word with my solicitor.' He was then taken to Brighton Central Police Station and booked into a cell.

I saw LEWIS again at 2.10 pm that day in the interview room, together with DC Libby. The interview was tape-recorded and ended at 2.25 pm.

At 4.45 pm on the 13th of May LEWIS was charged with robbery, the charge was read over to him, he was cautioned and made no reply.

Signed: D. Law
Signature witnessed by: A. Libby

STATEMENT OF WITNESS

Statement of:	Alan LIBBY
Age:	Over 18
Occupation:	Detective Constable 675P, Brighton C.I.D.

[Usual declaration omitted]

Signed by: A. Libby
Signature witnessed by: V. Worthy, PS 111P

Dated 18.5.05

At 6.00 am on the 12th of May 2005, I went to a private flat at 344 Lewes Road, Brighton, together with several other officers. The door was answered by a man I now know as Arthur DUKE. I said to DUKE, 'I have reason to believe that you were involved in an armed robbery last month on a Brighton building society. Have you got anything to say?' He replied, 'You've got the wrong man this time.' I asked if we could look round his flat and he said 'Yes'.

On the floor of a wardrobe in the bedroom I found a balaclava helmet. A shoebox in the same wardrobe contained six shotgun cartridges. Hanging in the wardrobe was a navy blue donkey jacket with an orange fluorescent upper half. I said to DUKE, 'Where did you get this jacket?' He said, 'I've had it for a while now. I wear it if I get any building site work.' I then showed him the balaclava and cartridges and said, 'How do you explain these then?' He did not reply.

I said, 'I am arresting you for robbing the South Downs Building Society in Brighton on the 17th of April this year.' I cautioned him and he made no reply. He was taken to Brighton Central Police Station.

At 2.40 pm on the same day, I was present when DS Law interviewed DUKE at Brighton Central Police Station. The interview was tape-recorded. I produce the master tape as exhibit AL/1 and the record of the taped interview (ROTI) as AL/2.

At 5.25 pm on the 12th of May DUKE was charged with robbery, the charge was read over, he was cautioned and made no reply.

On the 12th of May at 10.50 pm, I went to 65 Brighthelmstone Street where I saw a man I now know to be Leonard PETERSON. I said to him, 'Are you Lennie Peterson?' He said, 'That's right. Who are you?' I showed him my warrant card and explained that I was investigating the robbery of the South Downs Building Society.

I said, 'I have reason to believe that you garaged the car for the gang before the robbery. What have you got to say?' He said, 'I know nothing about it.' I said, 'It's right that you've got a lock-up garage at the back of the house, isn't it. That's where the car was kept.' He replied, 'Who's been talking out of turn?'

I said, 'The car was stolen on the 8th of April — that's a week before the robbery. It had to be kept somewhere, out of sight. I think you warehoused it for the gang. For all I know, you stole it, too.' He said, 'Look, I'm no car thief. Gerry ELLA asked me to keep it safe for him until he needed it. He brought it round on the 8th and took it away on the 17th. That's all I know.'

I told him he was being arrested for the robbery and cautioned him. He made no reply and was then taken to Brighton Central Police Station.

At 7.30 pm on the 13th of May at Brighton Central Police Station PETERSON was charged with robbery, the charge was read over to him, he was cautioned and replied, 'I've been very silly and it's all for nothing. What can I say.'

On the 13th of May at 2.10 pm, I attended an interview of Finlay LEWIS by DS Law at Brighton Central Police Station. The interview was tape-recorded and I produce the master tape as exhibit AL/3 and the record of the taped interview (ROTI) as AL/4.

Signed: A. Libby
Signature witnessed by: V. Worthy

Extracts from record of taped interview of Arthur DUKE by DS Law, produced by DC Libby (AL/2):

Q. Do you want us to wait for your lawyer?

A. No, let's get it over.

Q. As I mentioned on the way here, we've found some fingerprints on the Audi and it looks like they are yours.

A. Oh yeah.

Q. I'm serious. Those prints place you in the car. Take them together with what we found in your home . . .

A. All right. It was never meant to end up the way it did.

Q. What do you mean?

A. The old man. Finlay's always been stupid but that tops the lot.

Q. So it was Finlay that shot Mr Goodbody?

A. Yes.

Q. Is that Finlay LEWIS?

A. Yes. I should never have agreed to take part in it. Finlay had it all set up before I got invited. His original partner had to drop out — he's on remand in Brixton at the moment.

. . .

A. Finlay had Gerry ELLA and Len PETERSON lined up. He knew Gerry from Wandsworth and Len was a friend of Gerry's.

. . .

A. I kept watch while Finlay played the hard man with the cashier. Everything went smooth as silk until the old man grabbed Finlay's bag. I couldn't believe what they were doing. Just as I went back to help, Finlay's gun went off and the old boy went down. I don't know whether it was an accident or not.

Extracts from record of taped interview of Finlay LEWIS by DS Law, produced by DC Libby (AL/4):

Q. I am refusing to delay this interview so that you can have your solicitor present because I believe that delay may prevent recovery of the stolen money.

A. No reply

. . .

Q. . . . remind you that you are under caution . . .

Q. This was a very serious offence. I tell you now — I'm more worried about the guy that got shot than the money. Have you got anything you want to say?

A. No reply

Q. Look I'll be straight with you. We've got a confession from Arthur and he's dropped you right in it.

A. I don't believe it.

Q. Have a look at this. (Hands piece of paper to Lewis)

A. Well, it seems like you know it all. Why bother talking to me?

Q. We need to get your side of things, to see how everything fits together.

A. There's no point in holding back now — so much for honour amongst thieves. It was Arthur's idea — he'd planned it for weeks before he spoke to me. We decided that we needed a driver and I knew Gerry from our time in Wandsworth.

Q. You mean Gerry ELLA and HMP Wandsworth in South London?

A. That's right.

. . .

Q. Who got the car?

A. That's down to Gerry. I don't know where it came from — he just got it for the day. The first time I saw it was when I got in it after the job.

Q. Who did what in the shop?

A. I asked for the cash while Arthur kept everyone calm.

Q. With a sawn-off?

A. You don't want heroes in a situation like that.

Q. Like Reg Goodbody?

A. Is he the old boy? He never should have interfered. He got what was coming to him.

Q. From you?

A. No way. That was Arthur. I could have got the bag away from the old man but Arthur got impatient with him.

. . .

Q. So where's the money now?

A. Money? That's rich. Lots of it was cheques. The rest, well, I'll need a nest egg for when I get out, eh?

Q. So you won't tell me where it is?

A. No reply

. . .

Summaries of the antecedent histories of the accused men:

Finlay LEWIS (Age 40) Born Stornaway, Outer Hebrides.
18 previous convictions including 2 for wounding (s 18 OAPA) and 3 for armed robbery. Last conviction was at Portsmouth Crown Court for robbery in May 1998. Sentenced to 10 years' imprisonment. Released June 2004.

Arthur DUKE (Age 43) Born Catford, London.
8 previous convictions, mainly for offences of dishonesty. 1 recorded for robbery. Last conviction was at Brighton Magistrates' Court in February 1999 for a fraud on the Department of Health and Social Security. On committal to the Crown Court, sentenced to 6 years' imprisonment. Released April 2003.

Gerald ELLA (Age 26) Born Worthing, West Sussex.
6 previous convictions, all for theft of cars, except the last one. In 1997 a 3-year term of imprisonment was imposed by Inner London Crown Court. In September last year, Brighton Magistrates' Court fined him £250 and banned him from driving for 1 year for driving whilst unfit through drink or drugs.

Leonard PETERSON (Age 55) Born Brighton.
16 previous convictions, all for petty offences of dishonesty. Imprisonment has been ordered in the past, but the last conviction was in 1988 and resulted in a conditional discharge.

Optional exercise

If you would like to try your hand at drafting an indictment in a simpler case, try the following short problem.

R v Adams

Arthur ADAMS was charged with stealing from Jane BROWN a handbag containing a purse, lipstick and £20 in money. He elected for trial on indictment and he has recently been transferred for trial at Casterbridge Crown Court on that charge. The papers have been sent to you by the CPS and you have been asked to draft an appropriate indictment.

There is evidence to the effect that John SMITH was amongst the crowds in the area of Trafalgar Square at around 11 pm on New Year's Eve 2004 when he was suddenly jostled. He felt inside his jacket pocket, where he had been carrying his wallet, and found that it was missing. He reported the matter to the first police officer he saw. Jane BROWN's evidence is that at around 1 am on New Year's Day 2005 she was in Trafalgar Square when a youth violently wrenched her handbag away from her. Shortly after, she believed she saw amongst the crowds the person who had taken her handbag. She pointed him out to a police officer who arrested him. That person was Arthur ADAMS.

He was searched, and found to have £300 in cash on his person (none of which could be positively identified as having been stolen from either John SMITH or Jane BROWN) together with a wallet containing a cheque card personalised in the name of John SMITH. Subsequently SMITH confirmed that the wallet found in ADAMS' possession was the one which he (SMITH) had lost earlier that night.

ADAMS made a statement to the police in which he said that (i) he had found the wallet on the ground about half an hour before he was arrested and had been waiting for a suitable opportunity to hand it to the police (ii) the wallet was empty when he found it and (iii) he was not the person who had taken Jane BROWN's handbag, she being mistaken in her identification of him.

Having drafted the indictment, consider any objections which the defence might raise against it either on arraignment or at a pre-trial hearing.

Small Group Session 6   Sentencing (1)

Objectives

By the conclusion of this class you should:

- accurately explain the procedure between conviction and sentence;
- correctly determine the information which should be before the court to assist the sentencer;
- correctly identify the factors to be considered by the court when sentencing;
- understand the non-custodial powers of the magistrates' courts and the Crown Court when sentencing offenders aged 18 or over.

Research

Chapters 13, 14, 15 and **19**.
Blackstone's Criminal Practice, 2005 edn, sections D18 and D21, para D22.24, sections E4–E7, E10, E14–E15, E17–E18.
Powers of Criminal Courts (Sentencing) Act 2000, in particular ss. 12–15, 33–58, 81, 126, 130 and 156, and Criminal Justice Act 2003, Part 12.

Preparation

Read **Chapters 13, 14, 15** and **19** in the Manual. Prepare questions 1 to 5, ensuring that you consult *Blackstone's Criminal Practice* when researching. Attend the class with your notes on each question.

Tutorial questions

1. David is aged 22. He is employed as a painter and decorator earning £200 per week net. He is charged with one offence of theft. It is alleged that on 1 October 2005 he stole various items valued at £85 from a building site. He has the following previous convictions:

    (a) On 22 December 2004 at Greenacre magistrates' court he received a conditional discharge for two years for an offence of theft of paint and other materials.

    (b) On 2 September 2005 at Blackacre magistrates' court he was placed under a community order including a supervision requirement for two years for an offence of burglary.

    David appears at Blackacre magistrates' court and pleads guilty to the charge of theft. The pre-sentence report indicates that a financial penalty will be appropriate. What courses are open to the magistrates? What action can the court take relating to the conditional discharge or community order?

2. Ben, aged 32, pleaded guilty at Brentvale Crown Court to causing death by dangerous driving. He was driving his car within the speed limit at about 8 pm last November. He approached traffic lights which were showing red against him, drove across them and collided with a motor cyclist who was killed. He had drunk a pint-and-a-half of lager at about 6 pm but it was not suggested that he was driving whilst unfit through drink.

    Ben claims that he had failed to see the lights for some inexplicable reason and it was accepted by the prosecution that there was no evidence of bad driving before he had reached the traffic lights.

    Ben is employed as a surveyor and earns £30,000 per annum. He has one previous driving conviction for careless driving two years earlier, when he was fined £200 and his licence was endorsed with 4 penalty points.

    You appear on his behalf. His pre-sentence report is not of great assistance. What factors would you ask the judge to take into account when considering the appropriate sentence?

    What sentence would you suggest to the judge?

    Would your answer be any different if Ben had been over the prescribed alcohol limit?

3.   Jimmy, aged 22, pleaded guilty to one count of burglary at Romchester Crown Court. He was concerned in four dwelling-house burglaries in which various items of personal property were stolen. He admitted that he had acted as a lookout while other accomplices entered the houses. The sole count was charged as a specimen count.

He has two previous findings of guilt, when aged under 18, for theft for which he was conditionally discharged on each occasion and one for burglary when an adult for which he was placed under a community order for two years.

He is a self-employed window-cleaner and earns £300 per week take-home pay.

You appear on his behalf. His pre-sentence report confirms that he is suitable for a community order with an unpaid work requirment. What factors would you ask the judge to take into account when considering the appropriate sentence?

What sentence would you suggest to the judge?

Would your answer be any different if Jimmy had been responsible for cleaning the windows of the houses concerned?

4.   Edward (aged 22) and Frank (aged 21) both plead guilty at Casterbridge Crown Court to robbery. Prosecuting counsel, in summarising the facts of the offence, states that Edward and Frank stopped the victim (a Mr Brown) as he was walking along the street late at night. Edward held a knife to Mr Brown's throat while Frank searched Mr Brown's pockets, and took a wallet containing £100. They both then ran away. Defence counsel, in mitigation, denies that either of his clients had a knife or any other weapon, although he concedes that they threatened to 'beat Mr Brown's face in' if he struggled. The antecedents of the offenders disclose that Edward has two previous court appearances, one in March 2002 for taking a car without the owner's consent (conditionally discharged for one year) and the other in June 2003 for shoplifting (ordered to perform 80 hours' unpaid work under a community order, then known as a community punishment order). Frank has not been in trouble before. A pre-sentence report on Frank indicates that he would respond to a community rehabilitation order. In passing sentence the judge says:

What I find most disturbing about this case is the use of a weapon. I listened most carefully to what learned Defence counsel had to say on the matter of the knife, but I read the statement of Mr Brown before I came into court, and I am quite satisfied that a knife was used to threaten him. Reluctant as I am to deprive young men of their liberty, I would be failing in my duty to the public if I did not pass a sentence which will serve as a warning to others that this kind of conduct will not be tolerated. You, Edward, had the knife and you will be sentenced to a term of three years' imprisonment. In your case, Frank, I thought about making a community rehabilitation order. In some ways it is an attractive alternative to a custodial sentence, but I have to deal with you in a way which will be a deterrent and an example to others. I take into account your age and your not having committed any offences in the past, but even so the shortest sentence I consider appropriate is one of two years imprisonment.

Advise Edward and Frank whether they have any grounds for appealing against sentence. How long will they actually spend in custody?

5.   Lorna appears at Whiteacre Magistrates' Court and pleads guilty to an offence of criminal damage. She is in breach of a sentence of three months' imprisonment, suspended for two years, imposed by another magistrates' court. What action can be taken in respect of the suspended sentence?

Small Group Session 7   Sentencing (2)

Objectives

By the conclusion of this class you should understand:

- the principles involved in applying concepts of aggravation and mitigation to sentencing for offences reaching the custody threshold;
- the guidelines applied when anticipating courts' custodial sentencing decisions, including human rights considerations;
- the principles involved in imposing minimum sentences;
- the sentences available for young offenders according to their age — the principles involved in sentencing offenders aged 10–17 and 18–20, depending on their circumstances and the court in which they appear;
- the factors to be taken into account in determining the appropriate sentence for young offenders;
- long-term detention under s 91 of PCC(S)A 2000 (as amended).

Research

Chapters 14, 16, 17, 18 and **20**
Blackstone's Criminal Practice, 2005 edn, paras D22.22-D22.26, sections E1-E11, E13, E16 and E25.
Powers of Criminal Courts (Sentencing) Act 2000, in particular ss 76–111, 118–125, 151–152 and 161, and Criminal Justice Act 2003, Part 12.

Preparation

Read **Chapters 14, 16, 17, 18 and 20** in the Manual. Prepare questions 1–5, ensuring that you consult *Blackstone's Criminal Practice* when researching. Attend the class with your notes on each question.

Tutorial questions

1. On 19 November 2005 Rachel is convicted at Greenacre Crown Court of four offences of theft from shops. The offences took place on the same day and the total value of goods taken was £200. She has the following previous convictions.

Date	Court	Offence	Sentence
26 Feb 2000	Magistrates' Court	Theft	Community Order 2 years (probation, now known as supervision requirement)
5 April 02	Crown Court	Theft	Community Order requiring 120 hrs unpaid work
9 June 04	Crown Court	Criminal Deception	36 weeks' imprisonment suspended for 2 years

She was divorced in 1999 and is now 38 years old. Her two children aged 8 and 12 reside with her. Since her divorce she has suffered from bouts of depression. She has recently obtained employment as a nursing auxiliary and has formed a steady relationship with a man she hopes to marry. Her children are properly cared for and are doing well at school. According to her pre-sentence report she completed successfully and enjoyed the work she was required to do under the order for unpaid work, and it is likely she would 'respond positively to some form of supervision'. What factors will the judge take into account in determining the appropriate sentence to be passed on Rachel?

2.   Michael and Norman appear at Borough Green Crown Court jointly charged with theft of property valued at £1,600 from their employer. Both plead guilty. Michael is 35. He has three previous convictions for offences of dishonesty and is currently subject to a community order imposed at Doomchester Crown Court for handling stolen goods. When arrested he admitted the offence and gave the police information which led to the stolen property being recovered. Norman is 25. He has one previous conviction for common assault for which he received, and is now in breach of, a conditional discharge.

What sentence will the court consider in respect of both Michael and Norman and what factors will be taken into account in determining the appropriate sentence?

3.   Reggie, aged 19, pleaded guilty at Downtown Crown Court to supplying Ecstasy tablets in a nightclub. He has two previous convictions, one for being concerned in the supply of crack cocaine and the other for possession of heroin with intent to supply.

What factors will the judge take into account when determining the appropriate sentence?

4.   Barney is aged 17. He appears at Doomchester Youth Court charged with an offence of aggravated burglary which he admits. His only previous court appearance was nine months ago when he was conditionally discharged for 12 months for an offence of theft. A pre-sentence report reveals that Barney's parents are unable to exercise any effective control over him, and that he has now left school with little prospect of obtaining employment. What factors will the magistrates take into account in deciding the appropriate sentence, and what options are open to them in passing sentence?

Would your answer be any different if Barney appeared in the Crown Court?

5.   Scott, aged 15, has pleaded guilty at Brixgreen Youth Court to assaulting a PC occasioning him actual bodily harm contrary to OAP Act 1861, s 47. The facts were that when the officer stopped him in the street under the 'stop and search' provisions of PACE he picked up a piece of wood and struck the officer on the arm. Scott says that the officer made racist remarks and was just 'hassling me because I am black'. His pre-sentence report discloses that he has had a history of violence at school. His parents complain that he frequently stays out until the early hours of the morning. He has one previous finding of guilt when aged 13 for criminal damage, ie spraying graffiti on underground trains, for which he was made the subject of an attendance centre order.

What factors will the court take into account in determining the appropriate sentence to be imposed on Scott?

What would be the position if the prosecutor does not accept that the officer made racist remarks?

Would your answer be any different if Scott were aged 14? Aged 17?

6.   Marcina, aged 15, appears at the Toxtown Youth Court with two others, aged 15 and 16, charged with robbery. They attacked a 14-year-old girl at a bus stop and forced her to hand over £4.50. They are found guilty, and the evidence given indicates that

Marcina played a minor role in the offence. She has no previous finding of guilt, but the pre-sentence report discloses that she was sexually abused by her stepfather some six months prior to the offence and lives in an area of high delinquency.

What options are open to the court in dealing with Marcina?

Would your answer be any different if the victim had been an elderly woman?

Small Group Session 8

Objectives

By the conclusion of this class you should:

- understand the rules which govern trial on indictment;
- understand the principles applied by the Court of Appeal in deciding whether a conviction is safe;
- understand the procedural rules applicable in the Court of Appeal.

Research

Chapters 11 and **12**.
Blackstone's Criminal Practice, 2005 edn, section D23.
Criminal Law Act 1967, s 6(3).
Criminal Appeal Act 1968, ss 3, 4, 7, 19, 20, 23, 29.
Criminal Justice Act 2003, ss 57–97, 101.

Preparation

You will need to prepare tutorial question (brief in the appeal to the Court of Appeal against conviction — *R v Lewis and Duke*). This is a continuation of the case used in Small Group Session 5. In the brief are the papers that would normally be available to counsel in order to advise on appeal and settle Grounds of Appeal. For Lewis and Duke, prepare your appeal for the defence. Consider the arguments for and against the appeal.

Finally consider ancillary points — eg whether Lewis or Duke should apply for bail pending the hearing; whether they can (or must) be produced in court for the hearing. Lewis and Duke were convicted of the present offences on 5 January 2006. Lewis received an automatic life sentence and Duke received a substantial period of imprisonment.

Tutorial question

R v Lewis and Duke

Counsel has herewith extracts from notes supplied by N. B. Good, Esq. who was Defence counsel for the applicants at their trial.

Counsel is instructed:

- to draft Grounds of Appeal against conviction for the applicants, and
- to advise on the merits.

Both applicants were convicted by a jury at Lewes Crown Court of robbery, contrary to s 8(1) of the Theft Act 1968. Duke was also convicted of wounding with intent to cause grievous bodily harm; Lewis was convicted of this although not alleged to have actually committed the wounding.

Leave to appeal will undoubtedly be required from the single judge, no certificate having been granted by the trial judge.

As counsel was not instructed for the Defence at trial, instructing solicitors should make one or two points clear. First, the applicants were on trial for an armed robbery with two other men, Gerald Ella and Leonard Peterson, both of whom pleaded guilty to their parts in the incident. The applicants were separately accused of wounding Mr Goodbody with intent (OAPA, s 18).

Ella turned Queen's evidence at trial and appeared as a witness for the Crown. His evidence was potentially very damaging for the applicants.

The judge allowed the Crown to adduce Duke's and Lewis's interviews following a *voir dire*.

Duke did not testify in either his defence or on the *voir dire*. Lewis did testify in his own defence and on the *voir dire*, alleging mistaken identity and fabrication.

Extracts from Defence counsel's notes of the trial follow.

Prosecution Case

1. *Cross-examination* of Gerald Ella (for Lewis and Duke)

I am not making the whole thing up.

Lewis and Duke planned the thing from start to finish.

I am not lying about this, they know it's true.

It is right that I have not been sentenced yet, but I am only doing this because I want to tell the truth.

I was a willing party to the plot but those two schemed it all, without them it would never have come off.

---

2. *Voir dire* (on Duke's interview)

Examination-in-chief of DS Law

I told Duke that we had his fingerprints from the Audi TT.

At that time I thought there was a strong possibility that some of the prints we found might belong to Duke.

Some time after that interview occurred, I was informed by our forensic laboratory that none of the prints taken from the car matched Duke's fingerprints.

Cross-examination of DS Law (for Duke)

When I told Duke we had his prints, I genuinely thought that was the case.

It was not a deliberate lie.

I didn't need to lie, he knew what we'd found at his place.

I would describe it as unfortunate, that's all.

3. *Voir dire* (on Lewis' interview)

Cross-examination of DC Libby (for Lewis)

I regard your suggestions that I induced Mr Lewis to make a false confession as downright offensive. In 25 years as a loyal and upright police officer nobody has ever accused me of such a thing. The suggestion that I would threaten the defendant with the arrest of his partner on some trumped up charge is total rubbish.

Judge's decision on voir dire (Duke):

. . . I am not satisfied that it has been demonstrated that DS Law lied to the defendant, Duke. It seems to me that there was a simple error of judgment. DS Law made an assumption which was very likely to be correct but later proved to be incorrect. I am not persuaded that the confession has been shown to be so unreliable that I should exclude it from the trial . . .

. . . I am bound to say, in any event, that there is no basis for the exercise of any discretion that I might have under s 78 of the Police and Criminal Evidence Act to exclude the confession, as Mr Good argued.

Judge's decision on voir dire (Lewis):

I am not satisfied that the police made threats to Mr Lewis as alleged. It's possible this happened I suppose, but the defence have come nowhere near making me sure that anything happened to make his confession unreliable.

Defence Case

4.   Examination-in-chief of Lewis

I know nothing about this robbery except what I've read in the newspapers. I do know Gerald Ella but, until we were both arrested for this, I had not seen him for about 4 years.

5.   *Judge's decision on an application by Crown to cross-examine Lewis under Criminal Evidence Act 1898, s 1(3)*

I am satisfied that the cross-examination of both Gerald Ella and DS Libby was such that no jury could be left with the thought that Lewis alleged them to be merely mistaken. Indeed, Mr Good has not sought to persuade me to the contrary. I have no hesitation in permitting the Crown to use Lewis's criminal record to show the jury his true character.

---

6.   *Cross-examination* of Lewis

It is correct that I have several previous convictions.
About 18 altogether.
Some of them for robbery.
They were armed robberies.
Yes, they involved guns but no-one was ever hurt.
My last conviction was at Portsmouth Crown Court in 1997.
That was for an armed robbery.
I was sentenced to 10 years' imprisonment.

7.   *Judge's Summing-up* (Extracts)

. . .

You may have heard something about the standard of proof, members of the jury. Well, the Court of Appeal has said there is no magic formula to help us judges to help you. But I can tell you that the defendants should only be convicted if you are persuaded in your own minds of their guilt. If in doubt, acquit.

. . .

As to Count 2, wounding with intent. You've heard Lewis testify that he was not there, and I shall be dealing with his testimony later. As to the law — the Crown do not say he was the man who pulled the trigger but they do say that Lewis must have agreed with Duke before the robbery that, in the event of trouble, they would use their guns. Or else, why carry them?

Even if there was no agreement, which you may think is so unlikely as to be fantastic, the Crown say that simply by standing by and watching Duke shoot Mr Goodbody, Lewis is as guilty as Duke. It's what we lawyers call aiding and abetting.

. . .

Miss Penny was quite clear that the masked man who spoke to her had an Irish accent. Whatever it was, she picked out Lewis as that masked man at a parade, having heard him utter that same phrase. You may think she is unlikely to forget the sound of that voice, members of the jury. Anyway, you had the benefit of hearing Lewis for yourselves. We know he comes from the Outer Hebrides originally and he hasn't lost his accent. Could you have thought he was Irish?

. . .

Ella's testimony was, you may think, quite persuasive. He is, on his own admission, an accomplice of the others. Until recently, I would have had to give you a complicated direction about his evidence. Now things are simpler. We can look more realistically at each witness's evidence on its own merits.

I caution you to take care when examining Ella's testimony — he is, after all, a self-confessed criminal but I need say no more about it.

. . .

We heard the frank admissions made by Lewis in his taped interview once he was incarcerated in Brighton Police Station and realised the game was up. Your heard Mr Good suggest to DC Libby that he had induced the admissions by threatening to arrest Mr Lewis's partner — a suggestion hotly refuted by this officer who has many years' experience in enforcing law and order. You may think, as I do, that Lewis's interview had the ring of truth about it. That's a matter for you.

A similar point was put to Gerald Ella — that he was lying to lighten his own sentence. I shall be dealing with Ella at the end of this trial, members of the jury, so don't worry about that.

As a result of this cross-examination of the Crown's witnesses, I allowed the Crown's application to cross-examine Lewis about his chequered past. What did that tell you about the sort of man Lewis really is? A man experienced in the ways of violence and armed robbery? There it is, I say no more about it.

. . .

Finally, you must consider the evidence against each man separately and on each count separately. You may recall that we heard the interviews of Lewis and Duke in which each clearly damned the other as well as himself. What they say about the other one outside the witness box is not evidence in the case and you must do your best to ignore it.

Note for Appeal. After the jury retired to deliberate (2.15 pm), the usher caught one of them slipping back into the jury room. The judge was informed and, in court, asked the juror where she had been. She said she had left to telephone her husband to say she might be late home (this was at 3.15 pm). The judge rejected my suggestion to discharge her and allowed her back into the jury room.

The subsequent guilty verdicts (delivered at 3.45 pm) were unanimous.

APPENDIX 2
SAMPLE MULTIPLE CHOICE QUESTIONS

Question 1

Astrid is charged alone with shoplifting. She elects jury trial and is sent for trial to the Crown Court. She wants to get maximum publicity for the case in order to encourage any defence witnesses to come forward. She asks for reporting restrictions to be lifted. The magistrates:

    [A]   must grant her application unless the prosecution opposes it;

    [B]   must refuse the application if they believe it will prejudice her right to a fair trial;

    [C]   must grant her application;

    [D]   must grant her application if it is in the interests of justice to do so.

Question 2

Charles is charged in an indictment containing counts of causing grievous bodily harm with intent and forgery (the alleged offences relate to unrelated factual situations). At Charles' trial his counsel objects to the indictment on the ground that the counts are improperly joined. The trial judge (i) rules that the counts are improperly joined and (ii) orders that the indictment be severed.

  The judge was:

    [A]   Right on point (i) and acting beyond his powers on point (ii).

    [B]   Right on point (i) and acting within his powers on point (ii).

    [C]   Wrong on point (i) and acting beyond his powers on point (ii).

    [D]   Wrong on point (i) and acting within his powers on point (ii).

Question 3

Which of the following groups is not allowed into a youth court room during a hearing?

    [A]   Probation officers concerned in the hearing.

    [B]   Journalists reporting the hearing.

    [C]   Witnesses, after they have testified in the hearing.

    [D]   Barristers waiting for their case to start.

Question 4

Portia (aged 16) appeared with Quentin (aged 20) in the adult magistrates' court on a joint charge of theft. Quentin elected to be tried on indictment. The magistrates felt that it was not necessary in the interests of justice to commit Portia to the Crown Court for trial. Portia has now been tried and convicted by the adult magistrates' court. Which one of the following statements is correct?

[A] Portia must be sent to the youth court to be dealt with.

[B] Portia must be sent to the youth court to be dealt with if the magistrates do not think a custodial sentence is called for.

[C] Portia may be committed to the Crown Court for sentence if the magistrates think that a custodial sentence is called for.

[D] Portia may be dealt with in the magistrates' court or, if none of that court's sentences is appropriate, sent to the youth court to be dealt with.

Question 5

The police have reasonable grounds for suspecting that Edward has committed an attempted residential burglary. On a Monday morning Edward is arrested, cautioned and taken to the police station. He arrives at the police station at 11.30 am. The custody officer is of the opinion that there is not sufficient evidence to charge Edward. The same officer also has reasonable grounds for believing that the detention of Edward is necessary to obtain such evidence by questioning him. Edward is interrogated on a number of occasions. At 11.30 pm on the next day, Tuesday, what action should be taken?

[A] Edward should be released or charged unless his continued detention without charge for a further nine hours is properly authorised by the station superintendent.

[B] Edward should be released or charged unless his continued detention for a further 12 hours is properly authorised by the station superintendent.

[C] Edward should be released or charged unless earlier on Tuesday a magistrates' court issued a warrant of further detention authorising the keeping of Edward in police detention.

[D] Edward should be released or charged unless the police intend to apply to a magistrates' court for a warrant of further detention (authorising the keeping of Edward in police detention), in which case they may hold Edward at the police station overnight and should apply for such a warrant at the next scheduled sitting of the magistrates' court (which will be at 10 am on the following day, Wednesday).

Question 6

Kelvin is charged with, and acquitted of driving without due care and attention. He was refused publicly-funded legal representation on the 'interests of justice' test. He now makes an application for costs which the magistrates refuse because (a) Kelvin is a man of substantial means, and (b) Kelvin misled the prosecution into thinking that the case against him was stronger than it actually was. The basis of the magistrates' decision is:

[A] Correct as regards (a) but incorrect as regards (b).

[B] Correct as regards (b) but incorrect as regards (a).

[C] Incorrect on both points.

[D] Correct on both points.

Question 7

Andrew has been convicted in the magistrates' court of criminal damage to a bus shelter. The value of the damage done was £800. The magistrates decide to adjourn prior to sentencing, to enable a medical examination and report to be made. A fully argued bail application is made on Andrew's behalf but he is remanded in custody. Which of the following possibilities most accurately describes what Andrew may now do with a view to obtaining bail?

[A]   He may only apply for bail in the Crown Court.

[B]   He may only apply for bail in the Crown Court and if unsuccessful may then apply for bail to a judge in chambers in the High Court.

[C]   He may apply for bail to a judge in chambers in the High Court and if unsuccessful may then apply for bail in the Crown Court.

[D]   He may apply for bail in the way described in [B] or in the way described in [C], the choice being his.

Question 8

The Bail Act 1976, s 4, provides that a person to whom it applies 'shall be granted bail except as provided in Schedule 1'. In which of the following situations does s 4 preserve the right to bail?

[A]   When a person is convicted on indictment and his case is adjourned for reports prior to sentencing.

[B]   When a person, convicted and sentenced by magistrates, is appealing against sentence.

[C]   When a person, convicted and sentenced by magistrates, is appealing against conviction.

[D]   When a person, convicted by magistrates, is committed by them to the Crown Court for sentence.

Question 9

Jaspal Singh and Zahoor Choudhury have been charged with possession of indecent photographs of children and at the magistrates' court their counsel applied for bail on their behalf. Both the defendants are well-known television newsreaders. At the magistrates' court, the district judge grants unconditional bail. The prosecution wishes to appeal against the decision. Which of the following is the correction position?

[A]   The prosecution has no right of appeal against the decision.

[B]   The prosecution has a right of appeal against the decision but only if the offence charged is punishable with imprisonment of two or more years.

[C]   The prosecution has a right of appeal against the decision but only if it is conducted by the Crown Prosecution Service.

[D]   The prosecution has a right of appeal in all cases where bail is granted by the magistrates' court.

Question 10

Davis, aged 32, appears before the magistrates' court. He pleads guilty to assault. The magistrates are minded to pass a suspended sentence. Which one of the following orders is a valid suspended sentence order?

[A]   A custodial term of 24 weeks, an operational period of two years, and a supervision period of one year.

[B]   A custodial term of 24 weeks, an operational period of two years, and a supervision period of two years.

[C]   A custodial term of 48 weeks, an operational period of 18 months, and a supervision period of 18 months.

[D]   A custodial term of 48 weeks, an operational period of one year, and a supervision period of two years.

Question 11

Johnny, aged 19, appears before the Narrowview Magistrates' Court charged with three offences of theft (triable either way). He pleads guilty and asks for 20 other offences of theft to be taken into consideration. The magistrates are minded to impose a community order. Which one of the following is a correct statement of the law?

The magistrates:

[A]   Must obtain a pre-sentence report before sentence.

[B]   Must obtain, but need not consider, a pre-sentence report before sentence.

[C]   Must obtain and consider a pre-sentence report and may only impose a sentence recommended by that report.

[D]   Must obtain and consider a pre-sentence report unless they take the view that one is unnecessary.

Question 12

Colin is charged with criminal damage to David's Rolls Royce motor car. The value of the damage has been estimated by a Rolls Royce approved dealer at £5,579.86. Colin asks you about the appropriate court of trial. Which **one** of the following statements about this situation is correct?

[A]   He must be tried summarily.

[B]   He may be tried summarily but only if both he and the magistrates agree.

[C]   He may only be tried on indictment if both he and the magistrates agree.

[D]   He must be tried on indictment.

Question 13

Brian is charged with theft. He appears before the magistrates to determine the mode of trial. Which of the following propositions is **false**?

[A]   He may be tried on indictment if he so elects, despite the wishes of the magistrates.

[B]   He must be tried on indictment if the magistrates so decide whatever his wishes are.

[C]   He may only be tried summarily if both he and the magistrates agree.

[D]   He may only be tried on indictment if the prosecution is brought by the DPP, Attorney-General or Solicitor-General.

Question 14

Harry, aged 17, appeared at the Camberden Youth Court on a charge of unlawful wounding contrary to s 20 of the Offences Against the Person Act 1861. The maximum custodial sentence for the offence is five years. Harry pleaded guilty to the charge. What is the maximum duration of a detention and training order which may be imposed on Harry by the youth court?

[A] Six months.

[B] 12 months.

[C] 24 months.

[D] Five years.

Question 15

Oliver, aged 14, appears in the Newburgh Crown Court jointly charged with Ted, aged 15, and Charlie, aged 16, on an indictment containing three counts of burglary of dwelling houses (the maximum sentence for each offence being 14 years' imprisonment in the case of an adult). Oliver, Ted and Charlie are convicted of all three offences. Oliver is also subject to a supervision order for two previous findings of guilt for burglary. Ted and Charlie are given custodial sentences.

Which one of the following sentences will the judge not be empowered to impose on Oliver?

[A] A sentence of intermittent custody.

[B] A supervision order.

[C] A detention and training order.

[D] A sentence of long-term detention under s 91 of the Powers of Criminal Courts (Sentencing) Act 2000.

Question 16

Linzi appears before the Denton Crown Court to answer an indictment containing a single count of burglary, the particulars being that she entered the house of her next door neighbour and stole a hair-drier. Linzi says that the neighbour gave her permission to go into the house and borrow things whenever she wished, but admits that having borrowed the hair-drier she later decided not to return it. At her trial, her counsel asks the judge to direct the jury that it may acquit of burglary but convict of theft. Which one of the following statements correctly represents the law?

[A] The jury can only convict Linzi of theft if the indictment is amended so as to include a count alleging theft.

[B] The judge may direct the jury that it is entitled to acquit of burglary and convict of theft if he or she considers that it is in the interests of justice to do so.

[C] The judge must direct the jury that it may only consider the offence which appears on the indictment.

[D] The judge must direct the jury that it is entitled to acquit of burglary and convict of theft.

Question 17

Edward is convicted in the Middlemarch Crown Court of burglary and sentenced to two years' imprisonment. He appeals against his conviction. Depending on the facts and evidence put before the Court of Appeal, which one of the following options is open to the Court of Appeal?

[A]   Order a retrial.

[B]   Make a direction for loss of time.

[C]   Substitute a verdict of guilty of theft.

[D]   Exercise any of the above powers.

Question 18

Alphonse is convicted in the magistrates' court of theft. He wishes to appeal to the Crown Court against his conviction. Which of the following is the appropriate procedure:

[A]   Alphonse notifies the magistrates' court and the prosecution of his intention to appeal.

[B]   Alphonse notifles the magistrates and the prosecution of his intention to appeal, and sets out his full grounds of appeal.

[C]   Alphonse applies to the magistrates for leave to appeal to the Crown Court.

[D]   Alphonse applies to the Crown Court for leave to appeal to that court, stating brief grounds of appeal.

Question 19

Femi is convicted in the magistrates' court of two offences of handling stolen goods, and sentenced to two months' imprisonment on each offence, to run consecutively. He wishes to appeal against sentence. In dealing with Femi the Crown Court may:

[A]   Pass any sentence that it could have passed following a trial on indictment.

[B]   Pass any sentence that the magistrates could have passed.

[C]   Pass any sentence which is not greater than the sentence that the magistrates actually passed.

[D]   Treat the case as if Femi had been committed to them for sentence.

APPENDIX 3
VICTIMS AND OTHER WITNESSES

The purpose of this section is to alert you to the very particular and special problems faced by the victims and witnesses of crime, especially those who appear as witnesses in any criminal proceedings. It is a large and complex area, and this section can do little more than draw your attention to the issues involved. While it is intended as background reading only, you should not underestimate its importance in your professional life.

The word 'victim' is technically correct only after a verdict of guilt has been recorded. Until then, the word 'complainant' is probably more accurate. For the sake of simplicity, however, the word 'victim' is used throughout this section.

Much of what is said in this section relates to many witnesses, not just the victim, and this section should be read with that in mind.

History and background

Until the middle of the nineteenth century, the person primarily responsible for the prosecution of offences was the victim himself. Consequently he played a central role in the criminal justice system. With the introduction of efficient police forces, which took over the prosecuting role, the victim's main involvement in the criminal justice system was as (usually the chief) prosecution witness. Over time many rights he may have had came to be sidelined by the criminal justice system. Indeed, many victims found in the past that the criminal justice system has served them so badly that it was a more traumatic than the original offence. Some say that they would never report an offence and face the system a second time.

In recent years, a number of steps have been taken to redress the balance.

(a) 1964 saw the introduction of the Criminal Injuries Compensation Board (CICB) now the Criminal Injuries Compensation Authority (CICA) which has power to make payments to victims of crime following an application made to them by the victim. Many victims, however, neither knew of the scheme nor how to access it.

(b) In 1972, the court was given, for the first time, the power to make compensation orders to benefit the victim in suitable cases. Similar problems of ignorance existed as with the CICB. This power has been extended by the CJA 1988, and further amended by the Powers of Criminal Courts (Sentencing) Act 2000, and students should refer to the sentencing section of this manual for details, and see below, for a further discussion.

(c) In 1974, the first Victim Support scheme was established in Bristol. It is a national independent charity for people affected by crime. It provides a service in each community across England and Wales. It provides a free and confidential service, whether or not a crime has been reported, and regardless of when it happened. Trained staff and volunteers at affiliated local charities offer information, support and practical help to victims, witnesses, their families and friends. Victim Support works to increase awareness of the effects of crime and to achieve greater recognition of victims' and witnesses' rights. The organisation receives funding from the Home Office but also receives outside support. Each year Victim Support contacts over one million victims and works with over 300,000 witnesses. Particular skills have been developed to deal with more sensitive cases, such as cases involving racial harassment, the families of murder victims and child victims of offences. Research undertaken by Victim Support has established that those who have been contacted by Victim Support made a better recovery from the offence than those who did not.

(d) In 1988, a working party under the chairmanship of Lady Ralphs, CBE, JP, DL examined how a court appearance could be made less of an ordeal for the victim, and reported its findings under the title 'The Victim in Court'. Following this, in 1990, the government introduced the 'Victim's Charter: A Statement of the Rights of Victims of Crime'. In 1995 Victim Support published 'The Rights of Victims of Crime', which called for greater recognition of victim's rights. It stated five basic rights for victims:

1   The victim should not bear the burden of dealing with the offender.
2   The victim should receive information about their case, and be able to provide information for use in the criminal justice process.
3   The victim should be protected.
4   The victim should receive compensation.
5   The victim should receive respect recognition and support.

The latest version of the Charter entitled '*Victim's Charter: Statement on the Treatment of Victims and Witnesses*' was issued in 1996.

(e) Since then, a number of steps have been taken the most important of which are set out in detail below

Victim's Charter: Statement on the Treatment of Victims and Witnesses

The latest version of the Charter was issued in 1996. It will become defunct when the Victim's Code of Practice under the Domestic Violence, Crime and Victims Act 2004 (DVCVA) comes into force (see below). The Charter begins with the following propositions:

If you are a victim of crime you can expect:

- The crime that you have reported to be investigated and to receive information about what happens
- The chance to explain how the crime has affected you and your interests to be taken into account
- To be treated with respect and sensitivity; to be offered emotional and practical support if you have to go to court as a witness.

The Witness Service

The Witness Service, run by Victim Support, provides a free and confidential service in every criminal court in England and Wales. It aims to provide emotional support and practical information about court proceedings to both prosecution and defence witnesses. Further it provides a range of services including someone to talk to in confidence; a visit to the court centre, if possible a look round the court room before the witness is called; someone to accompany the witness into the court room when giving evidence and a chance to talk over the case when it has ended and get more help and information.

The Witness Service, produces a leaflet entitled 'Going to Court', which is information for witnesses and victims in either the magistrates' court or the Crown Court.

Information to victims

There has long been a concern that victims of crime have had very little information available to them, and very little opportunity to find out, or make any representations to the courts. Many will have had little or no contact with the police, the courts etc, and have very little idea as to how the system works. Further, information has been rarely been forthcoming about the progress of the case itself — whether anyone has been arrested, whether bail has been granted, when a trial is expected and so on.

In order to address this, the Home Office has produced two leaflets entitled 'Victims of Crime' and 'The Witness in Court'. The first should be made available to all persons who report to crime to the police. It explains how to obtain compensation (from both the CICA and the court) and how to obtain information about crime prevention and about the progress of the case. The second leaflet explains what is involved in being called as a witness and giving evidence in court.

The *Victims' Code of Practice*, when introduced, will require agencies to provide certain information to victims.

For victims of sexual and violent offences where the offender is sentenced to at least one year in prison (or where the court orders that the defendant be diverted to the mental health system in equivalent cases) the victim has certain rights to provide and receive information relating to the management of the offender. (Chapter 2 of the DVCVA 2004).

A Commissioner for Victims and Witnesses

Sections 48–53 of the DVCVA 2004 create the position of Commissioner for Victims and Witnesses — a champion for victims' interests across Government. His remit extends beyond criminal justice to include departments such as Work and Pensions, Health, and Education and Skills. He will be involved in promoting victim and witness rights at a general rather than individual level. There is no date yet for implementation of this provision.

Services to victims

The DVCVA 2004, s 32 provides that the Secretary of State must issue a Victims' Code of Practice. This will replace the Victim's Charter and place obligations on the criminal justice agencies and on Victim Support to deliver specified services to victims of crime.

The Home Office published a draft of the Victims' Code of Practice for public consultation in March 2005. The Code will probably come into effect at the end of 2005.

The Code provides for criminal justice agencies to provide special services to vulnerable victims. A vulnerable victim is defined as someone who is vulnerable by virtue of his personal circumstances or by the circumstances of the offence, including but not limited to a victim who is:

- under 17;
- suffering from a mental disorder within the meaning of the Mental Health Act 1873;
- has experienced domestic violence;
- has been the subject of recorded or reported incidents of bullying or harassment;
- has a history of self-neglect or harm;
- has made an allegation of an offence which is a sexual offence, or is aggravated on racial, religious, homophobic or transphobic grounds;
- is the family spokesman of one who died; and
- is likely to be subject to intimidation.

The obligations of the police include, some of them in conjunction with the CPS, explanation and information. Explanation is required about such matters as special measures provisions. Information must be given about each stage of the process such as any decision to charge or not to charge, bail, the outcome of any trial, and the process of any appeal.

The obligations of the courts include liaising with both the police and CPS to ensure that information is passed on to victims promptly, that victims have a separate waiting room from the defendant and defence witnesses, that special measures are available if required.

The obligations of the CICA include processing efficiently and sensitively all applications made to them, giving explanations for refusal or reduction of compensation, and informing the applicant of the right to apply for review if the application is refused.

The obligations of the prison service include maintaining a telephone helpline which can be sued by victims if they receive unwanted contact from a prisoner who had been convicted or remanded in custody in respect of relevant criminal conduct or have any concern about the prisoner's temporary or final release, and consider whether to impose additional conditions requested by the Probation Service or recommended by the Parole Board as a result of information offered by the victim.

The obligations of the Criminal Cases Review Commission include considering whether, during the course of a review of a case, contact with the victim should be made if there is a likelihood of the review coming to the victims' attention, and the result of any decision to refer the case to the Court of Appeal, unless the victim has made it clear that they do not wish to be informed or there is no identifiable victim.

All the obligations set out above carry strict time limits within which the information must be conveyed.

Failure to comply with these obligations does not render any individual liable for any offence, but may be taken into account in any proceedings where relevant.

The DVCVA 2004, s 47 enables the Parliamentary Commissioner for Administration (who investigates complaints about poor administration by Government department and agencies) to investigate breaches of the *Code of Practice*. Victims will need to make a written complaint to their Member of Parliament who will then refer the complaint to the Parliamentary Commissioner for investigation. There is no date yet for implementation of this provision.

Victim Personal Statements

Victims have expressed considerable concern in the past that the court, when dealing with the offender, has not heard anything from the victim on how the crime has affected him, nor has any opportunity to do so been available. After a good deal of debate, victim personal statements (VPS) are now accepted in court. A VPS adds to the information the victim has already given to the police about the crime. It enables the victim to explain how the crime has affected him, whether physically, emotionally or financially. The VPS then becomes part of the case papers and is seen by everyone involved with the case, including the CPS, the defence and the relevant court.

In the VPS, the victim may give any information that is not included in the evidential statement. It may include anything the victim thinks might be helpful or relevant, including, for example, that the crime has caused or made worse, any medical or social problems (such as marital problems), that the victim feels vulnerable or intimidated and that the victim is worried about the offender being given bail.

The VPS is not a victim impact statement and it was never the Government's intention to create a means by which the victim can influence a sentence. The VPS should not, therefore, include an opinion as to how the court should punish the offender, as this is a matter for the court, but the court will take into account how the victim has been affected. In addition, the court may use the VPS to decide matters such as bail.

The VPS also offers a means to record information in relation to the victim's needs and interests. As the VPS travels with the case papers, all agencies can respond to these needs. For example, the VPS may record the fact that the victim seeks a compensation order if the defendant is convicted. The VPS may also highlight the victim's vulnerability, prompting an application for special measures under the Youth Justice and Criminal Evidence Act 1999.

The Consolidated Criminal Practice Direction, issued on 29 July 2004, Part 3, para 28 provides as follows:

1 This part of the Practice Direction draws attention to a scheme which started on 1st October 2001 to give victims a more formal opportunity to say how a crime has affected them. It may help to identity whether they have a particular need for information, support and protection. It will also enable the court to take the statement into account in determining sentence.

2 When a police officer takes a statement from a victim the victim will be told about the scheme and given the chance to make a victim personal statement. A victim personal statement may be made or updated at any time prior to the disposal of the case. The decision about whether or not to make a victim personal statement is entirely for the victim. If the court is presented with a victim personal statement the following approach should be adopted:

(a) The victim personal statement and any evidence in support should be considered and taken into account by the court prior to passing sentence.

(b) Evidence of the effects of an offence on the victim contained in the victim personal statement or other statement must be in proper form, that is a witness statement made under s 9 CJA 1967 or an expert's report and served upon the defendant's solicitor, or the defendant if he is not represented, prior to sentence. Except where inferences can be properly drawn from the nature of or circumstances surrounding the offence, a sentence must not make assumptions unsupported by evidence about the effects of an offence on the victim.

(c) The court must pass what it judges to be the appropriate sentence having regard to the circumstances of the offence and of the offender, taking into account, so far as the court considers appropriate, the consequences to the victim. The opinions of the victim or the victim's close relatives as to what the sentence should be are therefore not relevant, unlike the consequence of the offence on them. Victims should be advised of this. If despite the advice, opinions as to sentence are included in a statement, the court should pay no attention to them.

(d) The court should consider whether it is desirable in its sentencing remarks to refer to the evidence provided on behalf of the victim.

Compensation

There are two separate considerations when dealing with the issue of compensation:

1 The making of a compensation order should be at the forefront of the courts mind when dealing with an offender. The Powers of Criminal Courts (Sentencing) Act 2000, s 1 provides that the court may impose a compensation order on an offender 'instead of or in addition to dealing with him in any other way'. This order may be made whether or not an application is made for it. The Act requires that the court should give its reasons if it decides not to make a compensation order.

   In the absence of an application, however, the court may not make an order. Prosecution counsel, therefore, may need to consider in advance of sentencing whether such an order should be applied for. This may involve discussion with the police who are likely to have had the closest contact with the victim, to discover whether such an application would be desirable.

2 A victim of crime may apply to the CICA for compensation for the crime to which he has been subject. Although an application may be made before trial, CICA will not make a decision until the trial has concluded. It may be appropriate to question a witness about any payment that has been made or promised to him, as it is relevant to the credibility of the witness. It is suggested, however, that great care should be taken when the victim of a violent or sexual offence is asked about any compensation that she or he has received. While it is known that allegations of rape are made for a variety of reasons, it is thought unlikely that it is in order for an application for compensation may be made. In some cases, the trial judge has intervened to stop this line of questioning, and prosecuting counsel may consider it appropriate to themselves challenge the questions or at least explain to the jury that the complainant has a right to compensation whether or not the defendant is even identified.

Reparation

Under the CDA 1998, the courts may pass two new sentences: the action plan order and the reparation order. The action plan order requires the offender to partake in specific activities, or to desist from specific activities, designed to achieve the offender's rehabilitation. The order may also specify that reparation is made to the victim of the offence (with his consent) or to the community.

The reparation order requires the offender to undertake certain work for the victim, provided that the victim agrees. This will be a maximum of 24 hours' work to be undertaken within a period of three months from the making of the order.

The existence of such order may be very beneficial to victims. Reparation may include writing a letter of apology to the victim or apologising in person, cleaning graffiti or repairing criminal damage. Any one of these may help in victim put the crime behind him. However, it is seen as very important that the reparation is something which is commensurate with the seriousness of the offence, is something to which the victim agrees and finally is tailor made for this offender, this crime and this victim, rather than a standard response to the type of crime.

See **Chapters 15** and **17** of this Manual for fuller discussion of these orders.

Conduct in court

It is important to be aware of the recent changes to the law which govern the way in which the witness may be cross-examined. Students are referred to the *Evidence Manual* for full details, but some of the most important are:

(a) CJA 2003, s 51 enables witnesses to give evidence from a location outside the court where it is in the interests of justice to do so.

(b) CJA 2003, s 116 allows for a witness's statement to be admitted as evidence where the witness is too frightened to give live evidence. The Act stipulates that the court should interpret 'fear' widely and consider whether admitting the statement as evidence is in the interests of justice.

(c) CJA 2003, s 137 provides for video recording of interviews with witnesses to be admissible where the witness's recollection of events is likely to be significantly better at the time of the recording than at the trial, and where this is in the interests of justice.

(d) CJA 2003, s 100 provides that witnesses other than the defendant may only be asked about previous character with the agreement of the parties or with the leave of the court and then only in specified circumstances.

(e) YJCEA 1999, s 41 restricted circumstances under which a victim's previous sexual history may be adduced as evidence.

It is also important to be aware of the provisions of the Code of Conduct. A barrister's first duties are to his client and to the court. See paras 302 and 303 of the Code of Conduct:

302   A barrister has an overriding duty to the Court to act with independence in the interests of justice: he must assist the Court in the administration of justice and must not deceive or knowingly or recklessly mislead the Court.

303   A barrister:
(a)   must promote and protect fearlessly and by all proper and lawful means the lay client's best interests and do so without regard to his own interests or to any consequences to himself or to any other person (including any professional client or other intermediary or another barrister);

While bearing these two duties in mind, a barrister must also act with sensitivity towards the victims of crime and other vulnerable witnesses. The Code gives some guidance in para 708 which provides:

708   A barrister when conducting proceedings in Court:
. . .
(g)   must not make statements or ask questions which are merely scandalous or intended or calculated only to vilify insult or annoy either a witness or some other person;
(h)   must if possible avoid the naming in open Court of third parties whose character would thereby be impugned;

(i)   must not by assertion in a speech impugn a witness whom he has had an opportunity to cross-examine unless in cross-examination he has given the witness an opportunity to answer the allegation;

(j)   must not suggest that a victim, witness or other person is guilty of crime, fraud or misconduct or make any defamatory aspersion on the conduct of any other person or attribute to another person the crime or conduct of which his lay client is accused unless such allegations go to a matter in issue (including the credibility of the witness) which is material to the lay client's case and appear to him to be supported by reasonable grounds.

These are reproduced in the Written Standards for the Conduct of Professional work issued on 31 October 2004.

These separate principles may cause some difficulty when making a plea in mitigation. The barrister acting for the defence must be careful that any plea in mitigation does not make defamatory aspersions on the conduct of the victim, which is very distressing to the victim, and in cases where the offence is murder, is very distressing to the family. A barrister acting for the prosecution must be alert to the mitigation which is being put forward, and correct any matters if necessary.

APPENDIX 4
TRIABLE EITHER WAY OFFENCES —
DETERMINING THE MODE OF TRIAL
(SS 17A–23, MCA 1980)

1 The usual procedure (ss 17A–21 and 23, MCA 1980)

If someone aged 18 or over appears or is brought before a magistrates' court on an information charging him or her with an offence triable either way, the magistrate (or magistrates) must determine the mode of trial: s 17A(1) and s 18(5). (A single lay justice may do this but it is unusual for this to happen.) The procedure is as follows:

2 Preliminary procedure for charges of criminal damage (s 22, MCA 1980)

For offences under the criminal Damage Act 1971, s1 (ie, destroying or damaging property), other than those involving arson, the following preliminary procedure must be used. This applies also to charge alleging that the accused attempted to commit such offence, or incited, aided, abetted, counselled or procured its commission (MCA 1980, s 22 sch 2).

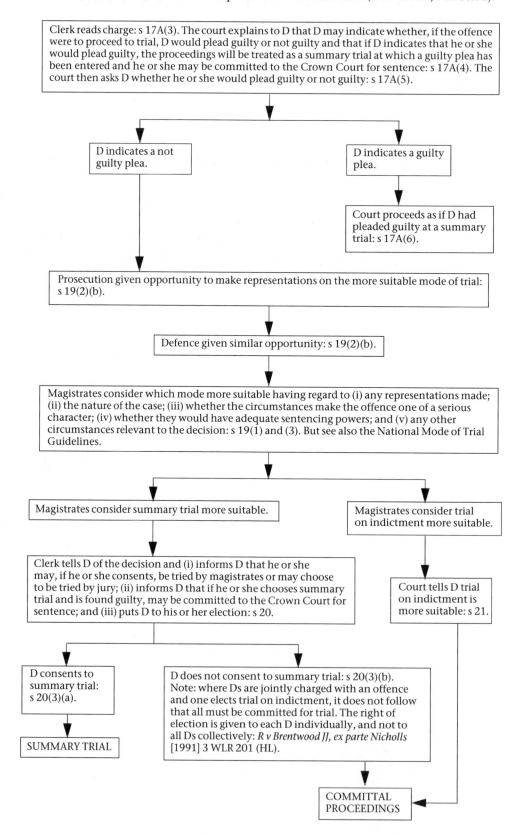

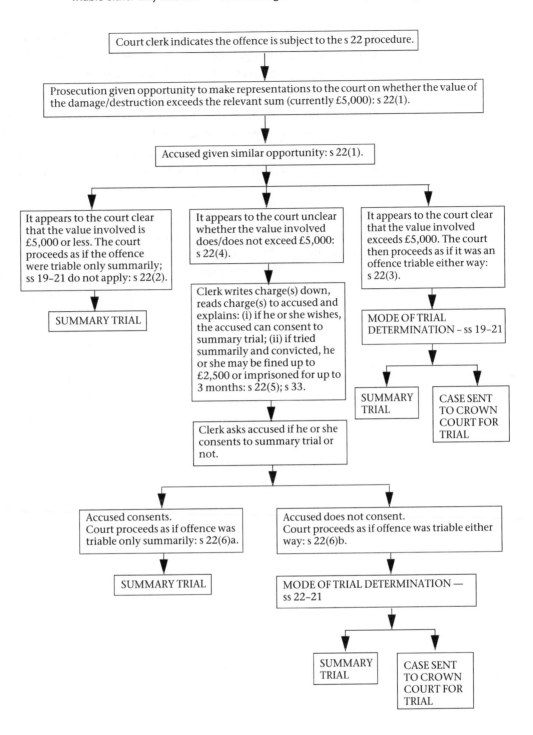

Cross-refer to **Chapter 4** (mode of trial), where offences which are triable either way are considered in more detail.

For charges involving allegations of criminal damage, there is a preliminary procedure which must be followed: MCA 1980, s 22.

Note that:

(a) The value involved is measured in accordance with MCA 1980, Sch 2. Simply, it is the cost of repair (if possible) or replacement, whichever is the less, at the time the offence was committed.

(b) Where two or more criminal damage offences are alleged against the accused on the same occasion **and** they form a series (or part-series) of offences of the same or a similar character, then the value of the damage/destruction which is used by the court is the aggregate for all the offences: s 22(11).

(c) The court must treat the offence initially as triable either way, and work through the 'plea before venue' procedure (see MCA 1980, s 17A; **Chapter 4**) with the accused. If the accused either indicates a plea of *not guilty*, or makes no indication as to plea, the procedure set out above will be followed in order to determine where the accused will be tried.

   If the accused indicates a plea of *guilty*, there is currently some doubt as to whether he or she may then be committed to the Crown Court for sentence if the value of the criminal damage is £5,000 or less (see, for example, *Blackstones' Criminal Practice*, 2005 edn, para D3.12). The offence is, of course, triable either way for purposes other than determining the mode of trial. It seems likely, though, that the procedure set out above will be followed up to the point where the value of the criminal damage is established. If the value of the criminal damage is found to be £5,000 or less, then the offence will continue to be regarded as summary only and there can be no committal for sentence under MCA 1980, s 38. Conversely, if the value clearly exceeds £5,000, then the defendant may be committed for sentence and appropriate representations should be made to the magistrates on that topic. One suggestion is that the magistrates' court should determine the value of a criminal damage charge before it does anything else. If the value is £5,000 or less, then mode of trial procedure would not apply, neither would committal for sentence nor plea before venue. See Inigo Bing, *Criminal Procedure and Sentencing in the Magistrates' Court*, Sweet & Maxwell, 5th edn, 1999, 4–14/6.

INDEX